Equality, Education and Physical Education

Edited by

John Evans

 The Falmer Press

(A Member of the Taylor & Francis Group)

London • Washington, D.C.

UK   The Falmer Press, 4 John St, London WC1N 2ET
USA   The Falmer Press, Taylor & Francis Inc., 1900 Frost Road, Suite 101, Bristol, PA 19007

First published 1993

A catalogue record for this book is available from the British Library

ISBN 0 75070 129 3 cased
ISBN 0 75070 130 7 paperback

Library of Congress Cataloging-in-Publication Data are available on request

Jacket design by Caroline Archer

Typeset in 9.5/11pt Times by
Graphicraft Typesetters Ltd., Hong Kong

Printed in Great Britain by Burgess Science Press, Basingstoke on paper which has a specified pH value on final paper manufacture of not less than 7.5 and is therefore 'acid free'.

Contents

Contents

Acknowledgments

My thanks go to Malcolm Clarkson, Falmer Press and all the contributors to this book, for their patience, persistence and unyielding commitment to this project. Special thanks are also due to Brian Davies for his editorial support and Marilyn Hayward and Joan Keeping for their technical advice, assistance and good humour throughout the production of this text. Finally, thanks to all the students, teachers and children who, over the years, have made equality, education and physical education such a challenging but rewarding issue to be involved with.

Introduction

John Evans and Brian Davies

Issues of equality of educational opportunity have long dominated debates about the goals and purposes of education in the British state system. In the last decade these have been aired even more openly, persistently and bitterly as both the form and content of education have occupied places high on the educational and political agenda. The time given to these issues in educational and political discourse is unsurprising. Once we accept the view that education is 'access to that which is worthwhile in a culture or an opportunity to develop one's intellect [and, we add, physical potential] and extend one's scope, it becomes a major further issue whether such assess or such opportunity should be made available to all pupils or only to a privileged few, whether, if the state is to finance educational provision, it should do so for the advantage of all children or only for those who will offer it some return for its investment' (Kelly, 1991, p. 40). Kelly contends that two major theories or conceptions of equality in particular have vied for dominance in the state education system over the last forty years, each struggling to determine and define how and what educational practice is and ought to be. The first of these, concerned with equality of opportunity, or equality of access, asserts that there are superior forms of human activity, a 'high culture', which requires high levels of intellectual activity if access to them is to be secured. Education involves initiation into those activities. Certain forms of knowledge, those which best develop the intellect, are deemed to be more important than others. This view of equality implies real danger for PE. The purposes of schooling reduce to a process of selecting and sieving out the intellectually 'able' from the so-called 'less able' and prohibiting the provision to the former of the opportunities and support they need to develop their intellectual capacities. Within such a context PE tends to function either to support and ape the actions and ambitions of the high-status subjects by stressing selection, competition, performance and reward in selected (high-status) physical activities, usually team games, or to help socialize and control children who have failed within this meritocracy, by keeping them busy, happy and involved in the practical and purportedly non-cognitive activities of PE and sport.

The second view of educational opportunity, by contrast, contends that 'every child is entitled to the fullest educational provision from which he or she is capable of profiting. On this view, educational provision is not tailored directly to economic productivity or even to high intellectual potential. Those children whose potential contribution to society seems minimal are regarded nonetheless as having the same entitlement to education as any others' (Kelly, 1991, p. 32). Many of the contributors to this book illustrate that this view has also found expression in the PE curriculum in programmes which lay less stress on competition and more on providing a curriculum which is both accessible and meaningful to all. This is the case despite the fact that debate about the issue of equality of opportunity and how this principle is to be expressed in PE programmes has not been greatly in evidence among physical educationalists. The likelihood is, however, that the Education Reform Act (ERA) 1988 and the implementation of a National Curriculum (NC) of core and foundation subjects for pupils of compulsory school age in England and Wales will bring about a change in this state of affairs.

On Wednesday 27 August 1991, the Physical Education Working Group established by the Secretaries of State for Education and Science and for Wales to advise on attainment targets and programmes of study for Physical Education in the National Curriculum, having received and considered 'a large amount of evidence ... from teachers, schools and colleges, local education authorities (LEAs), professional physical education associations, governing bodies of sports, national and regional sports and arts councils, dance associations and a wide range of other interested individuals and other organizations' (DES, 1991), submitted its final report to the Secretaries of State and the profession for consideration. It is difficult to overstate the potential significance of this document for the future of PE in schools in England and Wales. Its recommendations, as accepted by the Secretaries of State, will be taken to define what is to count as PE, and how teachers are to think and act in this subject for many years to come. For this reason it is of some import that a principle of 'Equal Opportunities' embracing the second view of educational opportunity described above, has been officially and forcefully established as a 'Guiding and Leading Principle for Physical Education' in its recommendations. This should present all parties concerned with the provision of PE in schools with enormous challenges over the next few years. As the report properly emphasizes,

> Working towards equality of opportunity in physical education not only involves widening and ensuring access. It also involves understanding ... of the range of pupils' responses to femininity, masculinity and sexuality, to the whole range of ability and disability, to the ethnic, social and cultural diversity, and the ways in which these relate for children to physical education. This will require both the initial and inservice training of teachers to promote a critical review of prevailing practice, rigorous and continuous appraisal and often the willingness to question long held beliefs and prejudices. These requirements should be shared by the whole school and relate to all aspects of the curriculum, not just physical education. They are the basis not only of commitment to providing equal opportunities, but also of the sensitivity needed for good and effective teaching. (DES, 1991, p. 60)

The contributions to this book endorse the sentiments contained in this statement and go some way towards outlining the range of identities and issues to which it refers. We have not set out to produce a 'how to do it' text on equal opportunities in physical education. This is neither possible nor desirable at this point in time. Our hope is that the papers in this book will help practitioners clarify their thinking on concepts and issues which are central to the task of effecting equal opportunities in programmes of PE and that this will in turn contribute to the formulation of PE programmes which routinely express the principles of both equity and equality. We explore the differences between these concepts in chapter 1, while Margaret Talbot examines the latter in chapter 5. In our view, creating equality and equity in PE will take time, experimentation, great patience and sensitivity to local school and community circumstances. It will also require the cooperation of parents, and of teachers in other curriculum areas. Perhaps most important of all it will need resources, in the form of time and money, at a level which will sustain and support appropriate work.

Although we come to the task of writing this introduction from different trajectories, we share a commitment to securing PE and sport in schools in a form that empowers children and young people. We take the view that PE and sport are social processes which can and do have a powerful and lasting impact on the identities of children, on their attitudes towards physical activity, themselves and others. In one way or another we have each been deeply influenced by the power of PE and sport in schools and the communities in which we have lived and our experience tells us that they have contradictory tendencies. On the one hand both have the capacity to empower, instil confidence, cooperation, sensitivity, dignity and pride in oneself and others; on the other they can alienate, promote insensitivity, exaggerate difference, foster selfish individualism, separate and divide. PE inevitably socializes as it skills: it helps lay down the rules of belonging to one's culture, gender and social class. Its social processes centre upon the display of physical ability and performance in which the relations and differences between individuals become much more vividly apparent than in other areas of the school curriculum (Hargreaves, 1990). Arguably, the way in which differences and relations are perceived lies at the source, if not as a cause, of prejudice and inequality in schools. In any programme of PE which proclaims the aims of equality and equity these differences and relations thus have to be addressed. We have to understand how social and cultural differences are constructed through various representations and practices in education and PE that name, marginalize and exclude the voices and actions of subordinate groups in Britain and elsewhere (Giroux, 1991). One of the themes of this book is that the differentiation of men and women, able from 'disabled', black from white, and their allotment often to antagonistic roles, their investment with rigidly separated predispositions, desires and emotions is not an expression of an underlying 'natural order' but a series of complex social artifacts. These processes are neither arbitrary nor immutable. They can be influenced, challenged and contested at least in part, through programmes of education and the curriculum of PE. Ironically, while the task of achieving this aim has not been made easy by the current political culture and the work conditions in which teachers operate, the principle of equality of opportunity is at least explicitly acknowledged in the Working Group's recommendations for the NC for PE (DES, 1991) (if not with the same integrity by the Secretary of State for Education and the National Curriculum Council),[1] and government policy on the provision of education for children with 'special educational needs' will force more and more teachers to confront their own attitudes towards 'ability', and their capacity to teach mixed-ability groups of children. While there is now no shortage of literature dealing with sexism, racism, disability and elitism, very little of it has placed PE, and the way in which the body is schooled, very high amongst its concerns. The aims of this book are thus very ambitious. They endeavour not just to raise issues and provide some practical guidelines for challenging sexism, racism and elitism for teachers to consider in their programmes of PE, but also deal with some of the fundamental concepts of social class, gender, 'race' and disability at a more theoretical level, with the perspectives which may inform our practical actions. We acknowledge that there are dangers in the way in which we have organized the book in chapters which appear to deal separately with class, 'race', disability and gender identities, conveying the surface impression that these identities are somehow a natural but separate set of 'policy problems' which can be placed together as 'equally troublesome areas demanding attention' (Arnot, 1985). The influences of class, 'race', disability and gender do not express themselves straightforwardly in classrooms. In our view they cannot be treated as either cumulative, parallel or mutually supportive. We see the relation between class, 'race' and gender as far more complex, problematic and contradictory than is suggested by parallelist theory. McCarthy (1980) invokes the concept of non-synchrony 'to advance the position that individuals or groups, in their relation to economic, political and cultural institutions such as schools, do *not* share the same interests, needs or desires "at the same point in time"' (p. 83). She goes on:

> The nonsynchronous approach to the study of inequality in schooling alerts us to the fact that different race-class-gender [and, we add, ability] groups not only have qualitatively different experiences in schools, but actually exist in constitutive tension, often engage in active competition with each other, receive different forms of rewards, sanctions and evalu-ation, and are ultimately structured into different futures. (p. 95)

It perhaps goes without saying that this conception of inequality complexifies rather than simplifies the task of promoting equity in the education system. We also acknowledge that as (relatively) physically able, white, middle-class, Anglo-Welsh men we cannot speak as, or for, 'the disabled', women, or other socio-cultural groups. We can, however, empathize with and cognitively accompany them with respect to issues of 'race', class, gender and disability and as Giroux (1991) stresses, 'work with these diverse others in order to deepen our own and their understanding of the complexity of the traditions, histories, knowledges (physical cultures and experiences) and politics that they bring to schools'. We endorse Giroux's view that 'while teachers may not speak *as* others whose experiences they do not share, they certainly can speak about and to the experiences of racism, sexism, class discrimination, and other concerns as histori-cal and contingent issues that affect public life' (p. 517). Indeed, we echo Cole's (1989) view that 'education is a meaningless process unless it is concerned with struggle against all forms of oppression and tyranny whether based on ignorance, oppression, inequality or exploitation' (p. 13). The contributors to this book offer a variety of perspectives on the forms which such a struggle should take, but together they share a view that education and physical education can be liberating. If this book goes some way towards helping others take this view and secure the expression of equality and equity in their programmes of PE then it will have achieved its aim.

Chapters 1 and 2 describe the socio-historical, political and ideological contexts in which teachers in the UK and the USA have had to work in recent years. They set the scene for the chapters that follow. In chapter 1 we trace the way in which the concept of equality has been contested and defined in the discourse of politicians in post-war Britain, and recently redefined by the New Right in a way which, we argue, impairs the achievement of equality and equity in the education system. In a discourse which confuses and conflates the role of the democratic citizen with that of the consumer, issues of 'race', social class, culture, and ability are marginalized, and the concept of equity is omitted from the agenda of political and educational debate. Patt Dodds in chapter 2 emphasizes this point by drawing attention to the debilitating 'back to basics' conservatism of Republican politicians in the USA, which has made it very difficult for PE teachers there to confront the variety of forms of oppression and disadvantage which feature in schools and society. In her analysis the concept of equity has to be positioned centrally in any debate or initiative aimed at achieving equality in PE. She goes on to outline some of the ways in which teachers can begin to confront sexism, heterosexism, racism, classism and motor elitism (the privileging of particular forms of skilled behaviour) in their PE programmes. Section One of the book deals specifically with the concepts of disability, social class, 'race' and gender, sources of oppression and discrimination that can be found in PE as elsewhere in the education system. In each of the chapters in this section the discussion is intentionally theoretical but never divorced from the range of practical issues and concerns facing teachers and students. Their tone is often polemical and critical as they challenge physical educationalists to problematize and appraise the assumptions, attitudes and beliefs which underpin their actions and initiatives. In chapters 3 and 4, Len Barton and Chris Shilling trenchantly attack both the individualism and the implicit conceptions of the 'ideal body' which have long been prevalent in PE, and which in their view continue to feature prominently in the PE National Curriculum and other recent PE initiatives. Lamenting the paucity of time and attention given in the work of physical educationalists working at all levels of the education system to the issues of disability in PE, Len Barton challenges the assumptions and practices in PE which locate 'problems' in individuals and their personal limitations rather than in the social and educational contexts which handicap individuals and create 'disability'. Disability, he argues, is 'a form of oppression' which entails economic and social hardships as well as assaults upon self-identity and emotional well-being. Contesting it will involve not only rethinking how we conceptualize ability and 'disability' but also reconstructing the 'unadaptive, unhelpful and unfriendly environments' which handicap and obstruct children's opportunities to enjoy and experience the education which they deserve and to which they have a right. Like Len Barton, Chris Shilling draws attention to the powerful impact schools and PE within them can have on children's developing conceptions of themselves, their own and others' bodies. He examines the way in which the issue of social class has been treated in the research and discourse of PE and he re-centres our attention away from issues of access and opportunity, long the focal point of analysts of social class in PE, to the way in which the body is schooled and 'classed' in processes of schooling. The body, he argues, has a far greater social significance than is often allowed in existing approaches to the study of PE. Physical educationalists unavoidably socialize as they skill individuals. They are heavily implicated in the way in which pupils 'internalize socially accepted ways of managing and maintaining their bodies' and in this way they differentially affect the ability of pupils to recognize and develop forms of attitude and behaviour (following Bourdieu, called 'physical capital'), which influence membership and access to particular social groups. Setting his analysis in the context of consumer capitalism and the social changes associated with late modernity, he implores us to examine the social nature and the class origins of definitions of the body, ability and skill conveyed in both long-established and more recent initiatives in PE, and consider whether, in conditions of late modernity, dominant definitions of what are to count as ability and skill can be sustained and legitimated. Like all the other contributors to this section of the book, Shilling highlights how PE can help either reinforce or contest stereotyping, discrimination and inequity in schools and society. Although his analysis centres on issues of class, it points to the way in which other identities are produced and reproduced in PE contexts.

Chapters 5 and 6 by Margaret Talbot and Peter Figueroa, by contrast, draw our attention to the way in which gender and 'race' enter into Physical Education and limit and constrain the opportunities available to children and young people. British PE is, as Margaret Talbot argues, deeply gendered 'in ideology, content, teaching methods and through its relationships with the wider dance and sport contexts', and she challenges teachers to examine the ways in which they may both conceptualize and explain perceived differences between the sexes. This paper not only forces home the important distinction between equal *access* and *opportunity*, stressing that achieving the former in a programme of PE is no guarantee that children have equal opportunities to experience different forms of PE, it also interrogates the merits of a variety of strategies that may be used to contest gender stereotyping and inequality in PE. Like others in this book, Talbot takes the view that the explicit commitment given to equal opportunity in the PE National Curriculum is an important development, and she argues that confronting sexism in PE will mean dealing with difficult issues because they are often deeply personal and political. As the paper points out, anxiety about sex identity in particular is usually much more acute amongst boys than girls, and the narrow range of acceptable 'masculine' behaviours which are presented to boys in PE does severely limit their opportunities for involvement in the so-called aesthetic physical activities. Evidently we cannot deal properly with gender issues unless we consider the social dynamic which constitutes the construction of female *and* male identities. Altering the opportunities available to girls and boys in PE will necessitate treatment of the way in which both females and males think about themselves and each other and in particular, as both Talbot and Dodds stress, the homophobia which is inherent in most portrayals of masculinity and its influence on the curriculum and teaching of PE. With Margaret Talbot and others in this book, Peter Figueroa in chapter 6 takes the view that conventional and stereotypical categories and labels are social constructions which define a 'reality' which individuals and groups, because of their differential power and resources, are differently able to alter and define. The curriculum of schooling, however, represents one important site for the contestation of conventional categories. It is therefore disappointing that the important and controversial issues of 'race' and racism have not featured prominently in the discourse of physical educationalists. Peter Figueroa's chapter makes an invaluable contribution to such a debate and to an understanding of key concepts such as 'race', racism, ethnicism, and pluralism, and the variety of approaches that have been and can be used to challenge racism in schools.

In chapter 10 Bob Carroll and Graeme Hollinshead provide empirical illustration of some of the issues raised in chapter 6, as they describe the dilemmas of following policies of equality of opportunity at the same time as multicultural and antiracist ones in PE. They highlight the slippery interplay of 'race' and gender issues and the way in which children can be caught between their own values and cultures and those of PE teachers. They then go on to outline some of the measures which have to be taken if racism is to be dismissed from PE in schools.

Section Two provides more focused discussion on the variety of strategies that teachers and teacher educators, working in each of the sectors of compulsory schooling, and in initial teacher education, can adopt to confront and contest the variety of forms of oppression which may feature in PE and society. The chapter by Sue Thomas (chapter 7), however, provides a backdrop to all the others in the section, dealing specifically with the requirements and the possible consequences of the 1988 Act. She raises the spectre of teachers desperately trying to resolve the tension between regulating and balancing their professional ideals and meeting the competing demands of surviving in the education market-place, circumstances hardly conducive to dealing with the complex curricular and pedagogical issues which have to be addressed if equality and equity in PE are to be achieved. Both Anne Williams and Sheila Scraton in chapters 8 and 9 emphasize this complexity in their respective discussion of primary and secondary schooling. They each illustrate that the adoption of mixed-sex grouping in PE does not signify the arrival of a decent coeducational PE, least of all one which expresses equality and equity. They point to the range of curricular, grouping, pedagogical, evaluation and cross-curricular issues that have to be dealt with if sexism and other forms of oppression are to be dealt with effectively in PE. The call for a more sophisticated pedagogy in PE which is inherent in their argument concurs with Anne Flintoff's analysis of teacher education in chapter 12. Her research reveals that many teacher educators are no more equipped than teachers in schools to deal well with equity and equality issues, and that Initial Teacher Education (ITE) courses in PE will have to change significantly if students and teachers are to be equipped with the understandings and skills required to promote them in schools. The chapters by Sheila Scraton and Anne Williams are a salutary reminder that current proposals by Conservative politicians to dissolve teacher education, to erode 'theory' and place student teachers in schools for 'practical experience' for the majority of their time, will neither help raise standards in education nor alter the educational opportunities of disadvantaged individuals and groups. Student teachers, under-trained and ill-equipped with ideas and strategies on action would serve only the interests of the status quo and the continuing reification of existing social hierarchies. Anne Flintoff's data are an additional timely reminder of the place and importance of ITE, strengthened with a curriculum and pedagogy capable of dealing theoretically and practically with equality and equity issues. Phil Hodkinson and Andrew Sparkes in chapter 11 direct our attention to the vocational thrust which has

7

increasingly featured in the curriculum of upper secondary and post-compulsory education. It has received scant attention in the discourse of physical educationalists. They emphasize the progressive possibilities in vocational education and illustrate how a vocationalized PE curriculum could be used to empower children and young people 'to act without constant dependence on others', liberated from the restrictive or oppressive features of the present and the particular. They advocate the 'deliberate education of generations who will think and do things for themselves, while recognizing the rights and needs of others'. This aspiration is also well expressed in Chapters 13 and 14. Barbara Humberstone celebrates and highlights the possibilities within Outdoor Education (OE) for both empowering all children and young people and challenging the stereotypical attitudes and expectations they often hold towards themselves and each other. She documents the struggle to retain OE in the school curriculum before and after the ERA and argues that both the NC for PE and the stringent budgets which some schools increasingly have to work with under Local Financial Management (LFM) may herald either the demise of OE in schools or very limited forms of Outdoor Pursuits which sustain rather than erode traditional male practices and gender hierarchies. Paula Halliday (chapter 13) advocates a form of practice in PE which assumes that all pupils, and not just those defined as 'disabled', have special educational needs and a right to a physical education. She points out that recent legislation in the UK will ensure that more and more children defined as having 'special educational needs', and previously educated in 'special schools', will enter the mainstream sector to receive their education. Many teachers in this sector will feel materially and pedagogically ill-equipped to deal with the range of pupil abilities and differences they will have to deal with in their classrooms. Her paper addresses many of the pedagogical and practical issues that teachers in mainstream schools will have to confront if they are to effectively realize the goal of providing a 'PE for all' and stresses that teachers should not and need not act alone in the reconstruction of their Physical Education. Meeting the special educational needs of all children will require cooperation and assistance from parents and other teachers outside the mainstream sector who have special knowledge and expertise in the Physical Education of pupils with 'special educational needs'.

Together the papers in this book address a variety of practical and theoretical issues. Some issues receive more attention than others. None is exhaustive. Our hope is that they will help practitioners identify and understand some of the common and key issues which have to be dealt with if equality and equity principles are to be adopted and expressed in PE. The strategies advocated for countering a particular form of oppression, for example sexism, in PE, cannot and should not simply or straightforwardly be applied to the treatment of other forms of oppression, for example racism in PE (see Carrington and Williams, 1988; Carrington and Leaman, 1986). But all need much more attention than they have received hitherto, in the immediate light of National Curriculum changes and the longer-term cause of achieving equality and equity in the field of PE, where nearly everything remains to be done.

Note

1   The 'recommendations' of the National Curriculum Council and the Secretary of State for Education have asserted that the rationale for PE outlined by the

Working Group in their recommendations for the PE National Curriculum (DES, 1991), and, we assume, all other non-statutory recommendations for PE, including the statement on equal opportunities, are to be omitted from the Statutory Order for Physical Education in the interest of making the NC PE programmes of study 'less detailed and prescriptive' (NCC, 1991, p. 16). This 'Order' and the statutory material it contains will effectively define the Physical Education National Curriculum. Although the 'non-statutory material' may be issued at a later date to accompany the statutory NC requirements, this deliberate separation of non-statutory 'principles' from the curriculum content of PE is unlikely to help secure a place for equity and equality issues amongst a teacher's concerns.

References

ARNOT, M. (1985) *Equal Opportunities Policies in Education*, Oxford, New York, Pergamon Press.

CARRINGTON, B. and LEAMAN, O. (1986) 'Equal Opportunities and Physical Education', in EVANS, J. (Ed.) *Physical Education, Sport and Schooling*, London, Falmer Press, pp. 215–17.

CARRINGTON, B. and WILLIAMS, T. (1988) 'Patriarchy and Ethnicity: The Link between School Physical Education and Community Leisure Activities', in EVANS, J. (Ed.) *Teachers, Teaching and Control* in Physical Education, London, Falmer Press, pp. 83–97.

COLE, M. (1989) *Education for Equality*, London, Routledge.

DEPARTMENT OF EDUCATION AND SCIENCE (1987) *The National Curriculum: A Consultation Document*, Cardiff, DES/Welsh Office.

DEPARTMENT OF EDUCATTION AND SCIENCE (1991) *Physical Education for ages 5–16*, DES/Welsh Office.

GIROUX, H.A. (1991) 'Democracy and the Discourse of Cultural Difference: Towards a Politics of Border Pedagogy', *British Journal of Sociology of Education*, **12**, 4, pp. 501–21.

HARGREAVES, J. (1990) 'Gender on the Sports Agenda', *International Review of Sociology of Sport*, **25**, 4, pp. 286–305.

KELLY, A.V. (1991) *The National Curriculum: a Critical Review*, London, Paul Chapman Publishing Ltd.

MCCARTHY, C. (1990) *Race and Curriculum,*, London, Falmer Press.

NATIONAL CURRICULUM COUNCIL (1991) *National Curriculum Council Consultation Report. Physical Education*, York, National Curriculum Council.

Chapter 1

Equality, Equity and Physical Education

John Evans and Brian Davies

Politics, Slogans and Physical Education

In the UK in recent years, the discourses of educationalists and politicians of the political Left, Right and Centre have often seemed to converge on the idea that 'equality', 'opportunity', 'freedom' and 'choice' are all inherently good things which should be sponsored through and expressed in the organization and content of the state education system. We would be particularly hard pressed to find a time when concepts such as these had featured so prominently in the discourse of the New Right.[1] The political message is frequently asserted that we live in an age of great consumer opportunities, in which individuals have the freedom and responsibility to create their own 'lifestyle', choose their own health care, their own housing, and their children's school. The apparent convergence in the thinking of politicians across the electable spectrum has led many (failing to note the connection between the political philosophy of Fabian Socialism and the Hayekian liberalism of Thatcherism; see Burden-Teh, 1991), to lament angrily that the political Right have 'captured their ground', stolen or borrowed concepts that are more appropriately associated with the politics of the Left or liberal centre (see Davies *et al.*, 1990) and wantonly redefined them in a way which has little to do with the achievement of 'real' equality, opportunity, or choice either in society or in schools. To be sure, in the staffroom and lobby discourse of educationalists and politicians, concepts such as equality, opportunity, freedom and choice can seem to have wings, when used in the manner described above, as popular slogans to arouse sentiment and the support of colleagues, or parents or the electorate, and to rationalize policies which forerun the implementation of educational and social change. This tendency to use slogans to define curriculum policy is not, of course, peculiar to the UK educational scene (see Werner, 1991). All dedicated engineers of the social know that the first rule of social change is to simplify both its necessity and possibility. In this sense, Thatcher's 'original' slogan call for reform, TINA (there is no alternative) was generated by the even more basic and potent belief in TINN (there is nothing new). Where there is 'nothing new', all attempts at change tend to be seen as potentially irrational and self-defeating attacks on how things must be, and their protagonists likely to be defined as both mad and bad. This ultimate rape of social reason is capable of generating an indefinite number of instances of defence of a 'natural' order (in Thatcher's case the sacred relation between shopkeeper and customer) starting from any point of privilege.

All such slogans need to be treated with interrogative caution not least because they intentionally simplify, reduce and thereby potentially obfuscate and distort the realities of the social world they purport to describe. Their meanings are conveniently transient and depend upon the specifics of social, political or fiscal interests which dominate political or educational contexts of the day. Because they derive their agendas from and are used in such contexts they are inevitably contested. Consensus over their meaning is unlikely to be achieved.

Margaret Talbot (1990) is right when she states that only once we begin to interrogate concepts such as equality does it become clear that people attach very different meanings to these terms and that these 'interpretations' can and do significantly effect the way in which the education system (and PE within it) is perceived and structured. It is for this reason that struggles over the language of education, over the meaning of the concepts which reside in the 'official discourse' (which defines what is to count as valid knowledge in PE and as culturally legitimate conceptions of the body, the individual, social order and society) are so important and as necessary and difficult to engage in as any contest over more practical or material matters such as the distribution of resources in schools. Beneath the rhetoric of these popular slogans lie deeply held values and conceptions of what individuals and society are and how they ought to be. It is their elaboration in policy and overall resource decisions which disposes of what counts as a level playing field upon which we make our marks.

Our task in this chapter is neither to command nor offer a consensus view on what is meant by equality in education. Our own perspectives and choice of company in this volume are informed by our value commitments to the politics and philosophies of democratic socialism. We reject Thatcher's selfish, now Major's putatively 'caring', materialistic individualism for the sort of democratic individualism which Leadbetter (1989) outlines. This places stress on collective and cooperative action, on universal rights and responsibilities and on policies which foster individuality, diversity and plurality both in and through the curriculum and schooling and in wider society. It is a view which has equity uppermost in its concerns. Others in the book claim feminist or liberal perspectives. We offer a generally critical reading of the education policies which currently are defining the work contexts of teachers in the UK and which, in our view, hinder the task of promoting equity and equality in the education system.

Equality of Opportunity Pre-Thatcherism

With Byrne (1985) we have taken the view that one of the weaknesses of the United Kingdom's attempts to achieve an educational equality programme in the state system in the 1960s and 1970s was its refusal to define what was meant by equality in education, and conceptualize its implications for the curriculum in schools. As we have argued (Davies and Evans, 1984; Evans and Davies, 1990), the patchy advent of comprehensive schooling in England and Wales produced neither organizational, curricular nor pedagogical reform capable of providing a common education for all. The Labour governments which introduced Circular 10/65 requesting Local Authorities to submit plans for comprehensive reorganization, and passed the 1976 Education Act, made no attempt to define or lay down guidelines for the provision of a comprehensive education. Caroline Benn (1979) makes the point that

It was impossible to ensure equality of opportunity without a definition of those minimum opportunities which should be available to all boys and girls in any school called a 'comprehensive'. To try to define them would have conflicted with the *laissez-faire* policy of governments in implementing the reform since 1965, a policy adopted by both political parties in the vain hope of appeasing two different kinds of political opposition. (p. 197)

Two powerful ideologies, those of human capital theory and of an 'access' version of equality, shaped the unsystematic development of the 'comprehensives' and the actions of teachers, including Physical Educationalists, within them. In the economic expansion and social optimism of the early 1960s it was widely believed that the educational system could be changed in such a way as to provide both greater equality in society and economic efficiency. Much of the ideological basis of this outlook in the UK as elsewhere (cf. Lauder, 1988) lay in 'human capital theory' and the view that 'investing in human capital not only increased individual productivity, but in so doing, also laid the technical base for the type of labour force necessary for rapid economic growth' (Chitty, 1987, p. 9). As Chitty points out, a version of this philosophy proved highly attractive to a Labour government which, in the 1960s (CCCS, 1981), was more committed to reform (for which the twin watchwords were social equality and economic progress) than to radical social and educational change. To the powerful Fabians who achieved dominance within the Labour Party, bringing children of different abilities and social backgrounds together within the comprehensive organizational form promised a means of not only moving the educational system in the direction of greater equality of opportunity and social justice but also of securing greater economic efficiency. It would help avoid the underskilling of children which was contingent upon the existing 'selective' school system and disastrous for an expanding and changing hi-tech economy. It would also begin to erode the unfairness of a system which denied to all children equality of access to a high-status grammar school education. The debates of the 1950s and 1960s, as Shilling notes in chapter 4, centred on issues of wastage of talent and equality of access to education and PE within it. Matters relating to what should be learned or how it should be acquired were of comparatively little concern. The early development of a comprehensive system was thus not grounded in anything approximating radical or even democratic socialist principles but in what Lauder (1988) has termed an 'enlightened individualism' which warmly embraced a commitment to a discourse which emphasized both the skilling of more children and a version of equal *opportunities* which, with its emphasis mainly on issues of *access*, had very little to do with egalitarian concerns with the structuring of opportunities both inside and outside schools. As Wilby remarks:

Educational equality was an attempt to achieve social change by proxy. More and better education was more politically palatable and less socially disruptive than direct measures of tackling inequality. So was

> economic growth. Even the most complacently privileged could hardly object to children attending better schools and to the nation producing more wealth. Equality of educational opportunity had an altogether more agreeable ring to it than any other form of equality, such as equality of income or equality of property. With its overtones of self-improvement, it could even appeal to the more conservative elements in society.... Ugly words such as redistribution and expropriation did not apply to education — or nobody thought they applied. Education was a cornucopia, so prolific of good things that nobody would need any longer to ask any awkward questions about who got what. (Wilby quoted in Chitty, 1987, p. 10)

The reforms of the 1960s were seen as a means of producing a greater degree of social harmony without in any way disturbing the basic class structure of a capitalist system (Chitty, loc cit). They were not concerned with issues of social class restructuring and on matters of gender, race and disability there was a resounding silence (see Arnot, 1991).[2] After twenty years of 'comprehensive schooling' in England and Wales, it is therefore unsurprising that such reports of social research that we have find selection largely intact. While comprehensive schools effectively undercut the more obvious forms of physical separation of pupils, they did not require or help teachers to reconsider their thinking about knowledge, the nature of ability, or the nature and purpose of secondary education (Davies, 1991).

We do not mean to denigrate the intentions and efforts of comprehensive reformers. Indeed we share the views of Hargreaves and Reynolds (1989), Simon (1988) and Kelly (1991) that the late 1960s and the 1970s were years in which widening educational opportunities, improved identification of educational talent, postponement and reduction of educational selection and differentiation and broadened curriculum entitlement did become issues, principles and goals. Although it is easier to create the impression of crisis than it is to romanticize the achievements of the comprehensive system, with these authors we would claim that inside many schools it was possible to find initiatives driven by concerns to express equality of opportunity in organizational and curricular terms, for example in the replacement of streaming with banding and mixed-ability grouping, by attempts to extend core and common knowledge contents for longer periods across a wider ability range and in challenging first sexism and then other forms of prejudice in the curriculum. It is, however, difficult to claim that such initiatives were ever widespread in PE, although moves towards a more pupil-centred education through access to a wider and less gendered range of physical activities for all pupils, the use of more individualized coaching techniques in the teaching of games and expansion of the media of educational gymnastics and dance were important though always piecemeal. They were persistently threatened by the criticism of conservative factions within the profession (see Kirk, 1990 and Evans, 1990b) and a well organized and vociferous political Right outside it. Those comprehensives reaching maturity in the late 1980s, schools in some measure actualizing an 'equal value principle' and endeavouring to effect a system of state education which was more democratic and capable of meeting the needs of all children, are, however, now in danger of being 'cut off in their prime' (Hargreaves and Reynolds, 1989). We have entered a period of decomprehensivization in which the concept of equality is being critically redefined.

Creating a Crisis

In the last decade, Conservative policy had systematically portrayed teachers in state schools in England and Wales as syndicalist obstacles to freedoms which could be better guaranteed by the principles of the market. This critique was not new. Reaction against so-called progressive developments in the state education system and a reassertion of arguments for a more selective and differentiated system, for more economic value and a proper return for investment of public money in the education system, had been voiced in earnest throughout the 1960s and early 1970s (see Kelly, 1991). The Black Paper writers (Cox and Dyson, 1969a, 1969b; Cox and Boyson, 1977) at this time did not reject the principle of equality of opportunity in the system but rather the means of its achievement and expression in schools. As one stated,

> Let us, however, clarify the term 'equality of opportunity'. It does *not* mean equality of education — rather the contrary, for equality of education would really mean the perpetuation of the social and economic inequality existing outside the school. Whatever the progressive ideologues may think, schools neither create nor preserve social and economic inequality: social divisions are a product of human society, and schools as creations of the same society, merely reflect these divisions. Education is not and can not be an instrument of 'social engineering'; its purpose is not the establishment of social equality — but it can play an important part offsetting the effects of existing social inequality. To quote Angus Maude: 'The object of the exercise is *not* to give every child an equal chance; it is to give every child the *best possible* chance to develop and make the most of his own special talents'. This can be accomplished only by an *unequal* differentiated educational system, which levels out the handicap created for the able pupil by the inadequacies of his family's social and economic position. (Szamuely, 1969, pp. 49–50)

It was ten to twenty years later before the policy objective of achieving equality through a more overtly differentiated school system could find expression in the legislative programme of a Conservative government. By then, in the eyes of the Right and some narrowed gazes of Left and Centre, the whole purpose of schooling had been distorted by teachers' preoccupation with promoting egalitarianism and by local politicians and professionals expropriating control of the service from its proper source, the parents. Teachers had too much control and they were insufficiently accountable to the consumer. Egalitarianism was 'on a crash course with freedom' (see McWilliam, 1987, p. 63). State management of education in the interests of justice and equality had to be supplanted by a consumer choice, cost-efficiency and the individual *opportunities* to pursue freely chosen differentiated interests in a differentiated system of schooling. The market would ameliorate society's inequalities and economic ills.

The case for such change had been brutally ideological in form and repeatedly directed at the actions of Physical Educationalists in schools. Teacher and system performance have been systematically denigrated to prepare the way for it. Indeed we have witnessed something profoundly disturbing about a form of political culture which gives license to a discourse in which 'facts' are rarely allowed to trammel the interests of a political judgment or opinion (Davies, 1988); a position which stems from a deeper conviction that only those engaged in changing the world can see it correctly (Evans and Davies, 1990); and where 'correctness' is monopolized by the 'naturalness' of market categories. We have the now familiar and transparent paradox that while the means of contestation are increasingly limited by authoritarian and interventionist measures of central government, its policy object is the dismantling of 'egalitarianism' in a school system which is antagonistic to personal freedom and liberty, a course which only 'decentralization' can redirect from calamity (McWilliam, 1987, p. 63). 'Decentralization' has altered its former meaning of empowering the local state capable of checking and balancing, as well as cooperating, to putting individual schools under direct central regulation and finance. A system that 'aped' the post-war grammar school for its new, non-selective secondary curriculum is now to copy the private sector in terms of governance with the DES stumping up the fees. It is in this sort of context that we find PE pictured as a hotbed of egalitarianism damaging Britain's children's health and economic wealth, an emblem as absurd as it is incorrect (see Evans, 1990b), but typical of the sort of change facing PE teachers in the last decade. Such myths are not concerned with facts but with meaning. Their key aspects are metaphors which not only profoundly and often unconsciously determine our attitudes towards the world, people, events and action but also 'obscure the interests of dominating elites and present particular, partisan views of the world as uncontestable descriptions of the way things are' and ought to be (Bates, 1986, p. 85).

Managing the Crisis: Equality after ERA

In the last decade or so, Conservative governments in the UK and elsewhere (see Dodds, in this volume) have taken a number of measures to reassert the economic function of the state education system and to create a context in which any endeavour to promote democratic or egalitarian principles and forms of schooling can be even more easily controlled and inhibited. Having created the idea in the public mind that crisis abounds in the educational world, that teachers are 'know-nothing, self interested, experts preventing sovereign parent consumers getting at the educational good' (Davies, 1988, p. 3), the 1988 Education Reform Act privileges the market as the natural solution to our economic and moral problems. The specific implications for PE are outlined by Sue Thomas in chapter 7. Everyone, regardless of social category, except the 'statemented' or those lacking in English as a mother tongue, is to get the same key curriculum contents, skills and processes from National Curriculum core subjects (maths, English, science and technology) and foundation subjects (modern languages, history, geography, art/music/drama, RE and PE). *Ad hoc* working parties have recommended programmes of study and attainment targets to the Secretary of

State for each. The curriculum is now a set of discrete and desirable contents in a structure 'given' to teachers and parents within which it is claimed 'the imaginative application of professional skills at all levels of the education service, within a statutory framework which sets clear objectives, *will* raise standards' (DES/Welsh Office, 1987, para 10, p. 5). Attainment targets have been set for children aged 7, 11, 14 and 16, to quantify 'improving performance'. Schools will provide information on outputs as raw data to which parents can directly relate, unpolluted by treatment for 'value added' or any other sort of social science sorcery. They will 'know better' what is taught and how their individual child, their class and school attain. Armed with this information, they can pick their schools so far as a system of 'open enrolment' permits. Thus 'good' schools will flourish and any except the small primary schools are already allowed to 'opt out' of LEA control and funding into grant-maintained status, directly funded by the DES, upon a simple majority vote of parents. Even if a change of political control halts grant-maintained status (GMS), Local Management of Schools (LMS) and Local Financial Management (LFM) signal a significant shift of power from LEAs to manage their systems which is unlikely to be reversed and may have severe consequences for the achievement of equality and equity in PE and sport. As Penney and Evans (1991) and Sue Thomas (in this volume) point out, LMS aims to make schools in England and Wales accountable for their operations and putatively encourage a more efficient use of resources. It makes fundamental changes in the financial and management structures in education, placing limitations on the function of LEAs and giving greater autonomy to schools and governing bodies. The two key features of this policy are *formula funding* and *delegation of management.* Formula funding introduces the allocation of school budgets on the basis of the number and age of pupils, with certain mandatory exceptions. Delegation of management makes governing bodies responsible for the management of school budgets, thereby significantly reducing the power LEAs have with respect to school finances, resources and personnel and giving far greater 'opportunity' and autonomy to governing bodies in these respects. The effects of these budgetary and management changes will take time to materialize. However, it has already been noted that they may not only exacerbate levels of competition *between* schools, but also create a competition *within* them. Schools will be 'forced' to vie with each other for a healthy supply of pupils, while subjects will have to compete with each other for resources in terms of staffing levels and financial support. Whilst all subjects will feel the effects of these policy changes, the potential implications for PE may be particularly serious since resources available are a key determinant of provision. The NC aims to ensure that a broad and balanced curriculum is available at certain standards, for *all* pupils, in the 5–16 age range, from within that provision. However, the phased implementation of the NC has created a situation in which curriculum subjects 'settled' first are already competing for timetable, staffing and physical resources at an advantage. The consequence for a subject late in the NC implementation process, with low-status subject matter, are potentially very severe. At face value, requiring schools to address the level of curriculum provision they are making for PE so as to ensure that it is 'broad and balanced' ought to have a positive effect on its provision in schools. In many primary schools where little or no provision is made for PE there may be increases in its *level.* Whether it achieves equality will depend on resources including opportunities for staff training. Whether the arrival of a National Curriculum for PE represents programme advance in the direction of equality of *opportunity* in the UK remains to be seen. Its continued stress on assessment, 'performance', and games may continue to disbenefit certain categories of child, particularly the physically less able or those with special educational needs. LMS and open enrolment may also make the face-commitment to a PE for all extremely difficult to achieve in practice. Open enrolment promises parents greater freedom to choose the school to which they will send their children. With the introduction of formula funding, this is likely to create a situation in which schools are competing for pupils. Schools will be forced to market their services and records, a key aspect of which may be their available facilities, including those in PE and sport. Pressures to increase pupil numbers may therefore have a direct influence on the provision of PE and sport in schools with unequal capacity to compete *qua* different size, location, and history (Penney and Evans, 1991).

Longer-term ERA outcomes are largely speculation. Elsewhere (Evans and Davies, 1990) we have suggested that they are likely to entail an increase in the number of more highly segregated schools as parents weigh issues such as racial mix, religion or culture in their choices. School differences in terms of social and ability mix which have bedevilled 'comprehensivization', a strong feature of our system, will accumulate even further. A future Conservative government will secure the return of a formally selective system based on testing at 11 as a 'welcome reintroduction' of variety and competition between different types of school. We may even have a system of payment by results re-echoing the Revised Code of 1862, when 'grants to schools were based on standards of attainment reached by children in a limited range of subjects' (Kelly, 1991).

Davies *et al.* (1990) suggest that a search for the concepts of freedom and equality operating in the ERA is pretty futile. They would agree that there is very little in the recent torrent of subject regulation to encourage teachers to tackle the issue of curriculum equality. They are likely to perpetuate rather than erode 'race', class and gender inequalities in education and in society at large. The 1988 Act neither acknowledged existing racial, sexual and class inequalities in education nor made reference to either the Sex Discrimination Act or the Race Relations Acts. The statutory changes embedded in the ERA and the NC were not designed to empower children or to raise or encourage critical thinking or challenge race, class, and gender inequalities. Indeed there is much in the legislation to reinforce stereotyping and disadvantage. As Davies *et al.* contend, the dedication to assessment predominantly through attainment levels and targets may not only set artificial limits to a child's learning but also exacerbate formal differentiation in the system and ossify labelling from an early age. Assessment and differentiation, much emphasized in the National Curriculum for PE, will be a routine teacher performance. It stresses that assessment at Key Stages One to Three will fall to the teacher alone and evidence of achievement will 'be gathered during the normal teaching programme over each key stage as a whole' (DES, 1991, p. 41). Will this process be free of cultural, class and gender bias? Who will be its beneficiaries? Having made individual difference 'an acceptable, discussable, legitimate agenda setting element of normal educational debate inside schools and out' (Davies *et al.*, 1990, p. 13) the issue must be not whether differences can be dissolved, a condition as inequitable as it is undesirable and impossible to achieve, but how they can be celebrated in ways which negate prejudice and stereotyping and at the same time respect individual cultural identity. This principal aim in any programme of PE is a matter to which we return below.

There is a conception of equality deeply embedded in the ERA. Its principal ideological thrust is that market forces can be applied as well to the education system as to any other site of production. Markets, it is claimed, are better than central planning authorities at coping with rapid social and technological change and at maximizing profits and benefits. 'Through the pursuit of selfish aims the individual will usually lead himself (sic) to save the general interest, the collective actions of organized groups are almost invariably contrary to the general interest' (Hayek, 1976, p. 138; quoted in Ball, 1990, p. 37). This is freedom *from* rather than a freedom *to*, that is, an absence of coercion. 'It is solely a freedom to have control of one's own behaviour, the removal of interpersonal constraints. It is a freedom to choose' (Ball, 1990, p. 37). In this perspective the power of the individual is celebrated, there is no one to blame for failure (in education, in leisure, in health, in housing, in wealth) but the failures themselves. Failure 'must lie in the culture, the family or the individual' (Ball, 1990, p. 37). The concept of equality embedded in the ERA connects very well not only with all this but also to the well-worn commitment to a meritocracy and equal opportunities in education which was expressed in a Fabian Socialist discourse some forty years ago. It is certainly not at odds with the individualism always endemic in PE (Hargreaves, 1986) and in the rest of the school curriculum. In a system which allocated children to different types of schools on the basis of different measured attainment/ability, the fee-payer and 11+ passer were always 'freer'. Our system is notoriously varied in its resourcing and delivery. The strains on an administered market in state education have led over many years to the variety of unequal school systems which characterize English and Welsh local provision, where *de facto* intake differences abound. Founded on residence, fuelled by insider trading in denomination and descent, the Wenglish middle orders practice effective togetherness in their offspring's schooling. The 'oversubscribed' and 'sink' schools of our system are not mainly or directly products of differences in managerial or pedagogical expertise among teachers. They are created by the unequal exercise of parental power upon old and new market rules. In principle the ERA promises a more overt shoppers' charter guaranteeing the right to see the inventory rather than the reserved purchase. The pain of refusal is to be assuaged by all establishments offering the same only different. The ERA re-celebrates equal opportunities of *access* for all children irrespective of their sex, ability or 'race', in any state school, up to the point where it is 'full'. This is not only not new but is a linchpin of our established 'comprehensive system'. What is new is that the principle of schools becoming 'more different' is out of wraps and the normal operation of social differentiation within administered markets is hidden and glamorized by Local Financial Management and 'opting out'.

A 'same for all thrust' would constitute progress in PE especially in secondary schools in England and Wales if it meant the end of ability- or gender-differentiated provision in Departments which are often separately staffed by males and females, usually with a man in overall charge. Unfortunately there is little in the recommendations of the NC for PE to ensure that the practice of differentiating the curriculum for boys and girls will not continue. Like Byrne

(1985), we take the view that equality does mean 'the same' for children of similar abilities and aptitudes whatever their sex, social class, 'race' or geographical background, but not uniformity across different interests or personalities. It does imply at least a common core of skills, knowledge, attitudes and experiences in PE and the wider school curriculum to which every child has a right and for which every school has a duty to provide (p. 98). But even securing for every child an entitlement of access to a common curriculum within whatever school they want will not end system inequalities. Successful removal of legal or procedural barriers is a critically important step in the direction of achieving equality whether in education or in wider society, but alone it is not sufficient to dissolve those attitudes and interests which underpin, sustain and in turn are fed by the structures and ideologies of oppression (Phillips, 1987). The quest to achieve and define equality in terms of formal rights of access remains quintessentially a liberal commitment, whether expressed in Fabian voices, feminist critiques or ethnic minority complaints about schooling in this country and elsewhere. It is rampant and reconstructed in the ERA and other New Right Conservative policies. As Apple (1989) points out,

> Equality no matter how limited or broadly conceived has become redefined. No longer is it seen as linked to past *group* oppression and disadvantage. It is simply now a case of guaranteeing *individual choice* under the conditions of a 'free market'. Thus, the current emphasis on 'excellence' (a word with multiple meanings and social uses) has shifted educational discourse so that underachievement is once again increasingly seen as largely the fault of the student. (p. 9)

There are severe limits to this liberal and individualistic perspective. As Phillips (1987) points out, its attraction lies in the claim that although people are different and occupy different positions in society these should be irrelevant. But if the implication of this is that differences in status or wealth or opportunity no longer matter, then we have a concept of equality that is profoundly unjust because it is abstracted from sources of privilege and relations of power. In short, there is a world of difference between achieving or being 'given' freedom from formal or legal constraints and having the power and the capacity to do as one wishes, as Margaret Talbot (1990) has stressed. The concept of equality as 'equal opportunities' is thus problematic for social and educational reformers. Indeed some have argued that in a highly competitive society it is an illusory goal because even if all individuals start from the same position and are given access to the same opportunities, the arrival of competitors in various states of fitness presupposes a race to be run in unequal circumstances (Fielding, 1987). Some years ago Rosemary Deem (1984) argued trenchantly that the sexes do not stand equal on admission to school and offering girls and boys the same opportunities and facilities cannot lead to equality of outcome. The tension between calling for equal treatment and insisting on the special needs of females, or any other social or cultural category, has featured most consistently in debates over single-sex or coeducational schooling. 'Going comprehensive' has largely meant going co-educational where boys have gained from the presence of girls in institutional circumstances whose codes remain dominantly male.

Re-Conceptualizing Differences

Post-ERA, 'sex division' is also high on the agenda of other cultural groups. As Sheila Scraton demonstrates in this book, the issue of whether to teach children in single-sex or sex-integrated groups is now a matter of great interest for teachers of PE. It is certainly difficult to contest the view that if women or girls are to have 'equal' opportunities there are times when they may actually need more of them than men, just as there are times when the 'disabled' may need more resources and help than the able-bodied. But acknowledging differences and arguing for separate provision can have distinct dangers. Once it is admitted that women and girls are different from men and boys, their chances for involvement in leisure, sport or work may be diminished if men or women continue to interpret 'difference' as evidence of less ability, skill, status and need. Certainly the dangers are many when advocating a policy of separate provision in a profession like PE which has long socialized its members into seeing and cultivating not the qualities and predispositions that men and women have in common but those which are thought 'naturally' to set them apart. If we reject the slippery interplay of competitive individualism and meritocracy in the ERA and address the important curricular, pedagogical and organizational questions of how and when children should be taught together or separately and why, we will need to bring principles to the surface as to how we can implement a form of practice capable of both bringing children (boys, girls, black, white, able, disabled) together towards a common culture and humanity, while at the same time respecting and educating them in all their diversity. We share Sawicki's (1991) view that all human differences are ambiguous and may be used either to divide or enrich our politics and daily lives. Perceiving 'differences' in this way, as a resource and a source of possibility, opportunity and creative change, rather than as a problem or barrier to be removed, is a necessary precondition to achieving equity and equality in PE. This would require, amongst other things, a critical appraisal of the value assumptions about ability, 'race' and gender differences which we hold.

The chapters in this book vividly illustrate how the PE curriculum is still strongly classed and gendered and fosters rather than contests sexism, racism and what Dodds in chapter 2 calls 'motor elitism' in the curriculum. The hegemonies of patriarchy, or class, and cultural anglo-centrism tend to ensure that some physical activities are given more status than others. Contesting this hegemony and the hierarchies it generates necessitates not only the provision of new activities but also the reconstruction of old ones around ideologies that stress the benefits of cooperation as much as competition. This requires confrontation of the nature of that authority and the values of those who define PE programmes inside and outside schools. If a commitment to equality and equity is to be more than a facade behind which old habits hide, it will have to go the heart of our thinking about cultural differences, ability, gender and knowledge. This will be slow and uncomfortable, as it will mean raising questions about distributions of power, status and reward in PE, about the knowledge and skills which teachers possess, about our capacity to effect desirable change. A recent report stated,

Many mature teachers feel that they lack confidence in the teaching of the opposite sex or dealing with the issues inherent in teaching mixed groups. Automatic adjustment does not occur and we recommend in-service training to give teachers the necessary outlook, confidence and technique which mixed ability/mixed sex physical education requires. (ILEA, 1988, p. 7)

Post-ERA the role of the LEAs in the provision of INSET has been severely diminished and the needs of teachers have become focused on the technical demands of delivering the National Curriculum and systems of testing. INSET in England and Wales is a Balkanized mess. Despite surface command of new contents and procedures, teachers will tend to know much more clearly what they are changing from than what they are changing to. A willingness and desire to effect equality and equity in PE may not be accompanied by any clear idea of how these commitments are to be expressed in practice. The PE National Curriculum recommended by the Working Group (DES, 1991) which properly commits PE teachers to the principle of equal opportunities goes some way to filling this lacuna at the level of principles and helpful recommendations, but it does not and could not provide detailed guidance as to how these are to be expressed programmatically. This gap will create a demand for support at both INSET and Initial Teacher Education (ITE) levels. Whether the latter is in good shape to meet this demand is also a matter of some concern, as Anne Flintoff demonstrates in chapter 12. In recent years the variety and pace of curricular and social change has often outrun the capacity and imagination of teachers and teacher educators to respond flexibly to them. The pursuit of equality and equity in PE teacher education may be particularly difficult. While the era of the single-sex PE college had long gone, as Anne Flintoff reveals, the residues of separation may still linger. There is little evidence to suggest that teacher educators have been any more willing or able than teachers either to confront sexism, elitism or racism in their curriculum or to address the pedagogical issues which the pursuit of equality and equity raise. Indeed, there is very little by way of a research basis upon which we can say anything about teacher education in Britain. We do not have the data to talk about how or whether teacher educators in PE have approached the issue of equality in PE, whether on gender issues or others. Some years ago Atkinson and Delamont (1985) lamented the paucity of interpretive research on teacher education, arguing that the sociology of education in Britain neglected occupational socialization in general and teaching in particular as an area for interactionist research. In their view research on socialization into teaching had lost its way. We may add that interactionist research on teaching and occupational socialization in PE never got to the start. Anne Flintoff's research is thus a timely and very important step in the direction of correcting this state of affairs. Like Atkinson and Delamont, we would contend that the separation of professional education and the investigation of education at school level may have contributed to stagnation in the former and impaired its ability to prepare teachers to promote equality and equity in schools. CATE (Council For the Accreditation of Teachers) requirements for IT courses, and the reports of HMIs (Her Majesty's Inspectors) who pliantly serve her, have all the dynamism of yesterday's shopping list. We need independent, research-based examination of the form, content and modes of educational practice in teacher education to ensure that they provide penetrations and paradigms of a kind required by student teachers in schools. Achieving this is likely to be as difficult and challenging for teacher educators as it is for teachers in schools, given the current emphasis and high status of the natural and physical sciences in PE teacher education in Britain and elsewhere. As Margaret Talbot (1990) has pointed out, students undervalue the human sciences in relation to the physical sciences and even question their relevance to professional training. There is a gendering of knowledge in PE which effects not only the choices male and female students make in their training but also their opportunities to develop their careers as PE teachers in the school system. Addressing the issue of how the hidden curriculum of teacher education impacts upon the identities of students is likely to be highly contentious. Raising questions about the nature of knowledge hierarchies will mean addressing questions about the social and status hierarchies which are contingent upon them. This will bring to the surface deep-seated values, vested interests and difficult issues of authority, power and control. It will mean examining how knowledge is selected, legitimated and transmitted and how these processes infuse the identities of young men and women. But unless these issues are addressed, we are not likely to find students in schools with the resources to deal with the social, ethical and curricular issues which will bear upon their work or to be able to give anything more than a rhetorical commitment to the pursuit of equality and equity in PE. Achieving an understanding of the social, cultural and political production of differences between individuals will require an examination of how 'representations and practices that name, marginalize and define differences as the "devalued other" are actively learned, internalised, challenged or transformed in and through educational practices' (Giroux, 1991) such as PE.

Equality and Equity in PE

It is evident in what we have said above that in our view equality and equity are not the same things and that it is their conflation in the discourse and policies of both left and right which has been so damaging to the cause of social democracy and citizenship in society and schools to the point where it is very difficult for teachers to conceive of the task of providing 'PE for all'.

In our view the failure to address the issue of how and whether equity is being expressed in the educational system is a matter of much greater concern than whether equality of opportunity in education is being achieved. Walter Secada (1989a) is correct to point out that equity in education has been uniquely an American notion. In the UK equality and equality of opportunity rather than equity have occupied the attention of educationalists and politicians. Equity refers 'to our judgements about whether a given state of affairs is just' (Secada, 1989a, p. 68). It goes beyond appeal to the application of a particular law or set of laws. As Secada notes, 'the heart of equity lies in our ability to acknowledge that even though our actions might be in accord with a set of rules or laws, their results may be unjust' (p. 68). Equality and equity ought to be viewed as complementary rather than conflicting alternatives (Byrne, 1985). As we have pointed out, British and US (see Dodds, in this volume) political–educational discourse of the Left and Right has converged to displace equity with a celebration and promotion of individual 'freedom', choice and opportunity. Equality in education has been defined purely as a technical concern with the distribution of opportunities amongst different social groups. With Byrne we can note that in England and Wales all children now have right of access by law to a National Curriculum for PE and go on to ask whether the curriculum to which they have access is just or equitable? Equity, says Secada, 'gauges the results of actions directly against standards of justice' (p. 68). It is used to determine whether or not what is being done is just. A good many chapters in this book clearly echo this view. It is critical to uphold a distinction particularly between equality of opportunity and equity because the achievement of the former is no guarantee that the latter is also evident. Equality in education, as Secada points out, tends to be debated and defined in terms of *inequality*. Typically 'groups are defined by some demographic characteristic: social class, race, gender, ethnicity, language background. Aggregate differences among these groups are then explored using some educationally important index. Group differences are interpreted to demonstrate the existence of inequality' (p. 69). In this view the concern for equality in education is registered as a concern that the 'goodss which the educational system can distribute are equally distributed in the aggregate among different groups of students' (p. 70). If, however, we take *equality* not only as 'the condition of being equal in quantity, amount, value or intensity', but also as 'the condition of being equal in dignity, privileges, power' (Byrne, 1985, p. 99), we are compelled to ask whether the planned provisions for different sorts of children in schools are equal at the level of what is invested in the processes of its delivery and in their justly differentiated learning outcomes? These are equity issues.

The question of whether there is both equality and equity in education and PE is more than ever a matter of considerable concern in a period driven by a discourse of injecting opportunity and choice in a system expected to incorporate a number of major initiatives with little or no preparation.

A National Curriculum may be a positive step in the direction of ensuring that a basic entitlement is established in PE but would be no guarantee of equity. The relationship is both complementary and profoundly problematic. As Secada points out, 'To ask a question based on equality, without first asking if that along which the equality is being measured is desirable and/or just, is to miss what equity is about' (p. 74). We might envisage a situation in which all children had equal access to a common PE curriculum and where teachers had developed a methodology to ensure that, across the ability range, they received more or less the same educational experiences and that the resulting distribution of measurable achievements showed no significant group differences based on sex, class or race. But this state of affairs would not be equitable if the curriculum which the children received either encouraged or helped sustain sexist, racist or elitist attitudes and behaviours. For example, the NC entitles all children (up to the age of 14) in England and Wales to Dance in school programmes of PE. But progress will be limited if they are introduced only to anglo-centred forms of dance expression which fail to meet the criteria of equity, or if the 'flexibility' demanded of the Physical Education NC in the secondary sector, by the Secretary of State and the National Curriculum Council (NCC, 1992), is used by teachers to provide or sustain a sex-differentiated curriculum in which boys have the 'opportunity' to opt out of Dance. Boys and girls may, however, in future have access to a common games programme. If racist, sexist or elitist attitudes and behaviours are expressed in these contexts then the educational experience they receive could hardly be said to be equitable. A commitment to equity demands that we scrutinize the nature of the experiences that are distributed through the curriculum. 'If we fail to ask whether or not the curriculum is just in what it legitimates as knowledge we may well achieve equality of education but it seems highly unlikely that that equality will represent a just distribution of knowledge' (Secada, 1989a, p. 75). Secada argues that such a focus on equality rather than equity brings a tendency to centre attention on how *groups* of people rather than individuals are benefited or disbenefited in education. This point is stressed by Paula Halliday (in this volume) who argues the importance of thinking about the 'special needs' of all children, not just of those who are categorized as such by legislation. To overlook the differences which exist amongst boys and girls, and within cultural groups, is potentially as damaging to the educational interests of children as it is divorced from the achievement of equity. Equality in education is then a noble and necessary concern but if unaccompanied by a commitment to equity it is also potentially damaging and conservative in its consequences because it is equity, not equality, which compels us to

> look at the justice of a given state of affairs, a justice that goes beyond acting in agreed upon ways and seeks to look at justice of the arrangements leading up to and resulting from those actions. . . . Equity inhabits this ground between our actions on the one hand and our notions of justice on the other. (Secada, 1989a, p. 81)

We contend that this is what the educational discourse and policy of the Conservative government in the UK has lamentably failed to do. The glory of the common law, much beloved of New Right ideologists, remains elusive and therefore deeply alienating for those left behind by economic and social competition.

In our view, then, the emphasis placed on free market principles and consumer choice in education are damaging to the expression of equality and equity in schools and cannot be equated with an education for democratic citizenship which would necessarily appraise and help reconstruct the way in which differences are conceptualized and constructed. We share Lauder's (1991) view that if notions of opportunity, choice and diversity are to be at all meaningful in a democratic system of education and Physical Education, then they have to be 'genuinely linked to the aspirations of ethnic minorities, women and the working class, rather than being used as code words designed to enhance the 'social wage' of the wealthy and the powerful' (Lauder, 1991, p. 428).

Notes

1 The two-winged (neo-liberal and neo-conservative) New Right has been most thoroughly analyzed by Stephen Ball (1990) developing Roger Dale's earlier ideas. The best brief summary of the recent literature is in Halpin and Whitty (1992).
2 Madeline Arnot (1991) argues that in the post-war period women's oppression was not only invisible but also silenced by the ideology of equality of opportunity. 'Female, and black and ethnic minority students were not even counted as significant participants within the sphere that was to help then achieve their "freedom"' (p. 452).

References

APPLE, M. (1989) 'How Equality has been Redefined in the Conservative Restoration', in SECADA, W.G. (Ed.) (1989b), pp. 7–26.

ARNOT, M. (1991) 'Equality and Democracy: A Decade of Struggle over Education', *British Journal of Sociology of Education*, **12**, 4, pp. 447–67.

ATKINSON, P. and DELAMONT, S. (1985) 'Socialisation into Teaching: The Research That Lost its Way', *British Journal of Sociology of Education*, **6**, 3, pp. 307–23.

BALL, S.J. (1990) *Politics and Policy Making in Education*, London, Routledge.

BATES, R. (1986) *The Management of Culture and Knowledge*, Geelong, Deakin University Press.

BENN, C. (1979) 'Elites versus Equals: The Political Background to the Comprehensive Reform', in RUBENSTEIN, D. (Ed.) *Education and Equality*, Harmondsworth, Penguin.

BURDEN-TEH, P. (1991) *Education and the Real World*, unpublished dissertation, University of Southampton.

BYRNE, E. (1985) 'Equality or Equity?: A European View', in ARNOT, M. (Ed.) *Race and Gender*, Oxford/New York: Pergamon Press, pp. 97–113.

CENTRE FOR CONTEMPORARY CULTURAL STUDIES (1981) *Unpopular Education*, London, Hutchinson.

CHITTY, C. (1987) 'The Comprehensive Principle Under Threat', in CHITTY, C. (Ed.) *Redefining The Comprehensive Experience*, Bedford Way Papers, London Institute of Education, pp. 6–27.

COX, C.B. and BOYSON, R. (1977) *Black Paper*, London, Temple Smith.

COX, C.B. and DYSON, A.E. (1969a) *Fight for Education: A Black Paper*, Manchester, Critical Quarterly Association.

COX, C.B. and DYSON, A.E. (1969b) *Black Power Two: The Crisis in Education*, Manchester, Critical Quarterly Association.

DAVIES, A.M., HOLLAND, J. and MINHAS, R. (1990) *Equal Opportunities in the New ERA*, Hillcote Group, Paper 2, London, Spider Web.

DAVIES, B. (1988) 'Destroying teacher motivation? The Impact of Nationalising the Curriculum of the Education Process', *Working Papers in Urban Education*, 3, King's College, London.

DAVIES, B. (1992) 'Social Class, School Effectiveness and Cultural Diversity', in LYNCH, J., MOGDIL, C. and MOGDIL, S. (Eds) *Cultural Diversity within Schools*, Vol. 3, London, Falmer Press, pp. 131–47.

DAVIES, B. and EVANS, J. (1984) 'Mixed Ability and the Comprehensive School', in BALL, S.J. (Ed.) *Comprehensive Schooling: A Reader*, London, Falmer Press, pp. 155–77.

DEEM, R. (1984) *Co-Education Reconsidered*, Milton Keynes, Open University Press.

DEPARTMENT OF EDUCATION AND SCIENCE (1987) *The National Curriculum: A Consultation Document*, Cardiff, DES/Welsh Office.

DEPARTMENT OF EDUCATION AND SCIENCE (1991) *Physical Education for Ages 5 to 16*, Department of Education and Science/Welsh Office.

EVANS, J. (1990a) 'Ability, Position and Privilege in School Physical Education', in KIRK, D. (1990) *Physical Education Curriculum and Culture*, London, Falmer Press, pp. 139–69.

EVANS, J. (1990b) 'Defining the Subject. The Rise and Rise of the New PE', in *British Journal of Sociology of Education*, **11**, 2, pp. 155–69.

EVANS, J. and DAVIES, B. (1990) 'Power to the People? The Education Reform Act and Tomorrow's Schools: A Critical and Comparative Perspective', in LAUDER, H. and WYLIE, C. (Eds) *Towards Successful Schooling*, London, Falmer Press, pp. 53–73.

FIELDING, M. (1987) ' "Liberté, Egalité, and Fraternité, ou la Mort": Towards a New School', in CHITTY, C. (Ed.) *Redefining the Comprehensive Experience*, No. 32, Bedford Way Papers, University of London.

GIROUX, H.A. (1991) 'Democracy and the Discourse of Cultural Difference: Towards a Politics of Border Pedogogy', *British Journal of Sociology of Education*, **12**, 4, pp. 501–21.

HALPIN, D. and WHITTY, J. (1992) *Secondary Education after the Reform Act*, Unit S1/2, *EP228 Frameworks for Teaching*, London, Open University Press.

HARGREAVES, A. and REYNOLDS, D. (1989) 'Introduction: Decomprehensivization', in HARGREAVES, A. and REYNOLDS, D. (Eds) *Education Policies: Controversies and Critiques*, London, Falmer Press, pp. 1–32.

HARGREAVES, J. (1986) *Sport, Power and Culture*, Cambridge, Polity Press.

HARGREAVES, J. (1990) 'Gender on the Sport Agenda', *International Review for Sociology of Sport*, **25**, 4, pp. 286–305.

HAYEK, F. (1976) *Law, Legislation and Liberty, Vol. 2: The Mirage of Social Justice*, London, Routledge and Kegan Paul.

INNER LONDON EDUCATION AUTHORITY (1988) '*My Favourite Subject*', Inner London Education Authority.

KELLY, A.V. (1991) *The National Curriculum: a Critical Review*, London, Paul Chapman Publishing Ltd.

KIRK, D. (1990) 'Defining the Subject: Gymnastics and Gender in British Physical Education', in KIRK, D. and TINNING, R. (Eds) *Physical Education, Curriculum and Culture*, London, Falmer Press, pp. 43–67.

LAUDER, H. (1988) 'Traditions of Socialism and Education Policy', in LAUDER, H. (Ed.) *Education in Search of a Future*, London, Falmer Press, pp. 20–50.

LAUDER, H. (1991) 'Education, Democracy and the Economy', *British Journal of Sociology of Education*, **12**, 4, pp. 417–33.

LEADBETTER, C. (1989) 'Power to the People', in HALL, S. and JACQUES, M. (Eds) *New Times*, London, Lawrence and Wishart, Ltd.

McWILLIAM, E. (1987) 'The Challenge of the New Right: Its liberty versus equality and to hell with fraternity', *Discourse*, **8**, 1, October, pp. 61–71.

NATIONAL CURRICULUM COUNCIL (1992) *National Curriculum Council Consultation Report, Physical Education*, York, National Curriculum Council.

PENNEY, D. and EVANS, J. (1991) 'The Impact of the Education Reform Act on the Provision of PE and Sport in the 5–16 Curriculum of State Schools, *The British Journal of Physical Education*, **22**, 1, Spring, pp. 38–44.

PHILLIPS, A. (1987) *Feminism and Equality*, Oxford, Basil Blackwell.

SAWICKI, J. (1991) *Disciplining Foucault: Feminism, Power and the Body*, London, Routledge.

SECADA, W.G. (1989a) 'Educational Equity Versus Equality of Education: An Alternative Conception', in SECADA, W.G. (Ed.) (1989b), pp. 68–89.

SECADA, W.G. (Ed.) (1989b) *Equity in Education*, London, Falmer Press.

SIMON, B. (1988) *Bending The Rules*, London, Lawrence and Wishart.

SZAMUELY, T. (1969) 'Comprehensive Inequality', in COX, C.B. and DYSON, A.E. (Eds) (1969b), pp. 48–57.

TALBOT, M. (1990) 'Equal Opportunities and Physical Education', in ARMSTRONG, N. (Ed.) *New Directions in Physical Education*, Human Kinetics Publishing, pp. 101–21.

WERNER, W. (1991) 'Defining Curriculum Policy Through Slogans', *Journal of Education Policy*, **6**, 2, April-June, pp. 225–39.

WILBY, P. (1977) 'Education and Equality', *New Statesman*, 16 September, pp. 358–61.

Chapter 2

Removing the Ugly '-Isms' in Your Gym: Thoughts for Teachers on Equity*

Patt Dodds

'Ellis ... Paul ... Eric ... Royce.' A pudgy third-grade boy stands fidgeting from one foot to the other, scuffing his sneakers in the dirt, fingers curled into fists and palms slightly sweaty. 'John ... Barbie ... David ... Sam.' Benjamin edges closer to the dwindling group, as if for comfort and protection. 'Susan ... Eddie ... Jamie ... Bobbie.' A small frown appears on the boy's face, his lips begin to quiver, his eyes look down at the toes of his shoes. 'Kim ... JoAnne' (longer pauses between the names, as team captains search the remaining children) ... and, at last: 'Benjamin!' He slowly trudges to the end of his team line, head hanging down.

A tall, scrawny teenage boy whiffs his bat at the ball. 'Out,' calls the teacher umpire. As the boy turns toward his bench, one of his teammates screams, 'You faggot! You made the last out and we lost the game'. On the adjacent field, a muscular teenage girl intercepts a soccer ball in front of a boy and shoots it toward the goal. Her reward is a loud 'Lezzie! Little dyke!' from her beaten opponent.

And so it goes, day after day, in typical physical education classes around the United States — children publicly choosing teams for game play, based on any of several possible factors: how proficient at the game children are, whether one is a best friend or not, if one is a girl or boy, to which race a child belongs, of which socioeconomic class one is a member, and many other features of which we are less aware. Each feature exemplifies an 'ugly ism', the major ones being sexism, heterosexism (homophobia), racism, classism, and motor elitism, which appear in every gym once in a while, but in many gyms far too frequently. Given the pervasive existence of these and other oppressive inequities in physical education, the purpose of this chapter is to encourage teachers and teacher developers to create physical education programmes where all students' interests

---

* Adapted from the 1984 Olympic Scientific Congress Proceedings, Volume 6, Sport Pedagogy (pp. 141–50) by Patt Dodds, 1986, Champaign, IL, Human Kinetics. Copyright © 1986 by Human Kinetics Publishers, Inc. Reprinted by permission.

are served and where all students have access to the rewards of the dominant social system.

Equity in the gym means providing fair, sensitive, respectful treatment of all students, regardless of their personal characteristics. As stated elsewhere (Dodds, 1986), *equity* is a way of looking at the world, an outlook, a cosmology, more akin to the overall tone of a symphony, a concerto, a string quartet, or to the idiosyncratic style of the conductor. As such, equity (or inequity) frames every aspect of one's teaching as an underlying theme, a ground bass easily recognizable in daily lessons, activity units, a year of skill themes work, or the entire elementary or secondary physical education programme. Equity is some-times subtle, sometimes distinctly obvious. It builds and fades, gradually or suddenly as it is always woven among the other elements of a lesson.

Why should physical educators be concerned about equity in the gym? While the answers are to some extent culturebound, and therefore differ from one country to another, all teachers who intend to help students learn will be interested in equity because it is their deliberate strategies which directly counteract and interrupt various forms of oppression in physical education. In the United States, oppression, and its alternative equity, remain emotionally loaded issues for educators in the early 1990s.

Until the past ten years, generous national and state educational policies and budgets were part of a general social liberalization built upon greater sensitivity to minority (subordinate) groups. Forty years of civil rights legislation had focused on each of these groups in turn. In the 1950s and 1960s laws were directed toward protecting the rights of African American (with other people of colour also benefiting), manifested in education by the forced integration of schools and colleges. The feminist movement of the 1970s highlighted women's issues (in education, for example, the federal Title IX Act of 1972 provided equal access for girls and women to sports and other education-related opportunities).

For disabled students, federal legislation 94-142 (1975) provided free public education in the 'least restrictive environments'. More recent state laws forbid discrimination based on sexual orientation (at least, in Wisconsin and Massachusetts), and several lawsuits over the past decade have reaffirmed the rights of lesbian and gay teachers and students (Harbeck, 1987). During these liberal years with strong social agendas and programmes, equity in education benefited from readily available federal grant money aimed at enriching teachers' strategies for coping with oppression. Six such grants were awarded specifically in physical education (Dodds, 1983).

Now, however, the current conservative Republican political climate, present 'back to basics' federal and state educational policies, declining monies for educational programmes for disadvantaged students (e.g. Head Start, Chapter I), and the marginal status of teachers and of physical education in the school curriculum make it difficult for physical educators to commit much energy toward combating oppression. To illustrate, the recent 'politically correct' (PC) movement,[1] particularly on college campuses (*Rothenberg*, 1991), is an ultraconservative backlash against four decades of gradual liberalization of education in the US. Along with the current PC agitation, increasing national political activity of fundamentalist religious groups (without exception ultraconservative), shrinking school and university budgets, dropping enrolments in colleges and universities, and declining secondary student achievement scores on national exams (e.g. Scholastic Aptitude Test, National Educational Assessment Program) have rapidly generated a fundamentals movement in US education which translates to increased concentration on the 'academic subjects' of reading, writing, maths, science and social studies to the exclusion of 'peripheral' subjects such as art, music, and physical education. The direct result of all these socioeconomic conditions is the elimination of elementary and secondary physical education programmes across the country, declining numbers of well-qualified teacher recruits, and minimal efforts by in-service teachers chronically tired from retrenchments, yearly pinkslips announcing unemployment, and constant bombardments of criticism from outside their school walls.

With social conservatism on the rise in education, the 'isms' in the gym also will almost certainly increase. One way for teachers to understand how the 'isms' operate is through oppression theory (Jackson and Hardiman, 1988), a theoretical framework encompassing all forms of inequity, including those that typically appear in physical education: racism, sexism, heterosexism (or homophobia), classism, handicapism, and motor elitism. Oppression, both a social condition and a process, is grounded in the identification of perceived (irrelevant) differences among groups which allow stronger groups to dominate society through ideology and control of the practices within society in general, and within each social institution such as education. In the gym, the prevailing white, male, heterosexual, middle-class, high-skilled ideology of elite performance in sport appears daily in physical education classes. Hierarchies among students are based on one or more of the 'isms' already mentioned: colour of one's skin, whether one is a girl or boy, one's sexual orientation, in which socioeconomic class one holds membership, whether one is disabled or not, and, of course, how well-skilled a sports performer one may be.

Physical educators should promote equity in the gym because educational rhetoric in the US holds that free public schooling for all children should create opportunities for each to maximize her/his individual potentials. Teachers, then, are obligated to design optimal conditions for their clients to learn. Maximizing students' opportunities to learn certainly includes minimizing restrictions and barriers to learning couched in oppression. Biases, prejudices, stereotyping and discrimination operate in the gym as the 'ugly isms' (racism, heterosexism, classism, handicapism, and motor elitism), promoting unfairness and inequities for many students. Each instance restricts some students, regardless of who imposes the limitations: teachers, fellow students, administrators, or the destructive cycle of a self-fulfilling prophecy.

Biases, prejudices, stereotyping, and discrimination are common manifestations of attitudes. Built over time into an array of coordinated beliefs about a particular object or person (Fishbein and Ajzen, 1975), physical educators' oppressive attitudes and behaviours translate to treating particular students unfairly based on characteristics which may or may not be accurate or true.

Biases and *prejudices* are beliefs and prejudgments about a person based on assumptions about the characteristics of particular groups to which the individual belongs, rather than on personal relationships with and knowledge about that individual. In the gym, such bias may take the form of sexism (judging that a girl cannot excel at upper body strength activities simply because she is female), racism (automatically expecting high performance from African American students in track and field [athletics] or basketball while holding lower expectations for them in tennis, gymnastics, or swimming), or motor elitism (using only one learning task, such as pushups, for a whole class when it is obvious that some students will be unable to perform that specific arm strength task at all).

Stereotyping, believing that every individual belonging to a group exhibits all the perceived characteristics of that group ('all African Americans dance well'), 'bangs people into shape with a cultural sledgehammer' (Pogrebin, 1980, p. 29). Stereotypes are based not on knowing an individual person, but upon knowing only the particular group into which an individual falls. Expecting a person to exhibit certain behaviours because she is a girl, he is Hispanic, or she is small, quiet, and bespectacled demands that each person act in accord with some mythical norm for a group. Out of the careless demands of such stereotypes one can create or sustain inequity of opportunity in the gym. Counselling all girls into field hockey units rather than flag football, placing all African American students in the low-skilled swimming section, or being totally surprised when the smallest boy in the class gets the best score on the fitness obstacle course illustrate ways teachers may perpetuate stereotypes in the physical education setting.

Discrimination restricts or denies rights, privileges, or choices of individuals because of their membership in subordinate groups. In the US, girls, students of colour, and poorly-skilled participants have been frequent victims in physical education classes. Even federal legislation has been unequal to the task of eliminating discrimination from the gym. For example, Title IX's first decade brought tremendous advances in equal opportunities for girls and women in sports, but today middle-class men once again dominate the decision-making, leadership, and budgets, thus eroding gains once made (Lopiano, 1989). Similar strides in equity for disabled students came through Public Law 94-142. Unfortunately, no law protects students with less motor ability against the apparent law of nature which guarantees that in the gym as in the wider world highly-skilled performers reap rewards while other students experience the psychological pain of rejection, ridicule, or just being ignored — unless, of course, sensitive teachers intervene to change the reward structure and help students celebrate more with each other than just 'being the best'. The end result of all the 'isms' is unfairness to some students, either from expectations too high, too low, or too different from the social norms of the dominant white male heterosexual able-bodied group.

Barriers and Problems: It's Not Easy To Be Fair To All

To become equitable physical educators teachers individually face three difficult tasks: recognizing and being sensitive to equity issues in their own classes; developing specific strategies to interrupt inequities and address oppression; and realizing that fully addressing inherent barriers to equity in the social system requires coordinated work with others. Being an equitable teacher is therefore a proposition far more complicated than mixing and matching a simple set of teaching behaviours at will. The contexts of teaching and of the gymnasium (Locke, 1975) create a long list of challenges for physical educators wishing to make their classes more equitable and less oppressive. The five outlined here may be addressed by individual teachers without additional help from others, though working together is advantageous for sustaining commitment, sharing specific contextual problems, generating multiple possibilities for strategies that work, setting realistic goals, confirming achievement of goals, and rewarding each other in collaborating toward equitable physical education.

Problem 1: Teaching is multidimensional

Teaching is never a single task attended by a teacher at a single moment. It is an ever-changing web of activities, varying from one instant to the next, characterized by multidimensionality, simultaneity, and spontaneity (Doyle, 1986). Teachers' repertoires do not include a single behaviour of 'fairness to all students', but must weave their focus on equity issues in and out of concerns for class management and organization, presentation and monitoring of student work, social and task-related interactions with individuals, and the constant flow of decisions which characterize each class session.

Because physical educators and their students live in incredibly complex environments where they must attend simultaneously to multiple events (Locke, 1975), equity imposes on teachers an entirely new framework for controlling the chaos of classes in movement environments. Teachers trying desperately to manage thirty or more children, distribute equipment, provide workspaces for all, monitor safety, record individual progress, and solve discipline problems may not believe they can really keep the lid on everything else — and still be equitable, too.

Equity requires adopting a different worldview in which the central question becomes 'how can I create a gym context that humanely serves the varying interests of all participants?'. Being an equitable teacher means far more than minor alterations in a few isolated teaching behaviours. Being fair to all may necessitate major changes in many teaching behaviours, as well as beliefs and attitudes. There is no simple cure for oppression, like retuning a viola between movements of a symphony. Many teachers fear losing control with one 'extra' thing to think about while performing their daily juggling acts. More attention to equity may feel like giving less to other aspects of good physical education classes. Continuous effort and attention to equity may feel too draining with so many classes each day. Even with good advice to start small with one step at a time, teachers may still believe becoming truly equitable requires too much change in their work.

Problem 2: Where and how to begin?

Even teachers aware of equity problems and possessing some knowledge about addressing the 'isms' in the gym may still be puzzled about the best time and place to start. Should they start revising the activity programme, reviewing grading standards, changing interactive verbal behaviours in one activity unit, rethinking their purposes for administering fitness tests, addressing all students more sensitively . . . or what?

One relatively benign place to start, requiring only persistent self-monitoring over time, is using inclusive language. When language habits change, so do our thinking patterns. In both written and verbal communication teachers can check themselves often in the course of a class, a day, or a week. It's easy to tell if you constantly bite your tongue as 'you guys' rolls out, use inclusive pronouns or plural structures to avoid the 'he' or 'she' applied to boys and girls collectively, or label sports terms generically rather than by gender stereotypes ('first base player' instead of 'baseman' or 'one-on-one defence' instead of 'man-to-man').

Beginning with language patterns allows teachers to practice frequently, self-check their own progress, model appropriate behaviours for students, and obtain feedback from others as they master at least one equity strategy. Lest changing language patterns be considered too trivial to count as a strategy to overcome oppression, remember that many linguists believe language shapes thought rather than the reverse. If changing language patterns is not a teacher's first choice, *any* equity strategy that seems reasonable to begin improving equality of opportunity in the gym is an adequate starting point. The energy required to make changes in teaching behaviours is considerable, so the choice of first focus ought to be self-generated.

Problem 3: How long must I continue?

The institutional nature of schools and the social characteristics of physical education classes dictate that significant changes in teaching will be neither quick nor easy, particularly when several simultaneous oppressions are apparent and the various strategies to address oppressions work differently for various students (and teachers). Educational change for teachers means not only adjusting one's own actions, but also convincing thirty students to act differently as well, and doing so in several classes per day.

Getting students to understand the reasons why teachers want them also to behave more affirmatively is both difficult and time-consuming. Teachers committed to equity often face the Herculean task of contradicting deeply ingrained social patterns students have learned since birth. It is difficult to overcome attitudes and behaviours which are reinforced daily by television programmes and commercials, by direct messages from adults, by family and peer values, and by the pervasive patriarchy of sport.

Further, when teachers stop addressing oppressions, they and their students gradually regress to former behaviours and attitudes. Without conscious maintenance and continuation, no equity patterns will long endure in the face of competing contingencies rewarding oppressions in the social context of the gym. Thus the question, 'How long must I go on?' is answered best by 'forever' if teachers are truly committed to increasing opportunities for all their students. The good news is that equitable teaching can become a good habit, demanding far less explicit attention later on than when first attempted.

Problem 4: What's in it for me?

Promoting teachers' commitment to greater fairness for all students is like convincing teachers that they ought to change anything: there must be payoffs or rewards for the new practices. As some of the most conservative educators, physical education teachers require powerful persuasion to alter traditional habits. Motivation thus becomes critical for inducing more equitable teaching practices in the gym.

Too often we assume automatically that all teachers are highly committed to their own professional development. While some certainly are, too many others are interested only in preserving their status quo. Capturing the attention of both groups and making it worthwhile to initiate more equitable treatment of students is easier when advantages for teachers themselves are enumerated. In one federally funded teacher development project designed to eliminate race and sex inequities in public school physical education (Project TEAM, 1983), the majority of teachers who completed training workshops and on-site practice activities already understood these advantages and were fine teachers eager to enrich their teaching repertoire. The greatest problem for the training pro-gramme was attracting less effective teachers not clearly convinced that greater equity for students would make their own work more rewarding as well.

Many teachers resist adopting more equitable teaching practices because they believe they may lose power by doing so. Whites, middle-class males, and highly- skilled performers (the dominant groups in our culture) are the teachers most likely to believe that they can only lose by treating subordinate groups of students more fairly. They don't understand the many advantages to themselves of addressing equity issues in their gyms, not the least of which is better cooper-ation by all students, which reduces class management problems and makes the gym a happier place for all.

To help teachers adopt more equitable actions, the present reward system for teachers must change. Now there are few financial reinforcers available for being especially good at teaching: rewards from students are too few, too infrequent, and too weak to sustain most physical educators. Administrative support, other than lip service, for acquiring new teaching worldviews or even isolated skills is generally absent. And often other teachers punish those who try to change. Thus, no simple answers to 'what's in it for me?' are possible.

Problem 5: Who's in charge of PE classes, anyway?

The last problem for teachers trying to eliminate oppression and inequity for students is that they alone do not control all the significant events in class. Chil-dren learn from each other as well as from their teacher. Their messages may overpower those of the teacher, particularly if the teacher is trying to change things to advantage more or different students than previously. Both congruent and dissonant messages reach students from their many 'teachers' and at differ-ent times.

If the teacher works intensively to help students treat each other fairly while the students continue to limit or discourage others, mixed and unclear signals wash out the effects of the teacher's messages. It is evident that enough students must support the teacher's equity efforts to ensure class-level changes. Other-wise, the teacher's battle will be long and lonely, intermittent schedules of reinforcement will maintain the status quo of relative inequity, and in effect the equitable gym will neither be attained nor continued.

The complex process of building equitable learning environments together, and the necessity for full participation by students as well as teachers require detailed analysis of how students affect each other if teachers are to have the strongest, most effective strategies for interrupting 'isms' in the gym.

Students' agendas of racism, classism, and motor elitism in elementary physical education, contrasting directly with the teacher's agenda of democracy and fair treatment for all, are tellingly documented in Wang's early participant observation dissertation (1977). The views expressed by secondary students, in one of the earliest in-depth interview studies (Kollen, 1981), provide dismal confirmation that physical education frequently has restrictive, limiting, negative effects, some of which can be traced to motor elitism. Currently, more promising research on cooperative learning demonstrates acquisition of both social and academic skills, happily for disadvantaged and less able students as well as high achievers (Johnson and Johnson, 1985; Slavin *et al.*, 1985). Teachers whose goal is real equity in physical education might draw advantageously on many of these cooperative learning strategies.

The five problems outlined above, only representative of the many barriers that prevent physical educators from confronting the oppressive 'isms' when they teach, are situated only in the most immediate context of the gymnasium as classroom. Long-lasting solutions for these problems must therefore be referenced within the wider social contexts of local, regional and national communities, although individual teachers may begin their equity work the very next time they teach a class.

Promising Research Addressing the 'Isms'

Scholarship in the US educational community addressing reduction of the 'isms' has depended in large part on limited government funding for small special projects rather than being systematically infused into education. While physical education is the context for a few pre-service and in-service teacher training projects, the vast majority of equity research over the last twenty years is classroom-based and focused only on sexism and/or racism. A 1983 equity research review (Dodds, 1982, 1983) is summarized below.

Researchers worked primarily in the positivist paradigm using experimental or quasi-experimental designs, usually included only observable and measurable teacher behaviours and student outcomes, and investigated teachers and students from preschool to college levels. Interventions included courses, workshops, and written materials, but very little supervised teaching practice with feedback for teachers actually addressing oppression in their classrooms. For students, teaching interventions generally involved modelling of appropriate equitable behaviours, audiovisual materials and prepared curriculum unit packages, and some simulation games.

Results were somewhat mixed for the principal dependent variables of teacher and student awareness, attitudes, and actions, with attitude changes being the most popular target of research efforts and behaviour change least represented in the literature. While some studies showed positive outcomes, many showed unclear or mixed positive and neutral results. Like the general state of teacher development research in the US, then, attempts to improve equity among teachers showed no powerful, consistent training strategies that were universally efficient.

Updating this research review during the early 1990s and narrowing the scope to physical education brings cause to celebrate greater sophistication and openness in equity research. In contrast to the general conservatism of our field (Bain, 1989), some researchers are now sufficiently bold to ask deeper, more important equity questions leading to faster, more substantial changes among teachers and students in the gym.

As the contributors to this book illustrate (e.g. Scraton in chapter 9 and Flintoff in chapter 12), qualitative/interpretive and participatory research/critical theory researchers now provide very different kinds of data from those derived from earlier, equally important positivist research, such as that reviewed above. Physical educators giving careful attention to these new portrayals of 'isms' in the gym can become smarter about the conditions necessary to create greater equity in the gym. Following are only brief research examples that centralize the experiences of teachers and students themselves within elaborated, richly detailed contextual descriptions to help readers understand more about equity issues. Although earlier qualitative studies generally only verify the presence of oppression by describing physical education situations, later researchers clearly have strong agendas for social change.

To illustrate only one 'ism' represented in research, several researchers during the past fifteen years have investigated heterosexism (homophobia), especially its implications for lesbians (and by extension, gay men and bisexual people) in sport and physical education (Beck, 1976; Bennett *et al.*, 1987; Cobhan, 1982; Gondola and Fitzpatrick, 1985; Guthrie, 1982; Hall, 1987; Lenskyj, 1986; Locke and Jensen, 1970; Woods, 1990). The earliest of these dared not even use the word 'lesbian' in their titles, instead euphemistically referring to 'never married women physical educators' (Beck, 1976) or reversing the real underlying question by the title 'Heterosexuality of women in physical education' (Locke and Jensen, 1970). The most recent work intensively captured the separate, dual lives of fifteen lesbian physical educators (Woods, 1990).

Griffin's research (1985a, 1985b, 1985c, 1985d, 1985e, 1989a, 1989b among others) best illustrates long-term commitment to questions about equity in the gym. Her earliest studies are qualitative descriptions of sexism and motor elitism in middle school (early secondary) physical education which segregates girls and boys into separate, distinct levels of participation in various activity units that were stereotyped as exclusively for girls or for boys (Griffin, 1985a, 1985d, 1985e). Next Griffin examined the experiences of two teachers, one openly strengthening sex equity in his physical education classes (Griffin, 1985b), and the other a white woman struggling to teach physical education effectively in an urban, multiracial junior high school (Griffin, 1985c).

Later Griffin advised a phenomenological interview dissertation (Woods 1990) of lesbian physical educators' experiences framed within oppression theory (Jackson and Hardiman, 1988). That study drew attention to teachers as victims rather than purveyors of oppression in physical education. More recently, Griffin herself shifted paradigms to participatory research with lesbian and gay teachers (including some physical educators). First these teachers collaboratively processed their own experiences as homosexual educators and then planned and carried out various social action strategies to continue validating themselves, as strategies for greater self-integration, and as tools for educating their students and the public (Griffin, 1991a, 1991b).

Griffin also has influenced other research related to equity now being conducted at the University of Massachusetts. Portman (in progress) is observing and interviewing low-skilled students in elementary physical education classes (effects of motor elitism), Sykes (in progress) is interviewing lesbian and gay pre-service teachers training to be physical educators (effects of heterosexism), and Carlson (in progress) is preparing an investigation of students alienated from physical education classes in various ways, searching particularly for evidence of motor elitism, sexism, racism, and heterosexism. Thus, Griffin's influence on equity-related research extends well beyond her own work.

Summary and Conclusion

This chapter has defined constructs important in understanding several forms of oppression occurring in physical education, presented illustrative examples of problems teachers face in making their work more equitable, and provided selective instances of physical education pedagogy research in the US that addresses equity in the gym. In the broad context of current conservative US educational policies and values for educational practice, it is clear that individual teachers working alone must generate their own commitment, strategies, and rewards for becoming more equitable with their students.

The vision is to create physical education classes where all children join a team without being subjected to humiliation or stress because their motor skills don't measure up; where African Americans, Hispanics, and Anglos play together peacefully without dwelling on cultural differences that might disrupt the game; where the norms are cooperation, sensitivity to others, appreciation of differences, and inclusion of students confined to wheelchairs or openly self-declared as lesbian or gay; and where every student can learn in an atmosphere of encouragement and joy for every social and academic achievement. Every teacher willing to pay the price necessary to be fair and affirmative for all students shares this vision. Although multidimensional equity in every gym may still be only fantasy, each teacher quietly removing the 'isms' from physical education moves us all one step closer to the dream.

Note

1 'Politically correct' is used by ultraconservative groups in the US as a demeaning, derogatory label for all who wish to liberalize society. 'Politically correct', or simply PC, is applied most frequently (as a backlash) against those advocating multiculturalism, lesbian and gay (or other oppressed groups) rights, revisionist history, or reorganization of the liberal arts college curriculum to include the experiences of women, or ethnic and racial groups other than white European males (Adler, 1990; Gibbs, 1990; Rieff, 1990; Rothenberg, 1991).

References

ADLER, J. (1990) 'Taking offense: Is this new enlightenment on campus or the new McCarthyism?', *Newsweek*, 24 December, pp. 48–55.

BAIN, L. (1989) 'Implicit values in physical education', in TEMPLIN, T. and SCHEMPP, P. (Eds), *Socialization into Physical Education: Learning to Teach*, Indianapolis, Benchmark Press, pp. 289–314.

BECK, B. (1976) 'Lifestyles of Never Married Women Physical Educators in Institutions of Higher Education in the US', *Dissertation Abstracts International*, **37**, p. 2715A.

BENNETT, R., WHITAKER, G., SMITH, N. and SABOLVE, A. (1987) 'Changing the Rules of the Game: Reflections toward a Feminist Analysis of Sport', *Women's Studies International Forum*, **10** (4), pp. 369–79.

CARLSON, T. (1991) 'A Critical Theory Analysis of Alienated Students in Secondary Physical Education', Amherst, MA, Comprehensive examination paper in progress.

COBHAN, L. (1982) 'Lesbians in Physical Education and Sport', in CRUIKSHANK, M. (Ed.) *Lesbian Studies: Present and Future*, Old Westbury, NY, Feminist Press, pp. 179–86.

DODDS, P. (1982) 'A Review of Sex Equity Training Programs *for Physical Educators*', Columbus, OH, Invited paper presented at the Teaching Research Workshop, Ohio State University, June.

DODDS, P. (1983) '*Equity Training Models: The Research Base*', Paper presented at the AAHPERD annual meeting, Minneapolis, MN, January.

DODDS, P. (1986) 'Stamp out the Ugly 'Isms' in your Gym, in PIERON, M. and GRAHAM, G. (Eds) *Sport Pedagogy*, The 1984 Olympic Scientific Congress Proceedings, Vol. 6, pp. 141–50.

DOYLE, W. (1986) 'Classroom Organization and Management', in WITTROCK, M. (Ed.) *Handbook of Research on Teaching*, 3rd ed., New York, Macmillan, pp. 392–431.

FISHBEIN, M. and AJZEN, I. (1975) *Belief, Attitude, Intention and Behavior: An Introduction to Theory and Research*, Reading, MA, Addison-Wesley.

GIBBS, N. (1990) 'Bigots in the Ivory Tower: An Alarming Rise in Hatred Roils US Campuses', *Time*, 7 May, pp. 104–6.

GONDOLA, J. and FITZPATRICK, T. (1985) 'Homophobia in Girls' Sports: "Names" That Can Hurt Us . . . All Of Us', *Equal Play*, **5** (2), pp. 18–19.

GRIFFIN, P. (1985a) 'Girls' and Boys' Participation Styles in Middle School Team Sport Classes; A Description and Practical Applications', *The Physical Educator*, **42** (1), pp. 3–8.

GRIFFIN, P. (1985b) 'Teacher Perceptions of and Reactions to Equity Problems in a Middle School Physical Education Program', *Research Quarterly for Exercise and Sport*, **56** (2), pp. 103–10.

GRIFFIN, P. (1985c) 'Teaching in an Urban Multiracial Junior High School Physical Education Program: The Power of Context', *Quest*, **37** (2), pp. 154–65.

GRIFFIN, P. (1985d) 'Boys' Participation Styles in a Middle School Team Sports Unit', *Journal of Teaching in Physical Education*, **4** (2), pp. 100–10.

GRIFFIN, P. (1985e) 'Girls' Participation Patterns in a Middle School Team Sports Unit', *Journal of Teaching in Physical Education*, **4** (1), pp. 30–8.

GRIFFIN, P. (1989a) 'Gender as a Socializing Agent in Physical Education', in TEMPLIN, T. and SCHEMPP, P. (Eds) *Socialization Into Physical Education: Learning to Teach*, Indianapolis, Benchmark Press, pp. 219–34.

GRIFFIN, P. (1989b) 'Using Participatory Research to Empower Gay and Lesbian Educators', Paper presented at the annual meeting of the American Educational Research Association, San Francisco, March.

GRIFFIN, P. (1991a) 'Identity Management Studies among Lesbian and Gay Educators', *Qualitative Studies in Education*, **4**, 3, pp. 189–202.

GRIFFIN, P. (1991b) 'From hiding out to coming out: Improving Lesbian and Gay educators', *Journal of Homosexuality*, **22**, 3/4, pp. 167–96.

GUTHRIE, S. (1982) '*Homophobia: Its Impact on Women in Sport and Physical Education*', Unpublished master's thesis, California State University at Long Beach.

HALL, M. (Ed.) (1987) 'The Gendering of Sport, Leisure, and Physical Education', *Women's Studies International Forum*, **10** (4) (special issue).

HARBECK, K. (1987) 'Personal Freedoms/Public Constraints: An Analysis of the Controversy over the Employment of Homosexuals as School Teachers, Vols. I and II', Palo Alto, CA, Unpublished doctoral dissertation, Stanford University.

JACKSON, B. and HARDIMAN, R. (1988) 'Oppression: Conceptual and Developmental Analysis', Amherst, MA, Unpublished manuscript, University of Massachusetts.

JOHNSON, R. and JOHNSON, D. (1985) 'Student-Student Interaction: Ignored but Powerful', *Journal of Teacher Education*, **XXXVI** (4), pp. 22–6.

KOLLEN, P. (1981) 'The Experience of Movement in Physical Education: A Phenomenology', *Dissertation Abstracts International* (University Microfilms No. 81-16272).

LENSKYJ, H. (1986) *Out of Bounds: Women, Sport and Sexuality*, Toronto, The Women's Press.

LOCKE, L. (1975) 'The Ecology of the Gym: What the Tourists Never See', *Proceedings of SAPECW*, Spring, pp. 38–50, also see *Resources in Education*, **10** (8), p. 179.

LOCKE, L. and JENSEN, M. (1970) 'The Heterosexuality of Women in Physical Education', *The foil*, Fall, pp. 30–4.

LOPIANO, D. (1989) 'The Foxes are Guarding the Hen House: The Current Reality of Title IX', Paper presented at the AAHPERD annual meeting, Boston, April.

POGREBIN, L. (1980) *Growing Up Free: Raising Your Child in the 80s*, New York, McGraw Hill.

PORTMAN, P. (1991) 'The Experience of Low-Skilled Students in Public School Physical Education Classes: The Significance of being Chosen Last', Amherst, MA, Unpublished dissertation.

PROJECT TEAM (1983) Teaching Equity Approaches in Massachusetts. Amherst, MA: University of Massachusetts, unpublished reports.

RIEFF, D. (1990) 'The Case Against Sensitivity: Are We Scrapping the First Amendment to Spare People's Feelings?', *Esquire*, **114** (5), pp. 120–31.

ROTHENBERG, P. (1991) 'Critics of Attempts to Democratize the Curriculum are Waging a Campaign to Misrepresent the Work of Responsible Professors', *The Chronicle of Higher Education*, 10 April.

SLAVIN, R., SHARAN, S. and KAGAN, S. (1985) *Learning to Cooperate, Cooperating to Learn*, New York, Plenum Press.

SYKES, K. (1991) 'Experiences of Lesbian and Gay Preservice Physical educators in a Teacher Training Program', Amherst, MA, Comprehensive examination paper in progress.

WANG, B. (1977) 'An Ethnography of Physical Education Class: An Experiment in Integrated Living', *Dissertation Abstracts International*, **38**, p. 1980A.

WOODS, S. (1990) 'The Contextual Realities of Being a Lesbian Physical Educator: Living in Two Worlds', Amherst, MA, Unpublished doctoral dissertation, University of Massachusetts.

Section One

Concepts and Issues

Chapter 3

Disability, Empowerment and Physical Education

Len Barton

The perspective adopted in this paper is only one of a number available on the issue of disability. Nor is it a popular approach. It is one which seeks to challenge the dominant assumptions and practices which locate the problems within the individual and their personal limitations. Increasing numbers of disabled people are subscribing to this position and it deserves to be seriously considered by all those who have a concern for the development of a just and equitable society. Whilst the issues and ideas in this brief analysis have an applicability to disabled people generally, it is specifically referring to physically disabled pupils and young people.

Disability is a complex issue. Definitions are crucial in that the presuppositions informing them can be the basis of stereotyping and stigmatization. One of the dominant influences shaping both legal and common-sense understandings of 'disability' has been the medical model. From this perspective an emphasis upon an individual's inabilities or deficiencies are central. Terms such as 'cripple' or 'spastic' reinforce such an individualized medical definition in which functional limitations predominate. Medical presuppositions have influenced the definition of 'disability' within the DES Final Report on PE and the National Curriculum, in which it is defined as 'the loss or reduction of functional ability' (DES, 1991b, p. 55, para 7).

Historically, disability has been viewed fundamentally as a personal tragedy, which has resulted in such people being seen as objects of pity or in need of charity. They have been subject to discriminatory policies and practices in which the predominant images of passivity and helplessness reinforced their inferior status. In a powerful critique of the medical model, Brisenden (1986) who was himself a disabled person vividly describes his feelings in the following way:

> We are seen as 'abnormal' because we are different; we are problem people, lacking the equipment for social integration. But the truth is, like everybody else, we have a range of things we *can* and *cannot* do, a range of abilities both mental and physical that are unique to us as individuals. The only difference between us and other people is that we are viewed through spectacles that only focus on our inabilities, and which suffer an automatic blindness — a sort of medicalised social reflex — regarding our abilities. (p. 175)

One effect of such a perspective is that it provides a variety of individualized responses to disabled people. For example, they are often viewed in heroine terms, as being brave and courageous. Their position is constantly being compared against an assumed notion of 'normality'. Indeed, it is the pursuit of this 'which leads to neurosis and is the cause of much guilt and suffering' (Brisenden, p. 175) on their part.

One of the most crucial limitations of this perspective is that it neglects any serious consideration of a socio-political dimension. This approach provides a very different understanding of disability and the issues involved. It entails an alternative set of assumptions, priorities and explanations. As Hahn (1986) maintains:

> disability stems from the failure of a structured social environment to adjust to the needs and aspirations of citizens with disabilities rather than from the inability of a disabled individual to adapt to the demands of society. (p. 128)

It is an unadaptive, unhelpful and unfriendly environment which needs to be examined and changed. Being interested in how disabled people suffer, requires an examination of those material conditions and social relations which contribute to their dehumanization and isolationism.

Participation in society is not contingent upon merely the individual limitations of disabled people, but rather the physical and social restrictions of an essentially hostile environment. Writing on the question of the politics of disability, Oliver (1990) summarizes the essential features of such an alternative position:

> All disabled people experience disability as social restriction, whether those restrictions occur as a consequence of inaccessible built environments, questionable notions of intelligence and social competence, the inability of the general public to use sign language, the lack of reading material in braille or hostile public attitudes to people with non-visible disabilities. (p. xiv)

He maintains that disabled people are involved in a difficult struggle in which they must strengthen their endeavours as a political pressure group. Disability is thus a social and political category in that it entails practices of regulation and struggles for choice, empowerment and opportunities (Fulcher, 1989).

In a society fundamentally organized and administered by and for able-bodied people the position of disabled people in relation to education, work, housing and welfare services is a matter of grave concern (Abberley, 1987; Oliver, 1990). Indeed, in many ways it is a scandal, and a reflection of their marginalization, low status and vulnerability as well as an indication of the power-struggle in which they are, and must continue to be, involved. Relationships with various professional agencies are often difficult and disabled people have vociferously argued for a range of changes. These include greater choice in the nature and amount of services provided, more control over the allocation of resources especially in relation to independent living and new forms of accountability of service providers to disabled people involving clear mechanisms for handling disagreements (Brisenden, 1986; Oliver and Hasler, 1987; Oliver, 1988). In an analysis of social policy in the past decade Glendinning (1991) discusses these and other issues and seeks to demonstrate that matters have actually got worse and that:

> The economic and social policies of the last decade have done little to enhance, and much to damage, the quality of life of disabled people. Despite the rhetoric of 'protecting' the most 'deserving', 'vulnerable', or 'needy', much of this 'protection' has been illusory. (p. 16)

Such events have resulted in a serious reduction in the degree of autonomy and choice of disabled people but an increase and intensification of 'scrutiny and control by professionals and others' (p.16). These forms of handicapping conditions and relations encourage passivity and dependency on the part of disabled people (Bishop, 1987). It is integral to the process of learned helplessness in which problems are depicted as personal troubles rather than public issues (Mills, 1970).

So far I have argued that disability needs to be understood as a form of oppression. Being disabled entails social and economic hardships as well as assaults upon self-identity and emotional well-being. However, it would be both disabilist and misleading to give the impression that disabled people are a homogeneous group. The reality and implications of this for the nature of the curriculum, teacher expectations and pupil opportunities, are not given serious consideration in the National Curriculum PE Final Proposals (DES, 1991b). Terms such as 'the disabled' are a catch-all and give an impression of sameness. But the difficulties of and responses to being disabled are influenced by class, race, gender and age factors. These can cushion or compound the experience of discrimination and oppression. For example, in a study of disabled women receiving care Begum (1990) maintains that:

> women with disabilities are perennial outsiders; their oppression and exclusion renders them one of the most powerless groups in society. The personal care situation encapsulates so many different dynamics that for many women with disabilities it becomes the arena where their oppression becomes so clearly magnified and distilled. (p. 79)

Supporting this perspective, Morris (1989) illustrates from the lives of a group of disabled women, including her own, that matters of privacy, body-image and sexuality are a source of tension and difficulties in relation to the care situation. Also, she highlights the disadvantages disabled mothers experience in having responsibility for the upbringing of the children and the general running of the home as well as maintaining some form of outside employment. The degree to which individuals can survive within these circumstances will be largely contingent upon their socioeconomic circumstances. The more they can afford, the greater the chances of coping. Unfortunately, few disabled people are in this position and therefore the overall situation is very bleak indeed. Many disabled people are therefore, as Borsay (1986) contends, 'located at the bottom of the income ladder, or out of work and dependent upon social security benefits' (p. 184). Given that the political discourse is now largely one of the market and that any policies have tended to 'have grown up in an ad hoc fashion without a coherent framework to guide policy development' (Borsay, 1986 p. 183), inequalities of provision and opportunity are being exacerbated. Questions of social justice and equality have become marginalized within this type of socioeconomic climate. In the struggle for empowerment, disabled people and able-bodied colleagues must strive to move the overriding interest in questions of *needs* to those of *rights* (Hudson, 1988). Critical attention can thus be given to those structural and institutional factors which constrain and serve the interests of the more powerful (Oliver, 1989a).

Diversionary Rhetoric

Official documents and policy statements contain a great deal of high platitudes, good intentions and appealing rhetoric. Sociologists have argued for the importance of recognizing the *real* as opposed to the *stated* outcomes of such material relating to special education (Tomlinson, 1982, 1985; Ford *et al.*, 1982). In an analysis of human services and their policies, Wolfensberger (1989) makes a distinction between manifest and latent functions. The manifest functions of such services contained in an avalanche of documents are:

> that services are beneficent, charitable, benign, curative, habilitative, etc. (p. 26)

However,

> while services may be some of those things some of the time, they also commonly perform latent functions very different from these proclaimed ones, including ones that are competency-impairing, destructive of independence, that are actually dependency-making and dependency-keeping, health-debilitating and outright death-accelerating, and thus killing. (p. 26)

Wolfensberger sets this argument within the context of what he calls a 'post-primary production economy'. In this contemporary historical period human service systems produce dependency. An important aspect of this process is persuading disabled people and society at large to recognize that recipients of such services ought to be grateful for what they receive. By this means the workings of service systems are depoliticized.

Whilst the previously outlined position may be viewed as extreme and mainly negative, from the perspective adopted in this chapter it has a number of advantages. First, it confirms that discussions relating to the experiences and well-being of disabled people *must* be part of a socioeconomic and historical analysis. This includes issues relating to the division of labour and its dynamic interplay on social status and opportunities. Secondly, and relatedly, disability is a political issue and entails seriously examining consumer-rights and raising questions about whose interests particular provisions serve and who benefits from them? Thirdly, that current ideologies and practices are neither natural nor proper and are a social creation and thus can be changed. Fourthly, that the struggle for change will be bitter and prolonged and will necessitate disabled people and their allies becoming increasingly politicized and vociferous in their demands. Finally, the position of government receives specific attention, in particular the political will involved in the development and implementation of appropriate legislation and policies. The overall impact of these factors give support to challenging individualized, mythical and deficit views of disabled people and priority to understanding and changing an offensive material and social world.

Dominant Images

One of the most powerful ways in our society in which particular images are promoted and legitimated is through the media. We live in a world in which physical appearance has become an obsession. Indeed, one writer maintains it is a form of narcissism which greatly exceeds any interest in fitness (Lasch, 1979). It consumes a great deal of people's time, money and effort. A whole consumer industry has been generated which is concerned with encouraging and maintaining an interest in attractiveness. This whole process has little to do with improving health and is often 'stressful and energy-sapping' (Lonsdale, 1990, p. 63).

Within a predominantly sexist society the significance of the issue of appearance in women's lives is considerable. In support of this viewpoint Lonsdale (1990) argues that:

> For boys and men body-image is primarily related to whether their bodies will *do* certain things, whereas for girls and women it is whether their bodies will look *right* and be acceptable. (p. 64)

In the stereotypes which are culturally reproduced through such activities as sport and leisure, girls are seen as being interested and successful in those activities which encourage 'grace, balance and aesthetic' qualities. In contrast, boys are best in those activities which require 'strength, stamina and aggression' (Carrington and Williams, 1988, pp. 93–4).

What is important as far as the question of body-image and disabled people is concerned is their powerful personal awareness that they do not, in various ways, match up to the physical ideals able-bodied society sets. Nor is there a single way in which disabled people deal with this. It is nevertheless a serious issue particularly for women, in that, as Morris (1989) notes in her book on the lives of a group of women with spinal injuries, including her own:

> One of the hardest parts of becoming disabled is acceptance of, and living with, a changed body-image. Our body shape and the aids we use (a wheelchair and crutches) are the visible signs of disability. Appearance plays a very important part in interaction with other people. What is more, women face an additional problem in that our physical attractiveness is generally the way our femininity and sexuality are measured by other people. (p. 60)

The accounts in this book illustrate that there are a range of responses with regard to the way and degree to which disability affects the individual's self-image. However, 'other people's reactions are a very important part of the experience of disability' (Morris, 1989, p. 78). Disabled people are measured against some unexamined, idealized notion of 'normality' including appearance and their difference is mainly seen in negative terms and results in offensive, condescending, patronizing encounters with able-bodied people.

In this brief overview the intention has been to present an analysis in which the issue of oppression is seen as central to an adequate understanding of disability. Social pathology models are a constant source of discrimination and dehumanization. Dominant images surrounding sexuality, attractiveness and the body-beautiful as well as the expectations, identities and practices associated with them are a means of oppression in the lives of disabled people. Nor must this be viewed as merely an attitudinal problem. It is rooted in real material, social conditions and relations. As such, it is a structural issue in which the pursuit of social justice, rights and empowerment must be essential motivational concerns of any serious and effective struggle for change.

The Education Reform Act, Physical Education and Disability

We are living in a period of unprecedented change in education. With the introduction of the Education Reform Act 1988, all aspects of state provision are being affected in various ways. These fundamental re-formulations have their justification in a series of criticisms of schools and teachers. These include issues of accountability, standards and discipline. The Government's interest is focused on how the system is to be managed and how educational success and effectiveness is defined and assessed. A particular market approach with an emphasis on parental choice, competition and individualism provides the basis for prophetic claims about improvement and greater opportunities.

Competition within and between schools, consumer choice and an increased diversity of school provision are central to these developments (Simon, 1988; Ranson, 1990). This has resulted in a world of enterprise culture supported by a new management language being applied to and used in discussions about schools. It includes such key concepts as efficiency, cost-effectiveness, targets, performance indicators, competences and appraisal. In such a highly pressurized world the task is to market or sell yourself. With the introduction of LMS, opting out and open enrolment, concerns over equal opportunity and social justice become increasingly marginalized (Arnot, 1991; Weiner, 1989).

Schools are not immune from external influences, nor can their activities be described as neutral. Schooling is a system of social practice which gives priority to particular forms of knowledge, evaluative procedures and outcomes. Schools are linked to other powerful institutions which themselves contribute to the generation and maintenance of social inequalities (Apple, 1990). Thus schooling 'is part of a larger process of winning consent to discrepancies in power and opportunity' (Johnson, 1991, p. 77).

When examining issues relating to pedagogy and curriculum it is therefore essential to think in terms that are less restrictive than much of the literature in the field of physical education. This is one of the reasons why Kirk and Tinning (1990) maintain that:

we cannot go on blissfully measuring the happenings inside physical education classes, counting students' 'motor-engaged' time or the amount of time teachers devote to managerial matters, without also taking account of the forces outside schools that are actually shaping the very substance of what we teach. . . . (p. 2)

This is a very apposite encouragement when trying to evaluate the DES Interim Report of the Physical Education Working Group (DES, 1991a). The Report attempts to depoliticize the notion of what constitutes 'a physically educated person' (p. 16). By underplaying the significance of existing inequalities and social divisions within society, an emphasis is given to individual ability and the acquisition of skills. In such a society, however, any success will be at the expense of others and the meanings of such key concepts need to be viewed as problematic. The process of understanding and interpretation involves contestation and conflict between parties operating from unequal standpoints. This struggle is evident when the following questions are asked with regard to physical education:

- Is such a curriculum enabling for disabled people?
- In what way does the curriculum deal with the issue of difference?
- why does the curriculum take the particular form it does?

The DES Report (1991a) maintains that teachers should remember that:

children are more important than the activities in which they are engaged. 'The game' is *not* the thing — the child is. (p. 16)

Whilst all service institutions claim to be enriching, supporting and enabling, their latent functions are often quite different, in that they become dependency-creating and stultifying (Wolfensberger, 1989). If we begin to make a distinction between the formal rhetoric and actual practice of school life, a quite different picture begins to emerge. In ascertaining the validity of the above statement from the Report, the following are among the factors needing to be noted and engaged with in a critical way:

(a) Physical education is the creation of and for able-bodied people.
(b) It gives priority to certain types of human movement.
(c) Individual success is viewed as a means of personal status and financial well-being. It is depicted as a way to the 'good life'.
(d) A whole consumer industry has been generated around such activities. Sport has become a commodity to be sold in the market-place.

The motivation to participate is encouraged through the articulations of idealized notions of 'normality' in which we can all, irrespective of race, class, gender or disability, benefit and be empowered. In the Final Report (DES, 1991b) the curriculum emphasis is on 'games' and 'performance'. It is not a curriculum which will easily accommodate physically disabled pupils. Whilst the rhetoric is on what teachers are supposed to do there are very serious grounds for concern.

Research has already begun to demonstrate that there are serious problems with regard to the values, expectations and experience of physical education for different groups of pupils. The result is often discrimination and stereotyping. For example, physical education tends to emphasize masculine values such as struggle and aggression (Bain, 1990; Kirk and Tinning, 1990; Carrington and Williams, 1988). Individualism and competitiveness are central values underpinning such activities (Leaman, 1988; Pollard, 1988). The Final Report of the National Curriculum for PE continues to emphasize these values. Although the report highlights the dangers of labelling and this is important (see p. 55, para 7) the definitions and distinctions made in the same paragraph between 'impairment, disability and handicap' will not help to avoid such problems or challenge discriminatory practices. The assumptions informing these able-bodied definitions are those which emphasize personal loss, inability and thus difference in essentially negative terms. Jenny Morris, a disabled analyst, discusses the nature of prejudice which disabled people experience and maintains that:

> Our physical and intellectual characteristics are not 'right' nor 'admirable' and we do not 'belong'. It is particularly important to state this because — having given such a negative meaning to abnormality — the non-disabled world assumes that we wish to be normal, or to be treated as if we were. (1991, p. 16)

A definition of disability which enables disabled people to take pride in their difference is essential.

We must not underestimate the concern of parents that their disabled child becomes as 'normal as possible'. The pressure to conform is immense and has led some parents and teachers to see Conductive Education as a means of achieving many of their hopes (Beardshaw, 1989). Many have visited the Peto Institute in Hungary to see what is involved in this philosophy and practice. Huge sums of money have been allocated for the training of conductive educators at Peto and a Centre has been established attached to the University of Birmingham. The method is concerned to enable the motor impaired 'to function in security without requiring special apparatus such as wheelchairs, ramps or artificial aids' (Oliver, 1989b, p. 197). Whilst recognizing the deep-felt concerns of these parents, Oliver (1989b) is nevertheless critical of these methods. He believes they detract from the struggle to change physical and social environments and

> The nightmare of conductive education is unachievable because nowhere in human history has the *different* been turned into the *normal*. . . . The reason is simple; normality does not exist. (pp. 199–200)

He also has

> an alternative vision where difference is just not tolerated but valued and even celebrated and where physical and social environments are constantly changing to accommodate and welcome these differences. (p. 199)

This struggle will be difficult and time-consuming and must not be side-tracked by those who would individualize the issues and advocate easy answers to complex problems.

Two main arguments are often used to justify the involvement of disabled pupils and young people in physical education and sports generally: that it will enhance the development of a more integrated society and that it could be the means to better status and a good standard of living. Both of these perspectives need to be critically analyzed. For those pupils who are in special schools the opportunity to engage in activities with able-bodied peers is basically nil (Rieser and Mason, 1990). Even those who would advocate that competitions at a more national or even international level will be important integrationally are largely offering a romantic vision. Disabled competitors, in almost all cases, compete against their disabled colleagues. Many of the spectators are parents or members of the family. Thus, there are strong grounds for being sceptical on this issue. Also, the prospect of the 'good life' for those who are successful needs to be challenged. Lessons can be drawn from those black young people who have followed such a dream and given their all in support of it, only to be disappointed. That physical education or sport at a professional level provides access to greater opportunities for black people is a myth. Few ever reach such a position. It is also important to remember that the money supporting such ventures for disabled people is far less than that for the able-bodied. There is neither the audience nor the commercial interest in such activities (Hahn, 1984).

The fact that some disabled people are involved in such activities is an illustration of the extent to which able-bodied values can become internalized in the lives of disabled people. This is what a disabled writer has called the process of internalized oppression (Crow, 1988). This analysis offers a model of four stages of adjustment able-bodied people go through when they become disabled. It is particularly applicable to newly disabled men who try to compete on able-bodied terms. The struggle to overcome these powerful pressures involves disabled people getting to the stage in which their sense of equal and difference goes beyond a sense of guilt, loss and inferiority. This will hopefully lead to that last stage of empowerment which rejects a self-diminishing or self-depreciating image. All these stages form a continuum and are part of the continual experience of a disabled person. Thus, the extent to which able-bodied values can be identified and challenged, especially in relation to physical education, is an enormously important issue.

In relation to the approach adopted in this paper, therefore, what is offensive is the uncritical emulation of non-disabled standards, the patronizing mentalities surrounding much of disabled people's involvement in these activities and the tendency to divert attention from, and the struggle for, changes in the social relations and environmental conditions of society. Supporting this position and seeking to offer an alternative approach influenced by socio-political concerns, Hahn (1984) himself a disabled person, raises some fundamental questions on these issues. He offers the following examples:

(a) the extent to which disabled persons wish to strive to emulate the values of the non-disabled portion of society through extensive participation in sports;

(b) the extent to which growing involvement in athletic competition might contribute to the inequality rather than to the equality of the disabled citizens without widespread efforts to modify the environment in which they live;

(c) the extent to which sports play a 'gate-keeping' role in society that may be detrimental to the interests of disabled men and women. (p. 3)

If the ultimate interest is in the extent to which such activities will contribute to the realization of a more humane society and the changes that this will require, then the careful consideration of such questions is essential. They certainly need to be integral to the discussions of all those involved in a professional capacity in the field of physical education.

Conclusion

The question of education and disabled children and young people needs to be set within an equal opportunities framework (Rieser and Mason, 1990; NUT, 1991). Thus the physical education component of the curriculum must be part of a wider whole-school policy on integration or education for all. It is not to be viewed in isolation. By being linked to such concerns as class, race, gender and ageism, prejudice, discrimination and oppression can be understood and challenged. This approach will provide a basis for identifying offensive features of policy and practice. It will be a means of developing connections between other discriminated groups in order that they can engage in common struggles. Finally, it will provide an antidote to those individualized and social pathology models that are central to a great deal of able-bodied thinking on this issue.

If Evans (1990) could argue that

> Effecting changes in physical education of a sort that would empower children and teachers irrespective of their social class, race or gender to experience and enjoy equality of opportunity in their work, health and physical education will not be an easy, a quick or a comfortable endeavour (p. 162)

and he could exclude any reference to disability in his discussion, then its introduction magnifies the seriousness, the complexity, the contentious nature, and above all, the urgency of the task ahead. Questions of rights, choice, power and change will be central to this emancipatory process. Part of this process involves the participation of disabled people in those decisions affecting their lives and over which they have expert knowledge. Merely adapting a curriculum for able-bodied people without some critical dialogue is unacceptable. The voice of disabled people needs to be heard and seriously examined. This is absolutely essential in the teaching of physical education.

Note

I am grateful to Richard Rieser, Jenny Corbett and John Evans for their helpful comments on an earlier draft of this paper.

References

ABBERLEY, P. (1987) 'The Concept of Oppression and the Development of a Social Theory of Disability', *Disability, Handicap and Society*, **2**, 1, pp. 15–19.

APPLE, M. (1990) *Ideology and Curriculum*, 2nd ed., London, Routledge.

ARNOT, M. (1991) 'Equality and Democracy: A Decade of Struggle over Education', *British Journal of Sociology of Education*, **13**, 4, pp. 447–466, Special Issue on Democracy.

BAIN, L. (1990) 'A Critical Analysis of the Hidden Curriculum in Physical Education', in KIRK, D. and TINNING, R. (Eds) *Physical Education, Curriculum and Culture: Critical Issues in the Contemporary Crisis*, London, Falmer Press.

BEARDSHAW, V. (1989) 'Conductive Education: A rejoinder', *Disability, Handicap and Society*, **4**, 3, pp. 297–300.

BEGUM, N. (1990) 'Burden of Gratitude: Women with Disabilities needing Personal Care', in *Social Care: Perspectives and Practice Critical Studies*, Warwick, University of Warwick.

BISHOP, M. (1987) 'Disabling the Able?', *British Journal of Special Education*, **14**, 3, p. 98.

BORSAY, A. (1986) 'Personal Trouble or Public Issue? Towards a Model of Policy for People with Physical and Mental Disabilities', *Disability, Handicap and Society*, **1**, 2, pp. 179–95.

BRISENDEN, S. (1986) 'Independent Living and the Medical Model of Disability', *Disability, Handicap and Society*, **1**, 2, pp. 173–8.

CARRINGTON, B. and WILLIAMS, T. (1988) 'Patriarchy and Ethnicity: The Link between School Physical Education and Community Leisure Activities', in EVANS, J. (Ed.) *Teachers, Teaching and Control in Physical Education*, Lewes, Falmer Press.

CROW, L. (1988) 'Raising Two Fingers', in DAVIES, C. and CROW, L. (Eds) *A Sense of Self*, London, Camerawalk.

DEPARTMENT OF EDUCATION AND SCIENCE (1991a) *National Curriculum Physical Education Working Group. Interim Report*, London, DES.

DEPARTMENT OF EDUCATION AND SCIENCE (1991b) *National Curriculum Physical Education for Ages 5 to 16. Final Report*, London, DES.

EVANS, J. (1990) 'Ability, Position and Privilege in School Education', in KIRK, D. and TINNING, R. (Eds) *Physical Education, Curriculum and Culture: Critical Issues in the Contemporary Crisis*, London, Falmer Press.

FORD, J., MONGON, D. and WHELAN, M. (1982) *Special Education and Social Control: Invisible Disasters*, London, Routledge and Kegan Paul.

FULCHER, G. (1989) *Disabling Policies? A Comparative Approach to Education Policy and Disability*, London, Falmer Press.

GLENDINNING, C. (1991) 'Losing Ground: Social Policy and Disabled People in Great Britain, 1980–90', *Disability, Handicap and Society*, **6**, 1, pp. 3–20.

HAHN, H. (1984) 'Sports and the Political Movement of Disabled Persons: Examining Non-Disabled Social Values', *Arena Review*, **8**, 1, pp. 1–15.

HAHN, H. (1986) 'Public Support for Rehabilitation in Programs: The Analysis of US Disability Policy', *Disability, Handicap and Society*, **1**, 2, pp. 121–38.

HUDSON, R. (1988) 'Do People with a Mental Handicap have Rights?', *Disability, Handicap and Society*, **3**, 3, pp. 227–38.

JOHNSON, R. (1991) 'A New Road to Serfdom? A Critical History of the 1988 Act', in EDUCATION GROUP II. *Education Limited: Schooling, Training and the New Right in England since 1979*, London, Unwin Hyman.

KIRK, D. and TINNING, R. (Eds) (1990) *Physical Education, Curriculum and Culture: Critical Issues in the Contemporary Crisis*, London, Falmer Press, Introduction.

LASCH, C. (1979) *The Culture of Narcissism: American Life in an Age of Diminished Expectations*, New York, Warner Books.

LEAMAN, O. (1988) 'Competition, Co-operation and Control', in EVANS, J. (Ed.) *Teachers, Teaching and Control in Physical Education*, Lewes, Falmer Press.

LONSDALE, S. (1990) *Women and Disability: The Experience of Physical Disability Among Women*, Basingstoke, Macmillan Education Ltd.

MILLS, C.W. (1970) *The Sociological Imagination*, Harmondsworth, Penguin.

MORRIS, J. (Ed.) (1989) *Able Lives: Women's Experience of Paralysis*, London, The Women's Press.

MORRIS, J. (1991) *Pride Against Prejudice: Transforming Attitudes to Disability*, London, The Women's Press.

NATIONAL UNION OF TEACHERS (1991) *Guidelines on Disability — An Equal Opportunities Issue*, London, NUT.

OLIVER, M. (1988) 'The Political Context of Educational Decision Making: The Case of Special Needs', in BARTON, L. (Ed.) *The Politics of Special Educational Needs*, London, Falmer Press.

OLIVER, M. (1989a) 'Disability and Dependency: A Creation of Industrial Societies', in BARTON, L. (Ed.) *Disability and Dependency*, London, Falmer Press.

OLIVER, M. (1989b) 'Conductive Education: If It Wasn't So Sad It Would Be Funny', *Disability, Handicap and Society*, **4**, 2, pp. 197–200.

OLIVER, M. (1990) *The Politics of Disablement*, London, Macmillan.

OLIVER, M. and HASLER, F. (1987) 'Disability and Self Help: A Case Study of the Spinal Injuries Association', *Disability, Handicap and Society*, **2**, 2, pp. 113–25.

POLLARD, A. (1988) 'Physical Education, Competition and Control in Primary Education', in EVANS, J. (Ed.) *Teachers, Teaching and Control in Physical Education*, Lewes, Falmer Press.

RANSON, S. (1990) *The Politics of Reorganising Schools*, London, Unwin Hyman.

RIESER, R. and MASON, M. (1990) *Disability Equality in the Classroom: A Human Rights Issue*, London, ILEA.

SIMON, B. (1988) *Bending the Rules: The Baker 'Reform' of Education*, London, Lawrence and Wishart.

TOMLINSON, S. (1982) *A Sociology of Special Education*, London, Routledge and Kegan Paul.

TOMLINSON, S. (1985) 'The Expansion of Special Education', *Oxford Review of Education*. **11**, 2, pp. 157–65.

WEINER, G. (1989) 'Feminism, Equal Opportunities and Vocationalism: The Changing Context', in BURCHELL, H. and MILLMAN, V. (Eds) *Changing Perspectives on Gender: New Initiatives in Secondary Education*, Milton Keynes, Open University Press.

WOLFENSBERGER, W. (1989) 'Human Service Policies: The Rhetoric versus the Reality', in BARTON, L. (Ed.) *Disability and Dependency*, London, Falmer Press.

Chapter 4

The Body, Class and Social Inequalities

Chris Shilling

Introduction

In studying the relationship between schooling and social inequalities, the sociology of education has tended to focus on cognitive development, certification and social mobility. As a consequence, little attention has been given to the role of physical education (PE) in the formation of social inequalities. Indeed, the complete neglect of PE in many sociology of education texts is symptomatic of a much wider underestimate of the importance of the corporeal in schooling.

The failure of most sociologists to examine the physical education of bodies compounds the mistaken view that schooling is concerned only with the mind, and with one sort of knowledge; the abstract and intellectual. This proposition is found in the writings of both liberals, who tend to equate education with *intellectual development*, and most reproduction theorists, who see schools functioning to inculcate dominant ideologies in the *minds* of pupils. Neither of these perspectives, which otherwise share very little in their analyses of the education system, take adequate note of the *embodied* nature of schooling or the *corporeal* implications of educational knowledge. A further problem with these approaches is that in divorcing the mind from the body, they tend to divorce knowledge from action. This has the effect of treating action as mainly a technical concern which is of secondary importance to the 'real' subject matter of the sociology of education.

Access to Physical Education

More suprising still is the relative lack of attention given to the body by those concerned with the social aspects of PE (cf. *Quest*, 1991). Instead, the dominant approach towards PE and social inequalities focuses on questions of *access*. A major issue here is the effect that mechanisms of academic differentiation can have in polarizing student attitudes towards, and involvement in, PE. Writers such as Whitehead and Hendry (1976) and Hendry (1978) have suggested that the middle-class values incorporated in schools may serve to alienate working-class pupils from sport and PE; a process which can be accentuated by organizational structures of streaming or banding (Hargreaves, 1967; Lacey, 1970).

In contrast, where there is mixed-ability grouping (i.e. less organizational differentiation) this is likely to encourage a higher incidence of involvement in school PE and sport (Ball, 1981). Mixed-ability grouping throughout a school remains relatively rare, though, and the negative experiences many young people have of PE serves to deprive them of the knowledge, skills and enthusiasm needed to make use of community sports and leisure resources. This, in turn, tends to compound the class-based patterns of leisure involvement among adults in society. For writers such as Hendry, this is an undesirable situation because of the close relationship which exists between someone's 'quality of life' and their participation in leisure activities.

The concern with access displayed by those interested in social class inequalities in PE has been reflected in policy initiatives stemming from the Sports Council's approach to sports and leisure facilities in England (Tomlinson, 1982). It is also a central concern of the final report of the National Curriculum Working Group on Physical Education (DES, 1991). However, questions related to access, although undoubtedly important, are not the only way of exploring the relevance of social class in school-based PE. Indeed, the 'access' approach can be seen as problematic in that it leaves unexplored central questions concerning the social significance of physical activities. First, it tends simply to assume that sports and leisure participation is a 'good thing' which can yield similar benefits to all sections of society. This assumption fails to explore how sports may carry different meanings and unequal benefits and risks for their participants depending on an individual's social class background. For example, middle-class (usually male) members of an elite golf club may not only relax and enjoy themselves over a round of golf, but may meet or make important business contacts in these exclusive social sites. In contrast, golf for members of the working class is, perhaps, more likely to mean a game of 'pitch and putt' on a municipal ground as a way of gaining short-term release from a mundane job or unemployment. The different meanings that physical activities have for groups in society are likely to have important implications for any programme which attempts to implement a policy of sport for all, yet this is not a concern tackled in the access approach.

Second, the access approach has gone only 'half way' in improving our understanding of 'ability' in PE. As mentioned previously, the access approach highlights how school organization can affect the motivation of pupils to participate in physical activities. This has usefully questioned the adequacy of accounts which explain the involvement or success of children in sport merely by referring to their physical abilities. Instead, it directs attention to the ways in which social criteria, such as teachers' values, enter processes of selection and differentiation in PE. This is extremely valuable. However, what the access approach does not do, or seek to do, is question the validity of the very notion of 'ability' in school PE and sport. Yet questioning existing definitions of physical ability might raise valuable questions concerned with the unequal opportunities pupils from different backgrounds have for becoming 'skilled' in an activity. Is the notion of 'skill' that PE teachers work with just a single definition from a multiplicity of possible definitions not presently recognized? If so, does the present dominant definition itself hamper any policy concerned with sport for all? Third, a focus on access serves to marginalize the social significance of what is the very object of PE — the human body. One only has to think of teachers' attempts to get pupils to sit still and be quiet in classrooms, and walk rather than run around corridors, to realize that the body is central not only to PE but to the very business of schooling. Ironically, though, the focus on access in PE tends to neglect the importance of education in forming among pupils particular orientations to their bodies. Furthermore, the education system not only 'moulds' bodies in certain ways, it also bestows different values on particular physical activities and bodily forms. One well-known example of this is the general value accorded to the mesomorphic bodily ideal by PE teachers over the fatter endomorphic, or thinner ectomorphic, body (Hargreaves, 1986). However, the only regular appearance made by the body in analyses of PE comes not in the access approach, but in the technically oriented work of those concerned with the 'body as machine' — focusing on how to maximize athletic performance and detailing regimented training programmes designed to achieve this end (see McKay *et al.*, 1990).

In this chapter I will argue that the body has a far greater social significance than is allowed by existing approaches towards PE. After outlining a view of the body as a form of physical capital, I then briefly suggest how this view of the corporeal may help us examine how schools have historically been involved in the production of physical capital in ways which bestow unequal opportunities on individuals from different social backgrounds. Here, the body is seen as fundamental both to schooling and to the social class location of different groups in society. I focus on social class in this chapter but this is for illustrative purposes only. This is not meant to downgrade the importance that cross-class gender and 'racial' influences have on people's orientations to their bodies. Elsewhere, I have explored in greater detail the importance of gender (Shilling, 1991b, 1993), and 'race' (Shilling, 1993) in the formation of physical capital. It is also worth saying something in this section about my use of the concept 'social class'. Social class is most commonly conceptualized in the sociology of education as membership of an occupational category and this is how the 'access' approach views class. In other traditions within the sociology of education class is also treated as a form of consciousness (as in segments of the 'New' sociology of education), or as a position within the relations of production (as in Marxist approaches). What I am attempting to do in this chapter, though, is to develop a notion of class which refers not only to factors *external* to the individual, such as occupational position, but to the *orientation that people possess to their bodies*.

The Body and Physical Capital

At one level, it is not difficult to envisage the body as a form of capital. One only has to think of the various rewards received by college athletes in the USA, and professional sportspeople across the world, to see how bodily performances can be exchanged for financial rewards. Furthermore, it is not only in sports that people use their bodies to earn money. Night clubs and discos frequently employ male bodybuilders as bouncers, while male and female prostitutes use their bodies in order to earn a living. Of course, these 'bodily exchanges' vary in the degree to which their owners profit from and are exploited by such transactions. Common to them all, though, is the use of the corporeal as a form of capital.

Schools are of obvious importance in shaping among pupils particular orientations to their bodies, and viewing the body as a form of physical capital highlights the possibility that formal education is involved in the production of corporeal inequalities. Schools may not only be involved in processes which lead to social inequalities in the acquisition of qualifications, they might also be involved in bestowing on pupils different quantities and qualities of physical capital. This approach to the body as a form of physical capital in and outside of schools can be developed further by drawing on the work of the French sociologist, Pierre Bourdieu.

Pierre Bourdieu is exceptional among contemporary sociologists in placing the body at the centre of his general theory of social reproduction. Bourdieu usually analyzes embodied or physical capital as a subsection of cultural capital (e.g. Bourdieu, 1986). However, I want to argue that the corporeal is too important to be seen merely as a subdivision of another form of capital. The development and management of the body is central in its own right to human agency in general, and to the attainment of status and financial capital. Indeed, the management of the body through time and space can be seen as the fundamental constituent of an individual's ability to intervene in social affairs and make a difference to the flow of day-to-day life (Shilling, 1991a, 1991b). Bearing this in mind, I shall now turn to Bourdieu's analysis of the production of physical capital and its conversion into other forms of capital.

The Production of Physical Capital

The *production* of physical capital refers to the social formation of bodies by individuals through sporting, leisure, waged and unwaged work (and all other body-implicating activities) in ways which *express* a social location (a social position marked by various cultural, economic and social opportunities and constraints) *and* which are accorded symbolic value. This social production of bodies is, of course, different from their biological reproduction and refers to the influence people have on their *already existing* corporeal selves. This includes how people develop, alter and hold the physical shape of their bodies, and learn how to present and manage their bodies through styles of walk, talk and dress. These activities enable people to communicate and interact with others — in short, to be social beings. However, Bourdieu argues that people both acquire and are socialized into *different types* of physical capital depending on their class position. This is because of the influence that individuals' *social location*, '*habitus*' and *taste* have on the development of their bodies.

Social locations refer to the degree of 'distance from necessity' that people have from financial and material want (Bourdieu, 1985). The fact that people's lives are characterized by varying degrees of distance of necessity means that individuals have unequal opportunities for acquiring that physical capital most valued in society. For example, the middle classes tend to have more financial and cultural resources than the working classes to keep their children in education for longer periods of time, release them from the need to work, and encourage them to engage in activities likely to increase their acquisition of prestigious types of physical capital. One obvious example of this is those parents who send their children to private schools, or daughters to 'finishing schools', as a way of 'improving' their deportment, manners and speech in ways which express, quite literally, a sense of class. However, there are numerous other ways in which middle-class parents are more able to buy pre-school or extra-school entry to activities conducive to acquiring certain forms of physical capital (e.g. horse-riding, tennis, ballet).

The social locations of individuals from different backgrounds is also important for Bourdieu's analysis as they provide the context in which the *habitus* and taste are developed. The *habitus* is a 'socially constituted system of cognitive and motivating structures which provide individuals with class de-pendent, pre-disposed ways of relating to both familiar and novel situations' (Brubaker, 1985, p. 758). It is constructed through children's experiences of socialization and their objective material environment, and is central to the reproduction of social inequalities. The *habitus* is not only inscribed in the mind, but is *embodied*, and the way people treat their bodies 'reveals the deepest disposition of the habitus' (Bourdieu, 1984, p. 190). 'Taste' is the conscious manifestation of *habitus* and refers to the processes whereby individuals come to prefer lifestyles which are actually rooted in material *constraints*. In other words, taste is making choice out of necessity. Adults may *feel* far removed from the circumstances in which they were raised, but it is common for people's habits and preferences to bear the mark of their early background.

Bourdieu's concept of taste represents an extension of the everyday mean-ing of this term, and the consumption of food is an obvious example of how taste is shaped by specific material locations. Throughout history, people's taste for food has developed in the context of its relative scarcity or surplus, and has been affected by the efforts of the dominant in society to appropriate certain foods in order to distinguish themselves from the dominated by what they eat (Mennell, 1985). These eating patterns have important consequences for bodily develop-ment. For example, in contemporary France and England the working class tend to consume more cheaper, fatty foods which have implications not only for their body shapes, but for their relatively high incidence of coronary disease in relation to the upper classes (Bourdieu, 1984; Townsend *et al.*, 1988). A further example of the development of taste concerns the relatively passive orientation to the body possessed by many women compared to the active bodily orientation more frequently developed by men (Willis, 1990). Here, tastes for physical activ-ities are frequently affected by the different options open to women and men which are strongly informed by dominant gender norms, and mediated through the gendered nature of the *habitus*. They are also reinforced by the unequal opportunities women and men have within the household to barter for leisure time (e.g. Barrel *et al.*, 1989). Furthermore, while contemporary consumer culture has promoted the slim, active, 'athletic' body for both women and men (Featherstone, 1982), it is still considered socially unacceptable for women to develop a heavily muscled body. These attitudes are reflected even in the very organizations which cater for women bodybuilders. The International Federation of Body Builders had the following to say about the criteria which should be used to judge women bodybuilders:

> first and foremost, the judge must bear in mind that he or she is judging a women's body building competition and is looking for the ideal femin-ine physique. Therefore, the most important aspect is shape, a femin-ine shape ... muscular development ... must not be carried to excess where it resembles the massive muscularity of the male physique. (quoted in MacNeill, 1988, p. 206)

As a result of the relationship between social location, *habitus* and taste, then, individuals from different backgrounds develop different orientations to their bodies which, in turn, lead them to acquiring specific forms of physical capital. Because the working class have less time free from material necessities, Bourdieu argues that they tend to develop an *instrumental* orientation to the body. The body is a *means to an end* and this is evident in relation to illness (e.g. 'getting well' is primarily a *means to* returning to work, getting ready for a holiday, or enjoying the weekend); and in the choice of sports for working-class men (e.g. in soccer, motor-cycling and boxing the body is mainly a *means for* the experience of excitement). Gender divisions mean that most working-class women have little time at all for sporting/leisure activities apart from those compatible with their waged *and unwaged* work. Even such 'low-key' activities as watching television tend to be accompanied by such chores as ironing or knitting (Deem, 1986; Green and Hebron, 1988). Working-class women, then, tend to develop an instrumental relation to their bodies marked by the need to earn money *and* service the needs of a household. This is evident in the widespread evidence which suggests that working-class women sacrifice their own bodily needs for rest, recreation and even food, in order to fulfil those of their husbands and children. These sacrifices have real effects on the bodily development of women, as evident by the disproportionately high incidence of physical (as well as mental) illness among mothers with children (Graham, 1984).

In contrast, the dominant classes tend to be further removed from the immediate demands of material necessity and therefore have the freedom to treat the body as an *end in itself* 'with variants according to whether the emphasis is placed on the intrinsic functioning of the body as an organism, which leads to the macrobiotic cult of health, or on the appearance as a perceptible configuration, the 'physique', i.e. the body for others' (Bourdieu, 1978, p. 838; 1984; pp. 212–13). Orientations to the body become more finely differentiated *within* the dominant classes. For example, fitness training for its own sake is often engaged in by the upwardly mobile middle classes who 'find their satisfaction in effort itself and ... accept — such is the meaning of their existence — the deferred satisfactions which will reward their present sacrifice' (Bourdieu, 1978, p. 839). In contrast, professionals in the field of cultural production, such as university teachers, tend towards activities which combine the health-oriented function of maintaining the body with the 'symbolic gratifications associated with practising a highly distinctive activity' such as walking in remote places. Such activities can be 'performed in solitude, at times and in places beyond the reach of the many' (Bourdieu, 1984, p. 214). Another distinction in physical activity is made for the elite, well-established bourgeoisie, who tend to combine the health-giving aspects of sporting activities with the social functions involved in such sports as golf, dance, shooting and polo (Bourdieu, 1987, pp. 839–40).

Orientations to the body, then, are central to the production of different forms of physical capital. These are shaped through the relationship between social location, the *habitus* and taste, but it is important to note that participation in body-forming activities is irreducible to the influence of these factors in the formative years of an individual's life. This is because a person's financial resources, their access to spare time and their life situation in general, continue to have an influence on their bodily orientation after initial tastes have been formed. For example, yachting and flying usually require expensive equipment which rules these activities out of reach of all but the wealthiest sections of society. Similarly, sports organized around elite clubs can require potential entrants to have acquired a certain status before they are able to join (e.g. applicants to prestigious golf or tennis clubs may require social contacts within the club and a suitable standing within the local community). Here, if an individual's stock of economic and social capitals has declined, both options may be ruled out and a taste for other activities and a new orientation to one's body may, eventually, be developed.

It also needs to be stressed that Bourdieu seeks to make his view of taste, sport and bodily orientation historically dynamic.[1] For example, the distribution of sporting activities between groups changes over time and between countries and regions, sports such as tennis can become 'democratized', and some activities will be characterized by genuine cross-class participation. However, sports are still likely to be viewed in different ways by social groups, be expected to produce different benefits, and are likely to be played on different sites. Indeed, the very search by the dominant classes for *distinction*, a way of marking themselves off from the rest of society, lends a dynamic to the 'who does what' in the sporting field. As one sport becomes commercialized, popularized and, consequently, changed, the dominant classes search out new activities which can serve similar purposes and provide homologous experiences (Boulanger, 1988).[2]

The significance of the bodily orientations and participation in sporting/ leisure activities described in this section is that they shape the formation of bodies fitted for different activities. The lifestyles of people from different social classes become *inscribed* in their bodies and it becomes more or less natural for them to participate in different forms of physical activity which are themselves invested with unequal social values. This is the *production* of physical capital.

The Conversion of Physical Capital

The relationship between social location, *habitus* and taste does not just produce different bodily orientations among social groups, it actually shapes the life-chances of people. This is because individuals have unequal opportunities for *converting* their physical capital into other forms of capital. Physical capital can be converted into economic capital (goods and services), cultural capital (e.g. it can aid entry into elite private schools), and social capital (social networks which enable reciprocal calls to be made on the goods and services of its members) (Bourdieu, 1978, 1984). So, working-class taste for accessible and affordable sports/leisure activities involves the production of physical capital which generally has less exchange value than that developed by the dominant classes. This does not mean, of course, that the working class lacks opportunities for converting physical capital into other forms of capital. For example, the instrumental approach towards sports as a means to particular ends provides the working class with the potential to convert physical capital into economic capital via entry into sporting careers. Here, the power, speed and agility invested in the body becomes the object of exchange value. However, this form of economic capital is limiting to the working class in several respects. First, only a small percentage of its members can hope to earn a living through sport. Second, this form of convertibility is usually partial and transient. It is partial because of its less frequent availability to the working class. Only a very small percentage of the working class become professional sportspeople, and these tend to be men, whereas members of the dominant classes have many more opportunities for converting their physical capital into other forms of capital. It is transient, as the capacity of the body is an important limiting factor even for those who do become professionals. For example, it only takes one injury to end a soccer player's career and the average length of sporting careers is low, leaving most ex-professionals needing to find work for the rest of their lives. Third, the time black working-class students spend on sports may affect detrimentally their acquisition of academic qualifications at school (Carrington, 1982). Fourth, this instrumental approach to their bodies can also steer working-class children away from activities engaged in by the dominant classes, and hence reinforce their class distinctiveness. McRobbie's (1978) work into working-class girls is a useful example of this phenomenon. The girls in McRobbie's study had an instrumental relation to their bodies and viewed them as a means to display adult forms of femininity and attract boyfriends. However, in possessing this relation to their bodies, working-class girls tend to reject the opportunities available to them in school PE and sport (Woods, 1979).

If there are limitations in the working class converting physical capital into economic capital, the same is true for cultural and social capital. Working-class physical capital is rarely converted into cultural capital in the education system. For example, it has long been argued that working-class speech forms and the linguistic codes which underpin them tend to be interpreted negatively by teachers (Bernstein, 1970; Keddie, 1971). In the case of social capital, working-class physical capital may lead to admiration among peer groups at school in terms of a prowess at fighting (Willis, 1977) or an ability to appear as adult and feminine as possible (McRobbie, 1978), but it does little to gain the support of teachers in helping with academic work. In sum, there tend to be high risks and opportunity costs associated with working-class efforts to convert their physical capital into other resources.

In contrast, the dominant classes in society have more valuable opportunities to convert physical capital into other material and cultural resources. Sport tends not to carry the same means or meanings of upward mobility for the children of the dominant class, and they tend mainly to engage in 'character-forming' sports and socially elite sporting activities which stress manners and deportment and hence facilitate the future acquisition of social and cultural capital. This is reflected in the PE curricula of elite private schools (Salter and Tapper, 1981). Developing a taste for elite sporting and leisure activities is also important as while these activities may not often represent a direct route to a career for the dominant classes, they can lead to social situations which indirectly facilitate entry into a profession or allow business contacts to be forged. For dominant groups, elite sporting activities also serve the purpose of finding marriage partners of their own class for their offspring, hence safeguarding the future transmission of their own economic capital (Bourdieu, 1986). Indeed, the prominence of elite sporting venues focused around such activities as eventing and polo in England can be seen as a contributory factor to the high degree of intra-class marriages among the dominant classes in this country.

The physical capital of the dominant class can also be converted into social and cultural capital. Elite social and sporting occasions tend to encompass strict rules of etiquette and allow for the stylized display of the body in formal contexts which allow members of elite groups to recognize and decode the body as a sign signifying that the bearer shares certain values (e.g. through modes of dress, methods of turn-taking and ways of speaking). Informal contacts can be made on these occasions which can be of great value in acquiring the services of others in such areas as law, finance and politics. Physical capital can also be converted into cultural capital. For example, the interview, in which the management and display of speech and the body is central, is still an integral part of the selection process for elite private schools and a number of universities in England (including Oxford and Cambridge).

To conclude, the potential exchange value of physical capital is much higher for the dominant class than for the working class. Furthermore, the development of physical capital for the dominant class does not usually carry the same risks or opportunity costs as working-class physical capital.

Schooling and Physical Capital

Having outlined Bourdieu's approach to the body as a form of physical capital, I now want to look at how this analysis might be used to illuminate the relationship between schooling, PE and social class inequalities.

In conceptualizing the relationship between schooling and the formation of physical capital, it is important to state at the outset that there can be no direct 'correspondence theory' between these factors (cf. Bowles and Gintis, 1976). The early development of physical capital takes place in a *variety* of contexts with the family being of obvious importance. However, educational institutions do contribute to the social formation of bodies. Moreover, PE is just one activity which affects how children perceive and treat their bodies. Teachers' attempts to get young pupils to dress themselves 'properly', ask to go to the toilet in time for accidents to be avoided, stay away from forbidden areas such as the car park, and even respect daily rituals such as morning prayers or saluting the national flag with bodily deference (eyes shut and hands together or appropriate posture and movement), all show how the body is centrally implicated in and constitutive of the daily business of schooling. Although seldom commented on in the sociology of education, schools in contemporary society are heavily implicated in attempts to internalize in pupils socially accepted ways of managing and maintaining their bodies (Kirk and Colquhoun, 1989). Crucial to this chapter, though, is not simply the point that schools are involved in the formation of bodies, but that they affect *differentially* the ability of pupils to recognize and develop specific forms of physical capital.

In what follows, I shall briefly sketch some of the ways in which English and Welsh schools have historically influenced the production of physical capital in relation to social class inequalities. The limitations of existing literature make this an inevitably cursory analysis, and I do not intend to provide an overview of the history of PE. However, I shall suggest that there has been a shift in the organization and control of knowledge about bodies in schools which has affected the ability of different groups in society to produce specific forms of physical capital and to convert this into other resources.

My general argument is that historically there has been a shift in the organization and control of educational knowledge about bodies. This has moved away from a position existing from the eighteenth century to the middle of the twentieth century where formal education established rigid boundaries between the bodies of different social classes, and schools were implicated in producing what I shall call 'disciplined bodies'. In the late twentieth century, in contrast, the tendency was for education to treat bodies according to individualist, rather then class-based, criteria. The body was seen more as a *shared* phenomenon whose biological characteristics and physical potential did not inevitably vary between the social classes. Instead, physical potential varied on the basis of *individual* characteristics (and, of course, between girls and boys). Here, schools were implicated in producing 'regulated bodies'. In conclusion, I will consider how the National Curriculum might be changing the contemporary situation.

Schooling the disciplined body

From the nineteenth century to the mid-twentieth century formal education established rigid boundaries between the bodies of working and middle-class pupils and the aristocracy, and between the bodies of girls and boys from the dominant classes. It also played a part in sorting out the bodies of the 'tidy' from the 'untidy' working classes (Evans, 1988). Separate forms of bodily development were seen as natural for different groups in society and these were designed to prepare people for particular categories of social positions.

In nineteenth-century England, sport was promoted in boys' private schools as a cultivator of character, moral values and 'manliness' which served to produce the corporeal qualities valued in elite jobs at home and across the Empire (Best, 1975). The educational theory implicit in the dominance of sport was that team activity trained individuals — and their bodies — out of individualism and into the corporate membership of a social class which led, and set an example to, the rest of the nation (Best, 1975). The 'cult of athleticism' prominent in these schools served also to promote a hierarchy of values and status built around a distinct orientation to the body which was used to devalue the meritocratic principles of mental (academic) performance promoted by the 'new' bourgeoisie (Bourdieu, 1978). Furthermore, these orientations to the body were reinforced by statutes which forbade commoners from wearing fabrics and styles which the aristocracy sought to reserve for itself (Davis, 1989). The bodily orientations produced among the English aristocracy by elite private schools were recognized by the higher professions as marks of distinction which were prerequisites for entry into elite occupations. Here, the physical capital which private schooling helped produce could be converted into economic capital through the labour market. As the century wore on, and the children of the industrial bourgeoisie started attending in significant numbers prestigious private schools, cultivation of the prestigious 'athletic body' was widened to sections of the middle classes and, ultimately, to the grammar schools.

Among the working classes, though, team games and the promotion of the athletic body were not considered suitable for those destined to follow rather than lead. Instead, a modified form of drill was introduced into state elementary schools for the working class in the late nineteenth century. Partly as a result of state concerns to maintain a 'fit', 'disciplined' and 'healthy' population that could be mobilized during times of war, drill was incorporated as a recognized subject in the payment-by-results scheme (McIntosh, 1952). This emphasis was continued in the early twentieth century and the 1933 Physical Education syllabus stressed the importance of discipline, alertness, precision, the soundness of body parts, and their harmonious functioning to produce a healthy and efficient whole (Hargreaves, 1986, p. 160).

These class divisions remained even after the establishment of universal secondary education. In the 1950s and 1960s, grammar and private schools continued to provide high-status team games such as cricket and rugby, while the secondary modern school PE curriculum tended to be dominated by games more popular among the working class such as soccer.

Schools were in the business of producing different bodies and forms of physical capital which had radically different exchange values. The corporeal was not something which people shared equally, but was divided by class. Furthermore, this division was not something over which teachers and pupils had much control. The view of the body as something divided by social class was so deeply embedded in English culture that headteachers attempting to change the games orientation of private schools met with overwhelming resistance (Mangan, 1975).

The education of bodies during this period was not, though, simply divided along class lines. Fundamental biological differences were seen to exist between the bodies of middle-class male and female pupils, the implications of which had inescapable social consequences. While the middle-class male body was moulded through athleticism, the Victorian image of a middle-class woman was of an invalid, ruled by her reproductive organs and limited by the finite amount of energy at her disposal (Atkinson, 1987). Even when PE did develop in girls' schools, this was within taken-for-granted assumptions about the innate limited capacities of women (Scraton, 1986; Hargreaves, 1986), and concern to counterbalance the strain of mental work for girls. For example, in the early twentieth century a number of girls' private day and boarding schools stressed the importance of *stylish accomplishments* for girls, rather than games, and in 1919 the Board of Education's Syllabus of Physical Training for Schools recommended certain activities as being more suitable for boys than girls (Scraton, 1986, pp. 76–7.) The Ling system of gymnastics, with its emphasis on remedial and therapeutic work, was recognized and promoted as being particularly relevant for promoting qualities of caring and helping others through physical education. These were qualities directly associated with the the ideal of perfect 'motherhood'. Indeed, the notion of woman as 'mother' became part of the general ethos of PE training throughout England.

It was not really until the late nineteenth century that there was a genuine shift towards sports, and even here most pioneers accepted the notion of 'limited games' for girls (e.g. hockey was often played on smaller pitches and for shorter periods of time than was usual when boys played the game, McCrone, 1988). Male sports were adapted to accommodate women's 'limited abilities' and new sports were introduced, such as netball, which did not carry the stigma of overt masculinity (Scraton, 1986).

Schools contributed to producing a form of physical capital among middle-class girls whose exchange value was limited mainly to marriage markets. The 'feminine accomplishments' encouraged in these schools prepared girls for future positions in society which were subordinate to men and ill-suited to the pursuit of work outside the limited sphere of the home. Gender inequalities in the education system of the nineteenth and early twentieth centuries, then, were evident not merely in the form of schooling open to the sexes or in the educational resources on offer to girls and boys. Instead, educational inequalities were, quite literally, *embodied*.

The education system of the late nineteenth and early twentieth centuries established clear divisions between the bodies belonging to people from different social backgrounds. *Natural* differences were posited between bodies belonging to different social classes and between those of men and women. However, there was a common approach which underpinned the educational treatment of bodies during this time. This involved the production of *disciplined bodies*; that is, an approach to the body which involved an increasingly better invigilated and rationalized process of adjustment between productive and reproductive activities (Foucault, 1982). Set categories of bodies had definite places in society (e.g. upper-class bodies were to lead whereas working-class bodies were to follow, middle-class men's bodies were primarily implicated in production whereas middle-class women's bodies were fitted for and limited by reproduction), and it was the job of schooling to assist in producing bodily orientations in line with these roles.

Schooling the regulated body

In the early years of the twentieth century the cult of athleticism came under increasing attack as academic and occupational pressures rose. Academic concerns came to occupy more of the school curriculum as the occupational system became increasingly bureaucratized and entry into elite jobs became more dependent on qualifications as well as on physical and social capital. Furthermore, by the second half of the twentieth century a new ideology of individualism competed with the team-oriented cult of the physical. During this time the production of disciplined bodies gradually gave way to the production of *regulated bodies*, with individual pupils given a role in *choosing* and *monitoring* their own physical development. Hargreaves (1986), following Durkheim, has described this shift towards child-centredness as helping to prepare young people for an increasingly complex division of labour in the occupational structure, and there arose a greater number of acceptable ways of organizing and controlling the body in schools. This was partly facilitated by the gradual 'merging' of separate female and male traditions of physical education which stressed gymnastics, dance and movement on the one hand and performance and measurement on the other (Fletcher, 1984; McIntosh, 1952, 1981). Although the latter, male, tradition gained dominance it did not obliterate completely the longer-standing female tradition.

By the late twentieth century there had been a fundamental shift in the educational treatment of bodies. The organization of bodies in schools no longer treated as *fundamentally* different pupils from separate class backgrounds. Although differences were not entirely eradicated, especially in the (by now less significant) private sector and in the case of gender where PE remained the most segregated subject in the school curriculum, there was a much greater variety of physical activities open to pupils from all class backgrounds than in the nine-teenth century. Curriculum options allowed students a degree of choice, and a growth in the number of health- and fitness-related initiatives available to schools gave teachers more control over how their work related to pupils' bodies.

The increased use of health-related physical education courses in state schools in England and Wales is a significant phenomenon worth focusing on, partly because it is paralleled in other countries such as Australia (Colquhoun and Robottom, 1990; Tinning, 1990). Evans (1988) has provided a useful review of two such courses currently in use in England, Health Related Fitness (HRF) and Teaching Games for Understanding (TGFU). TGFU seeks to offer pupils equality of access to activities for each individual irrespective of their level of ability, and some measure of equality of outcome. As Evans (1988, p. 179) notes, 'It is intended that everyone should experience a genuine (but not necessarily the same) level of success, achievement, satisfaction and enjoyment, along with an understanding of the principles which underpin different game forms.' In order to accomplish this, emphasis is placed on cognitive, rather than (but not at the expense of) technical aspects of games. Furthermore, mini-games with adapted rules and equipment are often used on the basis that they are more likely to provide all pupils with opportunities to participate and make decisions irrespec-tive of their physical ability. Health Related Fitness shares certain characteristics with TGFU such as avoiding labelling pupils as 'winners' or 'losers':

> It is against selection and the creation of ability hierarchies and for 'non-authoritarian', 'non-didactic' approaches to teaching. At the heart of this innovation (at least as officially espoused by the Health Education Council) is concern for the development of each and every individual's 'health career', their positive 'self-esteem' and 'decision-making skills'.... The aims are to create the habit of exercise and the belief that this can be fully integrated into one's life style. Within the context of PE ... emphasis is placed upon the development of individ-ual, personalized activity programmes designed to ensure a consistent involvement in physical exercise of an intensity which improves levels of fitness (especially cardio-vascular functioning). (Evans, 1988, p. 180)

In their approach to physical activity, both initiatives appear radically child-centred, rather than subject-centred (Payne, 1985). They appear to encourage pupils to develop individualized orientations to their bodily capacities and abil-ities which are not divided along social class lines. This emphasis on the individ-ual marks a shift away from the production of 'disciplined' bodies in schools. Instead, such initiatives are promoting among their pupils an attitude towards physical activities and health where they are encouraged to monitor their *own* performance and behaviour, and achieve their *personal* potential. In the terms of these initiatives, schools are no longer implicated in attempting to encourage orientations to the body rigidly divided by social class, but prepare pupils to *regulate* their own bodies on the basis of individual characteristics. This focus on individual regulations, though, does not necessarily remove completely class-based orientations to the body which were so evident in the nineteenth and early twentieth centuries. By focusing on the individual, these initiatives end up failing to confront inequalities in the extra-school opportunities open to people from different social backgrounds (Evans, 1988). They fail to question how they may be classed or gendered in terms of the unequal ability that pupils may have to attain the aims of these initiatives because of their previous development of physical capital. Furthermore, by developing in children flexibility and problem-solving skills, some commentators have argued that they are involved in developing characteristics required for a competent occupational performance among the new middle class (Hargreaves, 1986).

By focusing on the individual in this way, such initiatives run the risk of mystifying, and hence legitimizing, socially caused differences in the levels of physical capital open to people from different social backgrounds. Do TGFU and HRF tend to treat as *natural* and *individualistic*, what are in fact socially determined orientations to exercise and the body? Do such initiatives merely replace a prior notion of 'ability' with other versions which are equally biased in terms of the potential different pupils have for becoming 'skilled'? If so, is this merely replicating the problem of the access approach to PE and games by taking for granted, and treating as technical, concepts of skill which are, in fact, socially constructed and open to contestation? Does this serve to disguise both the body's implication in the production of social inequalities and the social causes and class- and gender-based incidence of mortality and morbidity patterns (as revealed in Britain by *The Black Report* and *The Health Divide* [see also Graham, 1984])? These are important questions which have yet to be explored in any depth.

Moving away from health-related initiatives in state schools, the continued existence of private schooling means that inequalities in the educational treatment of bodies *between* schools remains untouched. The scope of private schools has declined since the last century. However they cater for around 7 per cent of the school population in England (Walford, 1991) and can still be seen as aiding the development of physical capital (e.g. through insistence on 'correct' speech and manners) and instilling in pupils a particular confidence and orientation towards the body. This can help pupils acquire the confidence and pride valued in elite jobs (Salter and Tapper, 1981). Indeed, the importance of managing the body, dress, manner and speech in obtaining elite jobs is reinforced by those studies which suggest that qualifications serve only as an initial screening device, rather than actually determining employment selection decisions (Dale and Pieres, 1984; Moore, 1989). The informal aspects of employment selection relevant to bodily presentation can, then, play an important part in determining access to economic rewards. These may seem obvious points, but analyses of private schooling and the reproduction of class inequalities have focused on these institutions as providers of *cultural* rather than *physical* capital.

Conclusion

Having developed Bourdieu's approach to the body as a form of physical capital, I have briefly suggested how this analysis may help us illuminate the importance of the corporeal in education. In focusing on the treatment of the body in PE I have argued that historically there has been a change in the orientations schools have helped produce among pupils from different class backgrounds. In concluding this chapter, I want to say something about contemporary developments in PE.

Developments in the National Curriculum have dominated public and academic curriculum-related discussion over the past few years. The PE Working Group published its final report in 1991 (DES, 1991) and while the details of this document are examined elsewhere in this volume, it is worth saying something here about the report.

The Working Group identified a single attainment target which envelops three fundamental constituents of a PE curriculum: performing, planning, and evaluating physical activities. The Working Group also stressed the importance of equal opportunities in PE. While much of this is concerned with the provision of equal opportunities to pupils as *individuals* 'with their own abilities, difficulties and attitudes' (DES, 1991, p. 15), the report also expresses a sensitivity to some extra-school factors which may themselves shape individuals' orientations to the physical. For example, the report is concerned with the effects of some culturally restricted interpretations of masculinity on the place and value of dance in the schools curriculum, and on boys' opportunities of dance experience and education. This consideration of extra-school influences tends to exclude those related solely to social class, focusing instead on gender and 'race'. Furthermore, it fails to look in detail at the relationship between people's cultures and the curriculum. For example, the Working Group tends to treat 'Dance' as a relatively undifferentiated form. However, this disguises the degree to which the meanings and forms of dance change across ethnic and class-based cultures. Nonetheless, taken together with the relatively wide definition of PE adopted in the final report, the Working Group does lay out an approach towards PE which has the potential to scrutinize *some* of the social factors which shape orientations to the body. This is to be applauded as far as it goes. However, there is little evidence that the potential of the final report will be realized through appropriate in-service training. As the Working Group notes:

> Priorities for National Curriculum related in-service training are likely to be concerned with . . . helping teachers to become more aware of the components of planning, performing and evaluating, particularly in relation to dance, gymnastics and outdoor and adventurous activities. (DES, 1991, p. 52)

The danger is that such activity-centred training is likely to direct teachers towards *technical* concerns associated with conceptualizing and executing a performance, rather than the *social* concerns surrounding bodily dispositions.

Earlier in this chapter I stressed that there could be no correspondence approach to the relationship between schooling and physical capital. In concluding this chapter, it is worth tracing further the implications of this statement for the ability of different social groups to convert their physical capital into other forms of capital.

Irrespective of the effects schools may have in contributing to the production of physical capital, there is no guarantee that these will be maintained or amplified in the ability of social groups to convert this into other forms of capital. Just as aspects of cultural capital may fluctuate in value (e.g. the value of educational certificates may decrease because of qualification inflation [Dore,

1976; Collins, 1981]), so may the convertibility of physical capital (e.g. the earnings of professional sportspeople may decrease, individual sports may rise or fall in popularity, and changes in fashion may affect the symbolic value of certain styles of deportment, talk and dress [Featherstone, 1987]). It cannot simply be assumed that schools automatically produce in pupils forms of physical capital whose exchange value is guaranteed later on in life. The most important factor affecting the relative values of physical capitals at any one time, though, is the ability of the dominant class to define their orientations towards the body and lifestyle as superior, worthy of reward, and as, metaphorically and literally, the embodiment of class. This is a process constantly open to challenge and contestation. As those writers concerned with the development of consumer culture within late capitalism have argued, multinational corporate enterprises have become involved in the production of difference through assisting the proliferation of clothing styles and other signs of bodily identity to various groups within society (e.g. Jameson, 1984, 1985; Hall and Jameson, 1990; see also McRobbie, 1989). Though partly generated through global forms of post-Fordist industrial reorganization, this degree of proliferation and change poses threats to the ability of the dominant classes to continually impose their physical capital as of greatest social value. As Featherstone (1990) argues, the rapid internationalization and circulation of consumer and 'lifestyle' goods threatens the readability of those signs used by the dominant to signify their elite physical capital. This would 'threaten the logic of differences in which taste in cultural and consumer goods and lifestyle activities are held to be oppositionally structured' (Featherstone, 1990, p. 12).

In contemporary consumer society, then, it may be becoming much more difficult for any one group to impose as hegemonic, as worthy of respect and deference, a single version of physical capital. One consequence of this is that there is likely to be increased scrutiny of and disagreement over what PE teachers teach and how they teach it (see, e.g. Evans, 1990). If it is becoming more difficult for the value of forms of physical capital to be guaranteed, or even determined, then there is likely to be increased anxiety among groups in society to have their particular orientation to the body recognized as legitimate. No one in the PE profession should be surprised if dominant definitions of what counts as 'ability' or 'skill' in their subject come under even closer scrutiny, and even greater debate.

Notes

I would like to thank John Evans for his useful comments and suggestions on a draft version of this chapter.

1   For further analysis of Bourdieu's attempt to construct an approach to the body and sport which is historically dynamic see Shilling (1993).

2   This does not exclude the drive for forms of distinction that occur within working-class cultures (e.g. among sections of working-class men, for activities that display 'toughness'). However, in present circumstances, the drive for distinction among the dominant class is a pursuit for an elitism which contains the greatest potential for physical capital being converted into other forms of *high-value* capital.

References

ATKINSON, P. (1987) 'The Feminist Physique: Physical Education and the Medicalization of Women's Education', in MANGAN, J. and PARK, R. (Eds) *From 'Fair Sex' to Feminism*, London, Frank Cass, pp. 38–57.

BALL, S. (1981) *Beachside Comprehensive*, Cambridge, Cambridge University Press.

BARRELL, J., CHAMBERLAIN, A., EVANS, J., HOLT, T. and MACKEAN, J. (1989) 'Ideology and Commitment in Family Life: A Case Study of Runners', *Leisure Studies*, 8, pp. 249–62.

BERNSTEIN, B. (1970) 'Education Cannot Compensate for Society', *New Society*, 26 February, pp. 344–7.

BEST, G. (1975) 'The Ideal of "Manliness"', in SIMON, B. and BRADLEY, I. (Eds) *The Victorian Public School*, Dublin, Gill and MacMillan, pp. 129–46.

BOULANGER, R. (1988) 'Class Cultures and Sports Activities in Quebec', in HARVEY, J. and CANTELON, C. (Eds) *Not Just a Game: Essays In Canadian Sport Sociology*, Ottawa, University of Ottawa Press.

BOURDIEU, P. (1976) 'The School as a Conservative Force: Scholastic and Cultural Inequalities', in DALE, R., ESLAND, G. and MACDONALD, M. (Eds) *Schooling and Capitalism*, London, Routledge and Kegan Paul, pp. 192–200.

BOURDIEU, P. (1977a) *Outline of a Theory of Practice*, Cambridge, Cambridge University Press.

BOURDIEU, P. (1977b) 'Symbolic Power', in GLEESON, D. (Ed.) *Identity and Structure in the Sociology of Education*, Driffield, Nafferton, pp. 112–19.

BOURDIEU, P. (1978) 'Sport and Social Class', *Social Science Information*, **17**, 6, pp. 819–40.

BOURDIEU, P. (1984) *Distinction: A Social Critique of the Judgement of Taste*, London, Routledge and Kegan Paul.

BOURDIEU, P. (1985) 'The Social Space and the Genesis of Groups', *Theory and Society*, **14**, 6, pp. 723–44.

BOURDIEU, P. (1986) 'The Forms of Capital', in RICHARDSON, J. (Ed.) *Handbook of Theory and Research for the Sociology of Education*, New York, Greenwood Press, pp. 241–58.

BOURDIEU, P. and PASSERON, J. (1977) *Reproduction in Education, Society and Culture*, London, Routledge and Kegan Paul.

BOWLES, S. and GINTIS, H. (1976) *Schooling in Capitalist America*, London, Routledge and Kegan Paul.

BRUBAKER, R. (1985) 'Rethinking Classical Theory', *Theory and Society*, **14**, 6, pp. 745–74.

CARRINGTON, B. (1982) 'Sport as a Sidetrack', in BARTON, L. and WALKER, S. (Eds) *Race, Class and Education*, London, Croom Helm, pp. 40–65.

COLLINS, R. (1981) *The Credential Society*, New York, Academic Press.

COLQUHOUN, D. and ROBOTTOM, I. (1990) 'Health Education and Environmental Education: Towards a Shared Agenda and a Shared Discourse', *Unicorn*, 16, pp. 109–18.

DALE, R. and PIRES, E. (1984) 'Linking People and Jobs: the Indeterminate Place of Educational Credentials', in BROADFOOT, P. (Ed.) *Selection, Certification and Control: Issues in Educational Assessment*, Lewes, Falmer Press, pp. 51–65.

DAVIES, B. (1987) 'The Accomplishment of Genderedness in Pre-School Children', in POLLARD, A. (Ed.) *Children and their Primary Schools*, London, Falmer Press.

DAVIS, F. (1989) 'Of Maids' Uniforms and Blue Jeans: The Drama of Status Ambivalences in Clothing and Fashion', *Qualitative Sociology*, **12**, 4, pp. 337–355.

DEEM, R. (1986) *All Work and No Play?*, Milton Keynes, Open University Press.

DEPARTMENT OF EDUCATION AND SCIENCE (1991) *National Curriculum Physical Education Working Group: Final Report*, DES/Welsh Office.

DORE, R. (1976) *The Diploma Disease*, London, Allen and Unwin.

EVANS, J. (1988) 'Body Matters: Towards a Socialist Physical Education', in LAUDER, H. and BROWN, P. (Eds) *Education: In Search of a Future*, London, Falmer Press, pp. 174–91.

EVANS, J. (1990) 'Defining a Subject: The Rise and Rise of the New PE?', *British Journal of Sociology of Education*, **11**, 2, pp. 155–69.

FEATHERSTONE, M. (1982) 'The Body in Consumer Culture', *Theory, Culture and Society*, 1, pp. 18–33.

FEATHERSTONE, M. (1987) 'Leisure, Symbolic Power and the Life-Course', in HORNE, J., JARY, D. and TOMLINSON, A. (Eds) *Sport, Leisure and Social Relations*, London, Routledge and Kegan Paul, pp. 113–38.

FEATHERSTONE, M. (1990) 'Perspectives on Consumer Culture', *Sociology*, **24**, 1, pp. 5–22.

FLETCHER, S. (1984) *Women First: The Female Tradition in English Physical Education 1880–1980*, London, The Athlone Press.

FOUCAULT, M. (1979) *Discipline and Punish: The Birth of The Prison*, Middlesex, Penguin.

GOODGER, B. and GOODGER, J. (1989) 'Excitement and Representation: Toward a Sociological Explanation of the Significance of Sport in Modern Society', *Quest*, 41, pp. 257–72.

GRAHAM, H. (1984) *Women, Health and the Family*, Brighton, Wheatsheaf.

GREEN, E. and HEBRON, S. (1988) 'Leisure and Male Partners', in WIMBUSH, E. and TALBOT, M. (Eds) *Relative Freedoms: Women and Leisure*, Milton Keynes, Open University Press, pp. 37–47.

GRIFFIN, C., HOBSON, D., MACINTOSH, S. and McCABE, T. (1982) 'Women and Leisure', in HARGREAVES, J. (Ed.) *Sport, Culture and Ideology*, London, Routledge and Kegan Paul, pp. 88–116.

HALL, S. and JAMESON, F. (1990) 'Clinging to the Wreckage', *Marxism Today*, September, pp. 28–31.

HARGREAVES, D. (1967) *Social Relations in a Secondary School*, London, Routledge and Kegan Paul.

HARGREAVES, J. (1986) *Sport, Power and Culture*, Cambridge, Polity Press.

HENDRY, L. (1978) *School, Sport and Leisure*, Lepus Books.

JAMESON, F. (1984) 'Postmodernism: Or the Cultural Logic of Late Capitalism', *New Left Review*, 146, pp. 53–92.

JAMESON, F. (1985) 'Postmodernism and Consumer Society', in FOSTER, H. (Ed.) *Postmodern Culture*, London, Pluto Press, pp. 111–25.

JEFFREYS, S. (1990) *Anticlimax: A Feminist Perspective on the Sexual Revolution*, London, The Women's Press.

KEDDIE, N. (1971) 'Classroom Knowledge', in YOUNG, M. (Ed.) *Knowledge and Control*, London, Collier Macmillan, pp. 133–60.

KIRK, D. and COLQUHOUN, D. (1989) 'Healthism and Physical Education', *British Journal of Sociology of Education*, **10**, 4, pp. 417–34.

KIRK, D. and TINNING, R. (Eds) (1990) *Physical Education, Curriculum and Culture*, London, Falmer Press.

LACEY, C. (1970) *Hightown Grammar*, Manchester, Manchester University Press.

McCRONE, K. (1988) *Sport and the Physical Emancipation of English Women 1870–1914*, London, Routledge.

McINTOSH, P. (1952) *Physical Education in England Since 1800*, London, G. Bell and Sons.

McINTOSH, P. (1981, revised edition) 'Landmarks in the History of Physical Education since World War 2', in McINTOSH, P., DIXON, J., MUNROW, A. and WILLETTA, R. *Landmarks in the History of Physical Education*, London, Routledge and Kegan Paul, pp. 218–49.

McKay, J., Gore, J. and Kirk, D. (1990) 'Beyond the Limits of Technocratic Physical Education', *Quest*, 42, pp. 52–80.

MacNeill, M. (1988) 'Active Women, Media Representations and Ideology', in Harvey, J. and Cantelon, H. (Eds) *Not Just a Game: Essays in Canadian Sport Sociology*, Ottawa, University of Ottawa Press, pp. 195–211.

McRobbie, A. (1978) 'Working Class Girls and the Culture of Femininity', in CCCS Women's Group (Eds) *Women Take Issue*, London, Hutchinson, pp. 96–108.

McRobbie, A. (Ed.) (1989) *Zoot Suits and Second Hand Dresses*, London, Macmillan.

Mangan, J. (1975) 'Athleticism: A Case Study of the Evolution of an Educational Ideology', in Simon, B. and Bradley, I. (Eds) *The Victorian Public School*, Dublin, Gill and Macmillan.

Mennell, S. (1985) *All Manners of Food. Eating and Taste in England and France from the Middle-Ages to the Present*, Oxford, Basil Blackwell.

Moore, R. (1989) 'Education, Employment and Recruitment', in Cosin, B., Flude, M. and Hales, M. (Eds) *School, Work and Equality*, London, Hodder and Stoughton, pp. 206–22.

Payne, S. (1985) 'Physical Education and Health in the United Kingdom', *British Journal Of Physical Education*, 17, 1, pp. 4–9.

Quest (1991) 'Special Feature: Body Culture', 43, 2, pp. 119–89.

Radner, H. (1989) ' "This Time's For Me": Making Up and Feminine Practice', *Cultural Studies*, 3, 3, pp. 301–22.

Salter, B. and Tapper, T. (1981) *Education, Politics and the State*, London, Grant McIntyre.

Scraton, S. (1986) 'Images of Femininity and the Teaching of Girls' Physical Education', in Evans, J. (Ed.) *Physical Education, Sport and Schooling*, London, Falmer Press, pp. 71–94.

Shilling, C. (1991a) 'Social Space, Gender Inequalities and Educational Differentiation', *British Journal of Sociology of Education*, 12, 1, pp. 23–44.

Shilling, C. (1991b) 'Educating the Body: Physical Capital and the Production of Social Inequalities', *Sociology*, 25, 4, pp. 653–72.

Shilling, C. (1993) *The Body and Social Theory*, London, Sage/Theory, Culture and Society.

Tinning, R. (1990) 'Physical Education as Health Education: Problem-Setting as a Response to the New Health Consciousness', *Unicorn*, 16, pp. 81–91.

Tomlinson, A. (1982) 'Physical Education, Sport and Sociology: The Current State and the Way Forward', in *Physical Education, Sport and Leisure: Sociological Perspectives*, NATFHE Conference Report, pp. 44–54.

Townsend, P., Davidson, N. and Whitehead, M. (1988) *Inequalities in Health*, London, Penguin.

Walford, G. (1991) 'Private Schooling into the 1990's', in Walford, G. *Private Schooling*, London, and Chapman Publishing, pp. 1–13.

Whitehead, N. and Hendry, L.B. (Ed.) (1976) *Teaching Physical Education in England*, London, Lepus Books.

Willis, S. (1990) 'Work(ing) Out', *Cultural Studies*, 4, 1, pp. 1–18.

Woods, P. (1979) *The Divided School*, London, Routledge and Kegan Paul.

Chapter 5

A Gendered Physical Education: Equality and Sexism

Margaret Talbot

British physical education is gendered in ideology, content, teaching methods and through its relationships with the wider dance and sports contexts. While teachers of physical education may claim that they espouse equality of opportunity for all children, their teaching behaviours and practices reveal entrenched sex stereotyping, based on 'common-sense' notions about what is suitable for girls and boys, both in single-sex and mixed-sex groups and schools. The situation in physical education is complicated by its content. Competitive activities embody the end of exclusive success — on the face of it, antithetical to the aim of equality of opportunity.

While equality of opportunity is enshrined in the 1975 Sex Discrimination Act and in Department for Education policy, and now within the proposals of the Secretaries of State for physical education in the National Curriculum, the way in which the Sex Discrimination Act 1975 (SDA) is framed in relation to sport has given rise to a number of confusing anomalies. These anomalies are further compounded by the confusion shown by the Schools Unit of the Equal Opportunities Commission (EOC)[1] in its interpretation and advice, particularly with regard to curricular physical education and school sport.

As a result, the rights of girls and boys to equal access to a range of curricular physical activities are limited by practices, some of which were intended to protect girls' and women's access to competitive sport, but which were never framed to apply to educational programmes in curriculum time. There are also strong influences on school sport and physical education, exerted by sports governing bodies whose restrictive practices continue unchallenged by the legislation, and which cause further confusion for teachers of curricular physical education and competitive school sport.

This situation, with restricted *access* on the basis of *sex* for some children and adults to certain sporting activities, results also in restricted *opportunity* for both sexes, which is further compounded by the differential social value given to activities associated with girls and boys, women and men — with *gender*.[2]

In contrast, equal opportunities is, in National Curriculum Council[2] terms, like multicultural education, a cross-curricular *dimension* — which means that it should permeate all aspects of school life. The first section of the Education Reform Act 1988 (ERA) established general principles which must be reflected in the curriculum of all pupils. It *entitles* all children to a curriculum which is balanced and broadly based and which

(a) promotes the spiritual, moral, cultural, mental and physical development of pupils at the school and of society; and
(b) prepares such pupils for the opportunities, responsibilities and experiences of adult life.

This means, according to the Department of Education and Science (DES) document *From Policy to Practice* (1989), that pupils are *entitled* to an education which embodies the following principles, and that this is now established in law:

• that each child should have a broad and balanced curriculum which is also relevant to his or her particular needs;
• that this principle must be reflected in the curriculum of each pupil: it is not enough for such a curriculum merely to be *offered* by the school — it must be fully taken up by every individual pupil;
• that the curriculum should promote development in all the main areas of learning and experience which are widely accepted as important; and
• that the curriculum must also serve to develop the pupil as an individual, as a member of society and as a future adult member of the community with a range of personal and social opportunities and responsibilities.

Building on this principle, the National Curriculum Council's *The Whole Curriculum* (1990) establishes that

Dimensions such as a commitment to providing equal opportunities for all pupils, and a recognition that preparation for life in a multicultural society is relevant to all pupils, *should permeate every aspect of the curriculum* (our emphasis).

It should be emphasized that it is clear in these extracts that the essential distinctions between *access* and *opportunity* are recognized, as they are in the Proposals of the Secretaries of State for Physical Education:

it would be a mistake to equate **access** with **opportunity**, and it is important to appreciate the distinction between the two. In some schools pupils may be said to have the same **access** to curriculum physical education, regardless of their sex, religion, ability, or ethnic background. But it may not be the case that these children also have equal **opportunities** to participate in different activities. (DES, 1991, p. 15)

The distinction is a recognition of the power of the gendering of physical education, in the ways in which content, methods and social value are differentiated for girls and boys on the basis of gender expectations and assumptions, which in turn result in the perpetuation of various forms of sexism which in effect prevent physical education being delivered equitably to girls and boys in British schools.

On the face of it, the Sex Discrimination Act 1975 (Home Office, 1975) covers physical education in unequivocal terms:

sex discrimination [is] unlawful in employment, training and related matters, in education, in the provision of goods, services, and in the disposal and management of services.

In general terms, the Act requires that a person should be treated with reference to her or his own attributes, and not to those commonly associated with her or his sex. The Act thus recognizes biological sex differences, and does not seek to make sex differentiation unlawful, but is intended rather to prevent practices of discrimination related to cultural expectations (gender). These cultural expectations are usually dependent on restricted and polarized notions of female and male behaviour, often stereotyped as femininity and masculinity, and commonly justified as 'natural'.

What is the framework of beliefs within which physical education teachers work? There appear to be four main models used to make claims about the relative merits of gender groups:

1 **Women and girls are inferior to men and boys**.
2 **Women and girls are superior to men and boys**.

These two are often used in playground and staffroom battles of words, and my position on these is that no teacher should believe either; teachers who subscribe to either position should not be allowed anywhere near children! The third model is simple and unequivocal:

3 **Women and girls and men and boys are equal**.

Commonly, however, a condition is added:

4 **Women and girls and men and boys are equal — but different**.

This conditional approach is based on assumptions that sex category membership gives rise to differences *between* the sex groups which actually override individual differences *within* the sex groups: these category memberships are supported by claims that these differences are 'natural'. But for teachers, a central concern should be to distinguish between those aspects of a child's make-up which are *innate, inevitable and without exception*, and those which are *learned, rewarded and normative*: teachers' professional business is with the latter, while having due regard to the influence of the former — this is the central foundation for teachers' influence and contribution.

In 1988, at the NATFHE Dance Conference, a delegate asked this question:

Can the panel suggest a strategy for resolving the gender problem in dance? It is my opinion that dance will not be taken seriously in public debate either in the context of the school curriculum or any other context while this problem exists. (Curl, 1988, p. 59)

This question implies acceptance that there is a central 'problem', a conflict in the relationships between masculinity and dance: and yet the question was framed in terms of *gender* as a problem, rather than masculinity. This illustrates further dimensions which are beyond legislation, but which are influential in its interpretation — the dimension of social valuing and the ways in which issues come to be defined as problems. In physical education, these dimensions are further underlined by a range of other circumstances:

- the perceived low status of activities associated with women and girls;
- the reluctance of those identifying the 'gender problem' to focus on its source;
- the reluctance of those who, already struggling with the day-to-day difficulties of teaching physical education in schools, and now also with implementing the National Curriculum, fail to question the restrictive practices or ideologies within which they are working;
- the reluctance to recognize or acknowledge the influence on physical education practice of the dominant ideologies of sexuality and homophobia.

The so-called 'gender problem' is commonly cited and discussed among teachers of physical education. Yet there are so few references to gender or sexuality in any of the 'official' or academic physical education literature, even within perspectives related to personal and social education. Neither does there appear to be an understanding of the legal basis for practice and decision-making.

Under the terms of the 1975 Sex Discrimination Act, *sex discrimination*, the treating of people as unequal on the basis of their sex, is unlawful. There are general rules for educational establishments which make sex discrimination unlawful, although there are exceptions for single-sex and boarding schools, and for educational charities. Such establishments may continue to provide physical education and school sport in traditional ways, although of course state schools will still have to implement the statutory aspects of the National Curriculum.

Sex differentiation (treating people as equal but different by reference to their sex), however, is not in itself unlawful, as long as the differential treatment cannot be shown to result in disadvantage to either group. This distinction affects both curricular physical education and school sport, and, at first sight, could be said legally to support the continued provision of programmes of physical education differentiated in content and delivery for girls and boys, and further legitimated by expressed concern for fairness and prevention of injury in competitive activities. However, sex differentiation does not, and cannot, operate independently of *gender* expectations, which are culturally constructed and perpetuated. Sex differentiation is therefore often based on stereotyped notions of femininity and masculinity which perpetuate inequality. This is illustrated by practices in physical education which continue to label dance as suitable for girls but not for boys.

Many male physical education teachers have been criticized for their attitudes towards dance. It is certainly the case that several researchers (see Evans *et al.*, 1987) have observed that it is male physical education teachers who are least committed and even antipathetic towards equal opportunities. The proposals for the National Curriculum should help to challenge and confront such attitudes. As my colleague Anne Flintoff has commented:

> It is time for the outmoded, stereotypical attitudes towards dance held among some PE people to be banished once and for all, and for the profession to welcome dance within its remit, rather than suggesting that it goes elsewhere. (Flintoff, 1990, p. 88)

There have been arguments that dance should find its place with the arts (ignoring the framework given to it within the National Curriculum), and that, particularly for boys, dance should not take up precious time 'needed' for other aspects of physical education; there are even those who suggest that the term 'physical education' should be abandoned in favour of 'sports education' (see Alderson and Crutchley, 1990).

The different opinions around this issue are sometimes further polarized by the practices and ideologies of dance itself. Are teachers of dance themselves blameless? Are *they* willing to adopt the self-critical approach which is a pre-requisite for equal opportunities work? How many dance teachers, for example, see the failure of most people to conform with the restricted range of body shapes promulgated by some dance forms, almost as a moral fault? Royston Maldoom, a London dance teacher, has this to say:

> There's the feeling from the top that '*this* is what dance should look like, and this is what *dancers* should look like, and we'll do it *for* you'. Just as you can enjoy football, and play it, without becoming a professional footballer, so you can dance without becoming — or needing to look like — a professional dancer. Dance relates to life. (cited in Dougill, 1989)

The Equal Opportunities Commission (1988) has advised with regard to physical education that

> it is not unlawful to divide pupils by sex in co-educational schools but if pupils are taught physical education separately, this must not result in less favourable treatment on the grounds of sex. In view of the limited amount of case law on the subject it would not be safe to say that the same physical education must be offered to girls and boys but where different sports are offered they must be sufficiently similar as regards their relative merits. For example, if girls are offered hockey and boys football and all other things are equal, such as opportunity to play for the school or county, standard of coaching, time allocated, etc., it is unlikely that a court would find a girl was suffering a detriment by being banned from playing football. Our advice to schools is that *sports must be sufficiently similar to provide equal opportunities* and the safest way to ensure that they are sufficiently similar is to make equal provision for both sexes.

This paragraph illustrates several of the dimensions which make this issue so problematic and so interesting. If '*sports must be sufficiently similar to provide equal opportunities*' (and here the EOC does not distinguish between curricular physical education and school sport), a sex-differentiated curriculum can legally continue, as long as disadvantage is not present for either girls or boys.

It may even be problematic to assume, therefore, that team games traditionally associated with one or the other sex, especially in school physical education, do provide similar educational experiences. If this is indeed the case, then physical education teachers could (as many already do) legally offer soccer/hockey, basketball/netball sex-differentiated pairings for boys and girls. It would then be for a complainant to demonstrate that the educational experiences or resource bases for the girls' and boys' activities are not similar, or to show that the opportunities for future or higher-level participation in these sex-differentiated activities are not similar: further, the lack of similarity would need to be shown to be disadvantageous to the complainant having no access to the other sex-group activity. The place of girls' and boys' activities in resource allocation and in the ritual life of the school would thus need to be carefully monitored to avoid disadvantage.

But in the case of other traditional pairings of activities, for example, netball/ rugby, dance/sports hall games, the condition of 'sufficient similarity' would seem to be in doubt. Similarly, the flexibility offered at Key Stage Four (age 11–14) of National Curriculum Physical Education, for choice of any two activities from the five areas of experience (athletic activities, dance, games, gymnastic activities, outdoor and adventurous activities), could mislead some teachers of physical education into believing that it would be acceptable to offer boys different choices from those offered to girls. Selection of physical activities for physical education programmes within the framework of the National Curriculum, and with such advice from the EOC on the legality of differential provision, will require more considered criteria than those of tradition and 'common-sense' assumptions about what is suitable for girls and boys.

The power of the greater social value attributed to sports and games associated with boys and men is illustrated by the fact that the EOC have had a host of complaints from girls who are prevented from playing football in their physical education programmes or in school sport, but none from boys who are prevented from taking part in dance. The tradition of single-sex provision of physical education in the UK, for many years supported and reinforced by single-sex teacher training, has in fact resulted in a wider range of activities and teaching styles within physical education than might otherwise have been the case. It is therefore important to move forward towards extending equality of opportunity for children, without sacrificing some of the wealth of expertise which has accrued, and to avoid being too influenced by predominant sports cultures.

A clear example of sex discrimination in physical education would be for a male physical education teacher to offer a GCSE in Physical Education or Sports Studies only to boys: the single-sex tradition provides a context within which this, and the offering of GCSE Dance only to girls, may happen. Less clear examples relate, as already described, to the pairing of activities in sex-differentiated programmes, and to the different resources allocated for girls' and boys' school sport and extra-curricular physical activities.

This situation is compounded by the common confusion (shared by the Schools Unit of the EOC and various Ministers of Sport) between curricular physical education, which should be covered unequivocally by the terms of the Sex Discrimination Act 1975, and competitive school sport, especially that undertaken under the aegis and rules of sports governing bodies.

Competitive sport is affected by a General Exception to the Act (Section 44):

There is a general exception for acts relating to participation as a competitor in certain sporting events which are confined to one sex. The sports to which the exception applies are those in which the average woman would be at a disadvantage in competition with the average man. (Home Office, 1975, p. 32)

The effect of this exception is that most sports can legally be male (or female) exclusive, and that even small girls and boys may be prevented from competing with or against each other. David Pannick (1983) argues that this constitutes a conflict with the basic principle of the Act, namely that

people should be treated by reference to their individual attributes and not by reference to whether they are male or female. (Pannick, 1983, p. 68)

The case law here is limited to that of Theresa Bennett and the Football Association. The FA banned Theresa, aged 12, from playing in a football team of which she was the only female member. Supported by the Equal Opportunities Commission, she took her case to the courts and won her case on the grounds that as a pre-pubertal girl, she was not subject as an adult woman to the Exception, because she was not at a disadvantage in biological terms to her male peers.

The Football Association took the case to appeal and, in spite of overwhelming evidence from child development and football experts, that she was indeed not competing at a disadvantage to her male peers, Lord Denning overturned the previous judgment, because 'we do not enquire about the ages of ladies' (Court of Appeal transcript). The ideology of femininity embodied in this judgment is far from the biological sex differences of adults recognized in the Act: his further decision that the complainant should not have right of appeal to the Lords, on the grounds that the issue was 'of no importance whatsoever', also illustrates the distance between the spirit of the Act and its interpretation by an elderly male judge aged more than sixty years more than the complainant.

David Pannick (1983) quotes several other examples of the ways in which anachronistic ideologies of femininity and masculinity influence judicial judgments and decisions:

men and women should be equal certainly, but I sincerely hope that they will always be different. Merely to take the rather minor point of the sort of games they play, I cannot think of rugger as a very suitable game for girls, nor do I see boys taking to netball very successfully. (Lord Somers, House of Lords Debate)

there should be at least one island in the sea of life reserved for men that would be impregnable to the assault of women. (Lord Justice Tooze, on wrestling)

It is not as if the training of horses could be regarded as an unsuitable occupation for a woman, like that of jockey or speedway-rider. (Lord Denning)

Such lack of consistency in the interpretation of the law, and the failure of physical education as a profession to come to terms with the way it affects the subject in schools, mean that physical education teachers and often local education authorities are unsure or unaware of the legal position. Many therefore fall back on following the sports governing bodies' policies, especially where schools have no clear guidelines, and where physical education and school sport may be run on lines antithetical to schools' equal opportunities policies.

Some teachers do have genuine concerns for the physical safety of girls should they be offered access to physical contact games, but the long practice of physical matching to cater for the ranges of physiques and statures in most single-sex year groups would cater also for mixed-sex groups.

The EOC Schools Unit has shown confusion about the application of the SDA to curricular physical education, tacitly accepting that the Section 44 Exception may apply. Careful teaching, which is anyway always necessary in mixed-ability groups and groups of children with varying physiques, should ensure that learning games skills and tactics does not entail the kinds of risks which would be inherent in competitive contests, which are the situations which Section 44 was meant to cover.

Section 44 is problematic, especially for physical education. Its intention was to ensure fairness of competition in physical terms, but the ways in which it is commonly applied, based on illogical and ill-founded generalizations about girls and boys, women and men, means that physical diversity within the sexes is ignored, and a 'norm' of average woman and average man is set, which in fact rarely exists. The principle instead should be whether conditions for participation by all can be realistically set, and whether access can be extended without material disadvantage to others. For girls, who are so much more dependent on school sport than are boys for learning the skills, knowledge and confidence for further participation in sport, this is an essential and central aspect of physical education's contribution to equality of opportunity.

The Physical Education Association, in its response to the Interim Report of the Physical Education Working Group (PEA, 1991), supported the comments made in the short section on equal opportunities in the Report, and recommended that equal opportunity should be seen as a leading and guiding principle for physical education. The section in general was widely supported, with many respondents asking for further guidance in the final report. The question must be, to what extent physical education can be presented as inclusive rather than exclusive? The consideration of gender across the curriculum is relevant only if the promotion of equal opportunities is presented as an educational aim and therefore we need to understand the concept of equal opportunities rather better (for a fuller discussion of the interpretations of equal opportunities in physical education, see Talbot, 1990).

Many teachers argue that they always treat children identically. On the face of it, what could be 'fairer' than this — treating everyone the same, and offering them the same programme? But there are two basic faults to find in this claim, which make it unacceptable as a means of reaching equality.

First, the principle of equal treatment ignores the fact that young people differ in their abilities, interests, resources and previous experiences. This is particularly true of their experiences of physical activities. To treat children all the same would be to ignore their individuality and limit the extent to which they might all benefit from their various backgrounds, interests and abilities. The second criticism of the claim is that it simply does not happen in practice. No teacher treats all children the same. Classroom interaction studies show that teachers consistently give more attention to boys than to girls in coeducational settings; that their judgments of the same behaviour when displayed by girls or boys differ; and that interaction is similarly affected by factors of ethnicity, social class and age. When even committed teachers are made aware of this, first they find it difficult to believe; then, when shown the evidence of their own behaviour on videotape, they still find it difficult to change. The equal treatment claim ignores the pervasiveness and power of expectations of girls and boys, women and men. Nick May (1985) quotes from his own research on engendered teacher education:

> During the interview 'Mary' — who had last year been a school pupil and this year is a first-year undergraduate on the new degree in Education (with Teaching Certificate) — talked at some length, and with considerable feeling, about how her main frustration as a female pupil had been what she saw as her systematic disenfranchisement from influence over the content and process of the schools' curricula which she had pursued over the previous thirteen years. Although she felt that all pupils suffered this lack of influence she was convinced that girls suffered disproportionately. (Some time later in the interview), when talking about the 'teaching practice' she had recently completed, 'Mary' described how her 'music and movement' work had met with 'loud and disruptive' reaction from some of the boys in the mixed class of 7–8 year olds, even though the majority of the children had clearly enjoyed and been engaged by the scheme she had designed. Faced with this rejection, and experiencing some anxiety about how the teachers and her tutor would assess her potential as a future teacher if she was not seen to be exercising what they would count as 'good control' of the class, 'Mary' resolved her 'problem' by designing an alternative scheme which the few boys would not (and did not) reject. Although the girls had 'subsequently shown less interest', their quiet acquiescence to what she offered them reduced her anxiety about her assessment as a teacher. When she related her pupil experience to her teaching experience 'Mary' was dismayed to realise that she had 'reproduced for others precisely that frustration which (she herself) had experienced as a pupil'. (May, 1985, p. 79)

A further relevant question when claims for equal or the same treatment are made is 'the same as what'? The nature of the sameness of the treatment is itself open to examination, question and redefinition.

Teacher interaction with colleagues and pupils reveals much about the values and beliefs of that teacher. The kind of person that teacher is, also affects children's attempts to construct or respond to norms of behaviour and parity of treatment. Again, there is evidence that teachers will make more effort to accommodate boys' needs and demands in mixed classes than they will girls', partly because they are sympathetic to perceived gender conflicts for boys, but also to avoid potential disruption by boys. This relates to what might be described as 'me-too feminism', in which boys' activities are used as the norm, with girls forced into a 'catch-up' position, and boys' performances always regarded as the norm or bench mark against which girls' performances should be measured. This issue has important implications for the assessment and reporting of attainment in physical education, which anyway have to accommodate the whole range of ability.

We know that girls are more dependent on the school physical education programme for learning the skills and confidence needed for later leisure partici-pation than are boys, who have other agencies of learning outside the school. When considering the nature of the partnerships in provision which can be utilized to present a rich choice of physical activities at various levels, the paucity of community provision for girls, relative to that offered boys, must be borne in mind.

Another common interpretation of equality is that of *equal outcomes*; rather than ignoring individual differences in equal treatment, it accommodates these differences, to work towards a common outcome. But this approach overrides human potential, and in practice reduces performance to the lowest common denominator. Obviously, there are times when teachers will try to control or match differences between children in the same teaching group, in order to encourage progress among the less able or less confident, or to encourage the abler children to consider the needs of others, or to enlist their help in mentoring or helping others: but good teachers will not deny these differences in absolute terms — rather, they will try to help children to value and respect the different contributions of their colleagues. Equality of outcome is also difficult to deter-mine: when can it be judged to have been achieved? Again, I have seen the effects of this approach used implicitly in mixed classes, especially at student level, where skilled women students are prevented from achieving their best in mixed dance and gymnastics groups, either by the task which is set, or by their own perceptions that they should not 'show up' the men, who often 'ham' their way through their own feelings of inadequacy: collusion in this process by lectur-ing staff is understandable, but regrettable. As David Pannick (1983) has dryly remarked, 'It is not clear why a man's ego should take precedence over a woman's equality of opportunity'.

The basis of the constitution and sex discrimination legislation of many countries is that of *egalitarianism, or shared humanity*. As human beings, we all should enjoy the same rights and protections against discrimination. It can be a useful principle from which children can be encouraged to express and learn to value each other's differences, and discouraged from mistreating other people merely because of the category to which they belong. The film *One Flew Over the Cuckoo's Nest* shocked precisely because it portrayed the denial of a mental patient's essential humanity. It may also, if we allow it, provide us with the opportunity to confront our own presuppositions and prejudices, and to examine critically the ways in which our professional work informally or formally discriminates against certain categories of people. It furthermore gives us a firm foundation for refuting or challenging justifications of inequality as 'natural'. Such claims of 'naturally' determined differences affect girls and boys very differently and to different degrees. Anxiety about sex identity is usually much more acute regarding boys than girls: here, it is masculinity rather than gender which is problematic.

A girl may refuse the constraints of femininity during the period of childhood which the psychoanalysts have called 'latency' — that is, between the ages of about 7 and 11. She may climb trees, play football, get into scrapes and generally emulate acceptable masculine behaviour, *but only on condition that she grows out of it*. No such tolerance is extended to the male. He can never, even temporarily, abdicate from his role. The boy who goes around with girls, plays girls' games and rejects his male peers would probably be referred to Child Guidance. (Comer, 1974, p. 13)

It is not difficult to see how the narrower range of acceptable 'masculine' behaviour affects boys' opportunities for involvement in the so-called aesthetic physical activities and for dance experience, but it is much more difficult to challenge practices which are claimed to be natural and which have rarely been questioned hitherto.

If pupils are to have equal opportunities, presuppositions have to be confronted. This is not to argue that they must be made to conform to some other view, but they must, if education is to be anything other than a predictable channelling mechanism, be considered, examined, and, where necessary, challenged. (Pratt, 1985, p. 2)

It is even more uncomfortable to recognize and confront the homophobia inherent to most portrayals of masculinity and its influence on the teaching of physical education. Ian Day is researching on masculinity in physical education; he asked a male Head of PE in the school where he was observing why he constantly called young boys 'poofters', while claiming to be interested in equal opportunities. The teacher first was amazed at the question, but then justified his behaviour by claiming that he used to be worse — he used to call them women!

Of course, boys need not wait until secondary school before being subjected to these kinds of pressures:

as boys grow older, the majority are not allowed to show gentleness or sensitivity, unless they are willing or capable of stepping aside from the norm and accepting possible physical abuse and most certainly verbal abuse with names such as 'queer', 'puff' or 'queen'.... Rather than treating him as an individual with a personality of his own, his individuality has to be taken away so that he can be shaped into the male role model. The general belief is that sex-stereotyping is harmful to girls, but ... at this very young age it is also harmful to boys. (Hough, 1985, p. 18)

Walker (1988) has described how school sport reifies and entrenches this process:

the footballer culture tended to impose on other groups and individuals, with varying degrees of penetration, its definition of what it is to be a man. The material outcome of this is the assertion of a monopoly on achieved manhood, through the claim to exclusive possession of legitimate 'knowledge' of how men act. Practices which violated the dominant definition, as opposed to those of the dominant males, were labelled negatively, as 'poofter', just as those falling outside the dominant ethnic definition were labelled 'wog'. Sport, especially rugby football, was the focus of those practices which most coherently integrated the ethnic and gender elements of the cultural hierarchy. . . . The touchstone, often explicitly, was sexuality, postulated and perceived, enacted and avowed. (Walker, 1988, p. 5)

For such dominant cultures to be challenged, it is essential that challenge comes from more than one source, and that all teachers need to identify and nurture their allies in this process. To recognize homophobia in the classroom is one thing; to offer alternatives which are seen as possible and relevant by boys and male colleagues is quite another.

The most frequently used principle of equality is that of *equality of opportunity*. In education, the idea is to widen the franchise of opportunity by removing as many structural and social constraints to access as possible, so that no one is actively prevented from taking part. The problem with this interpretation is that *access* is not the same as *opportunity*. The distinction between access and opportunity is based on two aspects of freedom: freedom *from* constraint confers access, while freedom *to* do as one wishes confers opportunity. This active and positive definition of opportunity is crucial, because it relates to individual interpretations of what is possible, salient and relevant.

For example, we may claim that we have provided equality of opportunity to take part in programmes of dance or games, because the same programme is offered to all children, without regard to sex, ethnic or social background or religion. Equal access may, indeed, be the case: but the relevance of the sex of the teacher, the choice of physical activities offered, the interactions within co-educational classes and the previous experience and level of competence of the children have not been taken into account. Consideration has not been given to the ways in which the form of the lesson or its delivery could be seen by some of the potential participants as exclusive. If some boys, for example, see dance as antithetical to images of masculinity which have high social currency, and decide to avoid dance, or some girls see team games as conflicting with adolescent views of femininity, there is a tendency to label the whole sex group — 'boys won't dance', or 'girls don't like team games'.

Labels like these rapidly become myths, which may or may not depend on generalizable observations, but which are extremely difficult to challenge or disprove. Even if factually disproved, myths are still widely believed, especially when they are based on fear, or are embedded in the socialization processes and 'policed' by adolescent peer groups. When they are also embodied in the very culture of some of the activities we teach, with physical education teachers themselves demonstrating 'engendered' physical education, how can we possibly hope to promote equal opportunities in and through our subject? If as teachers we fail to recognize the culturally learned 'millstones' which children bring with them to their educational experiences, or the 'millstones' which we ourselves carry around, it is difficult to see how prejudice and entrenched belief can be confronted and challenged. John Evans and his colleagues (Evans *et al.*, 1987) have presented the process as shown in figure 5.1, and thus:

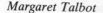

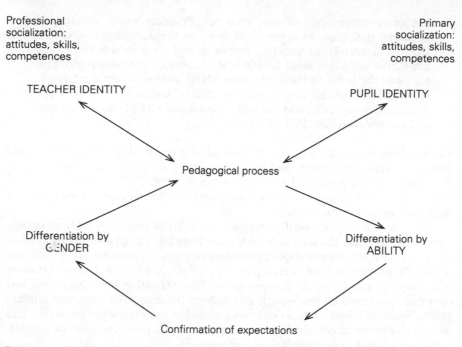

Figure 5.1   Teaching and Differentiation
(*Source:*   Evans *et al.*, 1987, p. 65)

Children do come to Physical Education deeply socialised into particular ways of seeing and doing physical activities, with images already worked out about what is appropriate for their respective 'gender'. Years of socialisation and practice have also differently pre-disposed them with the skills and abilities necessary for a competent performance in particular activities. Armed with this social and cultural 'habitus', this deeply sedimented package of attitudes, skills (physical as well as social), competences, teachers and pupils enter into the pedagogical process. (Evans *et al.*, 1987, pp. 64–5)

Recognizing some of these predispositions, we can begin to assess our own ability to bring about change. Of course we cannot change the world overnight, but we can perhaps identify those elements in the situation which are under our own control, and how our own behaviour as professionals and as social beings can help. Figure 5.2 is a basis for analyzing those aspects of schools and school life which are actually possible to control and manipulate. As reflective practitioners, teachers are obliged to recognize and address their strengths and weaknesses: the conventional wisdom is that where there is underrepresentation or relative underachievement (boys not taking part in dance, girls underachieving in competitive sport), then it is for the members of the group who do not take part or who underachieve, to change their behaviour in order to improve. Reflective teachers, however, can help to change the practices and images of activities to try to make them more boy- or girl-friendly.

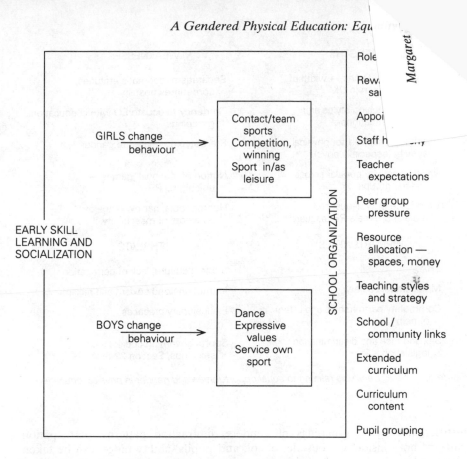

Figure 5.2   Gender and physical education: a model for change

SWOT analysis — STRENGTHS, WEAKNESSES, OPPORTUNITIES, THREATS — can be used as an evaluative tool to identify those aspects of performance which most require attention. The strengths and weaknesses are teachers' own, while the opportunities and threats are external, not under teachers' control, but requiring some response from them — they certainly must be aware of them and work out how to respond to them. A first attempt at SWOT analysis relating to equal opportunities and gender in physical education is given in figure 5.3.

Teachers can thus raise the level of their own knowledge, understanding and commitment. In accepting responsibility as educators to work towards achieving equality of opportunity, physical education teachers can unlearn some of the messages they themselves have learned, in order to confront their own beliefs and prejudices and how these are acted out in their teaching. The next stage is to identify the contextual factors in schools which affect teachers' ability to change — the school's commitment to equal opportunities; the status of physical education and its effect on the priority of equal opportunities work; the attitudes and commitment of PE and dance staff; the class norms; community support for physical education. Lastly, the appreciation of classroom variables like

STRENGTHS	WEAKNESSES
Single-sex traditions → width of PE curriculum in UK	Separatism, dogmatic attitudes, sometimes hostility
Range of teaching styles and learning situations	Tendency to equate EO with coeducational groupings
Peer group support for physical activity (especially boys)	Stereotyping related to gender
Physical activity popular across various groups	Notion of 'national' games — unicultural PE
Workforce of well-qualified male and female PE teachers	Homophobia: narrow range of concepts of masculinity
OPPORTUNITIES	THREATS
ERA	Subject culture; lack of permeation
Multicultural society	Institutionalized sexism and racism
Community partnerships and offers of help	Exclusionary practices
Sex and race anti-discrimination legislation	Sports governing bodies, single-sex clubs, Section 22 SDA

Figure 5.3   SWOT analysis relating to equal opportunities and gender in physical education

instructional styles, groupings of genders, interaction patterns, participation patterns both inside and outside school, and pupils' ability range, can be taken into account.

Section 1 of the Education Reform Act affirms the primacy of cross-curricular dimensions like equal opportunities. Structuring learning experiences on the basis of equality of opportunity is inherently good educational practice, and it assumes that children are more important than the subject matter to be taught. In accepting equal opportunity as a leading and guiding principle, physical education teachers would also be reaffirming a model for better, more sensitive and more effective teaching.

Notes

1   The Equal Opportunities Commission is a quasi-autonomous non-governmental organization (QUANGO), set up to monitor the effects of and interpret the legislation and provide advice relating to the Sex Discrimination Act 1975. The Schools Unit is the section of the EOC specializing in advice for and about school education. The EOC address is: Overseas House, Quay Street, Manchester M3 3HN.
2   The National Curriculum Council is a QUANGO, whose purpose is to advise on implementation of education policies. The NCC address is: Albion Wharf, 25 Skeldergate, York Y01 2XL.

References

ALDERSON, J. and CRUTCHLEY, D. (1990) 'Physical Education and the National Curriculum', in ARMSTRONG, N. (Ed.) *New Directions in Physical Education*, Rawdon, Leeds, Human Kinetics Publishers, pp. 37–62.

COMER, L. (1974) *Wedlocked Women*, Leeds, Feminist Books.

CURL, G. (Ed.) (1988) *Collected Conference Papers in Dance, Vol. 4*, Proceedings of the Conference on Dance and the Physical Education Curriculum with Reference to the National Curriculum, London, p. 59.

DEPARTMENT OF EDUCATION AND SCIENCE (1989) *From Policy to Practice*, London, DES.

DEPARTMENT OF EDUCATION AND SCIENCE (1991) *Physical Education for ages 5 to 16*, Proposals of the Secretary of State for Education and Science and the Secretary of State for Wales, London, DES/Welsh Office.

DOUGILL, D. (1989) 'Youngsters in a Popular Movement', *Sunday Times*, 15 January.

EQUAL OPPORTUNITIES COMMISSION SCHOOLS UNIT (1988) 'Sex Discrimination and School Sport', Paper presented to Annual General Meeting of Women's Sports Foundation, London, October.

EVANS, J., LOPEZ, S., DUNCAN, M. and EVANS, M. (1987) 'Some Thoughts on the Political and Pedagogical Implications of Mixed Sex Grouping in Physical Education', *British Educational Research Journal*, **13**, 1, pp. 59–71.

FLINTOFF, A. (1990) 'Physical Education, Equal Opportunities and the National Curriculum', *Physical Education Review*, **13**, 2, pp. 85–100.

HOME OFFICE (1975) *A Guide to the Sex Discrimination Act 1975*, London, HMSO.

HOUGH, J. (1985) 'Developing Individuals Rather Than Boys and Girls', *School Organization*, **5**, 1, pp. 17–25.

MAY, N. (1985) 'Engendering Teacher Education', *School Organization*, **5**, 1, pp. 79–87.

NATIONAL CURRICULUM COUNCIL (1990) *Curriculum Guidance Three: The Whole Curriculum*, York, NCC.

PANNICK, DAVID (1983) *Sex Discrimination in Sport*, Manchester, Equal Opportunities Commission.

PHYSICAL EDUCATION ASSOCIATION (1991) *Response to the Physical Education Working Group Interim Report* submitted to Department of Education and Science, unpublished.

PHYSICAL EDUCATION WORKING GROUP (1991) *National Curriculum Interim Report*, DES/Welsh Office.

PRATT, J. (1985) *Option choice*, NFER.

TALBOT, MARGARET (1990) 'Equal Opportunities and Physical Education', in ARMSTRONG, N. (Ed.) *New Directions in Physical Education, Vol. 1*, Rawdon, Leeds, Human Kinetics Publishers, pp. 101–20.

WALKER, J.C. (1988) 'The Way Men Act: Dominant and Subordinate Male Cultures in an Inner City School', *British Journal of Sociology of Education*, **9**, 1, pp. 3–19.

Chapter 6

Equality, Multiculturalism, Antiracism and Physical Education in the National Curriculum

Peter Figueroa

Introduction

If we are to develop a more sophisticated and coherent view of multicultural and antiracist education, and of its implications for physical education, it is important to examine a range of complex issues bound up in, but partly obscured by, the debate in Britain since at least the early 1980s of multicultural versus antiracist education (see, for instance, Sarup, 1991, pp. 29–42, and Figueroa, 1991, pp. 46–62). Multicultural education has been criticized for focusing only on culture, for being tokenist or trivial, and for ignoring inequality and racism. Antiracist education has been attacked for being 'negative' and ideological. Both have been criticized for threatening educational standards. Meanwhile, on the continent, intercultural education has likewise been opposed in oversimplified terms to multicultural education. Those who use the term intercultural education seek to highlight the (constructive) interaction between cultures. However, they tend to speak of 'foreign' or 'migrant workers'' children, and of promoting social integration. They are also likely to speak of preserving and developing cultural identity (see, for instance, Porcher, 1981, pp. 43–4).

However, the dichotomies sometimes set out between multicultural and antiracist education (for instance Brandt, 1986, p. 114), or multicultural and intercultural education (for instance Porcher, 1981), are simplifying and distorting. Rather than opposing multicultural to antiracist education, it is important to develop a conceptualization and practice based on articulated and critically explored concepts, on a commitment to certain social and educational values, in particular equity, justice, rights, openness, respect and constructive interaction, and on a sophisticated understanding of the social and educational contexts in which physical education occurs.

This paper thus seeks to explore and analyze antiracist and multicultural issues in relation to Physical Education in the National Curriculum by addressing mainly: the broad conceptual framework; the social and educational contexts; and the implications for policy and practice. Among the most crucial concepts that need to be explored are those of culture, equality, 'race', and racism.

The Conceptual Framework

Culture

Culture does not refer only to folklore, dress, diet or popular music. It embraces all that a group of people have together realized and pass on as part of their heritage. It refers especially to shared symbolic and cognitive systems, to language, beliefs, values, religion, way of life, and social institutions or patterns. Thus, as Banks (1981, p. 52) has pointed out, culture is a very broad term referring to all the 'human made components of society'.

Furthermore, 'multicultural' is ambiguous. It may for instance refer simply to the immediate presence of more than one culture, for example in the physical education class. It may, however, and perhaps especially, refer also to an openness towards other cultures, whether they are immediately present or not, since there are many cultures present in the society and the wider world. Moreover, this cultural diversity has implications beyond specifically intercultural relations, such as cross-cultural fertilization or cross-cultural mis-communication, for the groups that bear these cultures relate to each other not only in terms of actual cultural differences, but also in terms of their perceptions, of their definitions of the situation and of their relative positions in the society and its class system. Hence, multicultural education has many connotations going well beyond the multi-ethnic classroom and issues purely of culture. It is, for instance, very much concerned with issues of equality.

Equality

Equality refers not to sameness nor to some notion of the lowest common denominator, but to fairness or equity. It means the principle that relevant similarities and relevant differences should be given due recognition — while irrelevant similarities and irrelevant differences should be ignored — always within the framework of being fair to all parties. In social interaction, in the allocation of social 'rewards' and social position, and in education — in particular physical education — this means giving full recognition to everyone's rights and legitimate needs, and inseparably recognizing and taking into account relevant similarities and relevant differences, relevant resources and relevant disadvantages, but disregarding irrelevant ones.

One should seek 'to eliminate any unfavourable treatment of individuals based on their assignment to particular categories when membership is not a justifiable ground for differential treatment', as Banton says (1983, p. 396). Thus, for example, to encourage a child in physical education or sport at the expense of academic endeavour simply because the child is Afro-Caribbean is to take irrelevant differences into account. Beyond this, however, individuals should also be given equally favourable treatment when membership of some category is a justifiable ground for different treatment. For instance, Muslim girls who have strong religious beliefs might be allowed to wear tracksuits instead of regulation shorts during physical education classes. It is crucial that the notion of equality should include equal respect and equitable treatment for *difference*. The right to be different should not be denied because of abuses of it. A system such as apartheid violates the fundamental values both of equality and of freedom.

The National Curriculum, and Physical Education in particular, must thus be appropriate for *all* pupils in England and Wales as members of British society, *of Europe, of the North Atlantic and of the world today*. It must seek to meet both the needs of individuals, addressing their reality, and those of the society, addressing its reality, which includes its relation to the wider world. Physical education should contribute equitably to the full development of each and every pupil. It should be appropriate for the rights and needs of each pupil, and may need to be differentiated in approach, style and even content. Furthermore, it should seek to promote the values of equality and respect among all pupils.

If the principle of equality, that is of equal rights, is not accepted, everyone — indeed society itself — is potentially under threat. Ultimately this principle means a system is needed in which everyone has a fair say, for there needs to be some fair way of deciding what is a 'legitimate need' and what is 'relevant', and even of weighing one right or one relevant consideration against another. In the context of physical education 'everyone' would include teachers, parents and pupils. If any one party has control, in particular over decision-making, they could manipulate everything to their own advantage and to the disadvantage of others. In a racist system this is precisely what tends to happen.

The meaning of 'race'

'Race' and racism are sensitive and contentious issues, and antiracist education is often misunderstood. Perhaps the sensitivity of these issues relates largely to racism having negative moral connotations; it is often associated with such extreme phenomena as Nazism, the holocaust, apartheid, the Ku Klux Klan and virulent feelings of hatred and rejection. Also the concept of 'race' is widely used without the assumptions and images, indeed the paradigms, built into it being spelt out. Or people, somewhat uneasy about the notion of 'race', use instead those of ethnic group or culture, but in an uncritical way, and as apparently more innocent stand-in or surrogate concepts. Thus, ethnicism tends to come into operation, inexplicitly, and often as a deputy or proxy to racism.

As an authoritative publication (Hiernaux, 1965) indicated some years ago, 'race' has no scientific or biological validity. 'Race' is first and foremost a social construction, one of those categories, like gender or disability, that people use in defining the situation. Built into this everyday category is typically the notion of inherent features (such as social, cultural, psychological or intellectual features) assumed to be linked in some essential or deterministic way to some feature defined as 'racial'. This might be a phenotypical feature, that is a visible, physical feature, or it might be something else. This social construction is not just the accomplishment of individual actors, but rather of intra- and inter-group inter-action. Racist social constructions, where they take place, are themselves an important part of the mutual defining and differentiating of groups.

That 'race' is a social construction does not mean that 'racial' groups are just categories, just ideological constructions. Each actor's, and more importantly each group's, definition of the situation, and each group's assumptions and images — in particular any of a racist nature — inform social action and thereby social reality. Concrete social relations, and mechanisms of social ascription, mean that certain people end up sharing, or being locked into, an unequal situation, or are incorporated into the society in a subordinated location. The members of such a 'racial' group may thus share, or come to define themselves as sharing, common interests and a common identity. Although 'race' is not a scientifically objective reality, it may be a socially objective reality.

The meaning of racism

We can distinguish five dimensions or levels of racism, although they interact and are closely interrelated. Racism at the cultural level can be thought of as the operation of a shared racist frame of reference. This is a socially shared set of assumptions, beliefs, conceptual constructs, symbolic systems, values, attitudes and behavioural norms linked implicitly or explicitly to a concept of 'race', as explained above. Thus, this racist frame of reference can be thought of as a group myth, ideology, worldview, shared paradigm or embedded code in which real or supposed phenotypical or other features, taken as natural or inherent defining characteristics, constitute the key differentiating factor. It animates and constrains perception, interpretation and action, defines group identity, provides a rallying point for group loyalty and cohesion, structures social relations, provides a rationale for the existing social order, and performs a system maintenance function, serving the interests of those who hold power. It essentially operates at a tacit or taken-for-granted level (see Figueroa, 1974 and 1991).

At the individual level racism may manifest itself as attitudes, stereotypes, prejudice or hostility, and it may indicate particular psychological needs. However, racism often operates without any virulent feelings of hostility, and is not just a function of individual psychological factors.

At the interpersonal level racism refers to interactions and patterns of relations within the terms of the racist frame of reference. These include discrimination, harassment, avoidance, or certain interactions purely within the in-group. For instance, a racist joke or remark made entirely among in-group members about some 'racially' defined out-group or individual is a form of racist interpersonal relations. Indeed, it is largely through such in-group relations and discourse that racist definitions of oneself and of others, of the in-group and the out-group, are accomplished and sustained. It is important to remember this in 'all-White' educational settings.

Racism at the institutional level refers to the way the society, or particular institutions within it, such as the school, function to disadvantage certain groups or to advantage others by operating within the terms of the racist frame of reference, or by simply failing to take account of the relevant specific needs and rights of those defined as belonging to a different 'race'. Extreme and formal examples of institutional racism would be racist laws, as under apartheid. There are, however, more subtle, unintentional and insidious forms of institutional racism which might operate even where there is no overt prejudice or racism. An example would be the unthinking giving of intelligence tests, or of National Curriculum standardized assessment tasks, to minority ethnic children, even if such children were not adequately represented in the population on which these tests had been standardized.

Racism at the structural level refers to the way society is articulated by 'race' so that there is a differential distribution of resources, rewards, roles, status and power along racist boundaries. Such racist structures are the expression, outcome and source of racist thinking, behaviour and interaction.

Ethnicism parallels racism closely, the main difference between them being that in the case of racism the social defining, the attitudes, the interacting, the processes, the structuring are in terms of phenotypical features (real or supposed) or, in general, of features defined as 'racial'; whereas in the case of ethnicism all this is accomplished in terms of 'ethnic' features — and that means mainly in terms of cultural features (real or supposed and often distorted). Where the parallel between racism and ethnicism is imperfect is in the social significance which is inherent in culture — understood, as we have seen, to include the basic values of the society and its accepted ways of organizing and doing things — for there is no social significance inherent in phenotypical or superficial physical features as such. That 'colour' for instance only has the significance that it is given in a particular society can be seen by the fact that the same person might be classified — and treated accordingly — as 'coloured' in South Africa, Black in the USA or Britain, and perhaps White in Brazil.

The Context

Very closely related to and grounding these notions are the actual social and educational contexts within which Physical Education must take place, and which it must address and be appropriate to. The most relevant characteristics of these contexts for our purposes are cultural diversity, inequality and racism — though democratic, humanist and antiracist forces are also at work within these contexts.

Cultural diversity

Language is a very good indicator of cultural diversity. In the United Kingdom, for instance, apart from different dialects of English, there are, in varying degrees, such languages as Welsh, Irish, Scottish Gaelic and Manx. In addition, however, many other languages are spoken. The Inner London Education Authority (1989) found that among its 280,000 and more pupils, 184 different languages were in use in the home besides English. This did not include English-based or French-based Creoles, except for a small population of Krio speakers, since the relevant information was not collected, indicating at best an ambivalent attitude towards Creole. Undoubtedly, however, a substantial number of pupils did speak a Creole. Religion is another good indicator of cultural diversity. For instance in Britain today there are flourishing communities of Muslims, Sikhs, Hindus, Black Christians and Jews. The physical education teacher needs to be sensitive to such differences and to take them into account.

Moreover, these cultural differences may affect attitudes towards physical education, sport and other leisure activities. One can expect to find differences among school children in Britain today in, for instance, cultural forms of physical expression, ideas about desirable behaviour for males and females, and orientation generally towards exercise, sport and leisure. Verma *et al.* (1991, p. 10) point out that the 'concept of leisure as part of life and the belief that recreation is as inalienable a right as that of, say, justice or liberty is deeply embedded in the European ethos', but perhaps not in that of some sectors of the minority ethnic groups. Religion, and in particular Islam, was certainly associated with low participation rates in sports and various leisure activities (Verma *et al.*, 1991, p. 337). However, Verma *et al.* found that as far as people of Caribbean origin and their White British peers were concerned, their 'religious affiliation, their notions of gender difference, their approach to leisure and the place and nature of sport and recreation within it were comparable' (Verma *et al.*, 1991, p. 330).

Inequality

The unequal position of minority ethnic groups in Britain can be seen on various social indicators, such as unemployment rates and quality of accommodation. It can also be seen in terms of their position within the education system.

The most recent national survey of the Policy Studies Institute found that overall 'the quality of the housing of Black people is much worse' than that of people in Britain generally (Brown, 1984, pp. 305–6). Their density of occupation is much higher than average, and they 'more often share rooms or amenities with other households'. Brown (1984, p. 293) also showed that, on average, South Asians and Caribbean people in Britain 'are more likely than White people to be unemployed and . . . to have jobs with lower pay and lower status'.

In their recent extensive and thorough study referred to above, Verma *et al.* (1991) found some marked ethnic and gender differences in leisure and sporting activities. For instance, among males as much as 'a quarter of all Bangladeshis, West Indians, and Pakistanis took part in no [sport or physical recreation] activities' as against the much lower overall figure of 15 per cent for males who were inactive (Verma *et al.*, 1991, pp. 248, 251 and 334–5). Comparable inactivity figures for females were often almost twice as high: that is, almost 50 per cent for Bangladeshis and Pakistanis (although just under a quarter for West Indians), as against 29 per cent overall. Besides, Verma *et al.* (1991, p. 8), referring to the limited literature available, suggest that there is a lack of Black people 'in decision making positions, or positions of power in sport'. They are underrepresented or absent among coaches and sports managers and administrators.

Within the education system children of certain backgrounds, for instance Caribbean and Bangladeshi backgrounds, have been much more likely than others to be shunted into the bottom end of the education system — that is, for instance, into non-selective schools, lower streams and non-examination classes (see, for instance, Coard, 1971; Townsend, 1971, pp. 56ff; Townsend and Brittan, 1972; Tomlinson, 1982; Figueroa, 1984; DES, 1985; and Wright, 1986). A glaring distortion has been the overrepresentation of Caribbean pupils in schools for the 'educationally subnormal' in Britain. Various studies have indicated that Caribbean pupils, for example, are allocated fewer resources than many others, are unequally provided for in respect of language work, and unequally treated in curricular and assessment processes (for instance Bagley, 1982; Townsend, 1971; Little and Willey, 1981; Stone, 1981; and Wright, 1986). Some studies have shown that Caribbean-heritage pupils are often likely to be channelled away from academic endeavours and into sport (for instance Carrington, 1983). Yet, moreover, Black people are underrepresented among physical education teachers (Verma *et al.*, 1991, p.8).

Racism

There has been much evidence in the post-war era of racism, racist prejudice, stereotypes, discrimination and a racist frame of reference in British society (see, for example, Rose *et al.*, 1969, pp. 567, 569, 570 and 587; Bagley, 1970; Figueroa, 1974; Bagley and Verma, 1975; Verma and Bagley, 1975; Brittan, 1976; Husband, 1979; Sivanandan, 1982; Milner, 1983; Davey, 1983). In particular, the first national survey of Black minorities carried out in the 1960s by Political and Economic Planning (PEP, 1967; Daniel, 1968), and the second national PEP survey carried out in 1974 (Smith, 1977) provided evidence of the prevalence of prejudice, stereotypes, racism and discrimination. Almost twenty years later Brown and Gay (1985, p. 30), reporting on part of the third national survey in the same series, carried out by the Policy Studies Institute in 1982, and referred to above, concluded that 'racial discrimination has ... continued to have a great impact on the employment opportunities of black people'. Despite the existence for some seventeen years of an anti-discrimination Race Relations Act, there was in the field of employment 'no evidence of a decrease in the extent of racial discrimination over the past decade' (Brown and Gay, 1985, p. 31).

Verma *et al.* (1991, p. 12) state that Ouseley (1983) confirmed that institutionalized racism was common in the leisure services in Britain. Bayliss (1989) noted that Black athletes tend to be stereotyped as high in physical ability, but low in intellectual ability. Verma *et al.* (1991, p. 339) also present some limited evidence of Black people experiencing overt racism in sport or leisure, in particular a small number of claims by respondents of exclusion from a club or association because of 'racial discrimination'.

There is also a good deal of evidence, direct and indirect, of various forms of racism within the education system (see, for instance, Figueroa, 1991; DES, 1985, pp. 234–6; Gaine, 1987, pp. 2–8). For instance, some of the common stereotypes of pupils of Caribbean background as having 'natural' prowess in school sports and dance, and the way these may tend to function to channel such pupils away from academic endeavours, can be inferred from various studies reported by Taylor (1981, pp. 122–4). The remarkable thing is that Taylor reports these narrow stereotypes and the overrepresentation of such pupils on school teams and in dance simply as being positive. Other studies have documented stereotyping and the way it or various procedures in the education system seem to work to discriminate against Black pupils (see, for instance, Tomlinson, 1982; Brittan, 1976; Edwards, 1979). Furthermore, several recent studies have documented racist name-calling, harassment and violence in British schools (see, for instance, Figueroa and Swart, 1986; Kelly and Cohn, 1988; Tattum and Lane, 1989; Macdonald *et al.*, 1989).

There is, moreover, a good deal of historical evidence not only of the long-standing existence of a racist frame of reference in Britain, but also of its intimate link with racist social structures. Walvin (1973, pp. 173, 215) says, for example: 'From eighteenth-century plantocratic caricatures, to Carlyle and Trollope, through *The Times* of the 1860s to the more "scientific" apologists for racialism late in the century, common images of the Negro were passed on'; and: 'the events of the postwar years ... form a continuation of the well-established history of black people in this country, rather than being a new story'.

Multicultural and Antiracist Education

On the basis of the discussion so far, it can be stated that multicul'
is not just about cultural issues, as far-reaching and important as
about the relations between and the orientation towards groups with different
cultures, or groups seen in terms of cultural difference. This means that social
structural realities and relations are also central issues. In fact, in the historic
situations where the terms 'multiculturalism' or 'multicultural education' have
been used, issues of 'race relations' and inequality have been central. On the
other hand antiracist education is necessarily also concerned with promoting
equitable and fruitful relations between groups with different cultures.

Multicultural and antiracist education refer then to such things as:

- the promotion in and through education of equality, fulfilment and achievement for minority ethnic students — as for everyone;
- the reconstruction of racist and ethnicist beliefs, assumptions, perceptions, patterns of relations, and action of the majority — as of others;
- the promotion of constructive interrelations, for instance by encouraging the development of appropriate values and of personal, interpersonal and cross-cultural skills;
- the valuing and celebrating of cultural diversity;
- the benefiting from, and learning to be able to benefit from, cultural diversity.

Multicultural physical education does not therefore refer only to the sensitivities and the approach which are required when children of different cultural
backgrounds are present in the particular class or school; but also and perhaps
especially to awareness and valuing of cultural difference, to combating racism
and to promoting fruitful relations and equity, whether or not children of different cultural backgrounds are actually present.

Implications for Physical Education

The National Curriculum Physical Education Working Group in its Final Report
(DES, 1991, p. 5) gives as the overall rationale for Physical Education the
educating of people 'in and through the use and knowledge of the body and its
movement'. It also accepts the 'guiding and leading principle of equal opportunity for all pupils', stating that there should be 'no barriers to access or opportunity based on race, sex, culture or ability' (DES, 1991, p. 5).

This notion of equal opportunities is further discussed in chapter six and
in appendix A of the Final Report (DES, 1991, pp. 15 and 55–60). Equal
opportunities is there understood as all children being 'allowed access to and
given confidence in the different activities involved [in physical education],
regardless of their ability, sex, or cultural/ethnic background' (DES, 1991, p. 15).
Furthermore, the report, distinguishing between access and opportunities, points
out that participating in and benefiting from physical education activities can be
affected by such things as 'the attitudes and expectations of teachers; ... [and]

e interactions within ... multicultural groups ...' (DES, 1991, p. 15). Hence, such issues must be addressed.

The Working Group also highlights the other aspect of the principle of equality, namely that (equitable) regard should be given to differing backgrounds where they are relevant to physical education (or are of other educational relevance). It asserts that 'teachers should treat all children as individuals with their own abilities, difficulties and attitudes' (DES, 1991, p. 15). The children's various backgrounds — such as their religious and ethnic backgrounds — should be a source for enrichment and not 'a basis for restricting access' (DES, 1991, pp. 15, 55 and 59). Also 'an understanding and appreciation of the range of pupils' responses' to such matters as 'femininity, masculinity and sexuality' and 'ethnic, social and cultural diversity' are necessary, and physical education teachers 'should have regard to and respect for cultural and religious conventions' (DES, 1991, p. 59). For instance, girls from certain religious/cultural backgrounds may 'have to be taught in single sex groups, by same sex teachers, in private and without onlookers' (DES, 1991, p. 59). Of course, such single-sex groups would not have to be culturally homogeneous. Indeed, the Working Group stresses the basic principle that 'embracing the opportunities offered by diversity ... enable[s] children to learn both to accommodate variety and difference ... and to value the extension of their own experiences' (DES, 1991, p. 58). Besides, even where the class is more or less culturally homogeneous it is no less important for these goals of openness and enrichment to be pursued.

The Report stresses that the 'overriding aim' (whether there is diversity or not and whether differentiation seems necessary or not) is for 'young people and their teachers ... to respect and value each other' (DES, 1991, p. 15). It states that respect should be fostered, while stereotypes should be questioned and racism challenged. It also advocates cooperation, fair play and honesty in competition as primary aims. As it says:

> It is contradictory to expect children to learn to handle success and failure with dignity, and to embrace co-operation, respect for others, fair play and sporting behaviour, if they see honest competition or performance undermined by foul play or discrimination based on sex, class, colour or disability. (DES, 1991, p. 59)

In discussing equal access and opportunities the Final Report focuses mainly on issues to do with special educational needs, sex and gender, and cultural diversity. It acknowledges that the issues are complex, and that some 'values and principles may be seen to be in conflict' (DES, 1991, p. 59) — for instance gender considerations versus culture considerations? — but it does not elaborate. However, it is clear that in the view of the Working Group teachers should seek ways, through negotiation, to accommodate cultural and religious requirements without reducing access or opportunities. For instance, the Report suggests that where physical contact between the sexes is problematic, children of the same sex could be trained to support each other (DES, 1991, p. 59). Within this context, it also seems to imply that some games or sports might be avoided. This, however, could surely run counter to the principle of not restricting access or opportunities? Nevertheless, the Report does stress that the focus should be on enabling and facilitating participation (DES, 1991, p. 59).

   In doing this, in promoting respect for difference and in combating racism, it is important for the physical educationalist to be aware of and to take account of two basic phenomena. The first is that the way the body and physical activity are seen will differ from culture to culture. For instance there are differing concepts of decency, so that in some cultures it is indecent for girls to wear swim-suits or shorts: Muslim girls in purdah must keep their whole bodies, including arms and legs, covered. More fundamentally, perhaps, a culture less influenced by Cartesian dualism than Western cultures have on the whole been, might prefer to formulate the overall rationale of physical education less in terms of 'the use and knowledge of the body' (DES, 1991, p. 5), and more along the lines of educating people in and through physical activity by developing an active and reflective knowledge of self and others as embodied beings. In other words the emphasis placed in the Report on the 'use' of the body tends to reduce it to an instrument or object separate from ourselves, which is to be trained and manipulated. Instead, we are inextricably embodied, so that a balanced physical education must contribute to and be an integral part of the development of the whole person, who is inseparably physical, intellectual, spiritual, individual, cultural and social.

   The second phenomenon that has to be acknowledged is that stereotyped, differentiated body images play an important part in racist thinking. Physical educationalists should not perpetuate such racist thinking, for instance by channelling Afro-Caribbean pupils into sport rather than academic endeavours, or into athletics rather than swimming (see for instance Carrington, 1983, and DES, 1991, p. 59). More positively, physical education could make an important contribution to combating such racist thinking. 'There are many opportunities', as the Report says, 'to dispel myths and stereotypes through better acquaintance and information'. It gives as an example, 'learning through a range of dances and games and . . . using their place in religious festivals as a focus for multicultural education' (DES, 1991, p. 59).

   The Report also goes further, and suggests that references 'to "national games or dance" may be inappropriate', given the multicultural nature of society (DES, 1991, p. 59). However, it is important instead to see as an integral part of our national heritage the multicultural riches which now characterize our society. There is too frequently a tendency to use such words as 'our', 'national' and 'British' within a narrow frame of assumptions. Often such words are used in ways which assume a group or heritage or forms of activity exclusively defined by one or more of the following adjectives: white, English, Protestant, male, middle-class. Furthermore, combating racism in and through physical education is not only a matter of providing information, but also of involving parents and pupils along with teachers in arranging and planning cross-cultural and inter-ethnic activities and experiences of a positive nature. For instance, team activities provide many opportunities in a multi-ethnic school. Also, a shared, cooperative, well-planned and well-managed residential experience, the inclusion of which the Final Report recommends (DES, 1991, p. 13), could make a positive contribution to combating racist thinking and to promoting constructive interculturalism, especially where people of different cultural backgrounds took part.

   It is clear that the Physical Education Working Party seriously addressed issues of cultural diversity, equity and racism. Unfortunately, the 'advice' of the Secretary of State for Education and Science and of the National Curriculum

Council do not reflect the serious consideration of these issues by the Working Party (NCC, 1991, 1992). The National Curriculum Council (1992) simply advises that there should be no non-statutory statements of attainment for the Physical Education National Curriculum. The closest the National Curriculum Council Consultation Report — on which the statutory order, that is, the legal requirement, is based — gets to the issues of multicultural and antiracist education is in mentioning, sparingly and in the broadest terms, such concepts as 'fair play' and 'cultural issues' (NCC, 1991). Thus it goes no further than stating under programmes of study for pupils at Key Stage Two (7–11 years of age) that they should 'be encouraged to adopt good sporting behaviour and condemn anti-social responses including unfair play' (NCC, 1991, p. 22). It likewise goes no further under programmes of study at Key Stage Four (14–16 years of age) than stating that pupils should 'be made aware of the historical, social and cultural issues associated with the activities undertaken', and that they should 'be given opportunities to describe, interpret and evaluate all aspects of dance including . . . cultural . . . contexts' (NCC, 1991, pp. 30 and 31).

Of course, even these few statements are entirely capable of a purely monocultural interpretation. In fact none of the examples given in the National Curriculum Council Consultation Report highlight a multicultural, antiracist or equal opportunities context. Nevertheless, for the Physical Education teacher who is committed to multicultural, antiracist and equal opportunities education these ambiguities provide some openings. But Physical Education in the National Curriculum gives him or her very little positive lead in these crucial matters.

References

BAGLEY, C. (1970) *Social Structure and Prejudice in Five English Boroughs*, London, Institute of Race Relations.

BAGLEY, C. (1982) 'Achievement, Behaviour Disorder and Social Circumstances in West Indian Children and Other Ethnic Groups', in VERMA, G.K. and BAGLEY, C. (Eds) *Self-Concept, Achievement and Multicultural Education*, London, Macmillan.

BAGLEY, C. and VERMA, G.K. (1975) 'Inter-Ethnic Attitudes and Behaviour in British Multi-Racial Schools', in VERMA, G.K. and BAGLEY, C. (Eds), *Race and Education Across Cultures*, London, Heinemann.

BANKS, J. (1981) *Multiethnic Education: Theory and Practice*, Boston, Allyn and Bacon.

BANTON, M. (1983) *Racial and Ethnic Competition*, Cambridge, Cambridge University Press.

BAYLISS, T. (1989) 'PE and Racism: Making Changes', *Multicultural Teaching*, **7**, 2, pp. 19–22.

BRANDT, G. (1986) *The Realization of Antiracist Teaching*, London, Falmer Press.

BRITTAN, E. (1976) 'Multicultural Education 2. Teacher Opinion on Aspects of School Life. Part 2: Pupils and Teachers', *Educational Research*, **18**, 3, pp. 182–91.

BROWN, C. (1984) *Black and White Britain: The Third PSI Survey*, London, Heinemann Educational Books.

BROWN, C. and GAY, P. (1985) *Racial Discrimination: 17 Years after the Act*, London, Policy Studies Institute.

CARRINGTON, B. (1983) 'Sports as a Side-Track: An Analysis of West Indian Involvement in Extra-Curricular Sport', in BARTON, L. and WALKER, S. (Eds) *Race, Class and Education*, London, Croom Helm.

COARD, B. (1971) *How the West Indian Child is made Educationally Sub-Normal in the British School System*, London, New Beacon Books.

DANIEL, W. (1968) *Racial Discrimination in England*, Harmondsworth, Penguin.

DAVEY, A. (1983) *Learning to Be Prejudiced: Growing up in Multiethnic Britain*, London, Arnold.

DEPARTMENT OF EDUCATION AND SCIENCE (1985) *Education for All* (Swann Report), London, HMSO.

DEPARTMENT OF EDUCATION AND SCIENCE (1991) *Physical Education for Ages 5 to 16*, London, DES/Welsh Office.

EDWARDS, V.K. (1979) *The West Indian Language Issue in British Schools: Challenges and Responses*, London, Routledge and Kegan Paul.

FIGUEROA, P. (1974) *West Indian School-Leavers in London: A Sociological Study in Ten Schools in a London Borough, 1966–1967*, Unpublished PhD thesis, London School of Economics and Political Science, University of London.

FIGUEROA, P. (1984) 'Minority Pupil Progress', in CRAFT, M. (Ed.) *Education and Cultural Pluralism*, Lewes, Falmer Press.

FIGUEROA, P. (1991) *Education and the Social Constructioin of 'Race'*, London, Routledge.

FIGUEROA, P. and SWART, L.T. (1986) 'Teachers' and Pupils' Racist and Ethnocentric Frames of Reference: A Case Study', *New Community*, **XIII**, Spring/Summer, pp. 40–51.

GAINE, C. (1987) *No Problem Here: A Practical Approach to Education and 'Race' in White Schools*, London, Hutchinson.

HIERNAUX, J. (Ed.) (1965) 'Biological Aspects of Race', *International Social Science Journal*, **xvii**, i, pp. 71–161.

HUSBAND, C. (1979) 'Social Identity and the Languages of Race Relations', in GILES, H. and SAINT-JACQUES, B. (Eds) *Language and Ethnic Relations*, Oxford, Pergamon Press.

INNER LONDON EDUCATION AUTHORITY RESEARCH AND STATISTICS (1989) *1989 Language Census*, RS 1361/89, London, ILEA, December, report written by J. Sinnott.

KELLY, E. and COHN, T. (1988) *Racism in Schools — New Research Evidence*, Stoke-on-Trent, Trentham Books.

LITTLE, A. and WILLEY, R. (1981) *Multi-Ethnic Education: The Way Forward*, London, Schools Council.

MACDONALD, I., BHAVNANI, R., KHAN, L. and JOHN, G. (1989) *Murder in the Play-ground*, London, Longsight Press.

MILNER, D. (1983) *Children and Race Ten Years on*, London, Ward Lock.

NATIONAL CURRICULUM COUNCIL (1991) *Physical Education in the National Curriculum: A Report to the Secretary of State for Education and Science on the Statutory Consultation for the Attainment Target and Programmes of Study in Physical Education*, York, NCC.

NATIONAL CURRICULUM COUNCIL (1992) *Additional Advice to the Secretary of State for Education and Science: Non-Statutory Statements of Attainment in Art, Music and Physical Education*, York, NCC.

OUSELEY, N. (1983) *London against Racism in Sport and Recreation*, Report of a seminar on Sport and Recreation in London's Inner City, London, Greater London Council.

POLITICAL AND ECONOMIC PLANNING (1967) *Racial Discrimination*, London, PEP.

PORCHER, L. (1981) *The Education of the Children of Migrant Workers in Europe: Interculturalism and Teacher Training*, Strasbourg, Council for Cultural Co-operation, School Education Division.

ROSE, E.J.B., DEAKIN, N., ABRAMS, M., JACKSON, V., PESTON, M., VANAGS, A.H., COHEN, B., GAITSKELL, J. and WARD, P. (1969) *Colour and Citizenship: A Report on British Race Relations*, London, Oxford University Press.

SARUP, M. (1991) *Education and the Ideologies of Racism*, Stoke-on-Trent, Trentham Books.

SIVANANDAN, A. (1982) *A Different Hunger: Writings on Black Resistance*, London, Pluto Press.

SMITH, D.J. (1977) *Racial Disadvantage in Britain*, The PEP Report, Harmondsworth, Penguin.

STONE, M. (1981) *The Education of the Black Child in Britain: The Myth of Multiracial Education*, Glasgow, Fontana.

TATTUM, D.P. and LANE, D.A. (1989) *Bullying in School*, Stoke-on-Trent, Trentham.

TAYLOR, M.J. (1981) *Caught Between: A Review of Research into the Education of Pupils of West Indian Origin*, Windsor, NFER-Nelson.

TOMLINSON, S. (1982) *A Sociology of Special Education*, London, Routledge and Kegan Paul.

TOWNSEND, H.E.R. (1971) *Immigrant Pupils in England: The L.E.A. Response*, Slough, NFER.

TOWNSEND, H.E.R. and BRITTAN, E.M. (1972) *Organization in Multi-Racial Schools*, Slough, NFER.

VERMA, G.K. and BAGLEY, C. (Eds) (1975) *Race and Education across Cultures*, London, Heinemann.

VERMA, G.K., MACDONALD, A., DARBY, D.S. and CARROLL, R. (1991) *Sport and Recreation with Special Reference to Ethnic Minorities*, Unpublished research report, Centre for Ethnic Studies in Education, School of Education, University of Manchester.

WALVIN, J. (1973) *Black and White: The Negro in English Society, 1555–1945*, London, Allen Lane.

WRIGHT, C. (1986) 'School Processes — an Ethnographic Study', in EGGLESTON, J., DUNN, D. and MAHDU, A. *Education for Some: The Education and Vocational Experiences of 15–18 Year-Old Members of Minority Ethnic Groups*, Stoke-on-Trent. Trentham Books, pp. 127–79.

Section Two

Strategies for Change in Physical Education

Chapter 7

Education Reform: Juggling the Concepts of Equality and Elitism

Sue Thomas

Introduction

This chapter focuses specifically on the issue of elitism and examines the potential for equal opportunities within secondary physical education (PE) after the Education Reform Act (ERA) 1988. The political and ideological influences pervading the act generate a number of specific concerns for PE and the analysis begins by firstly locating PE within the policy, provisions and ethos of the Act. Secondly, the chapter considers the impact of selected policy recommendations of the ERA 1988, namely, Local Management of Schools (LMS), open enrolment, opting out and the National Curriculum, and draws out their implications for teaching and learning in PE. It is argued that the ethic of competition, private enterprise culture and market forces, which pervades the ERA, does not lie easily with the principle of equal opportunities and may camouflage some of the more ideological egalitarian aspects of, for instance, entitlement. Similarly, tensions within the Act may prove difficult to equate with egalitarian concerns. I suggest that there are certain structural and cultural features of the Act that will not only sustain elitist tendencies within PE, but also exacerbate them. Consequently, this chapter challenges the view conveyed through the official literature of the Department of Education and Science (DES) (renamed the Department for Education in 1992) and the National Curriculum Council (NCC) that the ERA 1988 will, in itself, bring about greater equality of opportunity and that 'all pupils, regardless of sex, ethnic origin and geographical location, have access to broadly the same good and relevant curriculum' (DES, 1987, p. 4).

The implementation of any new legislative measure is often a protracted affair and despite the quite unprecedented haste with which the Bill was processed, passed and adopted (see Deem, 1988; Edwards, 1989) it is probably true to say that the full force and impact of the ERA 1988 has not yet been felt in schools. In this respect and particularly with PE coming, as it does, at the end of the National Curriculum implementation process much of the comment on the policies of the ERA 1988 has had to focus on its 'likely' impact on teaching and learning. Subsequent events and the addition of more pieces to the jigsaw have, however, in many cases confirmed the early speculation of educational commentators (see Simon, 1987, 1988). It seems, however, that the consequences of the ERA 1988 are 'largely unpredictable' (Edwards, 1989, p. 65). This becomes all the more evident as we see the 'manicuring' of certain elements of the Act and the reaction from the teaching profession to the legislation of the Act. It is, therefore, most unlikely that the route mapped out by the DES in 'From Policy To Practice' will be slavishly followed, or adhered to, resulting in contrary directions and outcomes (Edwards, 1989). This is an important premise to establish because much of what follows in this chapter is, of necessity, speculative. My analysis, however, starts from the premise that 'what is provided in schools and what is taught in schools can only be understood historically' because 'earlier educational attitudes of dominant groups in society still carry historical weight' (Williamson, 1974, quoted in Goodson, 1988, p. 54). Furthermore, as Saunders (1986) suggests, 'in attempting to identify factors which will influence the future of physical education, we do not start with a blank card as future developments are bound up with past circumstances and present practices' (p. 9). Thus in contending that elitist tendencies and inequalities will not be dispelled, but reproduced and strengthened by the ERA 1988, support will be drawn from an analysis of the historical and contemporary practices and expectations of PE, both as a subject and as a process within the wider context of schooling.

The concepts of equality and elitism are somewhat contradictory terms and to appreciate the following discussion it is important to establish and clarify the relationship between them. To many working in education elitism has pejorative overtones. It would not elicit a favourable reaction from those who adhere to egalitarian principles. In the British education system, the framework of beliefs, within which elitism operates, manifests itself most obviously in some of the following ways:

(a) structurally: through the divisions of private (fee-paying) and state school provision and within schools in policies such as streaming and banding;
(b) culturally: through motor elitism, racism, sexism and classism.

Such practices, in their effect and outcome, can restrict the access to, and distribution of, certain educational goods and opportunities to particular children. It is, therefore, fundamentally incompatible with an ideology of equality.

Arguably elitist values pervade the whole British education system (Hoyle, 1969) and have consequently produced one of the most elitist systems of post-compulsory education in Europe (Green, 1988, p. 25) Almost entirely, this has been legitimized by, and institutionalized through, the examination system which has exercised a powerful grip on the curriculum content and pedagogy of secondary schools (see Broadfoot, 1984). Furthermore, the pressures on schools and subject areas to provide the consumers, and other professionals, with easily identifiable evidence of what has been taught and achieved has resulted in what Sockett et al. (1980) calls a 'public orientation'; a process in which performance becomes the main criterion of success. Not only is this process expressed in a product-orientated approach to assessment, but the pedagogical effects of such an accountability model based on performance and results may well be 'lessons in elitism' (Simon, 1987).

Elitism and Physical Education

With elitism institutionalized in the education system, it is hardly surprising that PE as 'one of a family of processes' which make up this system (Andrews, 1979, p. 4) also reflects this tendency. However, not all PE teachers hold an elitist ideology. Some evidently do (see Sparkes, 1989), but not all. Rather, as Hargreaves (1986) points out, elitism is locked into the system of constraints under which PE operates and is ultimately sustained by the structural and cultural processes which perpetuate educational ideologies, inform and shape teachers' thinking and makes access to PE knowledge and competence as privileged as in any other subject. Its roots can be traced to a number of diverse sources. While an extensive analysis is beyond the scope of this chapter, what follows seeks to flag the main issues and key points of interaction between origin and agencies.

The cultural transmission role of PE in schools, popularized and enshrined in the ethos of competitive team games and public school athleticism (Mangan, 1973, 1986; Treadwell, 1984; Kaye, 1990) which, in a modified form, has been absorbed into state schools (Hargreaves, 1986) has tended to embody and promote what Dewar (1990) has described as 'elitist, white upper-middle class, Anglo-Saxon, male values'. Additionally for some, the role of PE has been articulated in terms of safeguarding our British sporting heritage by inducting young people into a sporting culture determined and driven by:

(a) nationalistic fervour;
(b) the need to compete successfully in the international sporting marketplace;
(c) demands from the sporting world to produce excellence (see Kaye, 1990, p. 20).

Inevitably, therefore, a spectre of elitism becomes integral to the politics of nationalism and the desire for excellence. It likewise also demands an achievement orientation and sporting perspective (Sparkes, 1989) characterized by a narrow emphasis on traditional games, skill acquisition, sporting success and competition. This may be at the expense of the majority who fail to receive a physical education.

In a similar way, elitism can be seen as a response to the pressures and demands of the working environment, in particular those created by teaching and surviving in a marginal subject, and the need to meet accountability demands. The struggle of PE teachers to gain status for their subject, and for themselves as teachers, is well documented (Goodson, 1988; Bell, 1986). This has often been found to pivot around the production of sporting success providing a visible, tangible and objective measure which subsequently confirms the effectiveness of the school, department or teacher. Historically the worth of a PE department has often been judged on its ability to produce successful sports teams and high-level performances that bring prestige to the school (Sparkes, 1989). Male heads of department, in particular, may have benefited from this state of affairs. All this generates and perpetuates the demand for a sporting achievement orientation and hence shapes expectation as to the role of PE in schools.

There is little doubt that in the past some PE teachers and departments have been happy to be judged on the performance of their teams especially on occasions when PE is 'periodically elevated' (Woods, 1983) for public display, such as on sports days, or at gym displays etc. However, this only serves to perpetuate a notion that high-profile public sport performance is good 'currency' which can be exchanged for status or reward in the career stakes. It may also produce strong pressures towards a pedagogical elitism where sporting success becomes the litmus paper of effective teaching. Inevitably within such parameters, capable performers are seen as high credit units (see Sparkes, 1989), likely to produce good investment returns both personally in terms of teacher role satisfaction and collectively in terms of department and school status. Equally it is obvious that such a demand can only be met by concentrating on those who are identified as capable performers and in providing the resources and opportunities to nurture and develop this valued commodity.

In this respect, the compulsory PE curriculum has often been 'skewed' (Skinsley, 1987, p. 56) in favour of the physically able and school teams in terms of curriculum provision and orientation. Similarly, pedagogical practices have been shown to favour and privilege access for certain groups while oppressing and alienating others (see Dewar, 1990; Evans and Williams, 1989). Hence the teaching of PE has not been a neutral activity and access to, and consequently opportunities within it, have often benefited those who are strong, fast, co-ordinated (Vertinsky, 1983), mesomorphic (Hargreaves, 1986) and physically competent.

Likewise as an outgrowth from the PE curriculum, extra-curricular activities have often been biased, in terms of knowledge and resource allocation, towards physically competent pupils where access to instruction, coaching and competitive experiences have been limited to the more able performers. This leads to what Dodds (1986 and in this book) has called 'motor elitism'. Such practice reinforces the ideology of elitism at the expense of equal opportunities for all pupils.

As such then, the origins of elitism in PE can be located:

(a) in history, tradition and the need to maintain the competitive achievement-orientated sporting status quo;
(b) as a response to the nature of the workplace in PE and to the demands of teaching and surviving both personally and professionally within its constraints;
(c) in an ideological subscription to the concepts of competitive individualism;
(d) in the failure of the PE profession to adequately question and challenge the ideological basis of the PE curriculum — its content, organization, pedagogy and assessment — in an attempt to understand better the relationship between teachers' actions, practices, structural and occupational constraints.

The ERA and PE: Implications for Equality

The reconstitution of education according to 'new' organizing principles, values and provisions is a feature of the ERA 1988, and amongst its many and interrelated policy recommendations are those that will either individually or in combination have a significant impact on the practice, organization and provision of PE in schools.

The ERA 1988 is perhaps best conceived as a package of educational reforms and linked measures (Simon, 1987) that incorporates both curricular and non-curricular elements designed to meet the demands for greater efficiency and accountability in educational expenditure and pupil performance (Lingard, 1990).

Those aspects and provisions of the ERA identified (cf. Penney and Evans, 1991) as of particular relevance and significance to PE are:

- the Local Management of Schools (LMS) including financial delegation and formula funding;
- open enrolment;
- the provision for Grant Maintained Schools — opting out;
- the National Curriculum.

An analysis of educational policy-making illustrates that education has been, and still is, a deeply political issue and as Ball (1990a) suggests, 'as an educational innovation on a grand scale the ERA is a social process, a product of social and political interaction' (p. 133). Consequently there is a need to understand the ERA and its policies in the context of, and as an outcome of, the complex relationship between political, economic and social processes and education policy-making (Ball, 1990a). Whilst a detailed exploration of this issue is covered elsewhere (see Ball, 1990a; Flude and Hammer, 1990; Whitty, 1990; Lawton, 1989; Simon, 1988; Lawton and Chitty, 1988) in contending that the institutionalized elitism of PE will not be dispelled, but strengthened and exacerbated by the provisions and policies of the ERA (1988), it is important to make explicit the forces, processes and *priorities* that have shaped the policies. Beneath the veneer of a rhetoric of equality of access to educational opportunities, egalitarianism and entitlement it can be seen that the Act is not primarily about providing equal educational opportunities (Miles and Middleton, 1990), but rather:

(a) is a response to the demand to raise educational standards to meet the needs of the economy;
(b) reflects the values and principles of the political 'New Right', underpinned by the application and expansion of the free market forces of consumerism into the public sector; privatization, individualism and efficiency through diversity of provision (encouraging competition, parental choice and accountability);
(c) seeks to maintain and preserve the status quo through an emphasis on selection, tradition and cultural heritage to ensure 'social stability' (Simon, 1988, p. 41), through the policies and encouragement of differentiation in the educational market-place.

The values of the ERA 1988 are clearly reflected in its ethos and provisions which tend to support and celebrate a particular view of society, schooling and knowledge and the production of a particular kind of citizen (see Whitty, 1990; Carr, 1990) the embodiment of which is reflected in the traditions of the grammar and independent schools. As Ball (1990a) points out, the 'cultural restorationist mission is clear' (p. 48).[1] The re-creation and reconstruction, via a 'resuscitated academic grammar school, subject-based curriculum' (Hartnett and Naish, 1990, p. 4) represent values of a 'national identity based on a narrowly defined notion of "Englishness" (Hardy and Vieler-Porter, 1990, p. 184) and culture. This highlights the absence of neutral provision and signals the intention of an education for the minority. Concern for equality of opportunity does not seem to feature highly on the agenda, rather the ideological framework and major initiatives of the Act privilege some (the middle-class and able pupils), whilst at the same time oppressing others and displacing the ideal of equal access to education for all. Branded as elitist (Simon, 1987), it instead reproduces existing inequalities and legitimizes these.

The ERA 1988 makes certain provisions which it claims will:

● improve the quality of education;
● raise standards of achievement; and
● extend the freedom of choice in education. (Martin, 1988)

However, although the Act is made up of different reform initiatives, as a linked package a number of tensions (Troman, 1989; Hartnett and Naish, 1990), contradictions and paradoxes (Whitty, 1990) emerge that may well subvert the more laudable stated aims and intentions of the provisions, making these, as Green (1988, p. 29) suggests, 'quite unattainable'. At its worst, it may result in an inversion of these aims. For example, as Green observes 'testing combined with an open enrolment policy, will have the opposite effect from raising the standards. Whilst it may create some elite schools, it will be detrimental to most children, either labelling them as failures from an early age or confining them to unpopular and declining schools where the inevitable selection mechanisms of the more popular schools have excluded them' (1988, p. 29). Similarly, an obsession with competition, performance accountability, excellence and success does not bode well for minority groups or lower-ability pupils.

In the light of the potential implications a number of key questions emerge:

(a) What are the likely effects of the ERA 1988 on the provision of PE and sport in secondary schools?
(b) Who benefits from the education reforms and whose interests are served by the activities we will teach and by the revised curricular constraints under which PE teachers will now work?
(c) To whom will the fundamental principle of freedom of choice apply?
(d) Who 'has the cultural competencies and resources to succeed and benefit' (Evans, 1990a, p. 162) in PE under the ERA?

Policies and Provisions of the ERA: Implications for Teaching and Learning in PE

Local Management of Schools

The provision for the Local Management of Schools (LMS) needs to be viewed as a package within a package, the key elements of which are:

- formula funding;
- financial delegation and devolved responsibility (for the appointment and dismissal of staff and assessment of performance);
- open enrolment.

Ball (1990a) has argued that the LMS proposals represent the most significant aspect of the ERA 1988, 'certainly the most clearly ideological aspect, and the aspect likely to have the most radical, long term impact on the form and content of schooling' (p. 59). The tenet of LMS is that the application of market-style forces will function to secure greater educational accountability and more efficient use of resources and improve the quality of education and hence standards in general. Individual schools, via their governing bodies, are given greater autonomy through the policy of financial delegation and management of school budgets. This correspondingly reduces the control of the Local Education Authorities (LEAs) in terms of financial and resource provision. Additionally, the policy of formula funding involves the allocation of school budgets on the basis of the number, and age, of pupils enrolled. As such it can, therefore, be understood as a pupil-driven system of funding schools where pupils arrive with a 'price tag' and schools have an incentive to attract and retain them. Hence a school's popularity with the consumers will bring larger budgets with quite significant implications for resource provision, etc. Linked to formula funding is also the provision for open enrolment. This is designed to give parents a maximum degree of choice in the schools available to them. Together, these provisions force schools to compete in the market-place to attract pupils and hence funding. Thus schools, in order to compete and survive, are forced to market the service they provide. Quite clearly the LMS package (via the call for accountability, quality and standards) creates a framework in which, in order for some to succeed, others *must* fail.

The interpretation and implications of these enforced financial and management changes for PE and sport in schools has been a source of concern both to teachers in schools and outside agencies providing sporting opportunities for young people[2] (Sports Council, 1990a; Sports Council for Wales, 1990; Audit Commission, 1989). However, in relation to the provision of equal opportunity for all pupils in PE it is ultimately the translation of policy into practice that is the main issue. As already noted, a combination of measures has conspired to generate, and perhaps even encourage, competition both between schools and within schools. Events in the sporting world have illustrated that competition can take a variety of forms and induce a number of pressures (e.g. to win at all costs, or to adopt illegal and unfair performance-enhancing strategies). PE teachers, departments and schools may, through the competition generated by LMS, find themselves through their curriculum, pedagogy, organization and assessment being drawn as a matter of survival to the educationally unsavoury side of competition. This will work to the detriment of some pupils while privileging others.

The need to market the service provided in response to the competition to attract pupils will inevitably result in the cultivation of an image that conveys unequivocally the ethos of the school. In this respect, and for reasons outlined earlier, PE and sport will be seen as a highly marketable commodity. As examination results have tended to act as 'market indicators' of a school's quality, so will team success and the promotion and reporting of high-performance activities. Indeed, as Mangan (1973) has suggested, PE, and in particular competitive inter-school sport, function as symbols of 'structural solidarity' (p. 93). Equally, the ritualized procedures transmit a conspicuous value system rewarding conformity, discipline, standards, excellence and attainment — all ingredients of a traditional curriculum mode favoured by many parents (Whitty, 1990). The central concern here is that there will be a return to a technocratic mode of production (see Charles, 1979; Bain, 1990) with an emphasis on product, performance and physical skills. This will, as in the past, be inaccessible for many lower-attaining pupils and the attention on highly-skilled personal performers will leave them alienated in the process. In effect, PE may experience a distortion of much of the good practice that has characterized its development during the last decade.

In conjunction with the likely pressures on curriculum time in PE, will there be a return to selection, ability grouping and differentiated provision and resourcing based on physical ability and competence resulting in physical polarization and segregation? Will the demand to 'produce the goods' diminish the emphasis on physical education for all in favour of sport education for the few? Will those who are perceived as being physically less able receive a watered-down curriculum through differentiated provision and, therefore, reduced opportunities, as all efforts, energies and resources are geared towards the more able pupils? Finally, will the need to play its part in the marketability of the school force the PE department to divert the available resources away from curricular PE and towards extra-curricular sport? Whilst some pupils will be winners in this scenario, others will clearly be 'also-rans' through practices that will serve to perpetuate and legitimize inequality of curricular provision and an elitist orientation. Additionally, teachers may well find themselves victims of the tension that will exist between regulating and balancing their professional ideals with the competing priorities and demands of surviving in the education market-place.

The creation of an image requires the production and cultivation of that which is publicly valued and visible. In terms of PE this may determine and shape not only the curricular context, but also the learning process. For example, even within the parameters of the proposed PE National Curriculum and especially at Key Stage Four (age 14–16),[3] the curriculum as delivered and conceived may well be restricted to the traditional competitive forms of physical activity that have a currency in the middle-class, adult world of sport. As such, this may not have much relevance to those not of this group (see Jackson and Marsden, 1966, p. 123, in Saunders, 1986, p. 17). Bringing a socio-historical perspective both to the development of PE in state schools and to the influences which shape and form the school curriculum illustrates that there is considerable substance to what may appear a bizarre flight of fancy. The way in which nineteenth- and early twentieth-century minor public schools and aspiring grammar schools adopted the games tradition and ethic for the sake of acceptance and integration into the elitist public school system is well documented by Mangan (1982, 1986). Headteachers instrumentally used games, in particular, for publicity purposes and 'sensible self interest' (Mangan, 1982, p. 4). Games became the 'emblems of ideological subscription' (p. 7), symbolizing order, discipline, effort and excellence, and 'gave reassurance and satisfaction to middle class parents'

(Mangan, 1982, p. 7). In the same way, twentieth-century grammar schools adopted public school games, their associated rituals and elitist ethos so 'imitating their betters and disassociating from their inferiors' (Mangan, 1982) in the pursuit of acceptability, respect and status. One consequence of LMS may be that schools will be involved in utilizing similar strategies as 'specific instruments of institutional organization and publicity' (Mangan, 1982, p. 8) in an effort to attract parents to support the school. Edwards *et al.*'s (1989) research findings suggest that many (particularly middle-class) parents are looking for a traditional, safe curriculum model and ethos such as those embodied in the independent sector. The key point is this: headteachers and their governing bodies will need to construct their curriculum in the light of their conception of what the consumers demand, and are in this respect likely to be influenced in all areas by the model presented by the independent sector. Where curriculum provision is deemed to be an important factor in parents' choice of school it does, as Whitty (1990, p. 31) suggests, 'seem likely then, that the cultural pull of the public or grammar school curriculum (or rather the public perception of that curriculum)' could act as an organizing principle for the schools curriculum. Hence the effects of LMS are to generate a market-led curriculum that in practice could turn the PE clock back — to the unashamed, overt elitism of the mid-twentieth century, the marginalization of minority groups, and those with special educational needs (SEN).

LMS also increases the control that schools have over the use of their facilities out of school hours and provides for them to keep the income generated from 'hiring out'. This raises a number of equity issues that have a significant bearing on the provision of PE and sporting opportunities for young people both in curricular and extra-curricular time. The hiring out of sports facilities offers substantial potential for generating income. As headteachers become more aware of the cash potential lying within the gymnasium and swimming pools after 4 p.m., they may seek to make them available — but at a price. With entrepreneurial flair and a commercial approach encouraged through the market economy ethos of LMS, both PE departments and community sports providers could find their access to the school facilities reduced, limited or deemed financially unviable as governing bodies seek to maximize income from the hire of facilities.[4] Thus a school's need to generate income may find itself in conflict with both the PE department's and the community's expectations and demands. This could have implications for school and community links, partnership schemes and the breadth and range of curricular and extra-curricular provision. Community sports clubs may for financial reasons be forced to operate in alternative venues, in which case the 'community' element and links with the school may be lost. Consequently access may be restricted to those with the means and ability to travel away from the immediate environment. If schools are to avoid inadvertently disadvantaging some of their pupils in their leisure participation they need to consider the following equation: potential income generated, over responsibility to the community and their own pupils. Similarly, if the school's access is restricted to certain limited times there may be a tendency to orientate use towards those perceived to be best able to benefit from the precious resource — the most physically able?

Various strategies have been advocated by the Sports Council (see Sports Council, 1990a; Sports Council for Wales, 1990), to alleviate the anticipated problems which will be faced by both school and community providers of sporting opportunities as LMS takes effect. One such strategy seems to hinge around the concept of 'bartering' and the reciprocal use of facilities and resources. Essentially this could take the form of local clubs, in return for privileged access to the school's resources and facilities, offering their expertise in the form of coaching clinics, refereeing etc. Whilst potentially this could give a greater number of pupils access to resources that they have previously been denied, clubs may want to concentrate their efforts on those most likely to give good returns (i.e. the very able performers). As the Brighton and Hove Sports and PE Project (set up in 1990 and designed to establish an integrated and coordinated approach to sports provision for children by creating sporting links between schools and local authorities) showed, 'many clubs . . . do not share Sportslink's aims and continue to operate as bastions of elite exclusivity' (Sportslink, 1990, p. 31). Additionally, schools are not equal in their facilities and, logically, schools with good facilities have greater opportunities to generate extra income than those with poor facilities. Potentially, therefore, such schools will be better financially placed to resource the school and individual departments so attracting custom. Inequality thus now potentially manifests itself between schools as well as within schools. It follows that the extent to which schools can meet the requirements of, resource and provide the National Curriculum in PE, will be contingent on facilities. This is an area where deficiencies in 'plant' are not easily overcome. Hence, the extent to which 'a common threshold' of knowledge, skills and understanding can be achieved for *all* pupils is problematic. As Edwards (1989, p. 69) suggests, 'any such notion of common entitlement to a broad and balanced education is meaningless without reference to the threshold of resources below which it remains an empty promise'. Contrary to the apparently egalitarian objectives of the ERA 1988, it appears in this case that a pupil's quality of educational opportunity will be determined by the multi-faceted nature of LMS provisions. Pupils in poorly resourced schools whose parents, in reality, have limited choice as to which school their child attends *will* be denied the chance to reach their full potential by the accident of environment and geographical location.[5] Will poorly resourced schools be compensated or expected to trade equally in the unequal market-place?

Part of the LMS package outlined earlier involved the devolution of management to the headteacher and governing body. In essence, this represents a power shift in the 'ownership' of schools which has serious implications for all subjects, particularly marginal ones like PE. Parental representation on the governing body has been expanded and parent power increased. The key issue here, therefore, pivots around *who* are the new governors, whose interests do they serve and what are their likely effects on PE? Research (Deem, 1990; Golby and Brigley, 1989; Jefferies and Streatfield, 1989; Doe, 1988) has already suggested that the composition of governing bodies is skewed towards white, middle-class parents. As Deem (1988, p. 186) points out, 'parent power may turn out merely to add to the power of those parents who already have access to mechanisms of power rather than those who have little or no access at present'.

Governors' ideologies and perceptions, whether traditional, utilitarian or egalitarian (see Golby and Brigley, 1989) and their personal experiences and cultural values will inevitably shape their beliefs and behaviour. An elitist conception of what counts as valuable and high-status knowledge may condemn curriculum-time PE to an inadequate slice of the timetable cake.

Moreover in the effort to minimize the cost of providing the National Curriculum in the marginal areas, governors may resort to the appointment of less experienced or licenced teachers.[6] Concern over the appointment of licensed teachers has been voiced by Miles and Furlong (1988) who argue that if teachers train teachers in schools, where they have little opportunity for reflection on practice, inegalitarian practices may be reproduced rather than challenged. This holds true for PE especially where departments are strongly sports-orientated and where the hidden curriculum of motor elitism is most persuasive. Similarly, 'buying in' sports coaches who have not been exposed to courses addressing equality issues, and who are unaware of the effects of pedagogy and practice, may severely limit the PE and sporting opportunities of young people.

LMS also raises the visibility of the costs involved in the provision of certain educational opportunities, for instance, the use of off-site sports facilities. As Smith (in Rogerson, 1991) has pointed out, 'when you have only got a certain amount of funding the temptation is, of course, to satisfy your statutory obligations first'. In schools with limited on-site facilities, this could severely curtail both the range of PE activities available to pupils and their opportunities to participate in 'activities which meet their preference and personal exercise needs' (see DES, 1991, p. 33).

With economic rather than social and educational considerations beginning to surface as key factors in the community use of school facilities and the design of programmes of study (Sports Council, 1990a, p. 6), governing bodies may not be able to afford to plan a curriculum on the basis of educational and social criteria. In these circumstances PE teachers must be proactive in exerting some control over the destiny of their subject. They need to evaluate the perspectives of the governing body and communicate to governers the efficacy and the intrinsic and unique educational value of their subject in order to secure a budget to support existing good practice and develop new initiatives.

The National Curriculum

Chapter 1 of the ERA establishes the principle of a 'National Curriculum', the second major initiative to impinge directly on the provision of PE and sport in schools. A National Curriculum will, according to the DES literature, secure 'for all pupils in maintained schools a curriculum which equips them with the knowledge, skill and understanding that they need for adult life and employment' (DES, 1987, p. 3). This is to be achieved as 'all pupils study a broad and balanced range of subjects throughout their compulsory schooling' (DES, 1987, p. 3). The rhetoric is thus, that all pupils 'should be entitled to the same opportunities wherever they go to school' (p. 3) and that a National Curriculum will be an effective way of ensuring that good curriculum practice is much more widely employed (see DES, 1987, p. 3).

The National Curriculum requires schools to provide their pupils with a curriculum that comprises core subjects (maths, English, science) and foundation subjects (history, geography, technology, music, art and PE). Altogether there are three components of the National Curriculum that are specified for each subject:

- Attainment Targets — covering the range of knowledge, skills and understanding which pupils will be expected to show throughout their school career;
- Programmes of Study — which will set out 'the matters, skills and processes' which must be taught to pupils during each key stage in order for them to meet the objectives set out in the attainment targets (DES, 1991, p. iii);
- Assessment arrangements — for PE this will entail assessment of each child's achievement at the end of each Key Stage[7] in relation to the four statutory End-of-Key-Stage Statements. Additionally, the framework of the National Curriculum has provided for 'Levels of Attainment' which are defined in relation to the Attainment Targets and designed to reflect ten different levels of pupils' achievement, ability and progress according to age. For PE, these are intended to be non-statutory.[8]

In its content, hidden pedagogy, rhetoric and level of prescription, the National Curriculum transmits a number of contradictory messages. Whilst it has the apparently egalitarian objective of entitling all pupils to a much higher common threshold of knowledge, skill and understanding than available at present, its curricular content is, as Simon (1988, p. 16) suggests, 'unimaginatively academic'. Consequently this defines what it means to be educated in a very narrow academic and elitist way ignoring many of the recent curricular and pedagogical developments designed to meet contemporary social, economic and technological conditions. Similarly, its content and hierarchical organization reinforces the 'superordination and subordination' of some areas of knowledge (Hardy and Vieler-Porter, 1990, p. 180) over others; the academic continues to be privileged over the practical.

Similarly, the National Curriculum has been accused of being culturally imperialist, 'founded on the idea of one history, one set of values' (Ball, 1990b, p. 11) which is in Ball's view English, middle-class and white. In the light of this, its dismissal of the diversity of British culture calls into serious question the commitment to egalitarianism and the veracity of the term 'National' in the National Curriculum. The term is a misnomer because the legislation does not apply to the independent sector or to City Technology Colleges (CTCs).[9] The message, suggests Simon (1987) is quite clear; 'this is a curriculum for the masses. Its purpose is control' (p. 16). While the education of the elite remains free from prescription and Government control, Simon (1987) suspects that the education of 'ordinary people's children' (p. 15) will be subject to increased regulation.

The way in which the PE National Curriculum has been constructed and manipulated via its modified structure, vis-à-vis other foundation subjects, its position in the implementation process, DES imperatives and demands, has explicitly conveyed messages about the value of 'practical knowledge' within the hierarchy of knowledge and who is to control the PE curriculum. It is, therefore, important to understand and appreciate the PE National Curriculum in the context in which it was conceived and has emerged.

Firstly, the social and political context is one in which PE and sport in state schools have been heavily criticized for their purported failure to produce the calibre of sportsmen and sportswomen to allow Britain to compete successfully in the international arena.[10] Such an accusation clearly demonstrates the expectation that some have of the profession. Additionally, recent government measures and policies have had a serious impact upon both the working conditions of PE teachers in schools and the provision of resources for PE and school sport. For example, diminishing government rate support for local authorities has forced many to sell off playing fields to realize capital.

Secondly, there are those outside the PE profession, in the sporting world, who have consistently endeavoured to influence the role and curricular content of PE in schools. Their views have not always concurred with those of educationalists. Furthermore, the structure of the PE National Curriculum is 'less prescriptive ... than for other foundation subjects' (DES, 1991). This further differentiates PE from other curriculum subjects, and is likely to ensure that PE is seen by headteachers, governors and parents in less favourable terms. This could have implications for subsequent resource provision. Clearly, issues relating to resourcing will impinge directly on what is offered and for whom (see Penney, 1991, p. 36). If teachers have to work with barely adequate or impoverished resource provision, their opportunities and possibilities for change and innovation towards a more egalitarian curricular provision will be very limited.

The National Curriculum has raised issues as to what PE is and how achievement in the subject can be assessed. It has also highlighted current provision for PE and sport and prompted demand for increased support and resources for teachers, especially those working in primary schools at Key Stages One and Two. But, the Final Report of the PE Working Group (DES, 1991) is rather like the 'curate's egg' — good in parts. It not only expresses some of the struggles and differences which have been historically evident in PE;[11] it also reflects the difficulties in transforming principles, ideals and intentions into practice.

As well as providing a rationale supporting the entitlement of PE for all pupils (DES, 1991, p. 5) the report explicitly states that the focus of PE is wider than just the development of physical skills. It asserts 'Physical Education is achieved through the combination of physical activity with the mental processes of making decisions, selecting, refining, judging, adjusting and adapting' (p. 5), a process which involves pupils in 'planning, doing and evaluating' (p. 5). This commitment to education in and through the physical, rather than just education for sport, could help reduce elitist tendencies in PE. Similarly, in attempting to clarify the sport/PE interface (DES, 1991, p. 7) which has acted as a catalyst for many elitist practices, the report emphasizes a process-based and child-centred curriculum (see DES, 1991, p. 7). However, the sentiments of these principles may not easily find expression as practice in schools. There is a clear contradiction between a rationale which both broadens the notion of achievement in PE (see DES, 1991, pp. 5, 41) and challenges the perspective that 'performance' alone is *the* indicator of achievement and the notion that achievement can be expressed in a single Attainment Target, End-of-Key-Stage Statements and non-statutory Levels of Attainment. A single Attainment Target, which emphasizes participation and performance (DES, 1991, p. 17), will not help all children achieve and develop mental, social and physical skills and understanding through

PE. While the report recognizes that planning and composing, appreciating and evaluating are implicitly included in one Attainment Target, these important elements of achievement become hopelessly blurred. As a result the ghost of motor elitism may continue to haunt the PE curriculum. The report advocates that achievement in PE *should* be reflected in:

    (a)   the physical skill and ability of the pupil;
    (b)   the way in which the pupil has selected and organized the response;
    (c)   the recognition and appreciation by the pupil of performance of self and others (DES, 1991, pp. 41–2).

The key question, however, is whether the framework for the assessment of achievement in PE adequately values and reflects the intended process-based approach advanced in the rationale. For example, the concern with the personal and social education (PSE) of pupils referred to in the rationale is not sustained through the four Key Stages or right across the Levels of Attainment. Rather, references to collaborative working in groups diminish (at Key Stages Three and Four) as the End-of-Key-Stage Statements and Levels of Attainment assert the need for competition and individual activity. There is then a real danger that if the Levels of Attainment are uncritically applied they may perpetuate a concept of attainment in which tangible, visible outcomes of performance become the sole criterion of success.

    Paradoxically, however, the DES imperative that the statutory framework for the National Curriculum is 'sufficiently broad and flexible to allow schools wide discretion in relation to the matters to be studied' (DES, 1991, p. 3) and that, for PE, the statutory End-of-Key-Stage Statements 'are short and general in character' and 'less clearly identifiable with particular statements represented in the non-statutory levels' (DES, 1991, p. 87) certainly allows scope for a wide range of interpretation. There are dangers here on a number of levels. The generality of the statutory aspects of the PE National Curriculum may make it *more* difficult to interpret, administer and assess (see Curl, 1991, p. 11) and may not, therefore, provide the necessary support or incentive for teachers to challenge elitist tendencies in the traditional curriculum. Rather it may provide the scope and opportunity for teachers to act in ways that perpetuate rather than contest practices that are damaging. Whilst the legislation is intended to 'leave full scope for professional judgment and for schools to organise how the curriculum is delivered in the best way suited to the ages, circumstances, needs and abilities of the children' (DES, 1987, p. 11) the End-of-Key-Stage Statements (with the exception of those for swimming) are unsupported either by a clarification of what is to be provided or, more importantly, reference to the minimum level of resourcing below which entitlement remains an empty promise. This will pose problems for teachers in their application of the End-of-Key-Stage Statements and in formulating, assessing, resourcing and protecting their curriculum. For example, 'flexibility' integrated with the desire for 'generality' may not provide PE teachers with the protection needed in order to provide an entitlement and balanced curriculum for all pupils. There is a danger that the flexibility induced will lead to the provision of a very narrow range of activities.

    Flexibility may also mean that the further recommendations of the Final Report, which do not relate directly to the statutory requirements, but which nevertheless add to the educational experience and curricular entitlement for all pupils, are dismissed by teachers and governing bodies. For example, the National Curriculum recommends that all pupils receive a residential experience. This, however, is a non-statutory requirement and without the support structure of statutory status governing bodies may resource the subject at a minimal level, that which allows schools to meet the basic requirements of the National Curriculum, but little more. Because of costs and time, such opportunities may be driven outside the formal curriculum and outside the protective 'charging policy'.[12] This could subsequently severely restrict access to those who can afford to pay. The reality of entitlement may not materialize for all pupils.

The recommended Programmes of Study for the PE National Curriculum draw, in both content and ethos, upon an 'inherited selection of interests' (Goodson, 1983, p. 4) which seem to endorse the traditional elements of the PE curriculum (in particular the games and gymnastic/dance activities). Games are to remain compulsory until the end of Key Stage Three, thereby 'perpetuating the best of English (sic) traditions and cultural heritage' (NCC, 1991, p. 14). Although the report points out that 'the game is not the thing the child is' (DES, 1991, p. 15) it continues to place great importance on games, traditionally the site for the expression of ideologies of sexism, racism, classism and motor elitism. Although it advocates the progressive and developmental teaching of games, via 'small sided, simplified versions of recognized games' (at Key Stage Two) and 'small sided and modified versions towards the recognized form' (at Key Stage Three) to 'experience the full recognized version of a game' (in Key Stage Four), and thereby confirms and legitimizes as sound educational practice many of the innovations which have been attacked by the New Right in recent years (see Evans, 1990b), this may not be sufficient to contest the elitism which is endemic in the curriculum.

The National Curriculum is not silent on pedagogical matters. A faithful implementation of the Programmes of Study will necessitate, for some teachers, a change in their teaching methods. Didactic practices which emphasize performance, technique learning and the teacher as the only resource for learning may no longer be appropriate to the broadened definitions of ability, achievement, attainment and excellence which underpin the rationale for the proposed PE National Curriculum. However, there are all too few examples in the document to suggest how some of the social and cultural issues relating to PE and sport in the wider society are to be addressed by teachers *and* pupils. Although the report stresses that working towards equality of opportunity involves 'an understanding and appreciation of the range of pupils' responses to femininity, masculinity and sexuality, to the whole range of ability and disability, to ethnic, social and cultural diversity, and the way in which these relate for children to physical education' (DES, 1991, p. 15), little reference is given to how pupils or teachers are to deal with these issues. As a result, elitist and individualistic ideologies and practices may not in any serious or lasting way be challenged. While the discourse of the document reflects a genuine commitment and concern for equality issues, a form of practice in PE which is capable of providing an education for all may remain some distance away.

There is, of course, a limit to what can be achieved immediately. The process of change is multidimensional and cannot be hurried. Time and resources are needed and it has to be acknowledged that in the contemporary educational climate these may not be forthcoming. While teachers may wish to change their practice, the pressing demands to deliver the National Curriculum may constrain and lock them into the cycle of elitism that has traditionally pervaded the curriculum.

Conclusion

The ERA 1988 has the apparently egalitarian objective of providing an entitlement curriculum and equality of access to educational opportunities. This chapter, however, claims that a common curriculum may not erode institutionalized inequality. This is because, firstly, the ethos of the ERA 1988 articulates a value system that pays only lip service to equal opportunities. PE teachers may well find themselves juggling to balance, on the one hand, their professional integrity and ideals and, on the other, the competing demands of survival in the education market-place. Secondly, there may also be a disjuncture between the egalitarian intentions of the PE National Curriculum and practice in schools. Finally, legislation, per se, is likely to be insufficient to challenge inequalities which are an outcome of beliefs, values and ideologies that manifest themselves in social processes that are deeply embedded in the PE curriculum.

The sort of changes in thought and action advocated by others in this book may help teachers contest such processes, and constitute an important step in the direction of providing a physical education for all.

Notes

My thanks go to John Evans for his helpful comments on an earlier draft of this paper.

1 Ball is suggesting that the ethos and content of the National Curriculum reflects a strong desire to revive and restore the traditional moral and cultural values and standards of the grammar, direct grant and independent schools. It is felt by some (the 'New Right') that these elements have been absent in the progressive practice and curriculum of contemporary education.

2 The Central Council of Physical Recreation (CCPR) have even suggested that the responsibility for the sharp decline in sport in state schools is partly attributable to the LMS initiative (Rogerson, 1991, p. 11).

3 At Key Stage Four it is proposed that pupils should study at least two activities, but that these be drawn from one or two areas of activity.

4 The CCPR have continually voiced warnings about the possible impact of misplaced 'entrepreneurial zeal' (see Rogerson, 1991).

5 This state of affairs is contrary to the rationale outlined in 'The need for a National Curriculum' in the Consultative Document (DES, 1987, p. 4).

6 The Licensed Teacher Scheme was iniated by the DES in response to a perceived shortage in staffing levels and was designed to offer an alternative entry to the teaching profession and qualified teacher status (QTS). New recruits are over 26 years of age, and have spent at least two years in higher education. Training occurs 'on the job', in schools for two years under the supervision of that school.

7 Key Stages refer to the four periods in each pupil's compulsory education to which the elements of the National Curriculum will apply. These are: Key Stage

One from age 5 to 7; Key Stage Two from age 7 to 11; Key Stage Three from age 11 to 14; Key Stage Four from age 14 to the end of compulsory education.

8   The non-statutory status of the Levels of Attainment for PE has been a contentious issue during the evolution of the PE National Curriculum. For example, see the exchange of correspondence from the Chairman of the PE Working Group and the Secretary of State for Education and Science as reported in the Interim Report (DES, 1990).

9   City Technology Colleges (CTCs) were originally announced in 1986, at the Conservative Party Conference, to provide a new choice of school, raise educational standards, particularly in inner-city areas, and offer a curricular focus responsive to the needs of modern industrial society. CTCs represent a new category of independent school; independent of local authority control, intended to be financed primarily from industrial sponsorship and supplemented by government funding. In practice, CTCs have been substantially underwritten by government funding. CTCs were designed to offer free education for pupils of different abilities. As independent schools they are not subject to the requirements of the National Curriculum. The curricular focus is broad with a particular emphasis on science and technology. (See DES, 1986; Ball, 1990a, pp. 113–19).

10 For further discussion on the conflicts and crises in contemporary PE see Evans, 1990b; Kaye, 1990; Thomas, 1989; Hardy and Sparkes, 1987.

11 Such as those between rival groups to define the correct version of PE (see Kirk, 1990).

12 The ERA prohibits charging for any education provided in school hours at all state-maintained schools and also for out-of-hours provision where that provision is required to fulfil statutory responsibilities relating to the National Curriculum. Although the Act leaves LEAs and governing bodies free to charge for optional extras outside school hours (subject to the exceptions mentioned), there is no requirement for them to do so.

References

ANDREWS, J. (1979) *Essays on Physical Education and Sport*, Cheltenham, Stanley Thornes.

AUDIT COMMISSION (1989) *Sport for Whom? Clarifying the Local Authority Role*, London, HMSO.

BAIN, L. (1990) 'A Critical Analysis of the Hidden Curriculum in Physical Education', in KIRK, D. and TINNING, R. (Eds) *Physical Education, Curriculum and Culture*, London, Falmer Press, pp. 23–42.

BALL, S. (1900a) *Politics and Policy Making in Education: Explorations in Policy Sociology*, London, Routledge.

BALL, S. (1990b) 'A National Curriculum for the 1990s,' *The NUT Review*, **4**, 1, Spring, pp. 9–12.

BELL, L. (1986) 'Managing to Survive in Secondary School Physical Education', in EVANS, J. (Ed.) *Physical Education, Sport and Schooling*, London, Falmer Press, pp. 95–115.

BROADFOOT, P. (Ed.) (1984) *Selection Certification and Control: Social Issues in Educational Assessment*, Lewes, Falmer Press.

CARR, W. (1990) 'Citizenship and the National Curriculum', in *Autumn Conference Proceedings of the Exeter Society for Curriculum Studies*.

CHARLES, J. (1979) 'Technocratic Ideology in Physical Education', *Quest*, **31**, pp. 277–84.

CURL, G. (1991) 'Dance in the National Curriculum? — Yes Minister!', *British Journal of Physical Education*, **22**, 4, Winter, pp. 9–13.

DEEM, R. (1988) 'The Great Education Reform Bill — Some Issues and Implications', *Journal of Education Policy*, **3**, **2**, pp. 181–9.

DEEM, R. (1990) 'The Reform of School-Governing Bodies: the Power of the Consumer over the Producer?', in FLUDE, M. and HAMMER, M. (Eds) *The Education Reform Act 1988: Its Origins and Implications*, London, Falmer Press, pp. 153–71.

DEPARTMENT OF EDUCATION AND SCIENCE (1986) *City Technology Colleges: A New Choice of School*, London, DES.

DEPARTMENT OF EDUCATION AND SCIENCE (1987) *The National Curriculum 5–16: A Consultation Document*, London, DES.

DEPARTMENT OF EDUCATION AND SCIENCE (1988) *The Education Reform Act*, London, HMSO.

DEPARTMENT OF EDUCATION AND SCIENCE (1989) *From Policy to Practice*, London, DES.

DEPARTMENT OF EDUCATION AND SCIENCE (1990) *National Curriculum Working Group on Physical Education: Interim Report*, London, DES.

DEPARTMENT OF EDUCATION AND SCIENCE (1991) *Physical Education for Ages 5–16*, London, DES.

DEWAR, A. (1990) 'Oppression and Privilege in Physical Education: Struggles in the Negotiation of Gender in a University Programme', in KIRK, D. and TINNING, R. (Eds) *Physical Education, Curriculum and Culture*, London, Falmer Press, pp. 67–99.

DODDS, P. (1986) 'Stamp out the Ugly 'Isms' in Your Gym,' in PIERAN, M. and GRAHAM, G. (Eds) *Sport Pedagogy*, Champaign, IL. USA, Human Kinetics Publishers.

DOE, B. (1988) 'Good Turn Out For the Middle Classes', in *The Times Educational Supplement*, 16 December, p. 15.

EDWARDS, A., FITZ, J. and WHITTY, G. (1989) *The State and Private Education: A Study of the Assisted Places Scheme*, London, Falmer Press.

EDWARDS, T. (1989) 'Benefits, Costs and Risks: Some Expectations of the National Curriculum', *Curriculum*, **10**, 2, Autumn, pp. 65–70.

EVANS, J. (1990a) 'Ability, Position and Privilege in School Physical Education', in KIRK, D. and TINNING, R. (Eds) *Physical Education, Curriculum and Culture*, London, Falmer Press, pp. 139–67.

EVANS, J. (1990b) 'Defining the Subject; The Rise and Rise of the New PE', *British Journal of Sociology of Education*, **11**, 2, pp. 155–69.

EVANS, J. and WILLIAMS, T. (1989) 'Moving Up and Getting Out; The Classed and Gendered Career Opportunities of PE Teachers', in TEMPLIN, T. and SCHEMPP, P. (Eds) *Socialization in PE: Learning to Teach*, Indianapolis, USA, Benchmark Press, pp. 235–51.

FLUDE, M. and HAMMER, M. (Eds) (1990) *The Education Reform Act, 1988: Its Origins and Implications*, London, Falmer Press.

GOLBY, M. and BRIGLEY, S. (1989) *Parents as School Governors*, Tiverton, Fairway Publications.

GOODSON, I. (1983) *School Subjects and Curriculum Change: Case Studies in Curriculum History*, London, Croom Helm.

GOODSON, I. (1988) *The Making of Curriculum: Collected Essays*, London, Falmer Press.

GREEN, A. (1988) 'Lessons in Standards', *Marxism Today*, January, pp. 24–30.

HARDY, C. and SPARKES, A. (1987) 'School Sport and the Control of the Physical Education Curriculum', *Bulletin of Physical Education*, **23**, 1, pp. 28–31.

HARDY, J. and VIELER-PORTER, C. (1990) 'Race, Schooling and the 1988 Education Reform Act', in FLUDE, M. and HAMMER, M. (Eds) *The Education Reform Act 1988: Its Origins and Implications*, London, Falmer Press, pp. 173–85.

HARGREAVES, J. (1986) *Sport, Power and Culture*, Cambridge, Polity Press.

HARTNETT, A. and NAISH, M. (1990) 'The Sleep of Reason Breeds Monsters: The Birth of a Statutory Curriculum in England and Wales', *Journal of Curriculum Studies*, **22**, 1, pp. 1–17.

HOYLE, E. (1969) *The Role of the Teacher*, Routledge and Kegan Paul.

JACKSON, B. and MARSDEN, D. (1966) *Education and the Working Class*, Harmondsworth, Penguin.

JEFFERIES, G. and STREATFIELD, D. (1989) *Reconstitution of School Governors*, Slough, NFER.

KAYE, M. (1990) 'Participation and Excellence — The Legacy of Athleticism Within the Contemporary Debate', *Physical Education Review*, **13**, 1, pp. 17–23.

KIRK, D. (1990) 'Defining the Subject: Gymnastics and Gender in British Physical Education', in KIRK, D. and TINNING, R. (Eds) *Physical Education, Curriculum and Culture*, London, Falmer Press, pp. 43–67.

LAWTON, D. (1989) *Education, Culture and the National Curriculum*, Hodder and Stoughton.

LAWTON, D. and CHITTY, C. (1988) *The National Curriculum*, Bedford Way Papers **33**, London, University of London, Institute of Education.

LINGARD, B. (1990) 'Accountability and Control: A Sociological Account of Secondary School Assessment in Queensland', *British Journal of Sociology of Education*, **11**, 2, pp. 171–88.

MANGAN, J. (1973) *Physical Education and Sport: Sociological and Cultural Perspectives. An Introductory Reader*, Oxford, Blackwell.

MANGAN, J. (1982) 'Imitating Their Betters and Disassociating From Their Inferiors. Grammar Schools and the Games Ethic in the Late Nineteenth and Early Twentieth Centuries', in *The Fitness of the Nation: PE and Health in the Nineteenth and Twentieth Centuries*, History of Education Society.

MANGAN, J. (1986) *The Games Ethic and Imperialism: Aspects of the Diffusion of an Ideal*, Harmondsworth, Viking.

MARTIN, C. (1988) *Schools Now: A Parent's Guide*, Oxford, Lion Publishing plc.

MILES, S. and FURLONG, J. (1988) 'Teachers Training Teachers: An Opportunity for a Sociological Break in Educational Transmission?', in WOODS, P. and POLLARD, A. (Eds) *Sociology and Teaching*, London, Croom Helm, pp. 76–91.

MILES, S. and MIDDLETON, C. (1990) 'Girls' Education in the Balance: The ERA and Inequality', in FLUDE, M. and HAMMER, M. (Eds) *The Education Reform Act, 1988: Its Origins and Implications*, London, Falmer Press, pp. 187–206.

NATIONAL CURRICULUM COUNCIL (1991) *National Curriculum Council Consultation Report-Physical Education in the National Curriculum*, December, 1991, York, NCC.

PENNEY, D. (1991) 'Making a Case For Physical Education: Preparing For The National Curriculum', *British Journal of Physical Education*, **22**, 1, Spring, pp. 36–9.

PENNEY, D. and EVANS, J. (1991) 'The Impact of the Education Reform Act on the Provision of Physical Education and Sport in the 5–16 Curriculum of the State Schools', *British Journal of Physical Education*, **22**, 1, Spring, pp. 38–42.

ROGERSON, P. (1991) 'Sport for Some', *Public Finance and Accountability*, **1**, pp. 11–14.

SAUNDERS, E. (1986) 'Trends and Developments in Physical Education', in *Trends and Developments in Physical Education*, Proceedings of the VIII Commonwealth and International Conference on Sport, PE, Dance, Recreation, Health, pp. 7–19.

SIMON, B. (1987) 'Lessons in Elitism', *Marxism Today*, September, pp. 12–17.

SIMON, B. (1988) *Bending the Rules: The Baker 'Reform' of Education*, London, Lawrence and Wishart.

SKINSLEY, M. (1987) 'The Elite: Whose Responsibility?', *British Journal of Physical Education*, **18**, 2, pp. 55–8.

SMITH, A. (1991) quoted in ROGERSON, P. 'Sport for Some', *Public Finance and Accountability*, **1**, pp. 11–14.

SOCKETT, H. (Ed.) (1980) *Accountability and the English Education System*, Hodder and Stoughton.

SPARKES, A. (1989) 'The Achievement Orientation and its Influence Upon Innovation in Physical Education', *Physical Education Review*, **12**, 1, pp. 36–43.

SPORTS COUNCIL (1990a) *Education Reform and Sport*, Fact File No. **1**, Sports Council (North West).

SPORTS COUNCIL (1990b) *New Horizons, Education Reform and the Development of Sport in Greater London and the South East*, Sports Council (Greater London and South East).

SPORTS COUNCIL (1990c) *Education Reform — a series of three fact sheets for Governing Bodies of Sport and Local Sports Organizations, School Governors and Head Teachers, Local Authority Recreation Departments*, London, Sports Council.

SPORTS COUNCIL FOR WALES (1990) *Physical Education and Community Recreation Bulletin No. 1; The Education Legislation: A Guide for the Governing Bodies of Sport, Sports Clubs and Other Sports Organizations*, Bulletin No. 2, The Sports Council for Wales.

SPORTSLINK (1990) *Brighton and Hove Sports and PE Project*, Sussex, Hove Leisure Services.

THOMAS, S. (1989) 'Making Sense of the Public Image of the "New" Physical Education', in RAYMOND, C. (Ed.) *Physical Education Today*, Perspectives **41**, University of Exeter, School of Education, pp. 4–13.

TREADWELL, P. (1984) 'Victorian Public School Sport', *Physical Education Review*, **7**, 2, pp. 113–19.

TROMAN, G. (1989) 'Testing Tensions: The Politics of Educational Assessment', *British Educational Research Journal*, **15**, 3, pp. 279–93.

VERTINSKY, P. (1983) 'The Evolving Policy of Equal Curricular Opportunity in England: A Case Study of the Implementation of Sex Equality in Physical Education', *British Journal of Educational Studies*, **3**, pp. 229–51.

WHITTY, G. (1990) 'The New Right and the National Curriculum: State Control or Market Forces?', in FLUDE, M. and HAMMER, M. (Eds) *The Education Reform Act, 1988: Its Origins and Implications*, London, Falmer Press, pp. 21–37.

WILLIAMSON, B. (1974) 'Continuities and Discontinuities in the Sociology of Education', in FLUDE, M. and AHIER, J. *Educability, Schools and Ideology*, London, Croom Helm.

WOODS, P. (1983) *Sociology in the School*, London, Routledge and Kegan Paul.

Chapter 8

Who Cares About Girls? Equality, Physical Education and the Primary School Child

Anne Williams

While many have criticized secondary physical education practice for reinforcing sexism (Leaman, 1984; Talbot, 1985; Scraton, 1986; Evans, 1988) there has tended to be a tacit assumption amongst teachers and researchers, born possibly of a combination of ignorance and apathy, that all is relatively well in primary schools.[1] This assumption, which has only recently begun to be challenged, appears to be based on the premise that when or because the primary physical education curriculum is delivered to mixed groups, with the possible exception of some games work where 'equivalent' activities are undertaken by boys and girls, equality of opportunity is being expressed in practice. This rather naive view ignores a whole host of factors which result in the physical education curriculum experience of boys and girls being significantly different from reception class onwards. It is a view which is not limited to the physical education arena, as Skelton's (1989a) study of primary initial teacher training students reveals. I will refer to this later in this chapter.

It is suggested here that present practice in many primary schools ensures that pupils transfer to secondary school with their stereotypical attitudes (fostered, in many cases, from birth) towards physical education and sport not only intact but well reinforced by their primary school physical education, and that these attitudes disadvantage girls, and also set limits to the experiences of most boys.

There are many variables which can affect the interaction between teacher and pupil and thereby influence the learning process whether this be in the realm of knowledge, skills or attitudes. The relative importance of some factors appears to be constant while others will impact variably upon different children. Figure 8.1 presents a model which identifies some of these factors.

While many of the issues discussed in this chapter have been with us for some time and have been addressed in some primary schools (see, for example, Campbell and Brooker, 1990; Vick, 1990) there are new pressures emerging, primarily as a result of the introduction of LMS and the National Curriculum, which need to be addressed. It will be argued later that new and emerging forms of accountability support the promotion of equal opportunity policies.

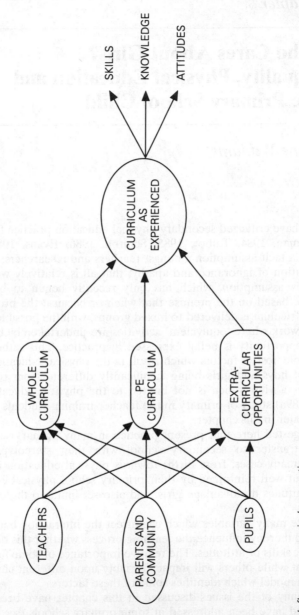

Figure 8.1   Influences on curriculum practice

Curriculum Access

First it is necessary to examine what is meant by equality in this context although this has been done more elegantly and more thoroughly elsewhere in this volume. It is axiomatic that equal provision does not mean equal learning or equal opportunity. This is graphically illustrated by the rather extreme but by no means unique example of offering opportunities in sport to both sexes given by May and Rudduck (1983). Their research describes a primary school where pupils had been told that football training was to be made available to all boys and girls.

> There was immediate uproar from the boys. They did not want girls to join in and showed marked hostility and antagonism to the idea. The girls were immediately put off and there was some ill-will and tension between the girls and the boys during the next few days. (May and Rudduck, 1983)

Predictably football training remained a male domain. It is encouraging to note that the proposals from the Secretary of State for Education for Physical Education in the National Curriculum emphasize the distinction between access and opportunity:

> it would be a mistake to equate access with opportunity and it is import- ant to appreciate the distinction between the two. (DES, 1991)

In some schools, girls and boys, able-bodied and disabled, from a range of cultures and ethnic backgrounds, may be said to have the same access to the physical education curriculum: no children are prevented by virtue of their sex, religion, or race from taking part. But even when this desirable state of affairs exists, questions have to be asked about whether children also have equal opportunities to learn and express themselves through and in physical activity.

Although equal access is demonstrably insufficient, it might nevertheless be a useful first step in the development of an equal opportunities programme, particularly if introduced with a little more subtlety than in the example above. While indoor primary school work is generally mixed-sex, games are still frequently taught to single-sex groups from top infant ages onwards. Moreover this differentiated curriculum diet is further reinforced in many schools by extra-curricular provision which, more often than not, favours boys. This point will be developed later.

A more difficult question is that of exactly what kind of curriculum we want to make accessible to pupils. It is argued that simply to ensure that girls have access to a physical education curriculum that reproduces and reinforces an essentially masculine world is not offering equal opportunity, even if such access were achievable. Available evidence about primary school physical education suggests that where resources are limited, be these physical or human, swim-ming tends to suffer both through lack of money for pool time or transport and through lack of expertise, dance is rarely taught unless there is particular exper-tise in the school, and gymnastics is also avoided by teachers who lack confidence and professional support. Leaman (1988) notes that the teachers he investigated expressed interest in introducing more work on dance and gymnastics into lessons but had little knowledge or understanding of how that might be achieved.

The result is the sort of games-dominated curriculum which has been much criticized at secondary level and which, while unsatisfactory for the school population as a whole, is particularly disadvantageous to girls in that they are denied access to the very activities which they can see as relevant to them as future adults. Swimming, dance or dance-related activities (including aerobics) are popular recreational activities for older girls and young women in the same way as soccer or cricket are popular with older boys and young men. Girls may not identify in the same way with team games, although they may enjoy their primary school experience of them. Implementation of the recommendations for National Curriculum Physical Education that six activity areas, gymnastics, dance, swimming, athletics, games and outdoor/adventurous activities, be included at Key Stages One and Two would go some way towards ensuring that the curriculum offered is of equal relevance to all pupils and would reflect existing good practice.

This is related to the next point which is that even within the limitations of a games curriculum, the social context of the games offered is problematic. Whether real equality of opportunity is provided by offering boys opportunities in high-prestige games such as football or cricket with obvious potential carry-over as an adult leisure activity, while the girls are offered at most arguably inferior games such as netball or rounders which they can expect to 'grow out of' at adolescence, is another matter. This point is also raised by Leaman (1988) who points out that in the local communities feeding the junior schools which he studied, the sort of competition which was prestigious almost exclusively took the form of boys' sports and games. Talbot makes the point that while boys' games and sports tend to lead into adult forms of the game, the same is rarely true of games and sports available to girls. Thus neither identical nor 'equivalent' activity offers equal opportunity in terms of relationship with adult or out-of-school physical activity.

This point can be further developed by pointing out that access to the curriculum is not synonymous with access to learning. Some pedagogical and behavioural impediments to equality will be examined later but for the moment the pupils' reception of the curriculum should be considered. Boys and girls arrive at school with very different pre-school experiences, both in terms of general behavioural expectations and in terms of access to physical activities. The tendency of fathers to encourage boys to play ball games while girls are socialized into more appropriate feminine and, by implication, less active pursuits is well documented. Boys and girls thus arrive in school with well-developed views of what constitutes appropriate activity for their own sex. This was well illustrated by some of the comments made by the 7-to-11-year-olds 'interviewed' by the author.[2] Some reveal stereotyped views.

Boys train for different things. They'd think, I'm not a girl, I'm not playing that game. (11-year-old girl)

Well the girls wouldn't want to play football as much as the boys would they? We don't want to play netball do we? (11-year-old boy)

I think girls are better at skipping and boys at football. (7-year-old boy)

Boys can't skip and they can't do much cartwheels and they can hardly do a gambol [forward roll]. (7-year-old girl)

Others show an awareness that social processes are at work.

> They say all the boys are better than the girls, but if the girls practised a lot they could be better. (11-year-old boy)

> Yes they [the girls] can play it [football] — I mean if they started at the time we started they could be just as good. (11-year-old boy)

> I suppose it depends — if you want to be as strong you can be as strong and if you don't, you don't. I don't want to be. (11-year-old girl)

It is interesting that the boys quoted above talk in terms of girls' access to the masculine world of football, while the girl's comment implies a rejection of access to this world while acknowledging that it exists as an option for her.

It should be noted of course that boys can be disadvantaged as well as girls where activities are sex-differentiated. Dance is the most obvious example of an activity seen as inappropriate for boys. The significance of the differential treatment generally meted out to boys and girls who fail to conform to gender stereotypes has not been given sufficient consideration by those demanding equality at primary level. Masculine behaviour is generally tolerated from girls at this age on the basis that they will eventually 'grow out of it'. The boy who is a cissy faces far more serious difficulties. While it is socially acceptable to be a tomboy it is demeaning to be effeminate.

Curriculum access therefore has to be considered both in terms of the extent to which curriculum experiences offered are gender-biased, and in terms of the way in which previous experience and upbringing will affect the way in which similar activities will be received and experienced by boys and girls. Curriculum content should be scrutinized in terms of its relevance both as a learning opportunity and as a foundation for lifetime activity for both girls and boys. The National Curriculum recommendation that games, gymnastics and dance should be emphasized, along with learning to swim, during the primary years offers the potential for a curriculum which does have equal relevance to both sexes. The range of games activities and skills proposed reinforce this with an emphasis on a range of games and games skills, as a foundation for later participation.

Extra-Curricular Opportunities

Activity opportunities outside the timetabled curriculum take the form of formally organized extra-curricular activity both at school and in the community and informal activity opportunities available at playtimes.

Since physical education post-holders tend to be male, and since more male than female teachers are involved in extra-curricular physical education in the primary school (Williams, 1980), there are likely to be far more opportunities for boys to take part in extra-curricular physical activities than there are for girls.

At the most basic level the school which can find someone to run a football team but cannot run a netball team as well is clearly failing the equal opportunity test. Leaman (1988) notes that extra-curricular physical education in the junior schools he investigated tended very often to take the form of provision by male teachers and male parents of football for boys, despite the questioning of the desirability of this by many teachers.

Differences are further reinforced by informal rituals such as playtime activity. Domination of playground space by boys has been well documented. For example, Askew and Ross (1988) observed that for the most part boys dominated the playground space and were active in physical pursuits in contrast to the girls who generally occupied the peripheral space and spent much time talking together. What seems to have been less well recognized is the direct relationship this may have with physical performance and attitude in physical education. It was clear from the comments made by pupils interviewed by the writer that playtime offered a significant opportunity to practise ball skills to the boys and that this opportunity was not available to the girls.

> We just walk around. They [the boys] take the whole field up playing football. (11-year-old girl)

> They should cut the playground in half so the girls can have one half and the boys the other. (10-year-old girl)

> Most of us play football. (11-year-old boy)

Where girls are involved in playground games, Roberts (1980) describes their ball games in terms of nimbleness and dexterity rarely matched by boys. However as Talbot (1985) points out, these are physical skills which are not, unlike boys' playtime activities, institutionalized into sports.

This unwitting reinforcement of differential treatment in terms of approved play activity is something which all primary schools need to consider. Girls are frequently denied access to the informal games played outside school by boys, because parents are less likely to allow young girls to be away from their direct supervision. Because boys tend to play ball games with their fathers and their friends and receive encouragement to do so they are likely to be more skilful and more knowledgeable about the game than their female peers. The reinforcement of this particular avenue of disadvantage during school playtime seems unfortunate, although the difficulties of remedying it should not be underestimated.

The pupils interviewed here also spoke of their experiences of watching sport on television, which in most cases served to further reinforce images of sport as a male domain.

> It's always football. It's boring. I usually go upstairs. (10-year-old girl)

> Sometimes I watch ice skating but when my dad comes in he puts the football on. (11-year-old girl)

The message from these children seems to be that teacher attitudes are critical. While not easy, it is not impossible to ensure that both boys and girls enjoy extra-curricular opportunities and that both sexes have access to playground space. It is, however, important to recognize the importance of involving parents and governors in the debate. If a successful football team is seen by these parties as a marketing tool for the school under Local Management of Schools where the budget is delegated to the head and the governors, then they will need to be convinced of the importance of offering girls similar opportunities and of the potential significance of extra-curricular provision for both sexes in marketing and promotion.

Pupils

It is now well established that, pre-puberty, there are no physiological differences to explain sex-related differences in physical performance. Indeed many girls will be bigger and stronger than boys at this stage. However the social mores and pressures which lead to different lifestyles, and which affect experience and attainment, operate from a very early age. Despite the lack of any physiological explanation, differences in fitness levels among 11/12-year-old boys and girls have been recorded by Eston *et al.* (1989). Wetton (1983) noted a higher incidence of chasing and vigorous activities among 4-year-old boys than among girls. Armstrong (1990) reports significant differences in activity levels, measured by heart rate monitoring over a one-week period, between boys and girls, with boys recording consistently higher levels than girls, although neither sex seems to undertake sufficient energetic exercise to protect against heart disease in later life.

Girls thus appear to be socialized into less active lifestyles and also appear to have fewer opportunities to acquire certain physical skills outside the school context. White and Coakley (1986) note that parents are much less likely to allow girls than boys to play unsupervised thereby denying the girls access to the sorts of informal ball games which are enjoyed by many young boys. The tendency of fathers to play games with sons and not with daughters is well known.

The primary school child's performance and apparent ability in physical education will thus be determined largely by previous experience, reinforced by continuing inequality in opportunity, for example, at playtime or in extra-curricular provision. Although performance differences between the sexes are often partly a result of differential teacher expectation, they are also a function of differences in previous pre-school and out-of-school experience.

It should be remembered that many aspects of classroom practice, over and above the actual lesson content, may affect the perceptions which girls and boys have of different curriculum activities. Requests for help with apparatus in PE from 'a couple of strong boys' have little logic in a class of pre-pubertal children where the strongest children in the class are quite likely to be female. Equally unsatisfactory in terms of the images of masculinity and femininity presented are organizational arrangements whereby some fourth-year boys have the task of putting out the large apparatus in the hall on designated days each week. Where boys and girls are ostensibly playing the same game, aggressive behaviour may be encouraged as appropriate for the boys while being condemned as unladylike if exhibited by the girls.

As has already been discussed, pupils arrive at school with fairly clearly formed ideas as to what constitutes legitimate activity and behaviour for the different sexes. Activities and procedures which challenge these ideas may not be well received, thus the pupils may well determine the success or failure of equal opportunity initiatives, unless the impact on them has been anticipated and strategies developed to overcome pupil resistance. Campbell and Brooker (1990) give many examples of blatantly sexist behaviour by primary school boys, which illustrate ways in which boys sought to control the educational agenda, including a boy feigning a sprained ankle rather than be beaten by a girl in an outdoor games lesson. In such situations the emphasis upon pupil decision-making which underpins many National Curriculum recommendations may have to be set against the consequences of giving pupils this responsibility, at least in the short term. For example, Campbell elected to choose all games teams herself in order to ensure that a balance of both gender and ability was achieved.

Other Curriculum Areas

The presentation of positive images should of course transcend subject boundaries. Lobban (1980) divided sex roles found in reading schemes into those prescribed for girls only, for boys only and for both sexes. There are no instances of sports activities being ascribed either to both sexes or to girls only, the nearest being skipping which is prescribed for girls. Under boys' activities or skills, in contrast, are found playing football, playing cricket, sailing boats and playing sports.

Mathematics workbooks have many examples of problems which use football as a context, e.g. finding the area of the field, using league scores for arithmetical calculations, but few which make equal use of examples from, for example, netball which would be equally capable of supplying a context for the application of mathematical concepts. Northam (1980), in an examination of mathematics texts notes that

> Maths in the junior school moves away from the domestic sphere and takes to the sportsfield, the battleground and worlds of business, space travel and machines where very few women are to be found.

Equal opportunity in physical education is a whole-curriculum issue and one which the primary school teacher, because of the class teacher system operating in the United Kingdom, is well placed to address.

Teachers

Teachers give messages to pupils by virtue of their position in the school, by providing role models and through their own attitudes and the teaching strategies which they employ.

The disproportionate number of men occupying senior positions, especially headteacher positions in primary schools, is well known. For example, statistics from 1985 show that while women constitute 78 per cent of the teaching force in primary schools, men hold a higher proportion (55 per cent) of headship (DES, 1987). The unequal opportunities offered to pupils in extra-curricular programmes as a result of the greater willingness of male teachers than female to become involved, has already been mentioned. There is no reason why male primary school teachers should not offer extra-curricular activity for girls as well as for boys or why parents should not help pupils of both sexes if they are interested in helping to provide additional opportunities through the auspices of the school. As important as the lack of opportunity for girls in a school where the only extra-curricular opportunity is football for the boys, is the picture given to the pupils of sporting activity as a male undertaking, run by men, for men and boys. This means that the suggestion above, while a useful first step, does not provide a long-term adequate answer to the issue of how to provide equal opportunities for both sexes.

Surveys of secondary school teachers suggest that there is support for equal opportunities in principle, but that teachers are disinclined to believe that schools actually favour boys and wary about interfering in the processes whereby girls make traditional career choices (Acker, 1988). While there is less information about primary school teachers, it seems reasonable to suspect that their attitudes will be similar. Skelton (1989b) suggests that primary initial teacher training students tend to respond to queries about gender by suggesting that it is a secondary school problem, connected with option choice or adolescent sexuality. Both she and Thompson (1989) contend that primary school teachers tend to be apathetic or hostile to suggestions that gender is a primary school issue. Moreover, Skelton (1989b) notes that students who could demonstrate an awareness of discriminatory practices and a willingness to confront sexist behaviour and attitudes while on campus, did not extend this into the school situation.

There are many issues involved in teaching mixed-sex classes which should concern the teacher committed to equal opportunity policies. A number of authors (Clarricoates, 1980; Shave, 1978; Delamont, 1983) have commented on the hostility found between male and female pupils. The educational consequences of this hostility, particularly the fact that, if forced to work in mixed groups, pupils frequently fail to carry out the tasks set, are considerable. The author's experience of teaching 10- and 11-year-old children supports this. If groups are to work successfully in mixed-sex settings, then the issues have to be confronted and time set aside with the specific aim of enabling and encouraging pupils to mix and work together. This aim has to have a high priority and there must be clearly planned strategies, if it is to be achieved. Games, such as sitting in groups of a specified number where each group must contain both boys and girls can be used. This may still lead to situations where a mixed sex-group of six sits in two separate subgroups to ensure that the boys and girls stay apart. An additional constraint such as sitting in a specified formation, for example a line or a circle, with identical distances between each member of the group may be needed. Discussion about the qualities needed in order to work together, such as cooperation, respect of others and so on will certainly be necessary to give a context against which future behaviour may be judged. Working together will not simply happen as a by-product of other activities.

Pollard (1988), in describing a student's problems with a movement lesson, highlights that boys' unwillingness to identify themselves with any activity interpreted as undermining their masculinity lay at the root of the difficulties encountered. Children's gender awareness can thus provoke particular problems of class control in physical education lessons. It is likely to be significantly more difficult to involve boys in activities perceived to be the province of girls than vice versa. Witness the earlier comment quoted which reveals one boy's view of netball. If this sounds rather pessimistic, it is worth mentioning that the author's experience of working with 11-year-old pupils with initial teacher education students in dance has been a positive one. The fact that the children are taught by both male and female students has undoubtedly helped to offer role models to all pupils. While this situation is clearly not available to everyone, there are many dance groups who can make inputs to schools in the form of practical workshops which offer the possibility of giving positive images to children of men and women who are involved in dance as a career.

Pollard also makes the point that teachers, like other people, will try to avoid situations in which they feel vulnerable. They will therefore adopt coping strategies in order to overcome perceived threats to their survival in the teaching situation. This is likely to include strategies which avoid disruptive behaviour by boys in a subject area where the teacher already tends to lack confidence, perhaps because of limitations of initial training, and which thereby accommodate the interests of the boys rather than those of the girls, whose behaviour is less likely to be seen as a threat, either to safety or to the teacher's self-esteem. Hence a game of football can provide a ready-made control structure but it also reinforces boys' gender expectations, especially where it involves, as in another example cited by Pollard, boys taking control of the majority of the available space by relegating the girls' game of rounders to one corner.

This all too common practice both reinforces social expectations and legitimizes, in the eyes of pupils, the equally prevalent playground practices commented on by the pupils here, whereby the lion's share of the space is occupied by boys playing football, leaving girls the periphery of playground space. Not only are the girls marginalized in terms of the space they are given, but in the case of the rounders lesson they are being offered a patently less prestigious game, one which has little if any carry-over into adult sport or recreation and one which is arguably less demanding both physically and in terms of skill.

All the examples given above illustrate the fact that asking teachers to take initiatives which will challenge gender stereotypes and sexist behaviours both implies criticism of their current practices and involves exposing them to situations which threaten their control and thus their confidence. Both of these characteristics of equal opportunity initiatives by their very nature are therefore likely to be resisted by teachers. Sensitivity in introducing proposals for change is therefore of paramount importance.

Shortcomings in initial training in physical education and in subsequent teaching in the primary school have been well documented (Williams, 1982; Leaman, 1988) and have a number of consequences related to equal opportunity. Leaman draws attention to a point made by others previously, namely that junior school teachers' commitment to child-centred teaching is rarely expressed in their physical education teaching. This is mirrored at secondary level in comments made by Evans *et al.* (1987), about the inhibiting effect the use of non-specialist physical education staff has on curriculum innovation. The use of non-specialist staff, in the view of one teacher, ensured an overproduction and overdependence on the use of competitive games which the helper teacher could simply supervise. Because there is activity and a semblance of order, and because the game itself is a useful control mechanism there will be great reluctance to dispense with it. Many primary school teachers find themselves in the same position as the 'helper' teacher. They may well have embarked upon their initial training course with very negative attitudes towards physical education. This is particulary true of many female initial training students. Time allocated to physical education in initial training is already severely restricted and the need to change attitudes and convince students that the subject is both valuable and enjoyable further restricts what can be achieved.

The relevance of this to the gender issue is that the tendency is to resort to lesson content and structures which reinforce rather than challenge social expectations regarding gender. This will mean competitive games rather than gymnastics or dance, and single-sex groupings within these games. For the teachers in Leaman's study, physical education teaching was constrained by what the teachers felt that they could do rather than what they would have liked to do.

The control problem is of course not only related to curriculum content and lesson organization. Boys who have been socialized into expecting the lion's share of attention also create difficulties for the teacher attempting to give equal attention to both sexes. In the hall using large apparatus, safety has to be taken into consideration. For the non-specialist teacher, older junior pupils who enjoy the physical challenge of using higher equipment or trying to see whether they can get further or higher are often a threat. Again they are often boys rather than girls who have, by the age of 11, all too often learned that physical challenges are not perceived as appropriate feminine pastimes.

A further avenue of teacher influence is in the role model which the teacher may provide. Again this is unlikely to benefit girls. The fact that girls tend to have less favourable attitudes towards their own physical education experience (Williams, 1988) and that adult participation is far lower among women than among men, means that female primary school teachers are less likely than their male counterparts to be active participants and also less likely to have favourable memories of school physical education.

Parental and Community Influences

Reference has already been made to Leaman's investigations which revealed a pattern of extra-curricular provision provided largely by male parents or male teachers exclusively for boys despite resistance to this by other teachers. Moreover, prestigious competition in the local community feeding the schools investigated took the form of almost exclusively boys' sports and games. The point is repeated here because of its relevance in the context of Local Management of Schools (LMS). The power of school governors and thereby of members of the local community has increased significantly with the introduction of budget delegation following the 1988 Education Act. Equal opportunity issues need governing body support. The second implication of LMS is in the pressure on schools to market themselves to prospective clients, that is, parents and thus to emphasize and encourage activities such as male competitive sport which is seen as valued by parents, even if teachers do not share such values.

It should also be noted that, while this paper has focused upon aspects of equal opportunity related to gender, race is of equal importance. For some cultural groups physical education has a very low priority and may be seen as undesirable for girls. In this situation there is a direct conflict between race and gender interests. This conflict will be difficult to resolve and absolutely impossible without the involvement and support of influential figures from the community.

There are many examples of good practice involving bringing parents into schools, for example to help to hear children read. An extension of such practice to involve physical activities could be highly beneficial in changing parental attitudes and educating them, where necessary about the benefits of a structured physical education programme for all pupils.

Conclusion

This paper has highlighted some of the issues facing the teacher related to identifiable influences on practice. Burton (1986) cites two major factors affecting girls' achievement in mathematics. These are:

(a) teachers, whose awareness of and sensitivity to the effects of their behaviour on pupils appears to be crucial; and,
(b) parents whose expectations of daughters and sons may differ markedly.

If we assume that these factors are of equal significance to physical education, and there seems to be no reason to suppose that the situation in physical education differs from that in maths, then there are important implications for the primary school teacher. We can see that, important as teachers' attitudes are, their impact will be limited unless the school makes conscious efforts to involve parents and community and to convince them of the relevance of such issues to their children. This is particularly significant at present given the increased responsibility of governors, including parent governors under Local Management of Schools. The teacher thus needs support from a range of agencies including parents and community if practice is to change.

There are of course ways forward. Because the primary school teacher has responsibility for the whole curriculum for one class, a coherent policy on equal opportunity is much more easily attainable across the curriculum than in secondary school. The primary school teacher can make significant progress towards offering equal opportunity by ensuring that girls have access to the same curriculum as boys and by considering curriculum content in terms of gender bias in order to facilitate equal access to learning. This implies far more than simply treating everyone in the same way and demands a whole-school, whole-curriculum approach. It would be in itself a significant achievement.

Notes

1   Children up to the age of 11 are taught in mixed-sex classes in mixed-sex schools within the maintained sector. Some schools cater for pupils aged 5–11, while others are subdivided into infant schools (5-to-7-year-olds) and junior schools (8-to-11-year-olds). A few local education authorities have adopted alternative age structures, for example, systems where pupils transfer from a first school to a middle school at age 9 and then to a high school at age 13.
2   This small-scale study consisted of tape-recorded 'interviews' with groups of 7-, 10- and 11-year-old pupils from two different primary schools. Pupils were recorded talking in groups of three children of the same age, in some cases in mixed-sex, in others, in single-sex groups. They were asked to talk about their

views of different physical activities, of whether boys or girls were better at some physical activities, of the sorts of activity which they would like to continue as adults, of their playtime activity and of TV viewing patterns.

References

ACKER, S. (1988) 'Teachers, Gender and Resistance', *British Journal of Sociology of Education*, **9**, 3.

ARMSTRONG, N. (1990) 'Children's Physical Activity Patterns: The Implications for Physical Education', in ARMSTRONG, N. (Ed.) *New Directions In Physical Education, Vol. 1*, Champaign, IL, Human Kinetics.

ASKEW, S. and ROSS, C. (1988) *Boys Don't Cry: Boys and Sexism in Education*, Milton Keynes, Open University Press.

BURTON, L. (Ed.) (1986) *Girls Into Maths Can Go*, London, Holt, Rinehart and Winston.

CAMPBELL, A. and BROOKER, N. (1990) 'Tom, Dick and/or Harriet: Some Interventionist Strategies against Boys' Sexist Behaviour', in TUTCHELL, E. (Ed.) *Dolls and Dungarees*, Milton Keynes, Open University Press.

CLARRICOATES, K. (1980) 'The Importance of Being Ernest ... Emma ... Tom ... Jane', in DEEM, R. (Ed.) *Schooling for Women's Work*, London, RKP.

DELAMONT, S. (1983) 'The Conservative School? Sex Roles at Home, at Work and at School', in WALKER, S. and BARTON, L. (Eds) *Gender, Class and Education*, Lewes, Falmer Press.

DEPARTMENT OF EDUCATION AND SCIENCE (1987) *Statistics of Education: Teachers in Service in England and Wales*, 1985, London, DES.

DEPARTMENT OF EDUCATION AND SCIENCE (1991) *Physical Education for Ages 5 to 16*, Proposals of the Secretary of State for Education and Science and the Secretary of State for Wales, London, HMSO.

ESTON, R., THRELFALL, T. and BRODIE, D. (1989) 'The Effects of Gender on Health Related Fitness Measures in Preadolescent Children', in *Physical Education Association Research Supplement*, No. 5.

EVANS, J. (1986) *Physical Education, Sport and Schooling*, Lewes, Falmer Press.

EVANS, J. (1988) *Teachers, Teaching and Control in Physical Eduation*, Lewes, Falmer Press.

EVANS, J., DUNCAN, M., LOPEZ, S. and EVANS, M. (1987) 'Some Thoughts on the Political and Pedagogical Implications of Mixed Sex Grouping', *British Educational Research Journal*, **13**, 1.

LEAMAN, O. (1984) *Sit on the Sidelines and Watch the Girls Play*, London, Schools Council/Longmans.

LEAMAN, O. (1988) 'Competition, Cooperation and Control', in EVANS, J. (Ed.) *Teachers, Teaching and Control in Physical Education*, Lewes, Falmer Press.

LOBBAN, G. (1980) 'Sex Roles in Reading Schemes', in REEDY, S. and WOODHEAD, M. (Eds) *Family, Work and Education*, London, Hodder and Stoughton.

MAY, N. and RUDDUCK, J. (1983) *Sex Stereotyping and the Early Years of Schooling*, Norwich, Centre for Applied Research in Education, University of East Anglia.

NORTHAM, J. (1986) 'Girls and Boys in Primary Maths Books', in BURTON, L. (Ed.) *Girls Into Maths Can Go*, London, Holt, Rinehart and Winston.

PHYSICAL EDUCATION WORKING GROUP (1991) *National Curriculum Interim Report*, London, DES.

POLLARD, A. (1988) 'Physical Education, Competition and Control in Primary Education', in EVANS, J. (Ed.) *Teachers, Teaching and Control in Physical Education*, Lewes, Falmer Press.

ROBERTS, A. (1980) *Out To Play: The Middle Years of Childhood*, Aberdeen University Press.

SCRATON, S. (1985) 'Images of Femininity and the Teaching of Girls' Physical Education', in EVANS, J. (Ed.) *Physical Education, Sport and Schooling*, Lewes, Falmer Press.

SHAVE, S. (1978) 'Ten Ways to Counter Sexism in a Junior School', *Spare Rib*, 75.

SKELTON, C. (Ed.) (1989a) *Whatever Happens to Little Women? Gender and Primary Schooling*, Milton Keynes, Open University Press.

SKELTON, C. (1989b) 'And So the Wheel Turns ... Gender and Initial Teacher Education, in SKELTON, C. (Ed.) *Whatever Happens to Little Women?*, Milton Keynes, Open University Press.

SKELTON, C. and HANSON, J. (1989) 'Gender and Initial Teacher Education', in ACKER, S. (Ed.) *Teachers, Gender and Careers*, London, Falmer Press.

TALBOT, M. (1985) 'Women and Sport: A Consideration of Gender Contradiction with Implications for Women's Involvement in Physical Activity', in *Physical Education, Recreation and Sport: Lifelong Participation*, Milton-under-Wychwood, International Association of Physical Education and Sport for Girls and Women.

THOMPSON, B. (1989) 'Teacher Attitudes: Complacency and Conflict', in SKELTON, C. *Whatever Happens to Little Women?*, Milton Keynes, Open University Press.

TUTCHELL, E. (Ed.) (1990) *Dolls and Dungarees: Gender Issues in the Primary Curriculum*, Milton Keynes, Open University Press.

VICK, H. (1990) 'The Use of Drama in an Anti-Sexist Classroom', in TUTCHELL, E. (Ed.) *Dolls and Dungarees*, Milton Keynes, Open University Press.

WETTON, P. (1983) 'Some Observations of Interest in Locomotor and Gross Motor Activities in the Nursery School', in *Physical Education Review*, 6, 2.

WHITE, A. and COAKLEY, J. (1986) *Making Decisions*, London, Sports Council.

WILLIAMS, E.A. (1980) 'Intention Versus Transaction — The Junior School Physical Education Curriculum', *Physical Education Review*, 3, 2.

WILLIAMS, E.A. (1982) 'Physical Education in the Junior School', *Education 3–13*, 10, 1.

WILLIAMS, E.A. (1988) 'Physical Activity Patterns among Adolescents — Some Curriculum Implications', Physical Education Review, 11, 1.

Chapter 9

Equality, Coeducation and Physical Education in Secondary Schooling

Sheila Scraton

Introduction

> When I first came here the PE was separate. It was not too good but then we tried mixed games and that was worse. I used to have to lock myself in the gym with these bad boys — fifth formers — because lads have a different set of standards. If it's going to be mixed its got to be from the start but I wouldn't want it. (PE teacher)[1]

Throughout the 1980s debates concerning coeducational PE were constantly on the agendas of both academics and practitioners concerned with the teaching of PE in schools (*BJPE*, 1987; Evans *et al.*, 1985; Graydon *et al.*, 1985). These debates were most pronounced in secondary schooling which has had a long tradition of single-sex teaching in PE which is recognized, increasingly, as an anomaly in otherwise coeducational school settings. In primary schools girls and boys are more frequently taught together for PE, although there is often a separation of the sexes for team games. It has been noted that this separation can result in the reproduction of ideologies of femininity and masculinity both overtly and covertly (Leaman, 1984; Pollard, 1988). In the 1990s there does not appear to be consensus about mixed-sex grouping being the norm for the curriculum 5–16. However, there does appear to have been a shift both in teacher education and in secondary school PE towards coeducational PE teaching, bringing it more in line with the experiences at primary level. With the advent of a National Curriculum in our schools (ERA 1988), the future teaching of PE (content, grouping, method) is likely to become both more standardized throughout the schools of England and Wales and more accountable to the Department for Education (DEF), governors and parents. Issues relating to both content and grouping will be central for all those involved in PE.

This chapter concentrates on the implications of a move towards coeducational PE for teachers and pupils, particularly in terms of how coeducation relates to equality and equal opportunities. The proposal put forward for the National Curriculum Physical Education for ages 5 to 16 states in its rationale:

> The physical education curriculum should enable all children to benefit.
> There should be *no barriers to access or opportunity based on* race, *sex*, culture or ability. (DES, 1991, p. 5; emphases added)

How these recommendations come to be interpreted in practice is crucial and relates directly to the debates concerning coeducational PE. This chapter addresses the complex issues thrown up by the equation of equal opportunities with coeducational PE and argues that we must not lose sight of some of the significant debates raised throughout the 1980s in relation to this area, particularly the contribution of critical feminist educationalists in problematizing the relationship between access, equality and mixed-sex groupings. The following discussion focuses on secondary schooling, not because the debates are any less significant for the primary age range, but because it is in secondary schools that I have had my teaching experience and it is the relationship between gender,[2] equal opportunities and secondary school PE which has been the centre of my research over the past decade including a major piece of qualitative research conducted in secondary schools in a large city education authority (Scraton, 1989, 1992).

The Rationale for Coeducational PE

The philosophy of equal educational opportunity, which was given formal recognition in the 1944 Education Act, was applied to opportunities afforded to girls and boys following the Sex Discrimination Act (1975). Coeducation became the norm in most state schools in order to ensure that girls and boys received the 'same' educational opportunities. As the Equal Opportunities Commission (EOC) stated:

> if true equality of opportunity is to be achieved for girls/boys then it is essential that during the schooling process boys and girls receive the same educational access. . . . (EOC, 1982, p. 1)

However, sport and physical activities were exempted from the legislation and PE retained its separate-sex grouping, with little critical consideration, until the early 1980s.

There have been no national developments in mixed-sex grouping for PE. Most initiatives originally developed on an ad hoc basis usually emerging from the enthusiasm and innovation of individual staff or for administrative convenience particularly in the top years of secondary schooling (Evans *et al.*, 1985). However, it was the recognition that PE was fast becoming the last bastion of single-sex teaching in many coeducational schools which led researchers such as Rosen (1987, p. 152) to comment:

> The case for mixed PE hardly needs to be stated. . . . The guiding principle in schools should be that pupils must never be segregated by sex (or 'race', colour or any other innate character) unless there are absolutely compelling reasons for so doing.

An equal opportunity rationale for coeducational PE developed which argued that mixed-sex grouping is a progressive development towards the fulfilment of a complete equal opportunities policy offering equal access across all areas of the curriculum (Browne *et al.*, 1985; O'Brien, 1987; Rosen, 1987). However, the equation of coeducation with equal opportunities is by no means straightforward or simplistic as research in other curriculum areas throughout the 1980s has highlighted (Mahony, 1985; Spender, 1982; Stanworth, 1981). The National Curriculum proposal (DES, 1991) appears to recognize that mixed-sex grouping is not an automatic route to equality between the sexes. It states:

> Choices of mixed sex or single sex groupings in physical education should be made for *educational reasons* and *after considering the conditions under which they might be most successful and appropriate* (DES, 1991, p. 57; emphases added)

This statement in the National Curriculum proposal highlights two major issues, both of which are of crucial significance in relation to coeducational PE. First, it states that there must be an educational rationale for any move towards mixed-sex grouping. However, the reality in many instances is that mixed-sex grouping is more to do with economic necessity and a rationalization of diminishing resources than because of a committed educational philosophy. Evans *et al.* (1985) in their study of mixed PE initiatives in three schools found that:

> The strategic response of mixed sex groupings at Marstons and Cherry Tree were the expression of the liberal, even radical, motivations of innovatory teachers. At Greenwood on the other hand, it was largely contingent upon conditions of severe financial or staffing constraint. (Evans *et al.*, 1985, p. 9)

My own research supports this recognition of the ad hoc basis of much of the educational 'innovation' in this area with the majority of mixed-sex grouping observed occurring in the upper years of the secondary school when 'options' were introduced. The reasons given for mixed grouping here were more to do with organizational convenience than a thought-through educational rationale. Attendance at PE was often optional at this stage and in order to offer a reasonable range of activities it was deemed more convenient to teach the boys and girls together.

The second issue raised by the National Curriculum proposals relates to their recognition that consideration must be given to the 'conditions' under which the choice of grouping for PE is made. The PE teachers in my research expressed a genuine concern about the potential problems that they identified in a move to coeducational PE. Some of these concerns and conditions have been raised in research studies relating to mixed PE (Evans *et al.*, 1985; Graydon *et al.*, 1985; Turvey and Laws, 1988), and by feminist educationalists concerned with the effect of coeducation in general on girls' experiences and opportunities in education (Deem, 1984; Mahony, 1985; Spender, 1982). It is these concerns that must be considered in detail before we can argue that coeducational PE is about the creation of equal opportunities for all pupils in secondary schools.

PE Subcultures — The Historical Legacies

The PE adviser interviewed for my research identified clear differences between women's and men's perceptions of PE. She commented:

I feel passionately that women's perception of physical education is at least as relevant as men's. We have quite different emphases — not just the activities we teach but also our whole ethos.

This view was reiterated by the majority of heads of department interviewed. Furthermore, the periods of observation confirmed that girls' PE remains separated from boys' PE not only spatially but also by perceived philosophy. Although the research study made no formal contact with the male PE departments, the girls' PE departments visited were considered by the female teachers to be engaged in separate and distinct areas of work. Evans *et al.* (1985) utilize the concept of subject subculture developed more fully by Ball (1987) in order to understand the differences between female and male PE. This analysis recognizes two distinct subcultures within the one subject area with male and female teachers having 'quite different conceptions of how and what to teach' (Evans *et al.*, 1985, p. 6). The concern shown by the female PE teachers in my research was that implementing organizational change would not result necessarily in a unified approach to teaching. The gender-specific subcultures of PE teachers would, as recognised by Evans *et al.*,

> tamper only with the surface of educational practice, leaving paradigmatic and pedagogic views and practices largely untouched. . . . (Evans *et al.*, 1985, p. 6)

This was highlighted in Lopez (1985) when she argued that the problem of attempting to combine two distinct subcultures becomes more intense when mixed PE initiatives are the result of organizational convenience and are resource-led rather than emerging from a shared philosophy and commitment.

Historically, girls' and boys' PE has developed separately with gender-specific activities and emphases (Hargreaves, 1979; Scraton, 1992). Fletcher (1984) traces the development of separate training for female PE teachers and identifies a distinct tradition for female PE, which whilst encouraging the development of confident, strong women also was underpinned by powerful gender expectations. The National Curriculum proposals recognize this legacy of single-sex teaching and training:

> The legacy of single sex teaching and teacher education on physical education, especially for secondary specialist teachers, means that there are still many teachers of physical education who were trained in single sex courses. The single sex tradition had meant that British physical education overall has greater breadth and balance than in many other communities. However, the *different ideologies and content of programmes of the former single sex institutions, and commonly for men and women in mixed courses, continue to affect not only teachers' attitudes but also the ability of both men and women teachers to teach across a balanced programme of physical activities.* (DES, 1991, p. 57, emphasis added)

The important issue is that underpinning girls' PE and the training of female PE teachers are dominant gender ideologies concerning expectations of women's physicality, their sexuality and their role as mothers and carers (Scraton, 1992). Current research suggests that equivalent gender expectations about dominant masculinities can be traced in the development of male PE and continue to be central to contemporary male PE teaching. If this is the case then it is not only historical traditions of separate activities and ethos that must be considered in any move to mixed-sex grouping but also the significance of *gender* for both staff and pupils when girls and boys are taught together.

Centralizing Gender and Sexuality

The National Curriculum proposals correctly recognize that in PE, although grouping is often by sex 'teaching and curriculum content have been differentiated according to gender' (DES, 1991, p. 57). In mixed-sex situations the significance of gender becomes intensified. Research into classroom interaction in mixed settings indicates that on the whole boys have far more contact with the teacher, receive more attention, talk more in class and are far more 'visible' (Spender, 1982; Stanworth, 1981). The evidence suggests that mixed PE is little different. Mixed PE generates problems concerning levels of participation and degrees of confidence. In principle there might be equal participation and certainly equal 'opportunity' to participate. In practice, however, girls are less involved. My observations of mixed lessons showed this to be the case. Observation of mixed basketball, cricket and soccer showed that in most situations the girls took a peripheral role. In basketball and soccer the girls spent the majority of time running up and down the pitch whilst the boys passed to each other! In several cricket games observed the boys started each lesson in the key central roles — batting, bowling, wicket-keeping and close fielding. Although these altered throughout the session the girls always had to wait for their opportunities. In most situations boys dominated the action with girls involved only occasionally as active participants. It is interesting to note that many of the mixed activities that take place in PE are the activities that have been traditionally male activities, for example, soccer, basketball, cricket. As Leaman (1984) notes, equal access in PE often means equal access for all pupils to male PE! As many of the male games played in schools have far greater cultural status and value, there is a danger that the traditional female games of netball and hockey may slowly die out if mixed PE were to become male PE offered to all children. The National Curriculum proposals recognise this potential problem and advise:

> Schools will need to include equal opportunities considerations among the criteria by which they select the content of physical education programmes, so that all children have the opportunity to experience a range of physical activities within both National Curriculum physical education and extra-curricular sport. (DES, 1991, p. 58)

In relation to pupil-pupil interaction in mixed settings this remains single-sex unless there is positive intervention by the teacher. When asked to work in pairs or small groups, the children organized themselves into single-sex groupings in observed situations of dance, games and gymnastics. In practice mixed-sex organization rarely means coeducational teaching and/or learning. This is not a surprising result given that Graydon *et al.* (1985) found clear gender-stereotyped attitudes from both boys and girls about the opposite sex. Both girls and boys considered that, in general, girls are less skilled and physically able than boys, thus boys are unwilling to partner girls and girls are less confident when working with boys. This is not solely an issue relating to attitudes. As the teachers in my research recognized, by the time children arrive at secondary school, physical skills have been considerably influenced by previous socialization and junior teaching. Many of the teachers noted that girls at 11, on average, do not start from an equal position to boys both in terms of physical skill and hand-eye coordination. In many cases girls have not been encouraged to develop ball skills and have been literally taught to 'throw like a girl' (Young, 1980, 1991). This does not mean that girls are incapable biologically of achieving similar skill levels but that mixed grouping without appropriate curriculum, pedagogical and attitudinal change, given the available evidence, would seem unlikely to assist in this development. As Deem (1984, p. 9) recognizes:

> the sexes do not stand equal on admission to secondary school, and offering both girls and boys the same opportunities and facilities cannot lead to equality of opportunity, still less equality of outcome.

Teachers in my research considered that the girls that they taught would not be enthusiastic about coeducational PE. The following quotes were typical:

> I am sure the girls themselves would not want to do it.

> The girls wouldn't be happy about it. They are terribly lacking in confidence and when the boys are around they're worse.

> It could be mixed but our girls have enough of the boys in class — our girls are quite happy to be on their own. How many times do you hear the girls ask to play with the boys? Never! They'll play out together at lunch and after school but girls don't want to be with the boys.

> It's the middle years really when they don't mix and want to be on their own with their own peer group. Girls don't want mixed games. They'd also be too embarrassed.

These comments made by women PE teachers raise a number of significant questions. The main reasons for believing that the girls would not want mixed PE relate to girls' embarrassment and lack of confidence during adolescence. Yet this is related directly to the behaviour and dominance of boys in mixed settings. Although these are teachers' perceptions rather than the girls' responses, the evidence from qualitative research into mixed-sex grouping in schools supports this concern (Mahony, 1985; Spender, 1982; Stanworth, 1981). Arnot (1984) succinctly sums up the major findings:

> We get glimpses of the extent of boys' disruption of the classroom: their noisiness, their sexual harassment of girls, their demands for attention and their need of disciplining and their attitudes to girls as the silent or 'faceless' bunch. (Arnot, 1984, p. 17)

Graydon *et al.* (1985) identify boys' control over the mixed setting as crucial:

> Generally we found that girls were tolerated by boys in the lesson as long as their contribution was kept within certain bounds and the boys didn't lose control.... Another issue in ball game situations is the girls' involvement in the game. Many complained that the boys wouldn't pass the ball to them in basketball and soccer. The boys freely admitted this to be the case. (Graydon *et al.*, 1985, p. 6)

Overall it would appear that in many mixed grouping situations boys control the learning environment. This can be achieved by physical control in specific activities or by verbal control. In most of the mixed lessons observed the boys tended to verbally dominate and order the girls about. If teachers challenged this, it simply resulted in the boys taking up a disproportionate amount of the teachers' attention. In these situations PE is reinforcing gender power relations with boys reproducing their dominant role and girls learning their subordination.

The serious problem of sexual harassment (verbal, emotional and physical) potentially is intensified when dealing with activities centred on the physical. There is growing evidence that girls and young women have to cope with sexual harassment throughout their daily lives, including during mixed settings in schools (Jones, 1985; Lees, 1986). Teachers confirm that girls and young women face similar problems in mixed PE. The annual mixed swimming galas and athletics meetings were identified as main foci of harassment:

> Oh the girls have to put up with remarks from the lads. That's why they all wear tee shirts over their costumes while they wait for their race.

> You can see the boys eyeing up the girls and comparing them. The girls are obviously aware of this — some of them just refuse to swim in the galas. I think at a certain age they just prefer to opt out.

In these situations girls run the gauntlet of persistent comment on their physical appearance and sexuality. The response is either to attempt to disguise their bodies by dressing in loose clothing or to opt out of the activity. During the sensitive years of adolescence when young women are physically and sexually developing, the ideology of woman-as-object becomes dominant in their lives (Coward, 1984; Lenskyj, 1986). Their bodies become the focus of comment, stares, admiration and/or criticism. This does not deny the problems faced by boys during adolescence with regard to their physique and sexuality, but while boys are judged by 'achievement' with regard to masculinity, girls are judged 'against' masculinity. Boys' masculinity is judged against other boys whereas girls are judged by boys in relation to 'desirable femininity'. They not only get defined as 'objects' but as the 'other', their reference point being men and men's attitudes, opinions and responses (De Beauvoir, 1972). As De Beauvoir states in her early and important writing:

> *Her* body is not perceived as the radiation of a subjective personality, but as a thing, sunk deeply into its own immanence; it is not for such a body to have reference to the rest of the world, it must not be the

promise of things other than itself: it must end the desire it arouses. (De Beauvoir, 1972, p. 178)

Given societal expectations of 'attractive femininity' or 'emphasised femininity' (Connell, 1987), girls are expected to respond to the stereotype in order to achieve male gratification. Their femininity is literally 'up for grabs' (Jones, 1985). There is a danger that mixed grouping in PE may provide a forum for an intensification of sexual harassment and abuse. The National Curriculum proposals (DES, 1991) do recognize the significance of sexuality in relation to equal opportunities:

> The physical nature of physical education, and the emergence of sexuality during Key Stages 2, 3 and 4, provide both problems and opportunities for physical education, in challenging body images, sex stereotypes and other perspectives which limit the choices and achievements of children with disabilities and of both girls and boys. (DES, 1991, p. 58)

While the recognition of sexuality as significant is to be welcomed, the previous discussion suggests that this area is complex and for young women is of particular significance in mixed settings. The proposal that 'a broad and balanced programme of physical education, sensitively delivered, can help to extend boys' restricted perceptions of masculinity and masculine behaviour' (DES, 1991, p. 58), is a positive ideal but there is a long way to go before this could be achieved through coeducation. It must be acknowledged that dominant heterosexual masculinity subordinates women, and other subordinate masculinities, through its structural location in patriarchal power relations, and is not simply attitudinal. Sport and PE have been shown to be an important site for the reproduction of hegemonic masculinity (Messner and Sabo, 1990; Scraton, 1989, 1992). Gender relations incorporating a subordinate femininity and a dominant masculinity are structurally located in PE teaching. However the emphasis on extending 'boys' perceptions of masculinity and masculine behaviour' (DES, 1991, p. 58) is a move in the right direction. The onus must shift to include male PE — teachers and pupils — if equal opportunities for girls are to be achieved. There needs to be a fundamental questioning about masculinity and acceptable masculine behaviour before coeducational PE can be seen as a positive progression towards equal opportunities. However teaching girls and boys together does highlight the significance of gender, and coeducational PE could force teachers and pupils to address the issue. As my research and the current work of Ian Day shows[3], the reproduction of dominant gender ideologies is fundamental to single-sex PE. The problem is ensuring that the reproduction of masculinity in a mixed setting does not oppress and subordinate young women to an even greater extent, but encourages young women to be assertive and allows them to develop through PE in a way that challenges patriarchal relations. It is vital that these questions are addressed and issues concerning gender and sexuality are considered before any move towards mixed-sex grouping in PE is instigated.

The notion of 'sensitive delivery' of PE, recommended in the National Curriculum proposals, is problematic in relation to gender stereotypes and teacher attitudes. My own research identified clear assumptions held by women teachers in relation to girls and boys physical capabilities:

Boys are stronger, taller, faster. Its just a physical difference.

Boys give girls more daring, adventure, excitement and of course girls can give grace and 'finish' to those things they are naturally better at.

Boys have a lot of 'natural' ability 'cos they do things on their own. Girls are more shy and timid. Most girls don't have a lot of natural ability.

Boys are more aggressive definitely — it's natural and shows in their physical abilities.

I support the fact that there are *clear* natural differences between boys and girls — most definitely.

The interviews indicate that there remain powerful attitudes, in the thinking of men and women, about boys' and girls' physical abilities and capabilities. Interestingly, although the interviews were conducted with female teachers who taught predominantly girls in single-sex groups, they responded by talking initially about boys and defined girls in relation to their perceptions of boys' abilities! Once more girls/young women become 'the other'. Furthermore, the stereotypes of boys were ones of dominance and physical 'prowess':

daring, exciting, rowdy, enthusiastic, strong, tall, fast, spunky etc.

Girls were stereotyped into quieter, subordinate femininity:

poise, subtlety, grace, finish, finesse, control.

Interestingly, the women teachers had far fewer definitions of female physicality than male physicality with many of their perceptions of girls' physical ability centring on appearance and presentation.

There has been little research on male PE teachers and gender, although a current study by Ian Day suggests in its preliminary analysis that male PE teachers not only hold similar gendered attitudes towards girls' and boys' physical abilities but, most importantly, male teachers and PE teaching continue to reinforce and reproduce dominant masculinities including ideologies of male sexuality, physicality, homophobia and mysogyny. Together with the conclusions of my research (Scraton, 1989), this would suggest that teachers continue to reproduce gender stereotypes which ultimately leads to a reproduction of gender power relations. These issues must be addressed and challenged before we can ensure that girls and boys would receive equal treatment and opportunities in mixed PE and that 'sensitive delivery' would be the norm in relation to gender and sexuality. Furthermore research by Flintoff (1990; 1991)[4] shows that gender and equal opportunities remain a problem in teacher education. If we are to produce teachers more sensitive to issues of gender and sexuality, who could work in a coeducational context and challenge gender stereotypes and thus offer an equal experience to girls and boys, then these debates must have a more central profile in teacher education. The advice given in the National Curriculum proposal in relation to the achievement of equal opportunities is most pertinent if coeducation is to be a part of equal opportunity teaching in PE:

> This will require, both in initial and in-service training, a critical review of prevailing practice, rigorous and continuous appraisal and *often a willingness to question long held beliefs and prejudices*. (DES, 1991, p. 15, emphasis added)

Staffing Issues

Gender does not affect only the teaching of PE and how it is received by the pupils. The staffing of PE, particularly if PE becomes coeducational, is an issue demanding attention. The PE adviser in my research noted her concern:

> One of my big worries is that there are already more men teaching PE than women for the 11 to 15 year olds. The problem I can see is that if it goes mixed then there will be fewer women teaching especially with the fact that a women's career structure is often interrupted. I can see men moving in if we aren't careful.

These serious reservations concerning women's jobs and status are justifiable and relate directly to equal opportunities for female staff. Statistics on the position of women teachers relating to pay, status and promotion point to considerable inequalities. In schools where there are separate PE departments the evidence shows that in the majority of cases the male is the overall head of department (Evans and Williams, 1988). Where there are separate heads of department for girls' and boys' PE, it is common for the head of boys' PE to be on a higher salary scale than the girls' head of department (Scraton, 1989). Thus, while women PE teachers hold status within their own female department, the male PE head of department had higher status in the overall context of the school which translates into power concerning decisions about PE. Given the evidence from coeducation in other subjects, there is a justifiable concern that a move towards mixed PE could have a negative effect on the career prospects of women PE staff and result in a potential loss of control and power for women in a joint PE department. The concern about the future career prospects of women teachers is exacerbated by the current economic constraints and cuts in educational funding. Women are more likely to take a career break than male teachers (Evans and Williams, 1988). Over one-third of the women heads of department in the research local authority had taken a break from teaching for childbirth or other family responsibilities. Evans and Williams (1988) found that the ideology of 'familism', the view that the family is where women should find their self-fulfilment, remains prevalent in attitudes to women PE teachers who are mothers. This ideology is taken up by both men and women as is evidenced by this comment from a PE adviser:

> After all women have far greater family commitments than men. Women used to take time out to have a family but now they stay with

maternity leave. Maternity leave is the biggest load of rubbish. I know that it might be old fashioned but I think no household should have both parents in full-time jobs. It is good for a child to have their mother round the house. I can see that it is good for women with small children to have part-time jobs. In fact that is very important for the women and the children but it is wrong to have full-time work. It is only storing problems for society.

Given the contemporary consolidation of ideologies of motherhood and domesticity and the substantial structural constraints on women, any move towards mixed PE must be treated with caution, particularly with respect to equal opportunities in status and career progression for women teachers.

Coeducation: A Move Towards Equal Opportunities?

Clearly, the simple equation of coeducation with equal opportunities is problematic. Equality of access in any aspect of schooling, including PE, does not result automatically in equality of outcome and practice. This is true particularly when the rationale for grouping is resource-led rather than the result of a clearly thought-through educational rationale. Girls and boys may have access to the same activities but their experiences will be very different. These differences may be a result of different physical abilities, class inequalities, racism and 'race' stereotyping and/or gender and sexuality. I have concentrated on gender and sexuality because coeducation is seen by many as a policy fundamentally concerned with equal opportunities between the sexes. However, mixed-sex grouping in PE does not necessarily create a less gendered structure and teaching context. By placing girls in a situation where ideologies of masculinity (especially those concerning physicality and heterosexuality) are reinforced and reproduced, they are in danger of losing out not only in terms of teacher attention, use of space, and inclusion in activities, but also by being the focus of sexual abuse and harassment — verbal and physical. Both girls and boys can learn in this context that the relations between the sexes are power relations with boys taking up the dominant role and girls being expected to retain a subordinate position. However, this is rather a deterministic and pessimistic view of PE given the evidence that single-sex PE also reproduces gender inequalities (Scraton, 1989). It does suggest that any moves towards coeducation must be cautious, with an awareness that coeducational settings can express and reproduce gender inequalities. However, this does *not* suggest a simple retention of the status quo of separate provision as this too is an arena for the reproduction of ideologies of femininity and masculinity. Furthermore, it does not mean that all girls and boys accept gender relations based on a 'hegemonic masculinity' and 'emphasised femininity' (Connell, 1987). Young women and young men do challenge the system and resist the determination of their position. But what occurs in PE does not happen in isolation divorced from the social, political and economic context in which it resides. PE is part of an educational system within a capitalist patriarchy based on inequalities of gender, 'race' and class. PE is also concerned fundamentally with the 'physical' which is of central significance to gender and sexuality. Therefore what happens in PE in schools is crucial to the reproduction of, or the resistance to, gender inequalities. The major consideration must be how PE can contribute to the challenge to existing inequalities and whether mixed or single-sex grouping is the most positive move towards equality and equal opportunities. I would suggest that the following are some of the 'conditions' (DES, 1991) that must be considered in relation to coeducational PE:

- **Teacher training** — gender and sexuality must be placed high on the agenda of initial teacher education and in-service education. Many of the staff in schools were trained years ago, often in single-sex establishments. As Deem (1986) emphasizes in relation to policy implementation, teachers must first admit that there is a problem before they will question their practice. There are powerful gender ideologies embedded in the traditions and teaching of girls' and boys' PE (Scraton, 1989). Although most teacher education courses are now coeducational, gender, sexuality and the broader area of equal opportunities remains marginalized in the training of future teachers (Flintoff, 1990). This needs to be altered if teachers in coeducational teaching contexts are to be sensitive to gender and gender relations in their 'classrooms'.

- **Stereotyping** — stereotypes of masculinity and femininity must be challenged through an awareness of language (Wright, 1990, 1991), the use of role models in demonstrations and direct intervention by teachers when pupils overtly stereotype. Gender stereotyping is a constant aspect of PE highlighted in my research by a comment from a female teacher to two girls who had opted to do a mixed soccer lesson:

    Football, you must be mad — you should have been born a lad.

    Even when equal access is available, stereotyping results in pupils having to run the gauntlet of comment from both teachers and pupils.

- **Sexuality** — sexuality and especially developing sexuality must be recognized. There needs to be an awareness that PE, as a subject dealing with the physical, provides the potential forum for sexual harassment and abuse. This must be recognized and clear procedures developed for dealing with reported incidences. In relation to this, young women must be given effective choice concerning clothes worn for PE. The National Curriculum proposals recognise PE dress as an equal opportunities issue:

    Children should be dressed appropriately for physical education activities. Considerations of safety, comfort and freedom of movement should override conventions associated with being female or male. (DES, 1991, p. 58)

    The earlier discussion argued that from puberty girls come to experience their bodies as 'public property' — defined, compared, criticized and often, degraded. Within PE, especially given the contexts of movement, girls need to have effective control over the 'presentation' of their physicality in dress. There needs to be a greater sensitivity to and awareness of the pressures on young women regarding body shape and appearance.

As argued previously, this is more acute for girls and young women in a mixed-sex setting. Young women's bodies are on display during physical activity and insensitivity in relation to comment or dress can contribute to the alienation of young women with regard to their bodies.

- **Masculinity** — the masculinity of both male teachers and pupils is a potential problem in mixed settings. 'Ideal' masculinity is concerned with power and control (Brittan, 1989) and in many contexts becomes the power *over* or the control *over* girls and women. If PE moves to a coeducational grouping from its traditional single-sex base, it becomes another context in which dominant masculinity can be articulated and played out. This must be challenged if equality for all staff and pupils is to be achieved. However, it must also be recognized that mixed PE can be problematic for some boys as well. Boys who do not fit into the dominant ideology of heterosexual masculinity are potentially marginalized and harassed. Their 'alternative' masculinities are highly exposed in coeducational contexts.

- **Staffing** — all staff changes and promotions should be monitored in the future. As has been noted, female staff may lose out in career opportunities or PE could become PE taught predominantly by male PE staff. Equal access must not become girls and boys playing men's games taught by male staff. Equally male and female staff must not be stereotyped so that the women teach only the gymnastics and dance and the men concentrate on team games and sport.

It is clear that there is no straightforward answer as to whether coeducation equals equality. If girls are not to lose out in any move towards coeducation then the issues raised above must be noted. In the short term girls require both the space and the time to develop their potential in PE. This will not be achieved by an uncritical move into coeducation. In some instances it may mean the retention of some single-sex opportunities on the PE programme. It will mean the retention of some female-only space. PE is in a fortunate position to learn from the experiences of other areas of study which have been coeducational for some time. In coeducational schools the evidence shows that boys and men dominate space — in all social situations — both verbally and physically (Spender, 1982; Young, 1980). In both single-sex and coeducational schools the main female-only space is in the toilets, changing rooms, cloakrooms. If PE becomes a mixed activity it would be positive if the girls and young women could retain their changing rooms not only for their official lessons but also as an area where they could chat, make plans or simply 'have a laugh'. Informal female-only space is crucial if girls are to develop confidence, realize their interests and control their social environment. They will need some space free from the dominance of boys and young men.

It is crucial that the politics of gender and sexuality are understood by the staff involved in mixed PE. With sensitive, understanding teaching, which may require positive intervention and leadership, mixed-sex grouping can provide the forum for increased pupil awareness of gender issues and the challenge to existing gender inequalities and expectations. If single-sex teaching and learning remains the long-term goal then the future is bleak for a comprehensive overthrow of gender inequalities in a mixed-sex social world. Yet there needs to be a short-term strategy to ensure that girls receive opportunities, time, space and understanding to redress the traditional base of gender imbalance. Equality, coeducation and PE are an ultimate goal although the road to its achievement is long and will require both short-term reforms within the school and longer-term structural change within the social, political and economic system.

Notes

1   See Scraton, S. *Shaping Up To Womanhood: A Study of the Relationship between Gender and Girls' Physical Education in a City-Based Local Education Authority*, 1989 PhD thesis, The Open University. This was a major piece of qualitative research involving interviews with all heads of girls' PE and other key personnel and extensive observation in four case study schools.
2   While recognizing the complex debates about the definitions of 'sex' and 'gender', for the purposes of this article the commonly used definition of gender as the social construction of female and male (femininity and masculinity) is used.
3   Ian Day is currently researching into 'Masculinity and PE' at Leeds Metropolitan University. He has undertaken extensive qualitative research in two case study schools including interviews with teachers, equal opportunity coordinators, boys across different age ranges and observation over a period of time with each of the PE departments.
4   See the chapter by Anne Flintoff in this volume. She is currently writing her doctoral thesis in the area of teachers education, gender and equal opportunities.

References

ARNOT, M. (1984) 'A Feminist Perspective on the Relationship between Family Life and School Life', *Boston University Journal of Education*, 166, 1 March, pp. 5–24.

BALL, S. (1987) *The Micro-Politics of the School*, London and New York, Methuen.

BEAUVOIR, S. DE (1972) *The Second Sex*, Harmondsworth, Penguin.

BRITISH JOURNAL OF PHYSICAL EDUCATION (1987) **18**, 5.

BRITTAN, A. (1989) *Masculinity and Power*, Oxford, Blackwell.

BROWNE, P., MATZEN, L. and WHYLD, J. (1983) 'Physical Education', in WHYLD, J. (Ed.), *Sexism in the Secondary Curriculum*, Harper and Row.

CONNELL, R.W. (1987) *Gender and Power*, Polity Press.

COWARD, R. (1984) *Female Desire: Women's Sexuality Today*, London, Paladin.

DEEM, R. (Ed.) (1984) *Co-Education Reconsidered*, Milton Keynes, Open University Press.

DEEM, R, (1986) 'Bringing Gender Equality into Schools', in WALKER, S. and BARTON, L. (Eds) *Changing Policies, Changing Teachers*, Milton Keynes, Open University Press.

DEPARTMENT OF EDUCATION AND SCIENCE (1991) *Physical Education for Ages 5 to 16*, DES Welsh Office.

EQUAL OPPORTUNITIES COMMISSION (1985) *Women and Men in Britain: A Statistical Profile*, EOC.

EVANS, J. and WILLIAMS, T. (1988) 'Moving Up and Getting Out: The Classed and Gendered Career Opportunities of Physical Education Teachers', in TEMPLIN, T. and SCHEMP, P. (Eds) *Socialisation into Physical Education*, Uckfield, Benchmark.

EVANS, J. *et al.* (1985) 'Some Thoughts on the Political and Pedagogic Implications of Mixed Sex Groupings in the Physical Education Programme', Paper presented to the Sociology of PE Conference, Manchester University.

FLETCHER, S. (1984) *Women First: The Female Tradition in Physical Education 1880– 1980*, Athlone Press.

FLINTOFF, A. (1990) 'PE, Equal Opportunities and the National Curriculum', *PE Review*, **13**, 2.

FLINTOFF, A. (1991) 'Dance, Masculinity and Teacher Education', *British Journal of Physical Education*, **22**, 4.

GRAYDON, J., GILROY, S. and WEBB, S. (1985) 'Mixed Physical Education in the Secondary School — An Evaluation', Paper presented to International Council for Health, PE and Recreation. World Congress.

HARGREAVES, J. (1979) 'Playing Like Gentlemen While Behaving Like Ladies', MA Thesis, University of London.

JONES, C. (1985) 'Sexual Tyranny: Male Violence in a Mixed Secondary School', in WEINER, G. (Ed.) *Just a Bunch of Girls*, Milton Keynes, Open University Press.

LEAMAN, O. (1984) *Sit on the Sidelines and Watch the Boys Play: Sex Discrimination in Physical Education*, Harlow, Longman.

LEES, S. (1986) *Losing Out*, Hutchinson.

LENSKYJ, H. (1986) *Out of Bounds: Women, Sport and Sexuality*, Toronto, Women's Press.

LOPEZ, S. (1985) 'An Innovation in Mixed Gender PE — With Special Reference To Whether This Form Of Grouping Can Undermine Gender Stereotypical Attitudes towards PE', Unpublished paper.

MAHONY, P. (1985) *Schools for the Boys*, London, Hutchinson.

MESSNER, M. and SABO, D. (1990) *Sport, Men and the Gender Order: Critical Feminist Perspectives*, Illinois, Human Kinetics.

O'BRIEN, D. (1987) 'Equal Opportunities in Physical Education', *British Journal of Physical Education*, **17**, 4, pp. 152–3.

POLLARD, A. (1988) 'Physical Education, Competition and Control in Primary Education', in EVANS, J. (Ed.) *Teachers, Teaching and Control in Physical Education*, London, Falmer Press.

ROSEN, D. (1987) 'An Outsider's View', *British Journal of Physical Education*, **17**, 4, p. 152.

SCRATON, S. (1989) Shaping Upto Womanhood: A Study of the Relationship between Gender and Girls' Physical Education in a City-based Local Education Authority, Open University. PhD. Thesis.

SCRATON, S. (1992) *Shaping Up To Womanhood: Gender and Girls' Physical Education*, Milton Keynes, Open University Press.

SPENDER, D. (1982) *Invisible Women*, Writers and Readers Cooperative.

STANWORTH, M. (1981) *Gender and Schooling*, Hutchinson.

TURVEY, J. and LAWS, C. (1988) 'Are Girls Losing Out? The Effects of Mixed-Sex Grouping on Girls' Performance in Physical Education', *British Journal of Physical Education*, **19**, Nov/Dec, p. 253.

WRIGHT, J.E. (1990) 'Remember those Skirts! The Construction of Gender in Physical Education', in SCRATON, S. *Gender and Physical Education*, Deakin University Press, Australia.

WRIGHT, J.E. (1991) *The Contribution of Teacher Talk to the Production and Reproduction of Gendered Subjectivity in Physical Education*, PhD thesis, University of Wollongong, Australia.

YOUNG, I. (1980) 'Throwing Like a Girl', *Human Studies, 3.*

YOUNG, I. (1991) *Throwing Like a Girl and Other Essays in Feminist Philosophy and Social Theory*, Indiana University Press.

Chapter 10

Equal Opportunities: Race and Gender in Physical Education: A Case Study*

Bob Carroll and Graeme Hollinshead

Equal Opportunities — Gender and Race in Education

It appears that gender and sexist issues, and race and racist issues have developed separately and have their different histories based in the context of their development (Gerwitz, 1991). However, their central concerns over inequalities in society and equality of opportunity would suggest they have similarities in approach to policies. The inevitable interrelationship between sex and race is bound to have repercussions at the general policy and practical levels which cannot be ignored. The research presented in this chapter supports this, and the need to combine the two at the practitioner's level.

The gender issue has led to feminist stances which are now well documented (Arnot, 1985; Weiner, 1985, 1990; ILEA, 1986; Delamont, 1990). There appear to be two main approaches, 'equal opportunities' and 'antisexist' (Weiner, 1990; Gerwitz, 1991). The former tends to advocate change within the system, such as greater opportunity of access and of representation, and changing stereotypical images, whilst the 'antisexist' stance advocates changing the unequal power relations in society between men and women. Thus it can be seen that the former has led to policies of accessibility and entitlement, whilst the latter has led to policies of empowerment, which, it is claimed, deal with the causes, not the symptoms, of injustice and inequality. In practice many of the policies of the two approaches come together and differences are blurred (Weiner, 1990).

There is a parallel with the issue of race. The concern with inequalities has led to two main stances in the antiracist movement. Again, the first can be classed as equal opportunities, and is concerned with issues of representation, access, entitlement, whilst the second is a stronger antiracist stance seeking positive action and empowerment to tackle white domination (Gerwitz, 1991). Again the distinction between the two 'groups' in pursuit of their policies is blurred and often comes together in the working situation as a practical solution, (see Troyna and Carrington, 1990).

* This is a shortened version of a paper entitled 'Ethnicity and Conflict in Physical Education' which is to appear in *British Educational Research Journal*, **19**, 1 (1993). We are grateful for permission from the Editor to reproduce extracts from that paper in this book.

The relationship between race and gender and the ensuing dilemmas and contradictions caused by accepting both equal opportunities and antisexist policies at the same time as accepting cultural norms of different ethnic/religious groups (e.g. Muslim) which are in conflict with those policies, are debated by Walkling and Brannigan (1987), Troyna and Carrington (1987) and Haw (1991). Problems, seem to revolve around the question of whether individual freedom and the rights of the individual are to gain precedence over the culture of the group, and there are clearly no easy solutions because it depends from which perspective one looks at the dilemma. It is all too easy to adopt a purely moral stance, ignore the political context, and take a Eurocentric view, which would be condemned by writers such as Brah and Minhas (1985) and Raval (1989), and by certain groups. The dilemma of adhering to multicultural and antiracist policies at the same time as antisexist and equal opportunities policies is raised by this research later.

Brah and Minhas (1985) illustrate how race, gender and class inequalities are produced through the education system and society. They argue that the structural context is often neglected in studies which reveal a 'cultural clash' (between ethnic minority culture and ethnic majority culture), and inter-generational conflicts (within Asian families). These latter studies usually locate the problem *within* the ethnic minority group culture and ignore inequalities and racism in society and therefore do not help an understanding of the conflict and its origins (Brah and Minhas, 1985). They stress the importance of rejecting a Eurocentric mode of thinking in order to initiate and operate equal opportunity policies.

Despite the Swann Report (DES, 1985) the government has failed to produce education policies for ethnic minorities and has left local education authorities to produce their own. Many LEAs have left it to the schools themselves to produce and provide more detailed guidelines. Thus racism has usually been seen as only a problem for those schools and LEAs who have a large ethnic minority group composition. It has not been seen as applicable to all-white schools. As far as multicultural or antiracist education is concerned it has not been an 'education for all' as Swann suggested.

The Context of Physical Education

In all the volume of literature on 'race' and racism in education there is little mention of physical education. The Swann Report does mention that particular conflicts can occur in PE because of pupils' religious beliefs (DES, 1985). Some LEAs have developed guidelines for PE teachers based on observations and problems met by teachers, but they lacked, as did Swann, the basis of detailed and systematic research (e.g. Coventry LEA, 1980; Rotherham MBC, 1986). Mullard suggested that these responses are merely assimilation policies in disguise to ensure harmony, and do not meet the real needs of the groups (Mullard, 1982). As Bayliss points out the emphasis is always on the ethnic group having a 'problem' and not on the concerns of racism and the curriculum (Bayliss, 1989).

There has been very little research into PE and ethnic minority groups. The type of work done by Ikulayo (1983) although welcome in some respects, adds little to our understanding of ethnic minority groups' perceptions, and it neglects the issue of racism, and may even help to perpetuate stereotypes. The work of Ikulayo (1983), Carrington and Wood (1983) and Cashmore (1982) point to the colonization of school teams by 'West Indians' and the channelling of 'West Indian' talent into sport and sporting careers. Although such effects may occur through equal opportunities and antiracist policies which are aimed at helping individual children, they often serve to perpetuate stereotypes based on myths of 'the black sportsman', depress academic attainment and narrow academic routes to success, and are a form of racism which does a disservice to the black community (Cashmore, 1982; Hargreaves, 1986). The teacher helps to reproduce, albeit unwittingly, the existing structures and inequalities in society (see Bourdieu, 1974).

The research most closely related to the study reported in this chapter was published whilst this research was in progress (Carrington and Williams, 1988). Carrington and Williams's work does show that South Asian Muslim children face difficulties in physical education, and that ethnicity heightens gender differences with girls facing more problems than boys. According to their study these problems are due to religious and cultural traditions which assign particular roles to men and women, and contain strict moral codes controlling behaviour and conduct, thereby restricting access to PE and leisure opportunities. Whether cultural tradition opens up other avenues is not discussed. Carrington and Williams show that, without taking into consideration these cultural and religious traditions and codes, equality of opportunity cannot be a realistic policy. These views are repeated in Carrington, Chivers and Williams's related research (Carrington et al., 1987), which is heavily criticized by Raval (1989). The basis of Raval's criticisms is that Carrington's model is based on a Eurocentric framework and definitions, fails to grasp the leisure experience of Asian women and fails to address the racist practice in British society. Carrington et al.'s explanations tend to locate the issues as problems for the teacher or child, and in gender relations in Muslim society. They have thus failed to locate the racist practices and the real conflicts which pupils and women face.

Bayliss (1989) highlights the use of stereotypes and stereotypical assumptions in PE and sport which shows how racism can unconsciously and unintentionally ensue. These are also often supported by so-called 'scientific' evidence to give them credibility (Bayliss, 1989). PE and sport is usually regarded as a sphere of activity where equality of opportunity and racial harmony exist, and the evidence is provided by the number of black children who do well in sport. Furthermore sport and PE is regarded as an integrative force (Mangan, 1973; Hargreaves, 1986). Consequently PE teachers would be reluctant to admit and believe that racist practices do occur and that sport and PE can be a divisive force. Fleming (1991) reveals the prevalence of racism amongst pupils in a case study in one school and community, and this is unlikely to be an isolated example, judging by reports of racism more generally by the media. However, there is no research in England to show to what extent racist practices do exist or what they actually are; and there is none which takes racist practices as the core, and examines policies in action. The neglect of PE is exemplified by Foster's case study of a school which looks at most subjects but ignores physical education completely (Foster, 1990). There is no reason to believe that physical education policies and departments have more success, in combating racism than other spheres of education.

A Case Study

Borin High School, a comprehensive school in Northern England, has seen a large increase in its intake of ethnic minority pupils. The vast majority of these pupils are of Pakistani and Bangladeshi descent, and represented 11 per cent and 37 per cent respectively of the total school population in 1989. Most of these pupils have parents who come from rural and hilly areas of Pakistan and Bangladesh, according to school sources and a Local Authority publication (LA, 1990). Many of the children were born in this country, but some were born in Bangladesh or Pakistan. All of them are Muslims, but not all practise their religion in exactly the same way or to the same level of devoutness.

Traditionally, in lessons at Borin High School, boys and girls have been, and still are, taught separately. Basically both groups follow a common core programme for years one to three with more variety and choice occurring in the fourth and fifth years. Different activities are taught to boys and girls as in most schools in this country, for example, soccer, rugby, basketball, cricket to boys, and netball, hockey, dance, rounders to girls. Both boys' and girls' includes gymnastics, athletics, volleyball, badminton and swimming. All pupils are expected to take part and to wear the school kit. For boys this is white vest and shorts for indoors, long-sleeved blue jersey for outdoor work, with appropriate footwear. Girls wear a plain white blouse and navy blue skirt for indoor and outdoor games, knickers for indoor gymnastics. The policy now allows tracksuit trousers or a shalwar to be worn by the girls. Pupils are expected to shower after a lesson for hygiene reasons.

The research was carried out within the social action perspective through observation and interviews with groups of boy and girl pupils and the PE staff. For further details see Carroll and Hollinshead (1993) and Hollinshead (1989).

The Problem Areas Defined

According to both teachers and pupils, taking part in games and physical activities caused some problems, which led to conflicts between pupils and their parents and the Asian community, between pupils and the staff of the school, and intra-role conflict within the pupils themselves as they tried to please two parties and two cultures. These problems were classed under the headings of PE kit, showers, Ramadan and extra-curricular activities.

PE kit

As one girl explained, it is not the activity or the exercise itself which is the problem but how they are dressed for that activity. This means keeping their bodies, arms and legs completely covered.

> you should really keep yourself fit. The only thing is that you have to cover your body. As long as you are in purdah you can do anything, as long as you are covered from top to bottom. (Naweeda)

Before the school recently changed its policy to allow girls to wear tracksuit trousers or a shalwar, the problem was particularly acute for the girls. For the devout Muslim there is a real feeling of guilt and shame at exposing their bodies and legs, which had not been fully appreciated by the teachers.

> 'At first, I didn't enjoy games because I had to take my shalwar off. I felt ashamed 'cause in junior school I was allowed to wear it or else wear a tracksuit when I did Physical Education, but suddenly, I had come to a new school and I couldn't say anything because I was the youngest and I actually had to wear a very short skirt and not wear anything to cover my legs. And that's what I really felt bad about but couldn't say anything.' (Morien)
> 'I felt the same.' (Naweeda)
> '... and when I came in and kept my shalwar on and went to the lesson I had to be forced back to change and take it off,' said another girl.

So not only were the pupils ashamed at their exposure and their breaking a religious code, they had to suffer the public humiliation of being forced to carry out the teachers' rule. The young children, having come to the school from junior school, felt helpless.

The problem is not totally confined to the girls. As these devout Muslim boys explain:

> '... only one thing put me off from games and that's shorts.'
> 'Yes me as well.'
> 'If we wear clothes we should wear them above the ankle and you shouldn't see the knee.'
> 'Our parents, they don't like it ... they don't like the idea of buying them [shorts].'
> '... because its against the religion.'
> 'In Islam it says that boys should get covered up as well.'

The problem is accentuated by having games lessons outside on fields which are accessible to public viewing. The pupils can be seen by the members of the community and the word will be passed on to parents and religious leaders, and the pupils are very much aware of this, for example, as one boy explains,

> Like even very religious people sometimes pass by the field and they see us playing with just shorts on and they talk with other people saying that it's against our religion.

The teachers confirmed this and said they had seen 'religious-looking gentlemen making notes' and the next day there had been complaints about the pupils' dress sent to the school.

The Muslim boys often put pressure on the girls to conform to the religious code, not only by their own beliefs about girls' conduct and dress, but by telling their parents. As one boy told us,

I don't feel that's right [referring to skirts] 'cause in Islam it says that you have got to cover the bottom parts of your legs, especially girls and most Muslim families apply that rule at home and they wish to apply it at school. Personally, my sister she does not wear a shalwar underneath and I have seen her once or twice and I have complained to my dad.

The less devout Muslim child may well decide to wear the school kit for various reasons — to be like the English child, to please the teacher — but is then, often, pressured by the parents or religious leaders to conform to Islamic practice.

Showers

It is not the shower itself which causes the problem, but communal showers, where pupils have to undress and shower with other children. The problem of exposing the body crops up at the end of every lesson when the teacher insists on the pupils having a shower. As Humera says,

> we are not supposed to show our bodies or expose it, even to another woman.

Although the problem is more acute with the girls, again, it is not entirely confined to them, as Hadiq states:

> according to our religion, you have got to cover your private parts.

Javid supports this:

> In Islam, it says you are not supposed to have a shower with other people. You are supposed to have it on your own.

Again, the devout Muslims' feelings are so strong, it is more than embarrassment, they feel a real sense of guilt and shame, as suggested by the following girls:

> We have this sense of shame. Really I don't think it is right. (Atia)

> We feel guilty because we are exposing ourselves in front of other girls. (Humera)

In addition to the shame and guilt felt within themselves, they incur the wrath of their parents if and when they get to know. Atia explained that her parents "don't think it is right" and because of this admitted,

> we don't really tell our parents what was happening.

Noreen stated:

> My mum was furious.

The teachers felt strongly that children should shower for hygiene reasons, particularly with the pupil population which they had to deal with over the years. It was part of their health education. Both male and female teachers said that white children did not always like the showers and felt embarrassed at first as they had not been used to them in the junior school. However, they felt this embarrassment was usually overcome after a short while. The teachers saw the same embarrassment in the Muslim children as in the white children and failed to see the deep feelings of shame and guilt.

Many of the children tried to avoid showers. As Javid says:

> usually when we do have a shower, we just stick our heads in, get out quickly and get changed, so it looks as if we've had a shower.

Some children go even further:

> You tried to avoid it — not come to school on those days — you know, miss school for one day just for ten minutes. (Zakia)

So, not only are some children put off PE lessons, some are losing other parts of their education. If this occurred on a regular basis then clearly the effects would be serious for a child, especially if they were already experiencing some difficulties elsewhere in the curriculum.

Ramadan

One of the features of the Islamic religion is the period of Ramadan which lasts for approximately one month. Almost all the Muslim families insist that their children fast from sunrise to sunset during this period, which means the youngsters must go without food and water for the whole of the school day. The problem is that a child can become very tired and strenuous physical exercise can cause discomfort and be distressing. As one boy explained,

> Really, when Ramadan comes it's quite a long day for us. We just eat once in the night and once when the sun has gone down and really . . . we have to come to school and doing games is a hard thing when we are fasting and we got really tired.

Ramadan has fallen during the summer term for the last few years, and athletics has been taught during this period. Athletics often demands intense physical activity for short periods of time so can be particularly distressing and tiring. Whilst the feeling of both pupils and teachers is that they should be allowed to do less strenuous activities or allowed to make less effort, this clearly has not been the practice in the past in many lessons. The pupils stated that the teachers have insisted on trying their best and making a full effort. This has resulted in the teachers antagonizing the pupils and either causing some conflict, or some pupils playing truant. One talented youngster, Abdul, related an incident which illustrates the pupils' dilemma and annoyance:

We want to do well in athletics but it's difficult. Like last year Ramadan came when I was doing running — sprinting with one of the teachers — and he kept saying, 'you can do better than that, why don't you?' And I kept telling him that I was fasting and that I could not run that fast, but he said that I had to try hard 'cause I was going to be in Sports day. So I thought, 'I'm in trouble now', so I kept going slowly but he kept saying, 'go on, go on', and I got mad about it but he wouldn't stop.

Swimming is a particular problem during Ramadan because water must not enter the mouth. As Naweeda says,

Yes, swimming is another major problem during Ramadan because we get the water in our mouth which is against the fast.

The teachers commented on the strange sight of the children struggling to swim whilst at the same time trying to keep their heads well above the water to avoid getting it in their mouths.

The dilemma for the pupils is a very real and agonizing one. Very often children are tempted to break their fast, particularly on games days, but then this will incur the anger of their parents if they find out. If they do not make much effort — in order to conserve energy or because they feel tired — the teachers can get annoyed. Naweeda and Sipia reveal the dilemma.

If you miss the fast the day you have games then your mum starts moaning. We want to do well sometimes so that we can join in Sports day but we hold back and don't give of our best. (Naweeda)

You feel guilty really because the teachers have difficulty understanding it but if we break the fast we feel guilty towards our parents. (Sipia)

Even where the pupils admit the teacher is more tolerant and says 'don't work as hard', as one boy said the pupils

still sweat and become thirsty and would like a drink of water.

Although the girls agreed with this, the women teachers were not aware of this as a problem. This is probably because, as Sipia says,

you don't really say anything. You tend to quietly get on with the lessons.

To avoid the temptation of breaking their fast and to avoid the conflicts with the teachers, some parents have encouraged their children to miss school on games days. Morian admitted:

My parents tell me not to go to school if I have games.

So once again children's education can be interrupted if this line of action is taken.

Extra-curricular activities

Staying behind after normal school hours to take part in extra-curricular activities proved an area of potential conflict for the Muslim child. Again it was more of a problem for the girls than the boys because the girls had more restrictions placed on how they spent their time. However, several boys said that until they had read the Koran they had to attend the Mosque, and missing a day could mean extra work at the Mosque the next day. Many of the boys would prefer to stay for games rather than attend the Mosque but parental pressure prevents them. As one boy explains,

> yes, we wanted to play games but then we are forced by our parents to go to the Mosque because we have to learn our religion. It's the only way we can pass it forward.

Presumably the Muslim community is aware of the attraction and lure of other activities to the boys as it is now organizing a recreation programme for the youngsters at the Mosque, so that they play pool, table tennis and badminton after attending religious instruction and prayers.

The girls have considerable restrictions placed upon them by their parents, and very few of the girls interviewed have taken part in extra-curricular activities, even though they would like to stay after school to take part in them. Their parents are particularly concerned about their daughters coming home from school or anywhere else by themselves, and about the development of social relationships with boys, both of which will damage their girls' reputation and their marriage prospects. Extra-curricular physical activities and leisure interests more generally are seen by parents as potential sources of danger in these respects. Therefore they are given a low priority and not seen as necessary for a girl to become involved in.

These views are illustrated by a number of instances recalled by the girls. Naweeda explains:

> Staying after school would be a problem 'cause it's not usual for a Muslim girl to go out on her own. She would have to go with her parents or with a brother and sister. When you go out on your own then people start talking about you and you get a bad name. It's a cultural thing. And it's against your religion 'cause you shouldn't go somewhere where you don't really need to.

The pressure from the community on parents and their children is very strong, as Amrean shows:

> the family are sort of branded for the rest of their lives. People would keep saying 'do you remember when your daughter did this', so parents are afraid of letting their daughters do what they want.

The Muslim Asian girls are often envious of their English friends' and Muslim Asian boys' freedom and independence and this is a potential source of conflict with their families. They often feel frustrated, angry and rebellious, as Zakia and Sameena show:

> Sometimes we rebel against it because my brothers are always going out, doing this and that, and I rebel against it sometimes. (Zakia)

> Sometimes, we feel angry when you see your friends going out and you want to join them but you can't because your parents' restrictions on you. (Sameena)

In spite of their frustration and anger, the comments of some of the girls revealed that parental expectations of their present teenage and future roles had rubbed off, as suggested by Sameena,

> it was not right for Asian girls to play about,

and again by Humera,

> you are grown up and you've got other work to do rather than sports. When I was small, then I was allowed to do things, now I've grown up you have got housework to do.

The boys have learnt the appropriate behaviour too. As Foyzur says,

> Like a girl at the end of school who comes home, she can't go out 'cause its strictly against their religion. When she gets married it's up to her husband if she can go out and she should be covered up.

> These comments show the context, value and relative unimportance of school sport and leisure activities in the role of Muslim women, and the relation of male and female roles. They raise questions of parental wishes and rights and children's wishes and rights, of the relationship of parents and children, of women's rights and male domination. These are commented upon in the discussion below.

PE Teachers' Values Versus Religious and Ethnic Cultural Values

What sort of physical education is it that, albeit unwittingly, produces forms of racism and practices which we have seen above, attacks the cultural and religious values of the child, causes the pupils severe conflicts, puts them off physical activity, and even encourages them to 'wag' PE lessons and school?

The PE teachers at Borin High School believed strongly in many of the traditional values of PE, such as the need to wear school and team kits, the need to shower after exercise for health and hygiene reasons, the provision of extra-curricular activities, the leading of an active lifestyle, making maximum effort, and development of physical potential.

However, there is a clash with Muslim beliefs and Pakistani and Bangladeshi cultural values when the teachers express their values in the traditional way, which they had done for many years before the arrival of ethnic minority groups. When the Bangladeshi and Pakistani children first arrived at the school they were expected to fit into the PE teachers' values and 'ways of doing things'. This was a simple integrationist policy based on a 'cultural deficit' model, which brought internal strife, pupil embarrassment, anger and hostility, and, as the female teachers admitted, it eventually brought open conflict between teachers and pupils.

As the numbers of Muslim children have increased, the PE teachers have felt it necessary to alter their policies, by, for example, allowing the wearing of tracksuit trousers or shalwars during the lesson, but this has resulted in some anomalies, such as one teacher following what can be described as a policy of positive discrimination towards the Muslims by not allowing other children to wear trousers in the sports hall whilst another teacher did allow this. The introduction of less strenuous activities such as table tennis during Ramadan is an example of teachers' modifications to their programme. However, in spite of these changes, the Muslim children still feel the teachers do not understand the importance of the Muslim religion in their lives or the problems that the PE policies have presented them. This was echoed many times by most of the children during the research and is borne out by their comments in relation to changing, showering and making an effort during Ramadan. If the children in this research are presented as 'victims', this is because this is how they themselves see the situation.

The changes made by the PE staff appear superficial, although they do represent a shift in the willingness of the staff to see the pupils' point of view. However, the practices themselves are still basically integrationist. In PE, the school had failed to develop satisfactory multicultural or antiracist policies. We have commented on the failure of the integrationist and multicultural policies in education more generally, so it is not surprising to have to acknowledge the failure of the policies in PE so far. What the research shows is the need to examine actual practices in the working situation rather than general policy statements and take cognizance of the views of the recipients of those policies, the pupils themselves. This is what the teachers at Borin High School are now doing.

The teachers themselves showed different levels of understanding of the importance of religion and cultural values and the impact of their PE policies upon the children. The teachers did not appreciate that the children felt shame and guilt and not just shyness and embarrassment over changing and showers. They failed to appreciate the conflicts caused through PE programmes and extra-curricular activities, and they underestimated the depth of feeling in all areas of concern.

Certainly, the teachers would now admit to not knowing enough about Muslim beliefs and values and the children's perceptions of the teachers' practices, and the need to know more. This is a matter of further education for the teachers. That is probably the easy bit. It will be somewhat harder for the teachers to formulate policies and practices which remain honest to their traditional values and to equality of opportunity and yet reconcile them within truly multicultural and antiracist programmes. It will be even harder to challenge those values and entrenched attitudes. The teachers cannot be divorced from their biography any more than the children can. Dealing with the policy and issues in the educationist context will be relatively straightforward; dealing with them in the moral context will be more tricky; dealing with them in the political context will be even more difficult and perhaps well-nigh impossible for the teacher (see Troyna and Williams, 1986, for a discussion of these different

contexts). This can be exemplified by the two issues of racist practices and policies of equality of opportunity.

The children themselves thought the teachers were being racist and grossly
unfair, in effect though not by intention, whilst the majority of the teachers did
not believe they were being racist. The teachers thought they were maintaining
values and being fair to all groups. They also believed that 'giving way' to
religious beliefs, although antiracist, was positive discrimination which would be
seen as grossly unfair to and by white pupils and would make the teacher's job
harder in the future. Making changes to policy and practice is a delicate job and
poses a moral dilemma.

Most of the teachers felt they were operating a policy of equal opportunity
though two of the teachers did acknowledge that this could not be so without
taking into consideration the children's Islamic and cultural convictions. Take
for example the extra-curricular programme aimed at development of potential
and leisure opportunities both for the present and future. The imposition of
restrictions by parents has been dealt with earlier. It is not merely a case of
accepting or rejecting something on offer. Clearly the girls from devout Muslim
families have no choice in the matter, and they can only express themselves
freely within the confines of the Islamic moral and cultural codes. However, like
other aspects of our education system which provide educational, career and
leisure opportunities, the teacher's policies are offering a potential attack on the
fundamental structure of the cultural values and differentiated roles of men and
women of this particular ethnic group. The PE teachers in presenting an equal
opportunities policy in leisure activities are hitting at what can be described
(from the Eurocentric view) as the sexist core of cultural tradition. It is understandable that the Muslim community wants to protect its tradition. They see the
so-called 'restrictions' not as restrictions but as positive action to protect values
and an essential part of their culture and the essence of its community structure.

This illustrates the dilemma raised in the debate by Troyna and Carrington
(1987) and Walkling and Brannigan (1987) mentioned earlier. It poses the moral
dilemma of individual freedom, equality of opportunity and life-chances in
society against the rights of the group to maintain cultural tradition and control
over its members in the political context of white domination. It poses a further
dilemma of how far parental rights, choice and control should go. It is complicated by the juxtaposition of male domination and the rights and equal
opportunities of women in white society which has been the subject of debate
and action. It can readily be seen that it is a complex political problem with
potentially hazardous solutions. The teachers are in the middle of this, and at the
forefront in the working situation, and have to take action. They are in danger of
being accused of being sexist if they accept cultural tradition and do not operate
policies of equality of opportunity, and of being racist if they do not accept
cultural tradition and go for equal opportunities. In this respect it would appear
that the teacher is always on sticky ground even with a weak version of antisexist
and antiracist policies such as representation, entitlement, access and elimination
of stereotypes. It would also appear that strong versions, that is empowerment to
both women and Muslim culture, would cause a cultural clash.

This research shows that Muslim children feel they are caught between the
school values and the community values, and, in spite of the racist practices,
clearly the children have been open to the influences of the English education

system and way of life and they often feel their parents' cultural values are restrictive, sexist and grossly unfair. They appreciate the moral and cultural code set by the community but resent it at the same time. For some children there is a clear crisis of identity, as Zakia shows:

> and that's just it because we have to play two roles — one as a Muslim child and one as being in the host community and joining in with them.

It leads to confusion and conflict with their families, as Humera admits:

> we are confused and we can't communicate with them [parents].

Both Morion and Naweeda complain that their parents, having lived most of their lives in Bangladesh, are too traditionalist, and they themselves are finding it difficult to accept the ways of their parents.

This supports the 'cultural clash' and 'intergenerational' conflict theories which Brah and Minhas (1985) have disputed and criticized. However, our evidence shows that this is the children's view and not merely the researchers' interpretation of the situation. 'Intergenerational' conflicts are not uncommon in white families, and neither are the perceived cause and sources of those conflicts in restrictions placed by parents or in religious practices where it is central to those families' lives. The teachers (quite typically, we believe, as do Brah and Minhas) hold a 'cultural deficit' view and see the problem lying in the Asian family and culture, and, more surprisingly, so do the children, at least in part, as evidenced by their criticism of their parents. However, we locate the beginnings of the conflict firmly within the school (along with other English/white influences on these particular children) as the socialization and acculturation agent because the teachers basically believe in integration. Perhaps the children should never have been put in such potentially conflicting situations. We agree with Brah and Minhas (1985) that the school is not neutral, but then, as a socialization agent, it is not meant to be. It is this function of the school which has led to the demands for separate Islamic schools which we have seen recently. This research shows that some acculturation has taken place and supports the findings by Ghuman (1991). This latter study shows that Asian children are in favour of acculturation in many aspects but did want to retain some of their own culture such as languages, though Muslims were 'less acculturated' and not as strongly in favour of acculturation as Hindus and Sikhs. It also found that girls were more strongly in favour of change than boys, particularly in relation to female roles. Ghuman's work lends support to the belief that potential 'cultural clash' and 'inter-generational conflict' exists on a wider scale than the sample at Borin High School. Therefore, in the short term we may hear of more evidence of these conflicts, but in the long term, according to Ghuman, these problems will be resolved as acculturation takes place with each generation as long as certain cultural traditions which are desired to be retained are allowed to do so. This is not the only scenario and the process may not be as smooth as Ghuman appears to make out. It may work this way for the less devout Muslims, but the more devout community may see the acculturation as eroding their tradition, values, parental and community rights. They may seek to protect and support them by placing more restrictions or putting stronger pressure on youngsters to conform, and by the demand for separate Muslim schools which has so far been resisted. Racist attacks portrayed continually in the media, economic recession resulting in loss of jobs, and events like the 'Salman Rushdie affair' serve only to reinforce the solidarity of the Muslim community and a desire for separatism in many spheres, including education and leisure activities. This could lead to sectarianism and conflicts between groups. A greater understanding of group interests is therefore required. This sort of possible scenario illustrates that what may appear to be relatively insignificant conflicts in situations like PE are part of a wider context and the effects are not always confined to the PE situation.

Conclusion

This research shows that the existence of general antiracist policies is not enough to ensure racist practices do not exist in the working situation. More detailed and carefully formulated guidelines related to the practical situation are clearly required for PE, taking into account gender and race together. Changing teachers' practices and attitudes is of fundamental importance. The evidence from this study highlighted the teachers' lack of understanding of the Muslim community and needs of the children, a lack of awareness of racism and antiracist policies and of the effects of their policies and actions. This, we suspect, might not be uncommon, as there appears to have been little done in initial teacher training or INSET in the past to confront racism in PE. It is now usual to include some element of multicultural and antiracist education in initial training courses but this is very limited. It would be naive to assume that the answers to the dilemmas and problems posed in this paper are simple or that schools can solve societal problems. Some of the dilemmas are deep-rooted, and the solutions are going to be long-term and political. However, some action can be taken at the educationalist and moral levels. Examples are:

- Better preparation of teachers in initial training, and a thorough programme of in-service training for those already in schools to deal with the multicultural issue which will be faced; awareness training related to cultural and religious practices, to draw up and operate antiracist, antisexist and equal opportunities policies, and to deal with specific issues in physical education as indicated in this paper;
- Stronger antiracist and antisexist policies such as positive action and empowerment must be examined for within school action, but the discussion of these in wider society could be discussed as part of a political education. This clearly calls for sensitive handling to avoid cultural clashes and offending individuals or groups;
- Closer links with the community, community representation or school governing committees, and more use made of community leaders, and local authority officers looking after ethnic group interests; where appropriate a greater understanding of the children's situation from parents and the Muslim community.

By taking the pupil perspective we have indicated the unintentional racist practices of the teachers, and the effects upon the children. Our action research perspective (Carroll and Hollinshead, 1993) allowed us to tackle these practices as we developed an understanding of the situation, and antiracist policies. This should lead not only to less conflict within the school, but also between children and their parents and community. This type of approach might well be fruitful elsewhere.

References

ARNOT, M. (1985) *Race and Gender: Equal Opportunities Policies in Education*, Oxford, Pergamon.

BAYLISS, T. (1989) 'PE and Racism: Making Changes', *Multicultural Teaching*, **7**, 2, pp. 19–22.

BOURDIEU, P. (1974) 'The School as a Conservative Force: Scholastic and Cultural Inequalities', in EGGLESTON, S. (Ed.) *Contemporary Research in the Sociology of Education*, London, Methuen.

BRAH, A. and MINHAS, R. (1985) 'Structural Racism or Cultural Difference: Schooling for Asian Girls' in WEINER, G. (Ed.) *Just a Bunch of Girls*, Milton Keynes, Open University Press.

CARRINGTON, B. and WILLIAMS, T. (1988) 'Patriarchy and Ethnicity: The Link between School Physical Education and Community Leisure Activities', in EVANS, J. (Ed.) *Teachers, Teaching and Control in Physical Education*, London, Falmer Press.

CARRINGTON, B. and WOOD, E. (1983) 'Body-Talk: Images of Sport in a Multi-Racial School', *Multi-Racial Education*, **11**, 2, pp. 29–38.

CARRINGTON, B., CHIVERS, T. and WILLIAMS, T. (1987) 'Gender, Leisure and Sport: A Case Study of Young People of South Asian Descent', *Leisure Studies*, **6**, 3, pp. 265–79.

CARROLL, B. and HOLLINSHEAD, G. (1993) 'Ethnicity and Conflict in Physical Education', *British Educational Research Journal*, **19**, 1.

CASHMORE, E. (1982) *Black Sportsmen*, London, Routledge and Kegan Paul.

COVENTRY, LEA (1980) *Physical Education in a Multi-Cultural Society*, Elmbank Teachers Centre, Coventry.

DELAMONT, S. (1990) *Sex Roles and the School*, 2nd ed., London, Routledge.

DEPARTMENT OF EDUCATION AND SCIENCE (1985) 'Education for All', Report of the Committee of Inquiry into the Education of Children from Ethnic Minority Groups (Chairman Lord Swann), London, HMSO.

FLEMING, S. (1991) 'Sport, Schooling and Asian Male Youth Culture', in JARVIE, G. (Ed.) *Sport, Racism and Ethnicity*, London, Falmer Press.

FOSTER, P. (1990) *Policy and Practice in Multicultural and Anti Racist Education*, London, Routledge.

GERWITZ, D. (1991) 'Analyses of Racism and Sexism in Education and Strategies for Change', *British Journal of Sociology of Education*, **12**, 2, pp. 183–201.

GHUMAN, P.A.S. (1991) 'Best or Worst of Two Worlds? A Study of Asian Adolescents', *Educational Research*, **33**, 2, pp. 121–32.

HARGREAVES, J. (1986) *Sport, Power and Culture*, Cambridge, Polity Press.

HAW, K.F. (1991) 'Interactions of Gender and Race—a Problem For Teachers? A Review of the Emerging Literature', *Educational Research*, **33**, 1, pp. 12–21.

HOLLINSHEAD, G. (1989) 'Problems Affecting the Participation of Muslim Asians in Physical Education', MEd dissertation, University of Manchester.

IKULAYO, P.B. (1983) 'Attitudes of Girls towards PE', *Physical Education Review*, **6**, 1, pp. 24–5.

INNER LONDON EDUCATION AUTHORITY (1986) *Approaches to Equal Opportunities in Secondary Schools*, Ed. C. Adams, ILEA.

LA (1990) *Interim Report of the 1989 Census of Bangladeshis in ... LA Research Department.* (Name withheld to protect anonymity of school.)

MANGAN, J.A. (1973) *Physical Education and Sport: Sociological and Cultural Perspectives*, Oxford, Basil Blackwell.

MULLARD, C. (1982) 'From Assimilation to Cultural Pluralism', in TIERNEY, J. (Ed.) *Race, Migration and Schooling*, London, Holt, Rinehart and Winston.

RAVAL, S. (1989) 'Gender, Leisure and Sport: A Case Study of Young People of South Asian Descent — A Response', *Leisure Studies*, **8**, 3, pp. 237–40.

ROTHERHAM, MBC (1986) *Physical Education in a Multicultural Society: Guidelines and General Information Leaflet*, Rotherham MBC.

TROYNA, B. and CARRINGTON, B. (1987) 'Anti-Sexist/Anti-Racist Education — A False Dilemma: A Reply to Walkling and Brannigan', *Journal of Moral Education*, **16**, 1.

TROYNA, B. and CARRINGTON, B. (1990) *Education, Racism and Reform*, London, Routledge.

TROYNA, B. and WILLIAMS, J. (1986) *Racism, Education and the State*, London, Croom Helm.

WALKLING, P.H. and BRANNIGAN, C. (1987) 'Muslim Schools — Troyna and Carrington's Dilemma', *Journal of Moral Education*, **16**, 1.

WEINER, G. (1985) 'Equal Opportunities, Feminism and Girls' Education', in WEINER, G. (Ed.) *Just a Bunch of Girls*, Milton Keynes, Open University Press.

WEINER, G. (1990) *The Primary School and Equal Opportunities*, London, Cassell.

Chapter 11

Pre-Vocationalism and Empowerment: Some Questions for PE

Phil Hodkinson and Andrew Sparkes

Vocationalism and PE

A great deal has been written in recent years about vocationalism and its relationship to schooling and education in Britain (Ball, 1990; Dale, 1985; Dale *et al.*, 1990; Education Group II, 1991; Gleeson, 1989; Holt, 1987; Pring, 1985; Watts, 1985). The rise of what has been called the 'new vocationalism' is often linked to the Ruskin College speech made by James Callaghan in 1976 voicing concerns about the relationship between schools and working life, although Marshall (1990) and Shilling (1989) indicate that the roots of this movement can be traced back to the nineteenth century. This often heated debate has become topical once more, with Government proposals for parallel vocational and academic pathways to Ordinary and Advanced Diplomas in Key Stage Four (age 14 to the end of compulsory schooling) and post-16 respectively.

The subject of PE has been conspicuous by its absence in this continuing debate about vocationalism. Exceptions include Carroll (1990) who considered vocationalism in relation to examinations and assessment in PE, with particular regard to City and Guilds and BTEC qualifications, pointing to the potential links in Further Education 'between sport and physical recreation and the growth of the recreation and leisure industries' (p. 148). Dickenson and Almond (1990) also draw attention to the growth of the leisure industry in discussing economic and industrial understanding as a cross-curricular theme that has a role for PE in terms of 'the increasing awareness of the role of exercise in maintaining a healthy state and in the management of work related stress' (p. 239). Similarly Sparkes and Dickenson (1989) mention links with the leisure industry but also raise concerns over the differential power resources with regard to schools-industry links and how this might shape the PE curriculum in the interests of the industrial employer rather than those of pupils.

The interim report of the National Curriculum Physical Education Working Group (DES, 1991a) included a small section devoted to vocational opportunities relevant to physical education. Again the leisure industry is earmarked as 'currently the fourth largest employer in the country. Within it there are many varied employment opportunities for those interested in sport education or dance' (p. 22). However, this listing is omitted from the later National Curriculum

Council proposals (DES, 1991b), where indicators of vocational concerns are more subtly located, for example the Level Eight Statement of Attainment suggests that pupils 'assess the leisure and vocational opportunities for one of their chosen activities in their own community' (p. 22). The programmes of study for Key Stage Four assert that 'Pupils should be shown how to use the various opportunities for physical activity in the local community, and how to choose their own activity(ies) for a healthy and enjoyable lifestyle. They should be made aware of the vocational opportunities in the sports and leisure industry' (p. 34). There is also a reference in the programmes of study to the latest government plans to introduce National Vocational Qualifications into Key Stage Four.

There have been few detailed case studies of the implementation and impact of vocational initiatives within specific PE departments. A notable exception is provided by Prince (1990) who illustrates how TVEI acted as a positive force for curriculum change in his own department. Here there was a shift from didactic to enquiry-orientated teaching styles, along with changes in course structure. He comments directly on issues of equality:

> TVEI also requires that all pupils have equality of opportunity in education. As a result of this I, as Head of Department, have been able to implement the process of change from a traditional segregated approach to an integrated mixed sex innovative approach. I have used our TVEI consortium policy to promote this philosophy in our structure. Through this vehicle we have also stopped the withdrawal of pupils with special needs and those who wish to follow a second language, both areas of inheritance for myself but areas that have quite rightly changed. My main argument has been equality of access for all. (p. 293)

This brief review highlights the difficult task that we as authors face in constructing this particular chapter. Vocationalism seems to have been peripheral to the concerns of mainstream PE, and there is little case study material available to help us tease out the relationships between these domains and how they relate to issues of equality. We have little empirical data to go on, so much of what we say is necessarily speculative. A further problem is the complexity of vocationalism, at the levels of both conceptualization and practice, and we must briefly turn to this next.

The Nature of Vocationalism

Various features have been attributed to the 'new vocationalism', and which of these are deemed important has varied with the ideological position of the writer. Liberal educators such as Bailey (1984) and Holt (1987) emphasize learning as a preparation for employment, which they see as narrow and instrumental, rather than open-ended and liberating. Inextricably linked with this instrumentalism is an emphasis upon practical skills rather than knowledge or understanding. This can be seen as a virtue (Jessup, 1991) or a vice (Wellington, 1987).

For others (McCullough, 1987; Alvis, 1991) the political origins of the new vocationalism are more significant, coming from the Department of Employment rather than the Department of Education and Science. The Technical and Vocational Education Initiative (TVEI) was a precursor of the centralized political control of the school curriculum now seen in the National Curriculum, although in other respects the principles of the National Curriculum and TVEI are at odds (Saunders and Halpin, 1990).

While acknowledging all these features of the new vocationalism, Pring (1985) highlights two others. For him, the new vocationalism epitomizes a student-centred approach, stressing individual learning and negotiation. He reminds us that its origins are found in post-compulsory and often low-status education and training, rather than in mainstream school-based education. Indeed, most vocational initiatives have been explicitly directed at post-14 age groups and lower-ability pupils.

Within this umbrella title of new vocationalism are lumped many different initiatives which share the features already identified to a greater or lesser extent. Many authors refer to all of the following as part of the same phenomenon: TVEI in both pilot and extension forms, the Certificate of Pre-Vocational Education (CPVE) and by implication its prequel the Foundation Programme, the Youth Training Scheme now reborn as Youth Training (YT), the Low Attaining Pupils Programme (LAPP) and National Vocational Qualifications. (NVQs).[1] Such portmanteau coverage can lead to confusion, especially if writers predominantly address a few of these schemes but then attempt to draw universal lessons across them all.

Hodkinson (1991a) claims that much of the debate over the new vocationalism effectively conceals some important differences in ideology and practice. He identifies two ideal types: the progressive trainer and the traditional trainer. The progressive trainer is primarily concerned with a student-centred view of vocationalism. While directly concerned with preparing young people for work, in intention at least it is the open-ended, personal development of the young person that is important. On the other hand, the traditional trainer puts the needs of employer or subject (such as typing or bricklaying) first. What matters is establishing the skills and understanding required for any particular job or qualification and then instilling them into the trainee. Hodkinson argues that this traditional vocationalism, often found in specialist vocational courses and highlighted in Youth Training and some aspects of NVQs, has more in common with the traditional teaching of academic subjects than it does with progressive vocationalism.

It follows from this analysis that different schemes within new vocationalism may have dramatically different principles, practices and outcomes and that to continue to deal with them all as if they were the same is at best misleading and at worst dangerous. In the rest of this chapter we are only concerned with what Hodkinson calls progressive vocationalism, with its student-centred focus. To make the boundaries of this ideal type easier to locate, we are also limiting our remarks to pre-vocational education, that is, those elements of new vocationalism that set out to prepare young people for the world of paid employment in general, and also for broader aspects of the adult world, including unpaid work, the family and leisure. These initiatives include CPVE,[2] the Foundation Programme and TVEI.

Issues of Equality

With the exception of the TVEI extension programme, which is cross-curricular in nature, pre-vocational education has almost always been associated with so-called 'less able' pupils. Thus the Foundation Programme was primarily, but not exclusively, targeted at those for whom academic GCSEs were inappropriate, while CPVE was designed to cater for the 'new sixthformers', for whom 'A' levels were unsuitable. This raises two apparently separate issues of equality that are in reality closely linked. These issues can be labelled personal empowerment and ghettoization.

Personal empowerment

Within the rhetoric of pre-vocational courses, there are clear intentions to equip the young people themselves for the adult word. Continuing efforts, for example by the Further Education Unit of the DES, have been made to develop these ideas, seeing education as student-centred with teacher as facilitator in the educational process. This places an emphasis on styles of teaching and learning which encourage young people to do things for themselves. In this sense, the programmes deliberately set out to empower the students, that is, to give them the independence to act without constant dependance on others. While several studies have shown that what actually happened in schools often fell well short of these ideals (Hodkinson, 1991b; Radnor *et al.*, 1989), there is also evidence of considerable achievement. While acting as a moderator for CPVE, Hodkinson saw a group of students in Cornwall organize a holiday for younger pupils from Bristol. The students, with teacher support, had organized visits, got industrial sponsorship, catered for and looked after their charges. He saw them collectively solving problems as they occurred, while teachers simply lent support. Their achievements had relevance to many aspects of their future adult life, not merely, or even mainly, paid employment. Similar points are made by Pring (1985), Hodkinson (1988) and Radnor *et al.* (1989). The last named authors report about CPVE that:

> First, there are concepts of negotiated learning, active learning and experiential learning and the shift in the balance of power that these suggest in the control of the curriculum. Students are to be involved in decisions about their own learning. The teachers must give up some aspects of their accustomed role in the classroom. In other words, there is an apparent shift of power. . . . Second, and related to the integration of subjects, is the use of team teaching. Teachers are encouraged to collaborate with colleagues in teams to plan, teach and evaluate CPVE work. . . . There is a change from assessment by examination to forms of profiling and the use of Records of Achievement. This is a change from assessment of failure, what the students do not know, to the recording of success, what they know or can do. . . . Assessment in the form of the construction of a profile is also related to student counselling. Once again there is a potential shift in the balance of power relations between student and teacher, whereby students are to be involved in forming and discussing their assessment. (pp. 108–9)

For advocates of pre-vocational education such empowerment, with its attendant growth in student confidence and independence, is a prime justification for these courses. In a sense, pre-vocational education is a compensation for three well-known perceived weaknesses in traditional academic education. The first is an emphasis on rote learning and the memorization of facts to be regurgitated in examinations, with the associated dominance of transmission styles of teaching (ILEA, 1984; HMI, 1979). The second is the concentration on knowing and understanding rather than doing (Burgess, 1986). The third is the emphasis on individual activity rather than collaborative group work (Resnick, 1987).

There are interesting parallels here between PE and pre-vocational education, which makes the lack of contact between the two at first sight rather puzzling.[3] PE involves the expression and development of practical knowledge, is inherently physical, is often creative, and can emphasize both team work and individual development:

> Physical Education aims to develop physical competence so that pupils are able to move efficiently, effectively and safely and understand what they are doing. It is essentially a way of learning through action, awareness and observation. (DES, 1991b, p. 5)

For many pupils it can be a source of confidence and self-esteem that is accessible to 'non-academic' pupils as well as others. The PE and sports community is proficient in arguing the need for their subject as a balance to other parts of the school curriculum, for example in ensuring that it remains a compulsory part of the National Curriculum even in Key Stage Four (age 14–16).

Other have vehemently attacked the view that pre-vocational education empowers pupils. Liberal educators, such as Bailey (1984) and Holt (1987), see such course provision as narrowly instrumental and argue that education should, in Bailey's terms, 'liberate from the present and particular'. That is, we should educate young people by developing their imagination and experience way beyond things they will directly meet in adult life. Such writers are equally dissatisfied with traditional academic education, but see pre-vocational provision as a dangerous distraction from what needs to be done.

Others go further. For Education Group II (1991) the focus on preparation for the world of work carries with it dangerous overtones of indoctrination and bias. For them, pre-vocational education presupposes a particular view of society based on classical economics. This view assumes that an individual is totally responsible for his/her own situation. For them, vocational training is a means of blaming the unemployed for their lack of jobs, by focusing on what individuals can/should do to remedy the situation. Furthermore, the focus on what pupils can do for themselves deflects attention away from more important questions, for example about the inequities in power or wealth distribution. They see vocational education as being for employers and others with an interest in preserving the status quo, rather than for the young people it is ostensibly aimed at. Once more, there are parallels in PE, or at least in health-related exercise modules, where a focus on personal health and fitness may distract attention from broader societal issues, such as the relationships between health, social class and living and working environments (Sparkes, 1989, 1991; Tinning 1990, 1991; Colquhoun, 1990, 1991).

These criticisms point up a crucial issue of equal opportunity for pre-vocational education. It could be argued that pre-vocational education undermines equality of opportunity if the result of such provision is the maintenance of inequalities in society, and the indoctrination of certain types of youngster to accept their lack of status. If, on the other hand, genuine empowerment resulted in greater awareness, greater confidence and ability to bring about change, then pre-vocational education might have a positive equal opportunity role to play.

Ghettoization

The second criticism of pre-vocational education concerns its ghettoization. Many writers (Raffe, 1985; Ball, 1990; Spours, 1988; Radnor *et al.*, 1989; Ranson, 1983; Hodkinson, 1991b) see pre-vocational education as separating its clients from academic education. Pre-vocational courses are low-status and for less able students. This means that despite the superficial attractiveness of the content of those courses for industry, in practice they hold very little currency in getting a job or in advancing further in full-time education. This is because, as Raffe (1985) first pointed out, users of educational qualifications tend to judge their value on the sorts of pupils recruited to the courses, rather than on the content. Thus, because pre-vocational courses like CPVE recruit less able youngsters, the qualification is seen as low status. We then enter a vicious downward spiral, where any pupil capable of following alternative higher-status courses will do so, thus further lowering the status of the pre-vocational course for those who have little other choice.

From this perspective, such courses reduce empowerment and self-confidence for those who follow them, because they bring stigma and lack of opportunity for progression. This downward and disempowering spiral is made worse by what Green (1991) has called the peculiarities of English education, with its excessive emphasis on status and academic elitism. A final twist is that the very strategies to achieve personal empowerment that pre-vocational courses emphasize are devalued by association. These may be all right for the less able, but are seen as a distracting waste of time for able youngsters who should be passing traditional examinations.

It should be remembered that the TVEI extension scheme is a cross-curricular initiative, designed to introduce pre-vocational approaches and perspectives into all parts of the Key Stage Four curriculum and to all pupils. For this initiative, the status issue is a slightly different one: the extent to which TVEI can counterbalance more traditional influences in the National Curriculum (Saunders and Halpin, 1990). However, with current government plans for parallel vocational and academic routes to the proposed Ordinary and Advanced Diplomas (DES, 1991c), the issues of ghettoization are returning once more to prominence.

Here also there are parallels with PE, which has also been historically defined as containing low-status practical knowledge, and being more appropriate for low-ability pupils. Even the emergence of examinations at GCSE and 'A' level in this subject fail to effectively challenge existing knowledge hierarchies (see Evans, 1990; Kirk, 1988; Sparkes *et al.*, 1990). However, PE is in

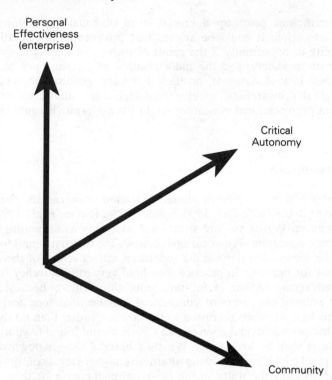

Personal
Effectiveness
(enterprise)

Critical
Autonomy

Community

Figure 11.1   Dimensions of Personal Empowerment

a stronger position than many pre-vocational courses. Firstly, it begins in the primary school, while pre-vocational education normally focuses on post-14 age groups. Secondly, PE contains high-status elements, through its links with team games and the prestige of a winning first team. PE is seen in all prestigious independent schools, where pre-vocational education is conspicuous by its absence. Finally, now the battle over the National Curriculum at Key Stage Four appears to have been won, all pupils in state schools must take PE at least until the end of compulsory schooling.

A Holistic View of Empowerment

An analysis of the strengths and weaknesses of pre-vocational education has been used by Hodkinson (1989; 1991a; 1991c) to develop a broader, more holistic view of empowerment, which is shown in figure 11.1. Empowerment is seen as consisting of three complementary dimensions, and we should provide young people with all of them, not choose one rather than another as some of the attacks on pre-vocational education imply. It is our intention in elaborating this model to raise some questions about the delivery of PE in schools.

Personal effectiveness

One dimension to empowerment is the practical ability to do things for yourself, a dimension we have already identified in pre-vocational education. Some writers call this being enterprising. Unfortunately, the term enterprise has become a rhetorical device (Francis, 1991) constantly used in association with running a business. Consequently, we prefer the term personal effectiveness, which, though clumsier, contains fewer political connotations.

The ability to do things for oneself can apply in any aspect of life or school. It might be running a business or organizing a playgroup. It might be making a sculpture, or putting on a play. In terms of PE, it might be planing a work schedule to reduce stress in your life, planning and sticking to a personal exercise programme, or organizing/running a club in the local community. We are concerned here with general qualities of personal effectiveness, rather than the ability to do specific things.

Johnson *et al.* (1987) list ten essential qualities for what they call enterprise, one of which is 'risk-judging'. By this they mean the ability to weigh up the chances of success or failure, and then be prepared to have a go without always playing totally safe. Central to this, and to personal effectiveness as a whole, is the notion of confidence in oneself and what Hargreaves describes as:

> motivation and commitment; the willingness to accept failure without destructive consequences; the readiness to persevere; the self-confidence to learn in spite of the difficulty of the task. (ILEA, 1984, p. 2)

Like him, we see these abilities as achievements that education should nurture, rather than innate personal qualities that some pupils have and others do not. The best examples of pre-vocational education did much to further this dimension of empowerment through the use of negotiated and experiential pedagogical styles. The importance of pre-vocational initiatives in changing pedagogy in schools was recognized in the final report of the National Study Group on Teaching and Learning Strategies in Physical Education (BAALPE, 1989).

If we accept the importance of this dimension to pupil empowerment, there are some obvious but important questions for PE teachers:

1 How can we help ALL pupils, regardless of gender, ability, ethnicity and sexual orientation, take some responsibility for their health, fitness and involvement in PE?
2 How can we instill the confidence in pupils to bounce back from apparent failure, and to go on to learn, rather than becoming demoralized and alienated from the subject?
3 To what extent can the pedagogical principles of pre-vocational education, with their emphasis on sharing responsibility and power with the learner, be further incorporated into PE teaching?

Critical autonomy

Another essential dimension to empowerment is the ability to think through issues and to form independent opinions. This perspective is often neglected within pre-vocational education, but is constantly emphasized by its critics. Some simple outcomes of such autonomy might be the ability to deal with advertising, propaganda, political polemic and religious beliefs. A central part of such independence of mind must be the ability to be critical not only of ideas but also of the context and culture in which we live. Citizens need to be aware of the cultural and historical influences which contribute to their understanding and that of others around them. They also need the ability to be critical of that context itself. To adequately address this dimension of empowerment, a PE module on health-related exercise would, for example, help pupils become critically aware of the historical influences that contribute to their current understandings of health issues. They need to be capable of making critical judgments for themselves of such contextual issues as the labour relations and working conditions that people operate in, the assumption of one dominant set of values towards health in a multi-ethnic society, or the social construction of women's role in our society and how this impacts on health (Sparkes, 1991).

While critical autonomy is intellectual, much so-called academic education in schools barely touches it. Traditional approaches to the curriculum, where the transmission of facts and theories-as-facts into pupils is the most important goal, contribute very little to critical autonomy. What matters is not that PE teachers tell young people what these issues are, but that they help equip them to think them through for themselves. This raises, therefore, three more questions:

4   To what extent can/should an essentially practical subject like PE concern itself with such critical intellectual activities?
5   What are the possibilities for addressing such critical intellectual activities via the involvement of PE in cross-curricular themes such as Health Education?
6   How far are PE teachers aware of the critical issues which surround their subject? Is there a danger of presenting to pupils a one-sided, if sincerely held, picture of issues such as sport, health and the place of competition in society?

If PE teachers cannot develop appropriate answers to these and other similar questions, then PE will be open to many of those criticisms now directed at pre-vocational education which were briefly summarized above.

Community

This third dimension to empowerment, like the other two, can be taken at either a trivial or profound level. More trivially, it is about working with and living with others. Resnick (1987) points out that

> The dominant form of school learning and performance is individual. Although group activities of various kinds occur in school, students ultimately are judged on what they can do by themselves. . . . In contrast, much activity outside school is socially shared. Work, personal life, and recreation take place within social systems, and each person's ability to function successfully depends on what others do. . . . (p. 13)

Consequently, it is important to educate young people to work with others. Pre-vocational education addresses the issue of community at this pragmatic level, as does much PE teaching if and when the emphasis is on group cooperation and team work.

At a more profound level, what we call community is about living as a social being, balancing personal desires with social responsibilities, and with empathy, understanding and sympathy for others. It entails the acknowledgment of conflict as well as cooperation. This is an essential counterbalance to individualism, for, as Ranson says, 'self-interest can be self-defeating' (1990, p. 152). Johnson (1991) identifies this flawed belief in individualism as the Achilles' heel of the now intellectually dominant New Right, and the same flaw can be found in the non-political writings of some of the early advocates of empowerment in education (Hopson and Scally, 1981).

There is a tension between individualism and community which cannot be easily resolved. Ranson (1990) addresses the problem in detail and concludes that in a participatory democracy there is a necessary duality in all of us, as individuals and as members of the community. He uses the term citizenship to cover an integration of both. It is impossible to live without being both, though the balance between self-interest and the need of the community varies both from person to person, and within each of us from time to time and situation to situation. To imagine empowerment without this more profound community dimension is to make it unreal and amoral, as if preparing pupils for life on a desert island.

Within PE, this broader community perspective raises many potentially troublesome issues. One is equal opportunity: not just making provision for pupils, but helping them to see and appreciate the different views and needs of others in society. Seemingly trivial examples, such as competition for facilities and players between different sports and teams, or the potentially off-putting effects of loud, mesomorphic successful athletes in alienating other groups from PE altogether, might prove a vehicle for raising such wider community perspectives. Once more, there are some difficult questions:

7 How far can/should PE in schools help sensitize young people to their wider community rights and responsibilities in a multicultural society?
8 Can the individualism that has been identified within the health-related exercise movement be transformed so as to address wider socio-political issues, that would include facing up to conflicting group interests and differing power relationships?

Conclusion

We claim that if empowerment incorporates all three dimensions, it can play an important if small part in addressing broader issues of equality of opportunity in society. We further suggest that PE can play an important part in empowering young people. It can stress the practical elements of what we have called personal effectiveness, which is an important balance to more intellectual elements of the curriculum. However, as conventionally provided, both PE and pre-vocational education give only a partial, and therefore sometimes distorting, view of empowerment. This gives rise to some quite difficult questions about the appropriate nature and balance of the PE curriculum, some of which have been raised.

One important lesson from pre-vocationalism may be that teaching styles and pupil-teacher relationships are of paramount importance if we wish to take empowerment seriously. The guidelines for PE published by the National Curriculum Council, while having pedagogical implications, seldom address such issues directly. It is therefore up to individual teachers and individual PE departments to develop their own approaches. We would suggest that some sharing of real responsibility with pupils, combined with a willingness to help them face situations and issues they might at first prefer to avoid are both essential. While these could be seen as mutually incompatible, we prefer to think that the way forward lies in negotiation between pupils and teachers, of the type pioneered on courses such as CPVE. Anne Jones (1990), while holding overall responsibility for TVEI, said that the real aim of the initiative was 'empowerment of the individual: helping young people call the shots' (p. 6). What we are advocating is that pre-vocational education should take this notion of empowerment more seriously. We support the cross-curricular approach of TVEI, whereby ALL education should actively address these issues. If PE can find satisfactory answers to the questions raised here, it could become a very effective part of pre-vocational education for all young people.

Finally, we must not delude ourselves. The agenda for empowerment presented here will be seen by many as subversive. What we advocate is the deliberate education of generations who will think and do things for themselves, while recognizing the rights and needs of others. Such pupils will challenge teachers and challenge aspects of school organization. But the opposite is, we believe, unsupportable, and is implied in the following quotation from Sheila Lawlor, of the Centre for Policy Studies, reacting to the riots in Newcastle in 1991:

> Much of the contemporary emphasis in teaching encourages debating and arguing and valuing pupil opinion, whether it is right or wrong. We are raising a generation of monsters who go back and challenge their parents. (quoted in *TES*, 20 September 1991, p. 6)

What we have done here is advance some of the elements of a pre-vocational education agenda for PE, to raise empowered citizens in a democratic society, not monsters.

Notes

1 Since we commenced work on this chapter, this list has been added to, by Government plans for a new General Vocational Qualification (GNVQ) and the decision by City and Guilds to replace both CPVE and the Foundation programme by the new Diploma for Vocational Education. The ephemeral nature of many vocational programmes in Britain vividly illustrates its relatively low status compared with academic education. It is much more acceptable to experiment with the former.

2   CPVE is used in this chapter as a 'typical' pre-vocational programme. It was originally designed, in 1985, as a full-time one-year course, including three elements: core skills, vocational skills and additional studies. The first two were to be integrated as far as possible, and additional studies were dropped in major amendments introduced in 1989, which saw the course as a minimum of 500 hours, normally taken over one year. Assessment was by means of a profile negotiated between the student and tutor, together with a portfolio of work.
3   The possible explanations for the virtual exclusion of PE from the pre-vocational debate are too intricate to explore fully here. We believe that it has much to do with the relative isolation of PE from other school subjects, together with attempts to academicize PE in order to enhance its status. Another possible explanation lies in the limited nature of the vocational debate, which some see as excluding apparently non-vocational subjects such as PE. We find this view unconvincing, because there is evidence of greater involvement in TVEI of other 'non-vocational' subjects such as geography and music. The Cheshire TVEI extension programme, for example, highlights 'understanding visual and performing arts' as one of eight common learning outcomes.

References

ALVIS, J. (1991) 'The Strange Fate of Progressive Education', in EDUCATION GROUP II *Education Limited: Schooling and Training and the New Right Since 1979*, London, Unwin Hyman.
BAALPE (1989) *Teaching and Learning Strategies in Physical Education*, Oxford, Alden Press.
BAILEY, C. (1984) *Beyond the Present and Particular: A Theory of Liberal Education*, London, Routledge and Kegan Paul.
BALL, S. (1990) *Politics and Policy Making and Education*, London, Routledge.
BURGESS, T. (Ed.) (1986) *Education for Capability*, Windsor, NFER/Nelson for Royal Society of Arts.
CARROLL, R. (1990) 'Examinations and Assessment in Physical Education', in ARMSTRONG, N. (Ed.) *New Directions in Physical Education: Volume 1*, Champaign, IL, Human Kinetics Press.
COLQUHOUN, D. (1990) 'Images of Healthism in Health-based Physical Education', in KIRK, D. and TINNING, R. (Eds) Physical Education, Curriculum and Culture, London, Falmer Press.
COLQUHOUN, D. (1991) 'Health-Based Physical Education, the Ideology of Healthism and Victim Blaming', *Physical Education Review*, **14**, 1, pp. 5–13.
DALE, R. (Ed.) (1985) *Education, Training and Employment: Towards a New Vocationalism*, Oxford, Pergamon.
DALE, R. *et al.* (1990) *The TVEI Story: Policy, Practice and Preparation for Work*, Milton Keynes, Open University Press.
DEPARTMENT OF EDUCATION AND SCIENCE (1991a) *National Curriculum Physical Education Working Group: Interim Report*, London, DES/Welsh Office.
DEPARTMENT OF EDUCATION AND SCIENCE (1991b) *Physical Education for Ages 5 to 16*, London, DES/Welsh Office.
DEPARTMENT OF EDUCATION AND SCIENCE (1991c) *Ordinary and Advanced Diplomas: A Consultative Document*, London, DES/DE/Welsh Office.
DICKENSON, B. and AMOND, L. (1990) 'Cross Curricular Issues and Physical Education within the National Curriculum', *British Journal of Physical Education*, **21**, 1, pp. 239–40.
EDUCATION GROUP II (1991) Education Limited: Schooling, Training and the New Right Since 1979, London, Unwin Hyman.

EVANS, J. (1990) 'Defining a Subject: The Rise and Rise of the New PE?', *British Journal of Sociology of Education*, **11**, 2, pp. 155–69.

FRANCIS, E. (1991) 'Making Rhetoric Real: Perceptions of Enterprise in Educational Contexts', *British Journal of Education and Work*, **4**, 2, pp. 21–34.

GLEESON, D. (1989) *The Paradox of Training: Making Progress out of Crisis*, Milton Keynes, Open University Press.

GREEN, A. (1991) 'The Peculiarities of English Education', in EDUCATION GROUP II *Education Limited: Schooling, Training and the New Right Since 1979*, London, Unwin Hyman.

HER MAJESTY'S INSPECTORATE (1979) *Aspects of Secondary Education*, London, HMSO.

HODKINSON, P. (1988) 'The Changing Curriculum at 16+: A Working View of CPVE', in MOLINEUX, F., Low, G. and FOWLER, F. (Eds) *Learning for Life: Politics and Progress in Recurrent Education*, London, Croom Helm.

HODKINSON, P. (1989) 'Crossing the Academic/Vocational Divide: Personal Effectiveness and Autonomy as an Integrating Theme in Post-16 Education', *British Journal of Educational Studies*, **37**, 4, pp. 369–383.

HODKINSON, P. (1991a) 'Liberal Education and the New Vocationalism: A Progressive Partnership?', *Oxford Review of Education*, **17**, 1, pp. 73–88.

HODKINSON, P. (1991b) 'Contexts and Innovation: A Case Study of the Use of CPVE with A-Level Students', *Educational Studies*, **17**, 2, p. 191–203.

HODKINSON, P. (1991c) 'NCVQ and the 16–19 Curriculum', *British Journal of Education and Work*, **4**, 3, pp. 25–38.

HOLT, M. (Ed.) (1987) *Skills and Vocationalism: The Easy Answer*, Milton Keynes, Open University Press.

HOPSON, B. and SCALLY, M. (1981) *Lifeskills Teaching*, London, McGraw Hill.

INNER LONDON EDUCATION AUTHORITY (1984) *Improving Secondary Schools*, London, ILEA.

JESSUP, G. (1991) *Outcomes: NVQs and the Emerging Model of Education and Training*, London, Falmer Press.

JOHNSON, C., MARKS, S., MATHEWS, M. and PIKE, J. (1987) *Key Skills: Enterprise Skills through Active Learning*, London, Hodder and Stoughton.

JOHNSON, R. (1991) 'My New Right Education', in EDUCATION GROUP II *Education Limited: Schooling, Training and the New Right Since 1979*, London, Unwin Hyman.

JONES, A. (1990) 'The TVEI Extension Post 16' in HODKINSON, P. (Ed.) *TVEI and the Post-16 Curriculum*, Exeter, Wheaton Education.

KIRK, D. (1988) *Physical Education and Curriculum Study*, London, Croom Helm.

MARSHALL, S. (1990) 'The Genesis and Evolution of Pre-Vocational Education: England', *Oxford Review of Education*, **16**, 2, pp. 219–34.

MCCULLOUGH, G. (1987) 'History and Policy: The Politics of TVEI', in GLEESON, D. (Ed.) *TVEI and Secondary Education: A Critical Appraisal*, Milton Keynes, Open University Press.

PRINCE, B. (1990) 'TVEI — Positive Experience So Far', *British Journal of Physical Education*, **21**, 2, pp. 293–4.

PRING, R. (1985) 'Curriculum for Ages 14–18 — "The New Vocationalism"?', Theodore Fink Memorial Lecture, University of Melbourne.

RADNOR, H., BALL, S. and BURRELL, D. (1989) 'The Certificate of PreVocational Education', in HARGREAVES, A. and REYNOLDS, D. (Eds) *Educational Policies: Controversies and Critiques*, London, Falmer Press.

RAFFE, D. (1985) 'Education and Training Initiatives for 14–18s: Content and Context', in WATTS, A.G. (Ed.) *Education and Training 14–18: Policy and Practice*, Cambridge, CRAC.

RANSON, S. (1983) 'Towards a Tertiary Tripartism: New Codes of Social Control and the 17+', in BROADFOOT, P. (Ed.) *Selection, Certification and Control*, Lewes, Falmer Press.

RANSON, S. (1990) 'Towards Education for Citizenship', *Educational Review*, **42**, 2, pp. 151–66.

RESNICK, L. (1987) 'Learning in School and Out', *Educational Researcher*, Dec., pp. 13–20.

SAUNDERS, M. and HALPIN, D. (1990) 'TVEI and the National Curriculum: A Cautionary Note', in *TVEI and the National Curriculum: Proceedings of a National Conference*, Exeter, Centre for Secondary and Teritary Inservice Training, University of Exeter.

SHILLING, C. (1989) *Schooling for Work in Capitalist Britain*, London, Falmer Press.

SPARKES, A. (1989) 'Health Related Fitness: An Example of Innovation Without Change', *British Journal of* Physical Education, **20**, pp. 60–3.

SPARKES, A. (1991) 'Alternative Visions of Health-Related Fitness: An Exploration of Problem-Setting and its Consequences', in ARMSTRONG, N. and SPARKES, A. (Eds) *Issues in Physical Education*, London, Cassell.

SPARKES, A. and DICKENSON, B. (1989) 'The Many Faces of TVEI: Some Possibilities and Problems for Physical Education', *British Journal of Physical Education*, **20**, 1, pp. 31–4.

SPARKES, A., TEMPLIN, T. and SCHEMPP, P. (1990) 'The Problematic Nature of a Career in a Marginal Subject: Some Implications for Teacher Education Programmes', *Journal of Education for Teaching*, **16**, 1, pp. 3–28.

SPOURS, K. (1988) *The Politics of Progression: A Discussion of Barriers to Student Movement and Continuity of Learning in the 14–19 Curriculum*, Working Paper no. 2, London, Institute of Education Post-16 Centre.

TINNING, R. (1990) *Ideology and Physical Education: Opening Pandora's Box*, Deakin, Deakin University Press.

TINNING, R. (1991) 'Problem-Setting and Ideology in Health Based Physical Education: An Australian Perspective', *Physical Education Review*, **14**, 1, pp. 40–9.

WATTS, A.G. (Ed.) (1985) *Education and Training 14–18: Policy and Practice*, Cambridge, CRAC.

WELLINGTON, J. (1987) 'Skills for the Future?', in HOLT, M. (Ed.) *Skills and Vocationalism: The Easy Answer*, Milton Keynes, Open University Press.

Chapter 12

Gender, Physical Education and Initial Teacher Education

Anne Flintoff

Introduction

Feminist critiques of schooling have been wide-ranging and varied, but it is only recently that there has been any attempt to consider issues of gender equality in Physical Education (PE) (e.g. Evans, 1989; Leaman, 1984; Scraton, 1989). Similarly, although the crucial role of teacher education in the process of challenging patriarchal gender relations has been recognized for some time, (e.g. Deem, 1980), it is only in the last few years that attention has been drawn to the way in which these courses address equal opportunity issues (e.g. EOC, 1989; Leonard, 1989; Mentor, 1989; Shah, 1989; Skelton and Hanson, 1989).[1] As Christine Skelton and Joan Hanson (1989) have suggested, unless teachers are 'born rather than at least partly 'made', then the initial teacher education (ITE) they receive has important implications for their future behavior in classrooms and their own development and careers' (p. 109).[2] The persistence of gender inequalities in secondary schools has caused renewed debate and concern over coeducation as it affects the educational experiences of girls in secondary schools (Deem, 1984; Mahony, 1985, 1989), and there has been some attention to the implications of moves towards coeducational school PE (Evans, 1989; Scraton, 1985). However, an understanding of the role of coeducational PE ITE in challenging or confirming gender inequalities has not yet developed as a line of enquiry.

This chapter aims to fill some of these gaps, drawing on some of the findings of a recent empirical study of the professional socialization of intending secondary school PE teachers in Britain.[3] It focuses on two aspects of the PE ITE curriculum; the selection, organization and timetabling of practical PE Studies, and the extent to which students are involved in addressing issues of gender equality.

The research included a term's observation in two case study institutions, together with semi-structured interviews with key decision-makers such as course leaders and heads of departments. The research also included interviews with leaders of courses in other institutions around the country. The two case study institutions central to the research offered both one-year, Postgraduate Certificate in Education (PGCE), and four-year undergraduate courses, in secondary PE ITE. They were chosen to reflect the separate and distinct historical development of the subject, and are typical of the institutions currently involved in the training of secondary PE teachers.[4] The institution I have called 'Heydonfield' had been a former men's college of PE and is now part of a university, whereas 'Brickhill' had been a former women's PE college, and is now part of an institute of higher education.[5]

The Context of PE Teacher Education

The history of PE teacher training in Britain shows its development along distinct gender lines. The professional training of PE teachers, until relatively recently, was carried out in separate institutions, producing two different types of PE specialists, not only in terms of the activities into which they were initiated, but also the educational aims and philosophies of their practice (Fletcher, 1984). Women were introduced to a range of activities deemed suitable for their 'different' physical capabilities, needs and their 'natural' role of motherhood; there was a strong emphasis on gymnastics, movement and dance, as well as a selection of 'appropriate' games (many of them versions of 'men's' games modified to make them less vigorous). In comparison, boys' PE developed largely in the public school system, without the help of specialist trained PE staff, and was based largely on competitive games. Boys' PE was dominated by 'an ideology of discipline, character building and camaraderie which emphasized and legitimated the development of a "culture of masculinity"' (Scraton, 1985), and it was not until much later that specialist colleges were set up for men's PE.

Recent research by Sheila Scraton (1989) shows that current practice in girls' PE continues to be underpinned by ideologies of femininity, and although there has been little empirical work focusing on the reproduction of ideologies of masculinity through boy's PE, work within the broader area of sport is beginning to explore and highlight this link (e.g. Bryson, 1987, 1990; Day, 1988; Connell, 1990; Whitson, 1990).

Sheila Scraton's work (1989, and see also her chapter in this book) has been important in highlighting the implications for girls of moves towards mixedsex/coeducational PE.[6] Coeducational PE cannot be equated simplistically with improved experiences for girls; much of the available research evidence shows how girls lose out in coeducational PE settings because of inabilities of teachers to effect curricular and pedagogical change, as well as the behaviour of boys in the class, who dominate the action, take up the lion's share of the working space, and demand most of the teacher's attention (e.g. Evans *et al.*, 1987; Evans, 1989; Scraton, 1985), mirroring their experiences within coeducational schooling more generally (e.g. Mahony, 1985, 1989). Whilst moves towards coeducational PE in schools continue on an ad hoc basis, with no national guidelines available from the profession, coeducational PE teacher education has been compulsory practice for some years, imposed on institutions as the result of the introduction of new European law.[7] This change could be seen as presenting an ideal situation for the breakdown of stereotypical images of 'girls'' PE and 'boys'' PE, but, as the evidence presented here will try and show, this has not been the case.

Gender and Teacher Education

The development of national criteria for ITE courses, controlled by the Council for the Accreditation of Teacher Education (CATE), established in 1984, means that all courses must include some attention to gender issues. Students need to 'learn to guard against preconceptions based on the race, gender, religion or other attributes of pupils and understand the need to promote equal opportunities' (DES, 1989, p. 10). However, research suggests that the implementation of this CATE criterion is far from adequate (EOC, 1989; Leonard, 1989; Shah, 1989; Skelton and Hanson, 1989). The EOC's (1989) survey of all teacher education institutions showed how little impact these criteria had had on the inclusion of gender issues in ITE courses. Whilst most institutions recognized the need for 'gender awareness', there was little evidence to suggest that this work was being systematically promoted; few courses had compulsory modules on gender, or assessed the effects of this work with students on teaching practice, and good practice owed more to the commitment and energy of individuals than to coherent planning. The report characterized the overall position towards the promotion of equal opportunities as 'benign apathy' (EOC, 1989, p. 7). Perhaps this should not be surprising, given the research which suggests that few teachers recognize or accept that schooling contributes to the processes by which girls are discriminated against (e.g. Adams, 1985; Kelly, 1985; Pratt *et al.*, 1984; Riddell, 1989). Although there has been no similar research which focuses on the attitudes of lecturers involved in ITE, it is unlikely that there will be significant differences from those of school teachers; indeed, there may be good reasons to suggest that the attitudes of lecturers involved in ITE might be *more* conservative than those of teachers in schools.[8] What then is the present situation in PE ITE?

Gender Issues in the Curriculum

'Core' courses within Professional Studies

How were gender issues addressed within current PE ITE courses and what were the attitudes of the staff to this work? Three out of the four courses in the case study institutions included a specific section of work where gender issues were addressed. (The PGCE course at Brickhill did not include any such work — see the discussion below). The undergraduate courses introduced students to 'equal opportunity' issues in short, compulsory modules, situated within the second-year Professional Studies element.[9] The PGCE course at Heydonfield included two lectures within the Professional Studies element of the course, one on gender stereotyping, and another called 'Fair opportunities for all' which made reference to girls' education (alongside issues of class and 'race').[10]

Both members of staff in charge of the undergraduate modules expressed some doubts about their role in running these courses. At Brickhill, where gender issues were addressed alongside 'race' and special needs issues in a twelve-hour 'Curriculum Access' course, the tutor admitted she was having problems getting someone 'knowledgeable enough' to lead it, since the tutor who had taught it the previous year was too heavily timetabled elsewhere. At this point, she asked me whether I would be interested in teaching the module!

The tutor responsible for the six-hour course at Heydonfield explained that this had been included for the first time that academic year, 'largely in re-sponse to CATE', and that he had been given responsibility for running the module chiefly because of his interest and expertise in multicultural education. Although he felt that it was an 'impossible' task to consider 'race', gender and special needs issues within this time allocation, he suggested that there was scope for students to develop their understanding and expertise further, should they wish, in the Multicultural Education and Sociology of Education option courses available in the third and fourth years of Professional Studies. He added that he thought 'it would be a bit tedious for students if these issues were "pushed down their throats" by making such courses compulsory'. By making third and fourth year work on equality issues 'optional' in this way, they effectively become just another educational issue which students might like to get involved with — a moral or voluntary involvement, rather than an integral part of their professional responsibility.

The fact that neither member of staff with responsibility for these short modules showed a particular sensitivity or commitment to gender equality suggests it would be highly unlikely that the work would be successful in raising students' awareness of gender issues. The location of the compulsory modules within the Professional Studies element of the courses — an area of work which students view as least relevant (see, e.g. Denscombe, 1982) — together with their 'one-off' nature, and their early placement within the course, are all factors likely to contribute to their overall ineffectiveness (Jones and Street-Porter, 1989; Shah, 1989). As Crispin Jones and Rosalind Street-Porter (1989) have concluded, short 'bolt-on' courses which deal largely with the mechanics of equal opportunities policies, or with raising 'awareness' of issues, without a theore-tical basis to help students appreciate and understand the *structural* frameworks of inequality, are unlikely to be effective in getting students to address the ways in which teachers and schools are part of this structure.

Gender as a cross-curricular issue

The EOC (1989) report noted that several institutions used 'permeation' as a major method by which issues such as gender equality were addressed, par-ticularly within the 'already overcrowded' curriculum of the PGCE courses. As noted elsewhere (e.g. Shah, 1989), 'permeation' seems to be accepted as a method of addressing equality issues within school or ITE curricula, despite a lack of clarity about what it *is*, or what the method entails *in practice* for teachers or lecturers. John Coldron and Pam Boulton (1990), for example, suggest that the effectiveness of permeation can be assessed in terms of how far the professional legitimacy of a concern with gender is conveyed through all elements of the course. More usually, and implied in the EOC (1989) report, permeation is used in a more modest sense to describe ways in which gender issues are raised with students throughout the course, other than in the 'core' modules specifically allocated to this task.

Adopting this definition, permeation as the sole method of addressing 'race' or gender issues in a course is unlikely to be successful. The Anti-Racist Teacher Education Network (ARTEN) (1988), for example, has suggested that whilst 'permeation' is often cited as the method used for raising equality issues, in reality it becomes a 'road to nowhere' — a way of avoiding them altogether. It also demands knowledgeable and sensitive staff, without which it can become less about *challenging* gender ideologies and stereotypes and more about their *reinforcement*. There is evidence to suggest that permeation *can* be a valuable method of addressing equality issues, if it is part of a well structured, planned and evaluated package, and used alongside specific 'core' modules addressing equality issues (Coldron and Boulton, 1989; Shah, 1989; Skelton and Hanson, 1989). However, it requires knowledgeable, sensitive and committed staff, and careful planning of when and where issues will arise, rather than leaving it 'to chance'. How then, did Heydonfield and Brickhill use permeation as a method of raising equality issues within other elements of the courses?

There were significant differences in the nature of course planning and construction at the two institutions. Taken together, the courses provided an excellent illustration of the overall lack of a coherent national system of teacher education in Britain (see, e.g. Whitty *et al.*, 1987). The tightly structured course documentation at Brickhill, written for Council for National Academic Awards (CNAA) validation, contrasted with the loose framework adopted at Heydonfield, where the different elements of the courses — PE Studies, Professional Studies and the Second Subject Studies — were planned largely independently of one another. There was no central course documentation and the PE staff admitted that they knew very little about the content of the other elements of the course. During the academic year of the research (1989/90); largely in response to CATE and the introduction of the National Curriculum in schools, the course management team had formed a committee to address 'cross-curricular issues' and collect information about where, or whether, these issues were addressed in the different Subject Studies areas. Up until this point, there had been no coherent planning as to where and how issues would be raised — as the head of PE admitted, although the management team 'had made us aware of the issues ... whether individuals put that into practice is a different thing ... how far people go in addressing gender issues is obviously up to them ... you know, because of the academic autonomy thing'.

In contrast, the BEd at Brickhill in particular, specifically identified permeation as a method by which 'cross-curricular issues' would be raised in the PE Subject Studies element of the courses, to reinforce the work in the Professional Studies outlined above. CNAA validation meant that, at least in theory, all members of staff had an overall view of the course structure, including where the permeation of 'cross-curricular concerns' including 'race', gender and special needs would occur. The CNAA course document included a matrix showing details of this. However, as Rosemary Deem (1991) has noted,

> policy, as we have begun to realise, is a process, not a statement and words have to be turned into deeds and the changes monitored and evaluated. Specific tasks have to be set ... if anything concrete is to be achieved or the fine words of the document remain just that. (Deem, 1991, p. 11)

There is a big difference between identifying where gender issues will permeate courses on paper, and how this is put into practice. Course documentation, for example, does not account for the difference between staff in terms of attitudes and value positions. As Ian Mentor (1989) has noted, one of the major barriers to the implementation of antisexist and antiracist work within ITE is the attitudes and value positions, as well as the interest and expertise, of the lecturing staff themselves. The next section explores the attitudes of staff towards gender issues.

The attitudes of staff towards issues of gender equality

The taped interviews with course leaders and heads of departments, together with observation of classes at both institutions, revealed both indifference and hostility on the part of staff towards addressing sexism within the courses. For example, the PGCE course leader at Brickhill suggested that gender issues were not explicitly addressed because of

> our background ... I mean we have always had more women ... in many ways we have had ... you know ... to have equal opportunities for the men ... we haven't been very good at that, like it was only last year that we got men's changing rooms. We have the opposite thing — in some ways we have taken it for granted because we have the women ... that's why they don't have much on gender. (taped interview, female PGCE leader)

The danger of viewing gender issues in liberal terms of access means that, as for this member of staff, in institutions like Brickhill which have always recruited large numbers of women students, 'gender' isn't a problem. Similarly, the head of PE admitted that she did not relate very easily to material addressing gender inequalities since it seemed to have had little relevance to her own teaching career:

> because of some quirk of circumstance, I have got where I have without even thinking that I am a woman, do you know what I mean? Got married, had my children and got a job ... whereas some people. REALLY get upset about the way in which women are treated ... I ... certainly working with Shirley [female sociologist] has been a real eye-opener for me because of this business of ... of you know, equal opportunities and discrimination against women, I just would not have THOUGHT about it! (taped interview, female head of PE)

She went on to stress that she doubted that she, or indeed the other teaching staff at Brickhill, were either 'sensitive or knowledgeable enough' to allow for effective permeation. There was little or no evidence during the observation period at both institutions of staff raising gender (or 'race') issues in a sensitive or informed way with students. On the other hand, there were many examples where stereotypical views of girls' and boys' physical abilities and behaviours in the classroom were actually *confirmed* rather than challenged, by both male and female lecturers. The following comments were typical:

> you will find that the boys will skip badly and the girls will throw badly . . . I might be making a sexist comment here but you will find it will be true. (female lecturer, Brickhill)

> what do the boys want to do when they start? . . . well yes, they want to play games . . . and sometimes some of the girls want to play games too, but more often the girls will do what the teacher wants them to do, but the boys will be more trouble and will need watching. (female lecturer, Heydonfield)

> in schools, girls are more likely to use creative movements whereas boys are more functional and straightforward. . . . (male lecturer, Heydonfield)

So although there was little evidence of gender being openly addressed and examined within the PE Studies, stereotypical assumptions such as these formed part of the hidden curriculum and would undoubtedly affect the future expectations and behaviour of the students in their teaching.

It is important to note that these kinds of comments were not always simply accepted by students (and as noted below, not all staff were involved in making these stereotypical comments). On several occasions students challenged staff over comments such as these, although one female student admitted to me that she had given up because the tutor 'didn't take any notice' and she was aware that she was getting labelled as the 'radical feminist' in the group by some of the male students.[11]

Some staff were quite openly hostile to suggestions that gender issues should permeate their PE modules. In a PGCE course committee meeting at Brickhill, cross-curricular issues were specifically raised as an agenda item. The course leader suggested that cross-curricular issues had been identified by the external examiner as an area which staff should try and strengthen that year, and her report also suggested that students had complained about the use of sexist comments by some staff. One man immediately retorted 'that assumes we know what a sexist comment is!' When the course leader suggested staff should consider how these issues could be more directly addressed in the course this year, he went on to complain that 'they cover "race" and gender issues in the Professional Studies don't they?' Another male lecturer protested that 'he wished he had known about this at the beginning of the year' so that he 'could have done something about it'. The report was largely dismissed by another female member of staff because the external examiner came from 'ILEA where these things are always high-profile'.

The external examiners for courses have important and powerful roles in making recommendations regarding course content and assessment procedures, and can have a crucial supporting role in reinforcing the development of critical work. However, the opposite may also be true. At Heydonfield the male head of PE considered that 'equal opportunities' was receiving too *much* attention within PE Studies, and that this had been noted by the external examiners, as the comment below illustrates;

> the point had been made, both internally and externally that we were asking that question far too often ... every time the papers were written there was one on equal opportunities ... more than any other subject ... Now Gill teaches the course (Curriculum Issues) and she obviously thinks that it is an important part of the course and obviously puts a question on it, but I mean it has been noted that too much attention has been placed on it, explicitly and it is ALWAYS examined ... the external examiners are saying, another question on equal opportunities! (taped interview, head of PE, Heydonfield)

This raises interesting questions, beyond the scope of this chapter, about who gets chosen as external examiners, and how this is done, as well as their expertise to act in this role.

This necessarily brief account shows how relying on permeation as a method of addressing gender issues is problematic. However, although the examples used here have demonstrated resistance or apathy by staff to gender issues, it would be wrong to suggest that this was characteristic of *all* staff. Whilst the study of teaching and teacher education as *structures* was central to this analysis, the practice of individual *actors* was also a vital ingredient, and it was clear that there were a number of different perspectives held by staff which need to be recognized and acknowledged. As Carol Smart (1984) has stressed, it is the study of individual actors which reveals the complexities of their ideological positions and the diversity of their practices, *as well as* their homogeneity, and 'it is these fragmentations and discontinuities which can give space to feminist ... struggles' (p. 152). A few staff worked hard to raise issues of equality in their work. For example, staff involved in the teaching of the sociology of PE 'option' courses in the second half of both undergraduate courses included work on equality issues, and these were also raised in the introductory, compulsory socio-historical modules in the first year. Each of these courses were taught by women staff. The difficulty of teaching this kind of knowledge within a subject dominated by the behavioural, 'hard' sciences (see, e.g. Dewar, 1987; McKay *et al.*, 1990) was reflected in a comment made by one woman, who admitted that 'it takes me more energy than all the rest of my courses to teach this module' (year one, socio-historical course).

This section has described the extent to which gender issues were given an official 'platform' in the courses. On the four-year BEd courses, students were involved in short modules within the early part of their Professional Studies element. Equality issues were also raised in the first-year socio-historical modules within Subject Studies. In contrast, the PGCE course at Brickhill did not involve the students in formally addressing gender issues at all; at Heydonfield, two lectures in Professional Studies focused on equality issues. The data collected from the observation of classes and from interviewing staff showed little evidence of gender issues raised as a cross-curricular issue. However, as Christine Skelton and Joan Hanson (1989) have noted, whether or not gender is given official status in this way, in terms of being directly addressed or not, gender can nevertheless occupy a crucial position in the underlying values or structures of the course. The next section considers how gender ideologies underpinned the structure and timetabling of the practical PE activities.

Practical PE Studies

The balance and range of practical PE activities included in the undergraduate courses reflected the gendered history of the institutions. At Brickhill, students followed a broad-based curriculum for the first two years, including a large emphasis on dance and gymnastics, traditional in the women's PE colleges, before specializing in two activities in the second half of the degree. In contrast, the curriculum at Heydonfield reflected the games-based curriculum of the former men's PE colleges, with games making up almost half of the total time allocated to practical activities. There were no opportunities within this programme for specialization in particular activities.

Similarly, the *form* of the activities students were introduced to corresponded closely to the institutions' historical roots. The different forms of gymnastics — educational and olympic gymnastics — which formed the basis of what Sheila Fletcher (1984) has called the 'movement/anti-movement war' within the PE profession during the 1960s, were still in evidence at the two institutions. At Brickhill, the gymnastics was educational gymnastics, based on the Laban-inspired 'movement' principles dominant in women's PE during the 1960s. Rhythmical gymnastics was also included. In contrast, the gymnastics at Heydonfield was heavily skills-based, reflecting the olympic gymnastics which characterized the male PE tradition (Kirk, 1990). A first-year 'foundation skills course' was followed by modules in olympic and acrobatic gymnastics in the second and third year of the course.

Since the move to coeducational ITE was imposed on, rather than chosen by, institutions, it was not surprising to learn from the interviews with staff that there was a general reluctance to make any changes to the courses, other than to 'tag on' 'appropriate' activities for students of the opposite sex. Since the *kinds* of practical activities and knowledge students are introduced to in their training will undoubtably be reflected in the shape and direction of their teaching, and the kinds of educational experiences they are able to offer children in school (as well as having implications for their status within the profession — see, e.g. Evans, 1990) the structure and timetabling of the practical activities within PE ITE courses is particularly significant. However, perhaps more significant than the differences in the balance, the range or the form of the activities included, was the differentiation of some activities by sex, and the rationales presented by staff for this. Although most activities were taught in mixed groups, male and female students were timetabled differently for some of the major games, specifically those which related to a social construction of 'appropriate' masculinity and femininity.

For example, rugby remained a male-only activity, and netball a female-only activity. At Heydonfield, the women studied lacrosse, whilst the men studied soccer, whereas other games traditionally viewed as 'male' or 'female', such as cricket and hockey, were taught mixed. At Brickhill, it had been decided that year to have single-sex groups for both hockey and soccer. This decision seemed to have been less about beginning to address gender differentiation in activities, more about satisfying the demands of incoming students. As one member of staff suggested, 'well, the men are playing much more hockey now, what with the Olympics and so on, and some of the girls have done soccer too'. At both institutions, male and female students studied dance, although male students in their final year at Heydonfield could 'opt out' of this activity if they wished.

However, as Scraton (1990) notes, it is not just important to identify and note gender differentiation in contemporary practice, but also vital to consider the ideological construction and reinforcement of gender through the teaching of PE. She argues that it is in the often extensive *definitions* and *justifications* of 'good practice' given by teachers that assumptions concerning the ideologies of gender can be found. How, then, did lecturers rationalize the gender differentiation in the timetabling of PE activities?

Preparation for teaching practice

The interviews with course leaders revealed that a major rationale for introducing men and women to different PE activities was the preparation for their teaching practice in schools. As one lecturer suggested, 'the women do not need rugby and the men don't need netball — they are *never* going to teach it on teaching practice'. Certainly, as others (e.g. Mentor, 1989) have noted, efforts by ITE institutions to be innovative and forward thinking are often thwarted by students' experiences on teaching practice, with many schools offering an experience which impedes, rather than helps, the development of critical, reflexive practitioners.

Whilst both institutions (rightly) felt it was important to adequately prepare students for their teaching experience in school, this rationale glosses over the question why *particular* activities become the province of one sex, or the implications of this differentiation for the reproduction of gender ideologies. Further questioning revealed more deep-seated rationales tied closely to these ideologies.

Women and contact sports

It was suggested that male and female students needed to be separated if the activity included physical contact, as the following comments made by staff illustrate:

> it depends on the activity . . . the swimming, the athletics, the gymnastics, it wouldn't cross my mind to separate them . . . the only thing where I have reservations about teaching mixed groups was if it was going to be a contact sport. . . . (male lecturer, Heydonfield)

> it's [single sex sessions] for the contact sports — you know, the athletics and the hockey and so on are mixed. (male lecturer, Heydonfield)

> obviously the women couldn't do rugby because of the injury factor. (female lecturer, Heydonfield)

> some of these lads are nutcases you know and they would think nothing about thinking it would be a good idea to crunch some girl. (male lecturer, Heydonfield)

As Sheila Scraton's chapter in this book shows, coeducational PE grouping *does* raise serious, major issues about sexuality and physicality, which need to be addressed by PE teachers and lecturers, rather than avoided or ignored, as the above comments suggest was the case here. As Scraton (1987, 1990) concludes, whilst the acceptance of physical aggression between boys and girls or men and women is in itself questionable, it is the double standard whereby it is only *women's* activity which is seen as in need of regulation which is so significant. She has identified how girls' PE contributes to an ideology of the physical which constructs young women as physically subordinate to men, and is closely tied to the development of female heterosexuality. Physical contact in PE for girls is considered inappropriate for reasons of safety, in terms of the potential physical damage girls could do to themselves, but also because

> any demonstration of power and assertion between women is not acceptable in relation to the social construction of female sexuality. Desirable female sexuality is a passive, responsible, heterosexuality and the engagement of girls or women in contact sports immediately raises doubts about the status of their sexuality. (Scraton, 1990, p. 28)

However, physical aggression and contact between men *is* considered acceptable and indeed *desirable*, since it is one of the ways in which men and boys can 'prove' their masculinity, a major feature of which is its link with physicality and physical prowess (Connell, 1987). A central process in the social construction of such hegemonic, or dominant, forms of masculinity is the way in which masculinity is more easily defined in terms of what it is *not* — that is, not feminine and not homosexual (Messner, 1987). Heterosexuality is central to hegemonic masculinity, as it is to dominant ideologies of femininity. Ideologies of gender and sexuality are, therefore, reproduced by the teaching of PE. By retaining soccer and rugby as male-only activities, the institutions ensured the involvement of male students in what Kessler *et al.* (1987) have called 'masculinizing practices', practices through which the reproduction of hegemonic masculinity, central to patriarchal gender relations, is maintained.

Aesthetic activities and masculinity

A third major rationale for the sex-differentiated timetable revolved around the 'inappropriateness' of aesthetic activities for male students. At Heydonfield, the staff had agreed, in response to complaints from male students, that the fourth-year course could become optional for men. At Brickhill, there was similar concern over the appropriateness of dance for the men students. As the Head of PE commented,

> although there is a strong dance ethos here, and the men *know* they have to do some . . . some of them are actually very good at it, not all of them obviously, but . . . it's just sort of . . . the social stigma attached to dance . . . they struggle to understand it, they struggle to teach it and then they don't have to teach it. (Head of PE, taped interview)

Similarly, there were doubts about the place of rhythmical gymnastics for the male students:

> we were worried ... about the men doing rhythmical gymnastics ...
> they are not too keen on rhythmical gymnastics, well it's not appropriate
> for them, and so we are trying to get some element of the martial arts in
> there for them. (Head of PE, taped interview)

Arthur Brittan (1989) notes that a major element in what he calls 'masculine identity work' — the way in which men and boys are involved in an almost continuous process of confirmation and construction of their masculinity — involves the rejection of 'feminizing practices'. The resistance of male students to the 'feminine' activity of dance needs to be seen in this light. Observation of dance classes showed how hard most male students worked to distance themselves from the activity, by laughing, 'fooling around' or exaggerating their lack of skill. Homophobic comments or gestures were common when men were asked to work together, since for men to touch one another in anything other than aggressive ways places their heterosexual 'masculinity' at risk (Askew and Ross, 1988).

The head of dance admitted that since the classes had gone mixed, dance teaching had become much more difficult, and that she had to 'change everything ... the music, the choice of material, the praise and the feedback ... to get the men to like the dance'. Despite these efforts, it was rare for any of the male students at Brickhill to opt to continue to specialize in dance in the final part of the course. Given the option, male students simply voted with their feet to reject any activity which would be likely to involve them in difficult 'masculine identity work'.[12] Although men were still very much in the minority on the undergraduate course at Brickhill, changes were being made specifically to meet their needs; another example of this was the way in which the 'striking-fielding games' option in part two of the course, written to include an analysis of the games of rounders, cricket and softball, was reduced to a cricket module, because the men 'didn't want to do rounders'.

As others have suggested, the move to coeducational PE has meant that it is a male-defined PE which is becoming dominant (Evans, 1990; Scraton, 1985). This trend is even more clear on the PGCE courses. The preoccupation of undergraduate PE programs with sport (see, e.g. Whitson and Macintosh, 1990), at the expense of a broader range of physical activities, including dance and gymnastics, affects the kinds of activities which can be included in PGCE courses. For example, at Brickhill, staff had decided to exclude dance from the curriculum, since so few students had experienced any dance in their undergraduate courses. The movement towards the PGCE route as the main route into ITE PE therefore has important implications, not only for the amount of time students have to develop an awareness of wider educational issues, but also for the types of activities which become defined as 'PE'.[13]

The implementation of the National Curriculum in PE may well contribute towards effective change in challenging the gender-differentiated curriculum — both at school, and at ITE level. For the first time, PE teachers (as well as lecturers) have a detailed national document, identifying equal opportunities as a 'guiding and leading principle' underpinning curriculum planning and provision.[14] The document states clearly, for example, that

> Sex differentiated programmes may be discriminatory, in that girls or boys may be prevented from learning certain types of skills. (DES, 1991, p. 58)

Teachers are asked to consider, and challenge, the way in which ideologies of femininity and masculinity associated with particular physical activities may affect the breadth of curricular provision for boys and girls. It will mean, too, that teachers will need to acknowledge, in their curriculum planning, the differential cultural values associated with different physical activities, and so avoid the situation where 'boys" and 'girls" PE are replaced simply by 'boys" PE. The report argues that 'sensitively' delivered, PE *can* provide opportunities for challenging body images and sex stereotyping which limit the choices and achievements of both girls and boys. But this will require

> both initial and in-service training of teachers to promote a critical review of prevailing practice, rigorous and continuous appraisal and often the willingness to question long held beliefs and prejudices. (DES, 1991, p. 15)

The position of teacher educators in this process is obviously crucial.

This section has focused specifically on the current sex-differentiated timetabling of practical activities in the undergraduate degrees of the case study institutions. It showed how particular activities — contact sports, and aesthetic activities such as dance — continue to be seen by teacher educators (if not always promoted) as 'feminine' or 'masculine'. However, wholesale moves to mixed classes were not necessarily the answer to breaking down these gender ideologies and to the provision of equality of opportunity for girls and women. Other research (e.g. Evans *et al.*, 1987) has shown how moves to implement co-educational PE classes, which have resulted from financial or staffing pressures, rather than on the basis of an *educational* rationale, are unlikely to be successful in challenging gender ideologies. The same scenario applied to the PGCE course at Brickhill. Because of the small numbers of students involved, all practical activities were timetabled in mixed groups, yet observation of classes showed how many — particularly the major games — were dominated by the actions of some of the male students, and, perhaps more disturbing, how members of staff rarely either acknowledged or challenged this behaviour. Most resistance observed was initiated from the students themselves. Some of the women students, in particular, resisted the ways in which they were often pushed to the 'margins of the classrooms' (Stanworth, 1983). As one woman commented angrily to me after a mixed soccer session in which the final 'game' had been dominated by three of her male peers, 'the girls just stood around and got bloody freezing — doesn't he realize that this will happen if we did this in schools? I said to them, 'did you enjoy your game lads?" but it mostly goes right over their heads'.

Conclusions

The extent to which PE students in the case study institutions were involved in addressing the ways in which gender inequalities are reproduced through the actions of teachers and the education system was minimal, and varied considerably between courses. On the undergraduate, four-year courses, students were involved in short compulsory modules in which issues of equality *were* raised. The effectiveness of these short, non-assessed courses, placed within the early years of the Professional Studies element of the course — the part students view as least valuable — was questionable, particularly given the contradictory 'hidden' messages reproduced through the timetabling and some of the teaching of the PE Subject Studies elements of the courses. The picture on the one-year PGCE courses was no more encouraging. At best, students at Heydonfield were involved in one or two lecture presentations where 'equal opportunities' issues for girls were raised; at worse, gender issues were not formally raised at all, as was the case at Brickhill.

If the practices and ideologies evident in the case study institutions are endemic in PE ITE, then ITE courses not only fail to raise students' awareness of gender issues, but also may *reinforce* ideologies of masculinity and femininity through the choice, timetabling and teaching of PE activities.[15] PE *can* play a major part in denying ideologies of femininity and masculinity, and in challenging physical power and sexual relations (Scraton, 1986), and, as the National Curriculum document suggests, ITE has a crucial part to play in preparing future PE teachers who are equipped with the knowledge, understanding and sensitivity to begin to do this. But there will need to be some important changes made before this is the case. The following would be some suggestions for the kinds of changes which need to be made.

Extending the legitimacy and visibility of equality issues within ITE

Issues of equality must be given a greater legitimacy and visibility within ITE courses as well as more generally within the institutions in which they are based. Teacher educators need to ensure that all students are required to study gender issues as a compulsory, and *assessed*, part of their course. The input needs to be carefully planned so that it is staggered throughout the course, rather than in a single block, and raised within all of the different components of the course (e.g. Subject Studies, Professional Studies, etc.) The work must be structured so that the issues are raised in a progressive way. As Sneh Shah (1989) notes, the level of discussion must match the level of professional development of the student, and recognize and take into account students' particular concerns at specific times during the course. It should also take into account their possible very different starting positions in relation to this work. It is important for issues of gender equality to be raised very early in the course so that students recognize the course's commitment to these issues. Similarly, they must be included within the structuring and evaluation of teaching practice, the central component of the courses, around which the rest of the course is organized. The promotion of gender equality in their work in schools needs to be one of the criteria by which students are assessed on teaching practice. As the study by Coldron and Boulton

(1989) has shown, with careful planning and coordination with the schools, this has the added advantage of involving, and giving support to, school teachers struggling to raise these issues in their own institutions.

These recommendations, however, may well become more difficult to implement satisfactorily, once the impending governmental changes to ITE are announced. Although the details are as yet unknown, it is likely that the current ITE provision will be subject to major change in the near future. Alternative routes into teaching alongside the conventional BEd and PGCE routes have already been adopted by the DES (although these have not so far included PE — at least at intending secondary teacher level). Both the Articled and, in particular, the Licensed teacher routes move towards a school-based model of teacher education. Although it is too early to assess the impact of these routes, the danger of the Licensed teacher route is that with 'teachers training teachers', existing inegalitarian practices will simply be reproduced (Miles and Middleton, 1990). In relation to PE, as I argued elsewhere (Flintoff, 1990), there is a danger that the current governmental support and encouragement for increasing the work of local authority sports development officers with schools may convince headteachers that such personnel could easily become 'Licensed' teachers, making trained PE teachers dispensable.

Whilst the Articled teacher route has more to recommend it, extending over two years and including a fifth of the time back in college, some (e.g. Hill, 1989) have suggested this does not give sufficient time for adequate reflection away from the classroom; also, there is a danger that students' experiences of schools might be more limited than on the current BEd and PGCE courses. As the evidence from my research has shown, the move away from the four-year BEd courses towards shorter, more school-based courses may squeeze the amount of time which can be spent addressing gender issues. Current PGCE courses are most likely to use 'permeation' as a method of addressing gender issues (EOC, 1989) which, as shown at Brickhill, can become a way of avoiding them altogether. Teacher educators, already under a great deal of pressure from having to accommodate increasing student numbers within a diminishing unit or resource, may find it difficult simply to maintain the present, limited provision, rather than to extend and develop it. As Sandra Acker (1988) has noted, in a situation where there are no *incentives* for teachers to develop this work, and where their role and workload have expanded and continue to expand, teachers and teacher educators may simply be too tired for 'optional' innovations in the area of gender equality.

Gender issues and PE

PE professionals working in ITE have an important role to play if future teachers of PE are able to implement gender equality as a 'leading and guiding principle' within their work in schools. They will need to critically evaluate their current practices and, in particular, question and rethink their sex-differentiated curriculum and grouping arrangements. In some senses, the National Curriculum in PE will help promote this reflection process, since teacher educators have been instructed to prepare students to take on board all aspects of the National Curriculum in their teaching (see NCC, 1991). However, unfortunately, whilst the National Curriculum in PE provides comprehensive *guidelines* for teachers in terms of equality issues, the *statutory* elements provide a flexible enough framework (particularly at Key Stages Three and Four) for much of the current poor practice to continue. For example, one male head of PE in school said to me recently that he had no intention of changing from his games-dominated curriculum, and that to 'get round' the 'broad, balanced' criteria which should underpin his programme, he would be offering his boys a trampolining course as their 'aesthetic' education.[16]

Teacher education needs to provide a lead in producing teachers who are prepared to teach across a range of activities, rather than the narrow, sex-segregated curriculum. If shorter, postgraduate courses in PE become the main route into teaching, which seems to be the case, then the profession will have to look critically at the undergraduate degree programmes, both in terms of students' practical experience of physical activities, as well as the kinds of (scientific, behavioural) paradigms which are likely to have dominated these courses. It may mean that the criteria by which students are selected to train to become PE teachers will have to change. If ITE in PE is to begin to break down gender stereotyping, and present positive role models (where women are not left to teach all the dance, or men the soccer, for example), we cannot continue to recruit students who have had only a narrow range of physical experience before they enter their training. Potential students will have to demonstrate a personal commitment to a balanced PE curriculum, *as well as* to gender equality, as key elements in good educational practice.

Finally, teacher educators in PE will also have to critically review their *own* practices, as well as those perpetuated within their institutions. For some, this will be difficult, for as Acker concludes,

> many of the reforms called for in the feminist literature are fundamental, and possibly threatening. Teachers' own gendered histories, roles outside schools and positions within the school, shape their beliefs about what reform is possible or desirable. (Acker, 1988, pp. 319–20)

And change within education alone will be insufficient. Schools and ITE institutions cannot be viewed as separate from the capitalist patriarchal society in which they are currently situated. Long-term change will need to happen at a structural level — political, social and economic change — as well as at the level of the attitudes and practices of individual educators. PE, however, with its close link to the body, physicality and sexuality, must be centrally involved in this process.

Notes

1 Since members of the black population are severely underrepresented on ITE courses, both as students and as lecturers, the research which is available focuses on predominantly white, if not all-white, groups. In this research, there were no black students on the PE courses at the institution I have called 'Heydonfield', and only a very small minority at the other, which I have called 'Brickhill'. Similarly, there were no black staff teaching on the courses at all. It is recognized that although the focus of this research was gender relations, these

will be cut across and compounded by relations of class and 'race'. However, as others (e.g. Dewar, 1990) have noted, it is often in terms of gender that an otherwise relatively homogeneous group of PE students might be differently positioned.

2 Although the term initial teacher *training* is more commonly used, like others (e.g. Mentor, 1989) I have chosen to use initial teacher *education* to reflect the kind of process I hope students would be involved in.

3 The research is a PhD project based in the School of Education, the Open University.

4 There are now only approximately twelve institutions which offer initial teacher education courses for intending secondary, specialist PE teachers. Although the material presented in this chapter derived specifically from fieldwork in the two case study institutions (and therefore it is wrong to generalize about the findings) interviews with lecturers in other institutions revealed not dissimilar attitudes and value positions towards gender issues, and curricular practices.

5 To preserve anonymity, all other names included in the text are pseudonyms too.

6 John Evans (1989) has suggested that it may be useful to distinguish between the terms 'mixed-sex' and 'coeducational'. He suggests the former should be used to refer only to a form of organization where children of both sexes are simply brought together in the same group for teaching purposes, whereas coeducational grouping should refer to situations where there is a sensitivity to the predispositions children bring to the lesson (abilities, physical strengths, cultural attitudes and expectations) which often serve to set boys and girls apart. I have chosen to use the term coeducation here, throughout, although in these terms I feel it may be a somewhat optimistic choice!

7 ITE courses in PE became coeducational as a result of the imposition of the 1976 European Equal Treatment Directive.

8 Research such as Pratt *et al.* (1984) found that females rather than males, and younger rather than older teachers were more likely to support the principle of sex equality, although subject specialism was more significant than either sex or age of the teacher. PE does not feature very well; PE teachers fell into the group of teachers who were least sympathetic to equal opportunities, a position which reflects findings in other research (e.g. Leaman, 1984; Scraton, 1989).

9 The ITE courses were made up of three major elements: Professional Studies, Subject Studies and Teaching Practice. On the undergraduate courses at both Brickhill and Heydonfield, PE students studied a second specialist subject as well as PE, although in both courses twice as much time was spent on their specialist Subject Study, PE, as on their Second Subject.

10 It is significant, but not surprising, that this work is couched in terminology central to liberal feminist critiques of education. The limitations of such an approach, based on issues of access and on changing stereotypical attitudes, are now well recognized (e.g. Arnot, 1981).

11 Comments such as these were made to me during informal conversations with students during the fieldwork. I did not interview students formally, but, particularly at Brickhill, spent a lot of time following groups of students to their various classes. I got to know the PGCE group at Brickhill particularly well, especially the women students, as my gender allowed me access to informal settings with them, such as the changing rooms, where the content and nature of their lectures were often the focus of discussion. Dot, the student who made the comment above, was one of the few students I met during the fieldwork who had a particular commitment to 'race' and gender equality. She confided in me that she had been on the point of withdrawing from the course several times because of the 'stereotypical and conservative' thinking of people involved with the course.

12 A more detailed overview of these issues is developed in Flintoff, 1991.
13 Although there are currently more PE (secondary) teachers trained through the four-year undergraduate route than the PGCE route, this balance is changing.
14 This is in contrast to other countries which have had these kinds of policies in place for some time, and where the government has taken a much more proactive stance on the position of women in education, and PE. For example, Australia, which passed a National Policy on the Education of Girls in 1985, sent guidelines to all schools about the implications of this policy for PE (see Ministry of Education, Western Australia, 1987).
15 Although there is no space here to discuss the findings, evidence gathered from observing classroom interactions suggests that ideologies of femininity and masculinity were also reinforced in the interactions between staff and students.
16 The framework presented in the final report may not necessarily be accepted in the final orders. Comments from the Secretary of State for Education to the working party about the interim report (in his letter included in the front of the final report) suggest that the final orders cut the numbers of activities included in Key Stage Three from five to four. This means that teachers will be able to use the flexibility offered in this statutory framework to avoid changing gender-stereotyped practice — for example, if this was the case, PE teachers could 'opt out' completely of providing a dance experience for boys.

References

ACKER, S. (1988) 'Teachers, Gender and Resistance', *British Journal of Sociology of Education,* **9**, 3, pp. 307–21.
ADAMS, C. (1985) 'Teachers' Attitudes towards Issues of Sex Equality', in WHYTE J., DEEM, R., CANT, L. and CRUICKSHANK, M. (Eds) *Girl Friendly Schooling*, London, Methuen, pp. 119–30.
ANTI-RACIST TEACHER EDUCATION NETWORK (ARTEN) (1988) *Permeation: The Road to Nowhere, Occasional Paper 4, Jordanhill College of Education.*
ARNOT, M. (1981) 'Cultural and Political Economy: Dual Perspectives in the Sociology of Women's Education', *Educational Analysis,* **3**, 1, pp. 7–116.
ASKEW, S. and ROSS, C. (1988) *Boys Don't Cry: Boys and Sexism in Education*, Milton Keynes, Open University Press.
BRITTAN, A. (1989) *Masculinity and Power*, Oxford, Basil Blackwell.
BRYSON, L. (1987) 'Sport and the Maintainance of Masculine Hegemony', *Women's Studies International Forum,* **10**, 4, pp. 349–60.
BRYSON, L. (1990) 'Challenges to Male Hegemony in Sport', in MESSNER, M.A. and SABO, D.F. (Eds) *Sport, Men and the Gender Order: Critical Feminist Perspectives*, Illinois, Human Kinetics, pp. 173–84.
COLDRON, J. and BOULTON, P. (1989) *The Implementation and Evaluation of an Action Plan to Develop the PGCE Curriculum so that the Professional Issues of Equal Opportunities are Effectively Addressed Using a Focussed Permeation Model*, Department of Education, Sheffield City Polytechnic.
COLDRON, J. and BOULTON, P. (1990) *Integrating Equal Opportunities in the Curriculum of Teacher Education: European Community Action Research Project, Phase Two Report (1989–1990)*, Department of Education, Sheffield City Polytechnic.
CONNELL, R.W. (1987) *Gender and Power*, Cambridge, Polity Press.
CONNELL, R.W. (1990) 'An Iron Man: The Body and Some Contradictions of Hegemonic Masculinity', in MESSNER, M.A. and SABO, D.F. (Eds) *Sport, Men and the Gender Order: Critical Feminist Perspectives*, Illinois, Human Kinetics, pp. 83–95.

DAY, I. (1988) 'Sorting the Men Out from the Boys: Masculinity, a Missing Link in the Sociology of Sport', MA dissertation, Dept of Applied Social Sciences, Sheffield City Polytechnic.

DEEM, R. (1980) 'Women, School and Work: Some Conclusions', in DEEM, R. (Ed.) *Schooling for Women's Work*, London, Routledge and Kegan Paul, pp. 177–83.

DEEM, R. (Ed.) (1984) *Coeducation Reconsidered*, Milton Keynes, Open University Press.

DEEM, R. (1991) 'Feminist Interventions in Schooling 1975–1990', in RATTANSI, A. and REEDER, D. (Eds) *Radicalism and Education*, London, Lawrence and Wishart.

DENSCOMBE, M. (1982) 'The Hidden Pedagogy and its Implications for Teacher Training', *British Journal of Sociology of Education*, **3**, 3, pp. 249–65.

DEPARTMENT OF EDUCATION AND SCIENCE (1989) *Initial Teacher Training: Approval of Courses*, Circular 24/89, DES.

DEPARTMENT OF EDUCATION AND SCIENCE (1991) *Physical Education for Ages 5 to 16, DES/Welsh Office*.

DEWAR, A. (1990) 'Oppression and Privilege in Physical Education: Struggles in the Negotiation of Gender in a University Programme', in KIRK, D. and TINNING, R. (Eds). *Physical Education, Curriculum and Culture: Critical Issues in the Contemporary Crisis*, Lewes, Falmer Press, pp. 67–99.

EQUAL OPPORTUNITIES COMMISSION (1989) *Formal Investigation Report: Initial Teacher Education in England and Wales*, June.

EVANS, J. (1989) 'Swinging from the Crossbar: Equality and Opportunity in the Physical Education Curriculum', *British Journal of Physical Education*, **20**, 2, pp. 84–7.

EVANS, J. (1990) 'Ability, Position and Privilege in School Physical Education', in KIRK, D. and TINNING, R. (Eds) *Physical Education, Curriculum and Culture: Critical Issues in the Contempory Crisis*, London, Falmer Press, pp. 139–67.

EVANS, J., LOPEZ, S., DUNCAN, M. and EVANS, M. (1987) 'Some Thoughts on the Political and Pedagogical Implications of Mixed Sex Groupings in the Physical Education Curriculum', *British Educational Research Journal*, **13**, 1, pp. 59–71.

FLETCHER, S. (1984) *Women First: The Female Tradition in English Physical Education 1880–1980*, London, Athlone.

FLINTOFF, A. (1990) 'Physical Education, Equal Opportunities and the National Curriculum: Crisis or Challenge?', *Physical Education Review*, **13**, 2, pp. 85–100.

FLINTOFF, A. (1991) 'Dance, Masculinity and Teacher Education', *British Journal of Physical Education*, **22**, 4, Winter.

HILL, D. (1990) *Something Old, Something New, Something Borrowed, Something Blue: Teacher Education and the Radical Right in Britain and the USA*, Paper 3, Hillcole Group, London, Tufnell Press.

JONES, C. and STREET-PORTER, R. (1989) 'The Special Role of Teacher Education', in COLE, M. (Ed.) *Education for Equality: Some Guidelines for Good Practice*, London, Routledge, pp. 211–29.

KELLY, A. (1985) 'Changing Schools and Changing Society: Some Reflections on the GIST Project', in ARNOT, M. (Ed.) *Race and Gender: Equal Opportunities Policies in Education*, Oxford, Pergamon, pp. 137–46.

KESSLER, S., ASHENDEN, D., CONNELL, R. and DOWSETT, G. (1987) 'Gender Relations in Secondary Schooling', in ARNOT, M. and WEINER, G. (Eds) *Gender and the Politics of Schooling*, London, Hutchinson/Open University Press, pp. 223–36.

KIRK, D. (1990) 'Defining the Subject: Gymnastics and Gender in British Physical Education', in KIRK, D. and TINNING, R. (Eds) *Physical Education, Curriculum and Culture: Critical Issues in the Contemporary Crisis*, London, Falmer Press, pp. 43–66.

LEAMAN, O. (1984) *Sit on the Sidelines and Watch the Boys Play: Sex Differentiation in Physical Education*, Schools Council, Longman.

LEONARD, D. (1989) 'Gender and Initial Teacher Training', in DELYON, H. and WIDDOWSON MIGNIUOLO, F. (Eds) *Women Teachers: Issues and Experiences*, Milton Keynes, Open University Press, pp. 23–36.

MCKAY, J., GORE, J. and KIRK, D. (1990) 'Beyond the Limits of Technocratic Physical Education', *Quest*, **42**, 1, pp. 40–51.

MAHONY, P. (1985) *Schools for the Boys? Co-education Reassessed*, London, Hutchinson.

MAHONY, P. (1989) 'Sexual Violence and Mixed Schools', in JONES, C. and MAHONY, P. (Eds) *Learning Our Lines: Sexuality and Social Control*, London, The Women's Press, pp. 157–90.

MENTOR, I. (1989) 'Teaching Practice Stasis: Racism, Sexism and School Experiences in Initial Teacher Education', *British Journal of Sociology of Education*, **10**, 4, pp. 459–73.

MESSNER, M. (1987) 'The Life of a Man's Seasons: Male Identity in the Life Course of a Jock', in KIMMEL, M.S. (Ed.) *Changing Men: New Directions in Research on Men and Masculinity*, London, Sage, pp. 53–67.

MILES, S. and MIDDLETON, C. (1990) 'Girls' Education in the Balance: The ERA and Inequality', in FLUDE, M. and HAMMER, M. (Eds) *The Education Reform Act, 1988: Its Origins and Implications*, London, Falmer Press, pp. 187–206.

MINISTRY OF EDUCATION, WESTERN AUSTRALIA (1987) *Equal Opportunity Legislation: PE and Sport Guidelines for Secondary and Primary Schools*, Education Dept, Western Australia.

NATIONAL CURRICULUM COUNCIL (1991) *The National Curriculum and the Initial Training of Student, Articled and Licensed Teachers*, York, NCC.

PRATT, J., BLOOMFIELD, J. and SEALE, C. (1984) *Option Choice: A Question of Equal Opportunity*, Windsor, NFER-Nelson.

RIDDELL, S. (1989) 'Teachers' Views and Gender Divisions in the Curriculum', in ACKER, S. (Ed.) *Teachers, Gender and Careers*, London, Falmer Press, pp. 123–38.

SCRATON, S. (1985) *Losing Ground: The implications for Girls of Mixed Physical Education*, Paper presented at the British Educational Research Association, Sheffield.

SCRATON, S. (1987) 'Gender and Physical Education: Ideologies of the Physical and the Politics of Sexuality', in WALKER, S. and BARTON, L. (Eds) *Changing Policies, Changing Teachers: New Directions for Schooling?*, Milton Keynes, Open University Press, pp. 169–89.

SCRATON, S. (1989) *Shaping Up To Womanhood: A Study of the Relationship Between Gender and Girls' Physical Education in a City-Based Local Education Authority*, Unpublished PhD thesis, School of Education, Open University.

SCRATON, S. (1990) *Gender and Physical Education*, Victoria, Deakin University Press.

SCRATON, S. (1986) 'Image of Femininity and the Teaching of Girls' Physical Education, in EVANS, S. (Ed.) *Physical Education, Sport and Schooling: Studies in the Sociology of Physical Education*, Lewes, Falmer Press, pp. 71–94.

SHAH, S. (1989) 'Effective Permeation of Race and Gender Issues in Teacher Education', *Gender and Education*, **1**, 3, pp. 221–45.

SKELTON, C. and HANSON, J. (1989) 'Schooling the Teachers: Gender and Initial Teacher Education', in ACKER, S. (Ed.) *Teachers, Gender and Careers*, London, Falmer Press, pp. 109–22.

SMART, C. (1984) *The Ties that Bind: Law, Marriage and the Reproduction of Patriarchal Relations*, London, Routledge and Kegan Paul.

STANWORTH, M. (1983) *Gender and Schooling: A Study of Sexual Divisions in the Classroom*, London, Hutchinson.

WHITSON, D. (1990) 'Sport in the Social Construction of Masculinity', in MESSNER, M. A. and SABO, D.F. (Eds) *Sport, Men and the Gender Order: Critical Feminist Perspectives*, Illinois, Human Kinetics, pp. 19–29.

WHITSON, D. and MACINTOSH, D. (1990) 'The Scientization of Physical Education: Discourses of Performance', *Quest*, **42**, 19, pp. 40–51.

WHITTY, G., BARTON, L. and POLLARD, A. (1987) 'Ideology and Control in Teacher Education: A Review of Recent Experience in England', in POPKEWITZ, T.S. (Ed.) *Critical Studies in Teacher Education: Its Folklore, Theory and Practice*, London, Falmer Press, pp. 161–83.

Chapter 13

Physical Education within Special Educational Provision — Equality and Entitlement

Paula Halliday

For an author to state the obvious can be risky. Firstly, because those who address issues at a surface level can congratulate themselves that they already know the nub of the issue and so stop reading. Secondly, those who are committed to the endeavour may see the statement as an insult to their understanding or exploration, and they too may stop reading. This author is going to take the risk, however, believing firmly that it is only by stating an obvious dictum that has been given lip service for the last twenty years that we can proceed to try to make it true. And the obvious ... what is it in a book which looks at equality of opportunity for all in physical education and in a chapter which deals specifically with needs of pupils with special educational needs? Quite simply it is that in order to meet the educational needs of pupils we must know what those needs are.

In April 1982, the Education Act 1981 came into force in England and Wales. For the first time, local authorities and schools were required to look at the individual curricular needs of pupils as a prerequisite to any decision about educational provision. Previously pupils had been assigned to categories outlined in the Education Act 1944, which were very much medically biased. Pupils would be variously described as physically handicapped, blind, partially sighted, deaf, partially hearing, speech defective, epileptic, maladjusted or educationally subnormal, whether mildly or severely so. Placement was often a routine response to a medical or psychological assessment both of which measured performance against norms and which assigned the pupils to one of the categories listed above rather than looking at their individual needs and competencies. In fact in some cases the cut-off point of categories was managed by local education authorities (LEAS) with regard to the provision available.[1] In some authorities children whose IQ fell below 90 could find themselves in a School for the Moderately Educationally Sub-Normal (ESN (M)), while in another LEA with fewer special schools pupils might only be so categorized if their IQ fell below 80. Little heed was paid to the profiles and individual circumstances of pupils. These individual strengths and weaknesses could mean that two pupils who scored identically on a standardized test would have very different curricular needs. This meant that special schools were often required to provide curricula for a tremendous range of pupil ability. This chapter will focus on pupils with physically disabling conditions in order to demonstrate the development from this position of place-ment according to category. This choice of focus on pupils with physical disabilities creates the greatest challenge for teachers whose emphasis is on developing physical coordination and skills within the context of the education of the whole child.

Legal and Historic Background — Reaction, Evolution and Resistance

Historically, young people who had a medically diagnosed condition which impeded their mobility, their motor control, their stamina or their general health were lumped together into a category called 'the physically handicapped'. Some young people's medical condition meant that they had complex problems with movement, learning and language, whilst others merely had a mobility difficulty and some merely a need for medical treatment or intervention. Once dubbed 'physically handicapped', however, most found themselves in a special school for the physically handicapped where the range of pupils' cognitive, language, move-ment, emotional and social needs lay in a continuum from minor to severe. Within such a school, designing a curriculum to meet all needs was difficult because as well as the range of needs represented, the population was small and often 'all-age', and even with high adult-pupil ratios this led to small staffing numbers with limitations to the specific expertise available. School priorities often dictated that the more 'academic' subjects, usually labelled 'basics' (i.e. English and Mathematics), should be seen as the priority for staff appointment, particularly in the many special schools where pupils remained with a class teacher for all subjects even within the secondary section of the school. In addition, the schools tended to be a geographical focus for paramedical services provided by the health authorities. Treatment provided at these centres was often seen as additional to, or in some cases was characterized by, its separate-ness from the educational endeavour, and so conformed to the medical model of intervention. In some extreme cases physiotherapy was seen as the prime or only necessary movement input to pupils. In the case of the special school of which the author was head, gym equipment fitted into the 'new' building twenty years previously was removed soon after on the assumption that it was surplus to requirements because the pupils had access to regular physiotherapy! PE and movement offered was, therefore, restricted by the paucity of equipment. Luck-ily the attitude that 'therapy was enough' had been eroded and an understanding that, although PE and movement might in fact sometimes be therapeutic, they were and are important components in curriculum. This had to be firmly enshrined in the ethos of the school and new monies found and dedicated to supporting the development of the curricular area.

The situation before 1981 was, of course, not static, as young people with less severe or complex difficulties tended to move to mainstream education as their treatment became more personally manageable. Young people with medi-cal difficulties (e.g. asthma, diabetes, cystic fibrosis) tended to be in the vanguard of this movement as they required little adaptation to building or equipment to access the curriculum and often had no associated cognitive difficulties. Teachers in the mainstream, therefore, were often exposed to pupils with 'hidden disabilities' which often meant that ostensibly their needs appeared to be in common with those of their peers. This may, in fact, have been inaccurate as many such pupils may have found that their medical condition restricted their stamina or strength and impeded their ability to participate fully in the curriculum on offer. Most importantly, the very hiddenness of their needs may have militated against the success of their integration. Sullivan (1990) who had a medical condition and who attended mainstream secondary education in the late 1970s, reported that she had frequent questions asked in her school reports about whether or not she was malingering because her condition limited her stamina, particularly on the sports field and increased her absence from school!

The 1981 Act endorsed the increasing realization that to assign pupils to categories was at best unhelpful and at worst counterproductive. It legislated for local authorities to look at the strengths of pupils and to involve a variety of professionals to include teachers, medical officers and psychologists as well as the child's parents in assessing needs. It requires schools and education authorities to identify any need which would get in the way of a pupil taking up the education experiences generally offered to pupils of that age group. Assessment of these needs is to result in provision which meets that individual's needs. The Act also acknowledges that some pupils' needs arise because of the environmental context of education. Pupils with any additional need, except second language requirements, are described as having 'special educational needs' and these needs may lie in the domain of cognitive, language, sensory, physical, motor, emotional or behavioural areas or in any combination of these. For those pupils with the most complex needs, local authorities must maintain and service a 'Statement of Special Educational Needs' which describes what provisions will be given to the pupil. This statement has legal status as a contract between the LEA and the pupil. Pupils with less complex needs are unlikely to have such specific protection but it remains the legal duty of governors and staff of all schools under the 1981 Act to ensure that pupils' needs are identified, assessed and met. The Act also lays an emphasis on meeting needs within the most normative educational setting. That is, most pupils should be educated in mainstream schools provided that this is within the LEA's perception of the efficient use of resources and to the best advantage of all pupils.

In spite of this 'escape' clause for local education authorities, many pupils with physical disability were transferred to mainstream schools and, as Howarth (1987) reported, 90 per cent of teachers were in favour of the integration of those pupils with 'physical handicaps'. Unfortunately, because of the dearth of essential facilities, those with multiple disabilities tended to remain in the special sector. In effect, therefore, pupils with physical disabilities in mainstream have tended to be those whose major difficulty in accessing curriculum is a mobility or movement disorder rather than those having a complex need with physical disability being compounded by communication, perceptual, cognitive or emotional difficulties. In addition to this motor disabled group, in most mainstream schools there will be other pupils with hidden disabilities due to medical conditions as described above, as well as a group of pupils described as 'clumsy' and those who have learned to be disaffected in physical education. Those groups of pupils who are clumsy or disaffected have been within the system for longer than those with motor disorders and have created a challenge for committed teachers of physical education. From this challenge, creative teaching strategies have evolved to ensure that their needs have been met. The range of responses to these needs have included assessment tools (e.g. Henderson, 1984), to ensure needs were identified and therefore effectively met, as well as active strategies for reducing disaffection by ensuring that pupils build positive self-images. In addition, cross-curricular planning across PE and Health Education has often meant that opportunities have been made for discussion not only of performance but of attitude and perception.

The new group of pupils with severe mobility difficulties who have moved into mainstream and who might use wheelchairs as their major means of mobility are sometimes not so lucky in teacher response in spite of positive teacher attitudes. HMI (1989) reported that, although pupils with physical disabilities in the mainstream had a wider choice of curriculum on offer, many had these choices restricted because of physical access or teacher anxiety. As Fisher (1988) suggested, integration for them could stop at the gym door, and many find themselves sitting in libraries or merely spectating as their peers participate in PE or sport.

The Physical Education Curriculum — Assessment, Attitude and Access

Such limitation of curriculum is not confined to PE, but in the case of this subject it is easy to see where the anxiety arises. Pupils with physical disabilities are by definition of their personal characteristics likely to have impairments to physical competence. These impairments will involve restrictions to mobility as well as difficulties with voluntary motor control, coordination or organization of movement. In the so called 'able-bodied population' such difficulties are also likely to be present, but to a lesser extent. People with 'physical disabilities' have competences which lie at a more extreme end of the continuum and like all pupils they may have a combination of motor, coordination and spatial difficulties. The majority of pupils with disabilities, however, will be in the same situation as their peers in that there is space for improvement in their physical coordination or performance which can be worked on through physical education. The key aspect, therefore, in identifying where that education can and should be targeted, is assessment. Teachers of physical education know about the development of physical coordination and sport skills and have practice and expertise in assessing the needs of pupils who fall within the average range of competence, but they can feel less than confident when assessing at extreme ends of the continuum or where movement is disordered. A prime need, therefore, is for those who teach physical education to upgrade or re-apply the assessment skills they have acquired to this wider pupil population. Some good teachers may even be unaware of the continuous assessment skills they exercise during the course of every lesson as they observe, intervene and challenge pupils. For these, assessment will need to be moved into conscious or formal control rather than remain at the intuitive or informal level at which they currently operate. For all teachers this enhancement or widening of assessment skills is imperative if they are not to be anxious about including pupils with greater degrees of movement or motor disorders. Otherwise, they may develop negative attitudes to those pupils who highlight their lack of confidence and competence (Doll-Tepper, von Selzam and Linnert, 1991). Luckily, additional expertise in this area is available to teachers from other professionals both on a formal and on a less formal day-to-day basis. Most pupils with physical disabilities will have contact with physiotherapists whose stock in trade is the assessment and improvement of competence at extremes of motor ability. Pooling this expertise with the teaching and learning expertise of trained educationalists will ensure that pupils have their needs met.

Direct access to another professional expertise is obviously a most potent form of support, but initial information on physical competence is available in the form of advice for 'statement' which should always be available to professionals who work with pupils who have a Statement of Special Educational Needs. A copy of the 'statement' should be lodged in the school. The advice is likely to include a medical diagnosis as well as description of motor competence, and, although reading about the condition can be helpful, teachers should remember that within most of these conditions pupils may be affected mildly or severely or may have some or none of the characteristics. (There is a list of helpful agencies who can supply information in an easily accessible form at the end of this chapter). Parents and the pupils themselves can and should contribute knowledge about competence and limitations, and pupils should be encouraged to take responsibility for working to, but not too far beyond, their limitations.

As the National Curriculum for Physical Education (DES, 1991) points out, INSET, too, is an obvious vehicle for ensuring that teachers learn or enhance their skills of assessment and class management to ensure that all pupils, including those with disabilities, are included into the physical education curriculum. Again, professionals from other disciplines can contribute their skills and experience to the pool of expertise to be tapped for such in-service training, but in-service training should offer much more. Teachers need the opportunity to discuss and resolve issues of curriculum planning, pupil grouping and delivery methods with colleagues whose experience may be different or wider than their own but whose approach issues from the classroom-based focus of educators. In addition, in-service training can be so managed as to provide 'safe', because guided and supervised, opportunities for teachers to work at first hand with pupils with disabilities. This can be enhanced if teachers from the mainstream, with their expertise in physical education, work alongside their colleagues from special schools whose PE expertise may be less formal but who have long-term experience with pupils with movement and motor disorders. In this way both sets of participants both give and receive skills. Such INSET has proved to be most effective and can also be very cost-effective. The author has contributed to such in-service training, arranged by the North West Regional Advisory Centre which set up such courses across a number of local authorities. If one teacher from a physical education department can become more expert, in the general sense, about pupils with physical disabilities, then perhaps a school could use such a member of staff alongside visiting therapists as a resource for the rest of the staff. Such school-centred expertise can be augmented by harnessing all LEA resources. These will include the contribution of inspectors/advisers for physical education as well as that of inspectors/advisers for special educational needs.

If the key aspects of pupil assessment, staff training and inter-agency consultation are optimized, then most pupils with physical disabilities can and should take part in some form of physical education alongside their peers (Hodgson, 1989).

Since the Education Reform Act 1988, all pupils have a curriculum entitlement which includes PE. This entitlement is discussed below, but the limitations of involvement only in mainstream physical education need to be examined further. Pupils with physical disabilities have historically participated in sporting and leisure opportunities and competed against others who were 'handicapped' (in the sporting sense!) to an equivalent degree as themselves. To this end a variety of bodies have been set up to regulate and promote physical and leisure activities for people with disabilities (see the appendix at the end of this chapter for contact addresses). Fisher (1988) reports that the British Paraplegic Sports have noted a decline in entrants to specialist events since the upswing in integration. He suggests that mainstream schools feel that their staff have not enough training or expertise to coach youngsters for these specialist games. Again, if this is so, expertise and training is available to schools through the specialist governing bodies. The National Curriculum Physical Education document (DES, 1991) suggests that both mainstream and special schools should foster links with clubs and associations to augment their own expertise and widen both current and future options for all young people in the areas of physical education and leisure. The secret of true integration into the PE curriculum in mainstream education must be the balance between enabling pupils to have two sets of opportunities. The first set of opportunities lies in giving access to the physical education curriculum the child shares alongside their peers. The second is in maintaining options for inclusion in specialist opportunities just as other pupils with particular needs are given access to non-routine events.

Doll-Tepper, von Selzam and Linnet (1991) suggest that aspects which may militate against complete access to the breadth of the physical education curriculum for pupils with additional needs are the large class sizes and high teaching loads which teachers often carry. Teachers of physical education must be prepared to confront these issues creatively by investigating and experimenting with varieties of pupil grouping and team teaching and by ensuring their involvement at the initial stages of school timetabling. The National Curriculum has given PE an increased and legal status within the school system which should be capitalized on. The National Curriculum for Physical Education also requires that the issue of 'special educational needs' be on the agenda of PE departments. If PE becomes or remains the timetable 'filler' or afterthought, then pupils' entitlement will be eroded. PE teachers must be willing to advocate for their needs within whole-school discussions about allocation of resources. In addition, PE teachers can and should see themselves as part of the advice-giving team for pupils with physical disabilities who are the subjects of 'Statements', and use such opportunity to outline the individual pupil's right to be included into the widest PE curriculum possible and the support needed for it. They may then find themselves in a position where some human support is focused on the PE session for a child with a severe disability. Again creativity needs to be exercised if such support is not to degenerate into 'minding' the pupil with a disability. This is both focusing on the pupil's 'specialness' and so compounding their difference but also could be a waste of resources. Two adults in a lesson must and should enhance the opportunities for all. By enhancing opportunities for all, we enhance opportunities for pupils with additional needs.

Good mainstream schools will have a broad and exciting PE curriculum. Pupils with physical disabilities should have access to such a curriculum, but we must accept that ensuring that all pupils participate in any PE lesson is no easy matter for a teacher. It demands first of all teacher commitment which will then result in appropriate assessment of need, good planning for differentiation according to pupil competences and finally, flexibility in delivery. If it is hard to achieve this for those whose physical competence falls within the 'norm', it is obviously more difficult when those who fall outside that range are included, but it can and should be done if we are not to deprive pupils of their legal rights.

Using others' expertise to add to the pool of teacher expertise in assessment and planning can and does help ensure that teachers are not alone in this endeavour. Good teachers can and do seize opportunities to extend their own competence and to widen the experiences of their pupils. The author recalls an excellent gym lesson where some young pupils with disabilities joined a larger group of pupils with 'able bodies'. The focus of the lesson was on movement through a variety of levels and in a variety of modes. The pupils with disabling conditions used wheelchairs for most of their mobility around school, but because of this had strong upper trunk and arm muscles. A decision was made that their wheelchairs would be parked outside the gym. At first the teacher was concerned that the pupils with disabilities might be at risk in her lessons but discussions with paramedics had assured her of their ability to understand and work within their own limitations. Her anxiety then moved to a concern that they might feel exposed, vulnerable and incompetent when deprived of their wheelchairs in the presence of their peers. Again her anxiety was alleviated by good professional collaboration. The lesson continued to her regular pattern and to her surprise the pupils with disabilities not only 'coped' but became excellent models of 'novel' modes of locomotion to their peers. The lesson, successful in completion, fed the confidence of the teacher and ensured her further endeavours were faced positively. More importantly the young people with disabilities had their self-image greatly enhanced not only by working successfully alongside their peers but because the teacher had the positive teaching strategy which encouraged the greater endeavour of all by pointing out models of good skills. She did this for all who demonstrated creativity and success without patronizing any whether they had a physically disabling condition or not.

Access to a Broad Curriculum: Context, Contacts and Cooperation

Perhaps it is the opportunity to be good models for their able-bodied peers, as well as to work with others who are good models of competence for themselves which is often missing in the education of young people with special educational needs who attend special schools. Often this access to different levels of competence and standards of performance is held up as a valuable learning opportunity for pupils in other aspects of education which are viewed as more realistically achievable by people with disabilities who are seen as people who need to develop sedentary skills (e.g. literacy, numeracy, word processing, computing) in order to compete in the job market. To this end even part-time integration often focuses on the more 'academic' aspects of curriculum. This may be more easily achieved as teachers are less anxious in subjects which have a lesser emphasis on the practical, but all people are entitled to opportunities to know themselves as whole people who do, as well as think, and who extend themselves to the optimum. In the case of some of the activities that are carried on even in segregated special schools, pupils have the right to know how competent they are in a realistic sense in all areas of development including motor performance. If I am an 'excellent swimmer' who has a disability, am I an excellent swimmer per se or an excellent swimmer for one who has a disability? In some sporting events in particular, my disability may not get in the way at all and my experience may even have left me with an advantage in terms of the development of certain muscle groups which others have not been obliged to develop. Those who sail, or canoe, or swim or shoot or dance, can and should compete or cooperate on equal terms. Special schools may not be able to give opportunities for their pupils to assess universal standards and although staff there understand the manifestations of disabling conditions, they may not be trained or skilled in the planning and developing of physical education. In addition the very existence of a segregated provision may lead not only to restriction in curriculum opportunities but also to a restricted world view which denies opportunities for testing oneself against the world, to take risks and to learn about pacing oneself.

Thus the opportunities for pupils with physical disabilities in either mainstream or special settings can be restricted. One sector can open avenues to wide opportunity whilst perhaps restricting access to specialist opportunities. The other offers expertise in accessing specialist events but has limitations in offering breadth of opportunity and access to opportunities where a disabling condition is no handicap to a sporting opportunity. As suggested above, both now have an additional mandate to ensure that they look to ways to redress this balance. The Education Reform Act 1988 requires all schools to provide a curriculum which is broad, balanced and relevant and which includes the subjects of the National Curriculum. These subjects obviously include a requirement to provide pupils with their entitlement to physical education. The legislation does not stop with the mandate that the curriculum be broad, balanced and relevant but extends this to include a requirement for the curriculum to be delivered in a way which is differentiated so that all pupils can take up their entitlement as individuals. This responsibility and requirement lies with all schools whether special or mainstream. A small minority of pupils may be exempted from all or some aspects of the National Curriculum. This may mean that they are not required to follow a particular programme of study and its assessment or that they might be working on programmes of study associated with an earlier Key Stage. Regardless of how the exemption/disapplication is described, it is illegal to deprive any pupil of their rights to a curriculum which is broad, balanced and relevant, whether their exemption is as the outcome of their Statement of Special Educational Needs, or of a temporary 'direction'. In effect this must mean that all pupils are entitled to a physical education curriculum which is in itself both broad and balanced, whether it includes the programmes of study described in National Curriculum Physical Education or not. The working group who designed the PE National Curriculum have worked with the experience of excellent physical educators. Schools will have to include the requirements of the PE National Curriculum into their personalized school curriculum and include any additional needs and responses required for the pupils who are educated in their own school context in order that the requirement for differentiation is fulfilled. This will be mandatory, as all pupils will need to have their individual needs met whether they have special educational needs or not. This is the key right of all pupils through the Education Reform Act. To ensure that this happens, good physical educators will continue to work hard to produce plans which challenge pupils in creative ways.

Planning for differentiation to meet individual needs may seem to be an additional burden on teachers who may feel undermined or constrained by a national framework. The opportunity to look at planning and practice in the light of such a framework should, however, be seen as an opportunity to ensure that new plans include all pupils whatever their physical, motor or spatial competence — why do only half the job! The effort to include all pupils into good and broad programmes of physical education, needs to be seen as an effort of will but one which is an equal opportunities issue. As Rieser and Mason (1990) point out, it is society's unwillingness to employ all and any means (and effort) to alter itself rather than constrain pupils to alter which causes our perception of disability. I am not disabled if I have the means to participate in society whether those means are technological, physical or as an outcome of teacher planning and effort. And the payoff? Cynicism may suggest that the only payoff is the compliance with both the spirit and the letter of the 1981 and 1988 Education Acts. Experience, however, shows that the rewards can be much more. The author has seen how professional competence has been extended as physical education teachers use their creativity to include more and more people with special educational needs into their lessons and so provided enhanced opportunities for all pupils, not just the 'special' ones.

The author's experience is not unique. Rieser (1990) who was engaged in some team teaching with a mainstream teacher as part of a disability awareness module with her and her class group, reports how a primary teacher described a PE lesson which included pupils with disabilities as her most creative lesson of the year! That is the payoff and, perhaps, the other one which he may have highlighted in that particular team teaching situation was one for the pupils as he supplied an excellent model of personal competence for all. His own disability proved a resource rather than a handicap. Valuing differences by collaborating and sharing the experiences of learners, teachers and other professionals can only enhance education and particularly physical education. We can all learn in spite of our imperfect bodies!

Note

1 Schools for pupils dubbed 'educationally sub-normal' were of two kinds. Those pupils whose IQ fell approximately between 60 and 90 were placed in ESN (M) schools, while those with profound and multiple difficulties or those whose IQ fell below the local cut-off point attended schools for the severely educationally sub-normal, ESN (S).

References

DEPARTMENT OF EDUCATION AND SCIENCE (1944) *The Education Act*, London, HMSO.
DEPARTMENT OF EDUCATION AND SCIENCE (1981) *The Education Act*, London, HMSO.
DEPARTMENT OF EDUCATION AND SCIENCE (1988) *The Education Reform Act*, London, HMSO.
DEPARTMENT OF EDUCATION AND SCIENCE (1991) *National Curriculum. Physical Education for Ages 5 to 16. Final Report*, London, DES/Welsh Office.
DOLL-TEPPER, G., VON SELZAM, H. and LINNERT, C. (1991) *Teach the Teachers — Including Individuals with Disabilities in Physical Education*, Presentation at the AIESEP World Congress, Atlanta, Georgia, USA.
FISHER, A. (1988) 'Just One of the Boys', in *Times Educational Supplement*, 25 November, p. 6.
HENDERSON, S.E. (1984) Henderson Revision of the *Test of Motor Impairment*, Windsor, NFER-Nelson.
HER MAJESTY'S INSPECTORATE (1989) *Educating Physically Disabled Pupils — A Survey*, London, HMSO.
HODGSON, A. (1989) Integrating Physically Handicapped Pupils, in COHEN, A. and COHEN, L. (Eds) *Special Educational Needs in Ordinary Schools: A Source Book for Teachers*, London, Harper Row.
HOWARTH, S. (1987) *Effective Integration: Physically Handicapped Children in Primary School*, Windsor, NFER-Nelson.
RIESER, R. (1990) 'Raising Disability in Primary Schools', in RIESER, R. and MASON, M. (Eds) *Disability Equality in the Classroom: A Human Rights Issue, London, ILEA*.
RIESER, R. and MASON, M. (Eds) (1990) *Disability Equality in the Classroom: A Human Rights Issue*, London, ILEA.
SULLIVAN, S. (1990) 'My School Experience, in RIESER, R. and MASON, M. (Eds) *Disability Equality in the Classroom: A Human Rights Issue*, London, ILEA.

Further Reading

British Journal of Physical Education, **21**, 4, Winter 1990, Special Edition: *Special Educational Needs in PE*, The PE Association, Ling House, London.
MEEK, G. (1991) 'Mainstreaming in Physical Education', in ARMSTRONG, N. and SPARKES, A. (Eds) *Issues in Physical Education*, Cassell, pp. 74–91.

Appendix: Useful Addresses

Asthma

Asthma Society & Friends of the Asthma Research Council, 300 Upper Street, LONDON N1 2XX.
Tel. 071 226 2260.

Brittle Bones

Brittle Bone Society, 112 City Road, DUNDEE DD1 2PW.
Tel. 0382 817771.

Cerebral Palsy

The Spastics Society, 12 Park Crescent, LONDON W1N 4EQ.
Tel. 071 636 5020.

Cystic Fibrosis

Cystic Fibrosis Research Trust, 5 Blyth Road, BROMLEY, Kent, BR1 3RS.
Tel. 081 464 7211/2.

Diabetes

British Diabetic Association, 10 Queen Anne Street, LONDON W1M OBD.
Tel. 071 323 1531.

Epilepsy

British Epilepsy Association, Crowthorne House, Bigshotte, New Wokingham Road, Berkshire, RG11 3AY.
Tel: 0344 773122.

Haemophilia

The Haemophilia Society, 123 Westminster Bridge Road, LONDON SE1 7HR.
Tel: 071 928 2020.

Muscular Dystrophy

The Muscular Dystrophy Group of Great Britain and Northern Ireland, Nattrass House, 35 Macaulay Road, LONDON SW4 OQP.
Tel: 071 720 8055.

Spina Bifida

Association for Spina Bifida and Hydrocephalus, 22 Upper Woburn Place, LONDON WC1H OGP.
Tel: 071 388 1382.

General

The Sports Council, 70 Brompton Road, LONDON SW3 1EX.

The British Sports Association for the Disabled, Sir Ludwig Guttman Sports Centre, Harvey Road, AYLESBURY, Bucks.

Royal Association for Disability and Rehabilitation, 25 Mortimer Street, LONDON W1N 8AB.

Royal Yachting Association, Victoria Way, WOKING, Surrey.

Wheelchair Dance Association, 30 Templar Road, PAIGNTON, TQ3 1EL.

British Ski Club for the Disabled, Corton House, CORTON, Near Warminster, Wiltshire.

Riding for the Disabled Association, Avenue R, National Agricultural Centre, KENILWORTH, Warwickshire, CV8 3LY.

Equipment for the Disabled, 2 Foredown Drive, PORTSLADE, Sussex, BW4 2BB.

Chapter 14

Equality, Physical Education and Outdoor Education Ideological Struggles and Transformative Structures?

Barbara Humberstone

The boys say, 'Girls can't play football'. They still say it even though we are in the '90s! (Claudia)[1]

In this chapter, I will briefly examine the complex issues of equality in relation to physical education (PE) and outdoor education (OE). In so doing, I will not only consider the construction of particular gender identities and the transmission of gender and educational codes but also draw attention to what is perceived to constitute valid knowledge and skill and by whom. The contradictions surrounding OE, its position in the National Curriculum (NC) and the particular form and content of OE and its relations to social change are important issues which are raised.

Introduction

Is there any reality in talking of correspondences between the structure of gender relations, of masculinity and femininity and the divisions of school knowledge? ... The school's gender code sets up the categories of masculine and feminine as well as the boundaries and relations of power between them. (MacDonald, 1980, pp. 36, 38)

Clearly, we live in a gendered society in which particular forms of knowledge and ways of knowing are privileged over others. In such a society taken-for-granted assumptions about the naturalness of prevailing forms of masculinity and femininity contribute toward the concealment of, and de-fusion of resistances to, inequalities of race, sex and class (James and Saville-Smith, 1989). Simplistically, gendered societies are characterized by structures which largely depend, for their continuance, upon the maintenance of 'hegemonic masculinity' and 'emphasized femininity'.[2] These forms of femininity and masculinity are stereotypical and 'their interrelation is centred on a single structural fact, the global dominance of men over women' (Connell, 1987, p. 183). This pattern of dominance is realized throughout society in the unequal material conditions between men and women in which women are generally paid less and work longer hours and through the manifestation of male public and private, real and symbolic violence which affects both men and women on a world scale (Walby, 1990). These patterns are enacted through sports-associated cultures where there continues to be significant underrepresentation of women in decision-making positions and women's access to facilities is limited (cf. Ball, 1986; Green *et al.*, 1990; White and Brackenridge, 1984; White, 1988; Wimbush and Talbot, 1988).[3]

Historically, traditional sport has provided a visible powerful symbolic and material milieu through which male privilege and prestige have been supported, bolstered and naturalized and in which male aggression and violence, if not sanctioned, are considered 'natural' (Connell, 1987; Dunning, 1986; Whitson, 1990). Sport is a domain in which hegemonic masculinity and, through the processes of exclusion or incorporation, emphasized femininity (Dewar, 1991) are constituted and even celebrated. But traditional and, perhaps even more so, alternative forms of sport may also be significant sites of contestation of oppressive forms of gender and other relations (cf. Hargreaves, 1990; Humberstone, 1990b; Messnor and Sabo, 1990).

School physical education curricula and the curriculum more generally are media through which the complex web of interrelations between the development of gender identity and relations, cultural values and gender stereotypes embedded in sport are mediated (Humberstone, 1990a). PE or OE may provide the space in which girls and boys can accept, reject or accommodate to cultural and ideological messages conveyed through media and other representations of sport. Evidence suggests that many young people, but particularly girls, have in the past been discouraged from participating in physical activity. We see the ways in which young sportswomen, even today, must struggle against inbuilt prejudice and discrimination in order to pursue their interest and display their expertise.

Claudia,[4] a young working-class sportswoman, describes proudly how in her primary school she went about getting the boys to let her play football with them at break times:

> At break ... at first ... [the boys] used to say, 'no you're not playing football with us'. So what I did to get around that was I bought a new football ... Then they [the boys] said, 'can we borrow your football'? and I said, 'Yes, you can play football with me!', and so that was how that was resolved ... But that came to an abrupt end when a muddy football was thrown at the dinner lady. I had to stand in the hall. I didn't do it but it was my football! (Claudia)

At one level and in terms of gender, equality means not only providing the opportunities for girls to learn the same knowledge and skills as boys and vice versa (whilst compensating for previous lack of experience in any particular activity), but equally importantly it means educating boys as well as girls to recognize and value girls' abilities. It also means providing an educational environment in which young people (girls and boys) acquire respect for themselves and each other, regardless of racial difference or disability. Equality in education does not solely involve liberalizing access but it must also encompass reciprocal understanding and valuing between girls and boys.

At another level, any material and substantive move towards long-term equality can only occur through a recognition of the structures of oppression by those white men (and some white women) in positions of privilege within institutional structures and more importantly a personal commitment to act and to reposition themselves, and to reject hierarchies of race, sex and class, in the struggle for a fairer, more just society. This means not merely writing and theorizing about equality but 'doing' equality in both personal *and* professional lives, and it means taking action to draw attention to and to counter oppressive practices in sporting and educational contexts at all levels.

Providing equal access to all types of activities, then, is, although a positive step towards equality, inadequate if we are concerned to challenge sexism and all other kinds of discrimination in schooling and in PE in particular. It is also unsatisfactory if the majority of girls and boys continue to view involvement in forms of sport and PE as inappropriate for girls. Weiner (1985) argues that a major restructuring of all institutions, including schools, is what is required if real equity is to be achieved. Change cannot occur until there is a paradigmatic shift in the ways in which men/boys perceive and respond to girls' and women's abilities. It means then not only a change in the form and content of PE in schools but also a change in the deep structures of communication throughout education and society.

The National Curriculum and Physical Education

Schools are experiencing considerable pressures as a consequence of the Education Reform Act (ERA) 1988 and the National Curriculum (NC). Underpinned by a market forces philosophy, these are unlikely to provide the material resources or to foster a climate which will support curricula which could directly or indirectly break down barriers which prevent the promotion of equality for all (cf. Davies, *et al.*, 1990).

The NC, as well as creating an overemphasis on testing, has led to a more compartmentalized approach to knowledge 'delivery'. The bulk of school time is being taken up by a core of rigidly defined traditional subjects which, it is argued, are based upon assumptions about what constitutes valid knowledge and modes of learning and a privileging of one particular value system over another (cf. Davies *et al.*, 1990).

The privileging of aspects of PE and its compartmentalization has been clearly evident in Conservative government interpretation of PE in the school curriculum and its response to the PE interim working group report. Far from wishing to provide a broad, balanced and worthwhile PE curriculum for *all* pupils (girls and boys), what, for this Conservative government, constitutes valid knowledge and skills in PE is categorized and legitimated largely as one area of traditional team games and this is consequently strongly male-orientated. This was evident when the Sports Minister, Mr Atkins, stated that he had 'made it his personal crusade to reverse this decline [in young people's participation in sport], particularly in school cricket, soccer and rugby' (TES, 1991). He had suggested that some sort of national lottery might be initiated through which monies might be collected which could help to sponsor this crusade. Clearly, he was neither aware nor concerned about promoting team games in which young women have substantial representation, nor was he interested in promoting a broader, more holistic PE curriculum. Rather, his views of sport and PE seem somewhat limited and without vision, concerned with the celebration of a few (males) whilst largely ignoring the participation, physical and emotional development and excellence of the majority of our pupils.

The education minister, Mr Kenneth Clarke, showed a similar reluctance to recognize and support the diversity of PE. This was evident in his response to the PE Working Group Interim Report. His response clearly showed a lack of support for dance, swimming and OE and was based largely upon both resource implications and upon a limited conception of what should constitute valid physical education experience. Clearly, in Clarke's perception, OE is not to be an entitlement for every pupil:

> I do not consider that residential experience should be an obligatory part of the PE curriculum — *or for that matter a compulsory element of any part of the statutory curriculum.* I should like you to reconsider the feasibility of compulsory inclusion of outdoor education in the statutory PE curriculum. (DES, 1991a; emphasis added)

In the final proposals for the PE curriculum, outdoor education is replaced by outdoor and adventurous activities (cf. DES, 1991b).[5]

The National Curriculum and Outdoor Education

> I was tremendously impressed with the quality of experience offered to the children and the total commitment of the centre's staff. . . . Why are establishments of such proven worth constantly under attack for the shoddy, limited reasons of short term profit and loss?
>
> I saw how young, nervous children grow in courage and self-confidence, tackling assignments that they never had the opportunity to face before. . . . It would not be an exaggeration to say that, for many youngsters, even a brief (residential) stay at the centre has the possibility of changing the direction of their lives. Who would dare put a price on that? (Governor, a middle school, 1990)[6]

As a consequence of the implementation of funding arrangements initiated by the ERA and the effects of government policy on local authority financial management, a substantial number of outdoor/adventure and field study centres have been closed or were under extreme threat of closure during 1991 (cf. McMorrin, 1991a, 1991b).[7]

The Association of Heads of Outdoor Education Centres reported on the plan by Cumbria resources working party to close and sell two of the three residential centres (cf. Stansfield, 1991). The need to reduce spending by £3 million, it was claimed, had forced council members to consider such measures.

> The response to the threatened closure was enormous from both schools and national bodies and the size and tone of the response was instrumental in the Education Committee deferring a decision . . . to give supporters of the centres time to evolve a plan under which they would become self-financing. (Stansfield, 1991, p. vii)

As a consequence of this plan only one centre was closed and the remaining two were to become self-financing from September 1991.

Clearly, despite grass-roots belief in the value of the learning experiences made available through outdoor education centres and through the medium of outdoor education more generally, the ERA and the implementation of the NC have placed the provision of OE very much under attack.

If we look at early NC documentation, we find that OE is not identified as a core or foundation subject, nor even a cross-curricular theme, skill or dimension, but it can be found under the title 'extra-curricular' activity in the document concerned with the whole school (NCC, 1990).

> Outdoor education can make a significant contribution as a focus of cross-curricular work. . . . There is value in sampling activities which may become the basis of life-long outdoor pursuits: in addition outdoor education provides an ideal opportunity for field work in geography, science, physical education, environmental education and for education for citizenship. (NCC, 1990, p. 6)

Further, the document states that extra-curricular activities

> are so familiar and have so successfully formed part of the curriculum of every school as not to require detailed examination. (p. 6)

This latter statement glosses over the effects of local financial management of schools (LMS), teachers' contracted time and the vast increase in paperwork (all products of the ERA) which have deleterious implications for the provision of all forms of extra-curricular activities (cf. Humberstone, 1992). It implies that OE does *not* belong in the NC but as an afterthought — after school hours. However, the PE Working Party Interim Report identified extra-curricular as not necessarily outside of school hours but as part of the formal curriculum which is undertaken 'off-site', that is, in residential or sports centres (cf. DES, 1991a, p. 19). The PE interim report strongly supported the inclusion of outdoor/adventure education and residential experience both within the PE curriculum and through its contribution to the education of the whole child more generally:

> Both living and travelling out of doors can include *residential experiences*. These provide opportunities for pupils to learn more about themselves as individuals and in relation to their peers and adults. Such experiences can prove an effective means of consolidating and extending school-based personal and social education. (DES, 1991a, p. 14)

Despite these recommendations, the Secretary of State for Education and Science is clearly adamant that OE should be an entitlement for every child. Considerable confusion and contradiction, then, have existed in formal documentation and government perception as to where OE should be positioned within the NC, if at all.

An HMI report (1991a) concerned with teaching and learning in primary PE makes a very brief mention of observing OE in some of the schools visited and makes reference to the utilization of residential experience for enhancing school work and for personal and social education.[8]

In response to the PE interim report and its subsequent discussion, the proposals of the Secretary of State presented in the NC document (DES, 1991b), recommends that outdoor and adventurous *activities* should form part of the statutory requirements of the PE curriculum rather than OE.

In making this distinction, the document states that

> Outdoor Education is not a subject but an approach to education which is concerned with the overall development of young people. It is an organised approach to learning in which direct experience is of paramount importance. (DES, 1991b, p. 12)

In so doing it legitimates the whole-school and holistic approach propounded by outdoor educators for so long and endorses that, whilst residential experience is not to be a compulsory element of the curriculum, such experience is an 'excellent cross-curricular educational practice' (DES, 1991b, p. 65).

However, by limiting the scope of the recommendations to 'those aspects of physical education which are clearly part of physical education ... that are almost entirely physical in content, such as orienteering, rock climbing, skiing, hiking and canoeing' (p. 12), the non-macho approach to the provision of these activities, which many were developing in and through a holistic outdoor education pedagogy (DES, 1975; Mortlock, 1984) may be ignored. As a consequence, there is grave danger that traditional exclusively male images and attitudes may re-emerge and these activities may become expressions of male bravado and ego boosting.[9] Most outdoor educators would argue that these activities are not 'almost entirely physical in content', but have equal components of aesthetic, emotional, spiritual and intellectual content as well as aspects of such subjects as geography, environmental issues, mathematics etc. which are accompanying parts of the learning experience (cf. Mortlock, 1984).

The majority of providers of outdoor adventure activities are men, particularly at the more prestigious and influential positions such as in teacher education and outdoor centre management and teaching; whereas, at grass roots (that is, in the less well paid, less secure teaching, instructing and youth work positions) where the interpersonal and holistic approach is valued and less emphasis is placed upon technical skills, there is a higher percentage of women utilizing these activities safely and competently.[10] A valuing of technical skills at the expense of interpersonal, decision-making skills made available within a sensitive holistic approach would most certainly disadvantage girls and women and further limit boys' and men's experience.

Outdoor Education and Social Change

> I don't think it [OE] is about physical fitness. It's more than that. It incorporates the ethos of group work; learning to cope as a group and problem-solving. (Anne)[11]

The historical background and philosophical basis of OE tend to be concerned with aspects surrounding group work which it views as central to its aims, which include valuing individuals and encouraging individuals to take responsibility for their own learning. The now classic qualitative research of Roberts, *et al.* (1974) found that staff in the residential centres under investigation held what appeared to be progressive ideals. They found that a major concern of the staff was to provide challenging situations to an individual, 'that would encourage the development and appreciation of 'his (sic) abilities' (p. 16). Like much of the research and writing at that time women were generally invisible (cf. Green *et al.*, 1990; Humberstone, forthcoming).

Roberts *et al.* (1974) found that the residential experience providers' objective was to foster personal and social change and this they felt they were achieving within their institutions. Furthermore, this positioning of the individual as the focus of the learning experience is emphasized by outdoor educators working with secondary pupils with learning difficulties as well as more generally (Loynes, 1984). Loynes emphasized the importance of providing stimulating adventurous situations and a supportive cooperative social environment in which to foster the confidence and self-esteem of these pupils (cf. Loynes, 1984).

Person-centred learning, in which individuals feel valued and in which trust is communicated between teachers and pupils and between pupils and pupils is, in a sense, essential in much of the work in OE. It is essential because of the possibility of physical or psychological harm occurring as a consequence of badly organized and/or poorly taught hazardous activities. Accidents which have occurred have frequently been a consequence of bad communication or miscommunication between teacher and pupils (cf. Report of the Altwood Schools Inquiry Panel, 1989). Consequently, it is not just for ideological but also for pragmatic reasons that OE pedagogy tends to be child-centred. An examination of past texts, DES and HMI documentation and reports concerning OE clearly identifies this underlying principle (cf. Humberstone, 1992). Evidence suggests that the promotion and provision of OE at the present time is founded upon

> a consensual, coherent and powerful ideology whose underlying values appear strongly democratic and child-centred. The associated pedagogic approach is concerned to empower pupils and to value individual needs and capabilities. Outdoor educators see the need for this approach, with its experiential and challenging style of learning, to permeate the whole of the school curriculum. (Humberstone, 1992)

Not only does OE subscribe to a 'progressive' ideology but also its cross-curricular applications are strongly promoted and emphasized by many outdoor educators (cf. Keighley, 1991). Furthermore, it is strongly argued that OE is not a subject but an approach to education (cf. HMI, 1977; Hunt, 1989, p. 53; DES, 1991b, p. 12).[12] Both ideologically and, in some cases, in practice, OE appears to cut across subject boundaries; it has a holistic, integrative approach to education. Within an external framework of physical and psychological safety, the predominant pedagogy is one which encourages personal responsibility and is concerned to empower the pupil, at least in terms of developing pupils' confidence in themselves and their peers. Thus the pupils' actions are strongly framed by common sense and visibly explicated rules of personal and group safety or care for oneself and others in hazardous situations. There is generally weak framing in social relations between the teacher and pupils (cf. Humberstone, 1986, 1990b). Evidence from one particular case study suggests that the form and content of the hidden and overt curricula in the OE centre under investigation held positive implications for pupils' learning and confidences (see also the letter from a governor which refers to the same centre). An unintended consequence of the 'progressive' approaches realized through the particular material conditions, social relations and ethos was a shift in the gender relations and identities during the experience (Humberstone, 1990a; 1990b).[13] However, one cannot generalize from one case study and there is a need for further research of this nature. We also do not know whether there is any 'carry-over' of this shift into other situations.

One important aspect which is frequently taken for granted when OE is considered is that underlying the pragmatic need for care for oneself and others is also a care for the environment (cf. Mortlock, 1984). This focus upon caring not only for humans, but for all that makes up life, if only in the immediate vicinity of the pupils' experience, is a significant encompassing and integrative ideal of what constitutes valid knowledge and skill.[14]

Outdoor Education in the National Curriculum: Contradictions and Dilemmas

Even at a surface level, the forms of experiential learning promoted through OE convey values which, I would suggest, are counter to those prevailing within patriarchal and capitalist ideologies underpinning the Conservative concept of a NC.

This visible conflict of values has created something of an identity crisis for OE. Pre-ERA DES documentation saw OE as cross-curricular in delivery, maintaining it to be more of an educational medium than a subject. The flexibility of the curriculum enabled OE to be made available by enthusiastic and appropriately qualified teachers, if the school felt it was worthwhile. However, post-ERA NC documentation renders OE almost invisible except for the more recent PE document (cf. DES, 1991b). Any rigid implementation of core and foundation subjects and LMS makes the inclusion of OE difficult (cf. Humberstone, 1992) other than within the PE curriculum. The latter inclusion defined as 'outdoor and adventurous activities' (DES, 1991b, p. 12), however, may well diminish its value. Unless carefully implemented within the PE curriculum OE may re-emerge as 'technical skills' based rather than person-centred and consequently redevelop as a 'macho', oppressive subject with little understanding or concern for the ideology which has underpinned it.[15]

To prevent this occurring, teachers of outdoor and adventurous activities need to be fully aware that they are teaching individuals as well as activity skills. These types of activities can provide contexts in which the pupil may experience fear in relation to an apparently hazardous situation. Each pupil is different. Cultural and social influences, particularly in relation to gender, will engender different feelings and reactions to fear which may manifest themselves in various ways. Pupils may express a range and variety of emotions under the same circumstances. The support, encouragement and trust which all pupils can give to each other is of paramount importance. It is vital for teachers to recognize that fear is subjective to each child and involves not only fear of physical harm to themselves, but also fear perhaps of not being adequately able to take the responsibility for another's safety. For boys and young men particularly, there is the fear of showing themselves to be frightened in front of their peers; fear of appearing cowards. These emotions may be felt or expressed even at levels of little potential physical risk and teachers need to be extremely sensitive to each individual pupil.

The form of interaction or manner of communication between pupil and teacher has particular implications in promoting equality. An interpersonal and non-authoritarian teaching approach (cf. Bernstein, 1977) which fosters collaborative learning situations in which everyone is valued is significant (cf. Salmon and Claire, 1984), as is the ability of the teacher to foster independent learning and decision-making.

There is also a danger that, with the growing awareness of gender influences (at least as they affect women and girls) and in some cases the concern to take seriously girls' and young women's cultural needs (cf. Hunt, 1989), a simplistic or superficial approach to the issue may be adopted. We may well return to a situation of understanding, by providers (mainly men), in which the physical, emotional and intellectual capabilities of girls and young women are perceived to be different and less valuable compared with those of boys and young men. There would be nothing more inhibiting to the progress made in challenging gender stereotyping through adventure education (for both girls and boys) than for 'equal but different' to become 'different and less challenging' for girls (cf. Humberstone and Lynch, 1992). Teachers need to take seriously the needs and capabilities of all our pupils, recognizing not only the way in which societal concepts of gender, racial and cultural stereotypes shape our understanding of those needs, but also acknowledging that the intellectual, emotional and physical differences within a particular sex, racial or cultural group may be at least as great as that between groups.[16]

The NC imposes upon teachers a market forces ideology which encourages destructive and divisive forms of competition rather than collaborative enterprises in the pursuit of balanced worthwhile educational experiences for pupils. Some schools (cf. Thompson, 1990) which have developed an outdoor education programme argue its value in terms which are incompatible with those promoted through rigidly controlled and bounded NC policies. The head of outdoor education in one such school argues:

> It [OE] represents a subject amalgamation, an applied area of know-ledge which draws from several established parts of the school curriculum. This interdisciplinary integrated approach reflects the views that such knowledge and experience cannot or should not be put into separate and rigid subject categories. (Thompson, 1990, p. 37)

This version of the form and content of OE appears incongruent within the prescribed NC. It appears as an oppositional educational paradigm (cf. Giddens, 1982). Consequently, it seems that proponents of OE have found considerable difficulty transposing their conceptualization of what constitutes valid OE in a language which would be compatible with those values articulated through the

NC.[17] The powerful ideological commitment to a permeation of subject bound-aries and to the empowerment of young people is antithetical to the ideological commitment underpinning the NC. Nevertheless, not only are outdoor educators attempting to maintain OE in the school curriculum on its own terms, but they are finding alternative routes to providing these experiences for young people.

Community, Schools and Outdoor Education

OE can be seen to support a holistic approach, crossing many subject bound-aries. The overriding aim of OE, some proponents believe (cf. Hunt, 1989), is the personal and social development of young people through the provision of adventurous, challenging activities, in a wide variety of environmental contexts. These can include not only the rural outdoors or wild country settings, but also urban sites and even locations under cover.[18]

There has been a trend for those from different work cultures who utilize OE to come together to share ideas and resources. Consequently, outdoor educa-tion work is now frequently seen as a collaborative venture between teachers and voluntary or LEA youth workers. One example of this is the Outdoor Education Policy document developed by Surrey County Council in 1990 (cf. Surrey County Council, 1991). When collaboration occurs, often in inner-city areas, OE is most certainly perceived to be a medium for personal and social development and almost always it is the 'less privileged' young person for whom the experiences are made available. One can, of course, argue that these initiatives are merely concerned with social control rather than providing posi-tive opportunities and experiences for young people. In these contexts, the most successful ventures, it is believed, are those in which workers are drawn from the local community and are known and trusted by the young people and in which the challenging experiences are seen as worthwhile and enjoyable by the young people themselves.

There are strong moves from within the very broad spectrum of people who constitute the various outdoor education interest agencies to provide oppor-tunities of an adventurous challenging nature to all young people (cf. Hunt, 1989).[19] Moreover, among some teachers, but more particularly among youth workers, there is considerable concern not only to empower disadvantaged young people but to overtly challenge sexism and racism in and through their work.[20]

HMI (1991b) describes a collaborative project between teachers and de-tached voluntary youth workers from the 'youth reach narrow boat project' in Bradford. This involved a school group of Asian young women aged 14–16 years and a day visit. The report, somewhat patronizingly, believed the project had been successful as the young women had expressed 'positive' reactions to their experiences and they had the opportunity to broaden their experiences and 'learn to mix with strangers'. The report maintains its success was due to it being

> part of a long-term planned programme. The youth worker was skilled and well known to the school staff and pupils, and the day was appropri-ately paced to maintain and encourage a sense of success.

The report goes on to state,

Effective work of this kind illustrates the benefits of youth workers and teachers working closely together and sharing the experiences with the young people. When this happens it is possible to integrate the experiences into the pupils' school learning, and, if appropriate, modify school approaches in the light of pupils' experience. (HMI, 1991b, p. 5)

We see then that in this form of education the 'everyday community knowledge' of the pupils is apparently perceived to be valid and worthy of recognition. However, there is still a long way to go before all outdoor education providers are able to fully understand and respond successfully to the needs of different ethnic groups and cultures.

Concluding Remarks

I have argued that OE has the potential for creating social change. However, for the potential of OE to be realized not only within the 'classroom', but also in wider society, action must be taken at all levels. Women and others from underrepresented groups with appropriate qualifications should not be excluded from privileged male work contexts because they bring a different (threatening?) perspective to those environments. Provision needs to be made for individuals from underrepresented groups to have fair and equal representation in PE and outdoor education work at all levels.

Teachers of outdoor and adventurous activities *can* help to bring about a more caring, just and balanced society in and through their teaching by adopting a sensitive, holistic and child-centred approach. Potentially hazardous activities made available within supportive and aware social contexts can provide unique opportunities for pupils to experience physical, emotional and intellectual challenges positively. Such experiences, at their most potent, can foster self-esteem and empower pupils to understand and value individual needs and capabilities whilst also enabling them to take responsibility for their own actions. Providing access for all pupils to the positive experiences which these activities can foster and creating equal opportunities within the 'classroom' context for all pupils to participate fully, 'regardless of their sex, religion, ability or ethnic background', is no easy task. But if teaching is underpinned by democratic and child-centred values and carried out sensitively, with the desire to challenge inequalities and stereotypical assumptions, its potential for social change may be realized more readily in practice.

Notes

1 Claudia is 14 years old, working-class, and a sportswoman who hopes to make her career in sports journalism. We talked about many things, some of which are made available in Bradshaw and Humberstone (1991), the first edition of the publication 'Women and Sport' which is concerned to promote all aspects of support for women in sport.

2   Hegemonic theory is important in that not only can it conceptualize processes of gender and other relations of inequality, but also there is a recognition that hegemonic control is tenuous and always struggles to maintain its oppressive control (cf. Hargreaves, 1990).
3   Note the MCC's vote by its members to keep out women in April 1991!
4   See note 1.
5   Despite the publication of these proposals there is no guarantee that the statutory orders regarding the PE curriculum due in Spring 1992 will not be significantly changed. At a Department of Education and Science conference on Outdoor Education, Professor Denys Brunsden explained that the NC PE working party (of which he had been a member) was told that educational aspects were not PE's responsibility and that outdoor education could only be included as outdoor and adventurous activities. However, the NC PE proposals were designed to emphasize the whole-school and cross-curricular dimension of outdoor education. The conference supported the view that outdoor education should be 'anchored' in the PE curriculum as outdoor and adventurous activities but that it had a significant contribution to make to schools in the broader perspective as required by section 1 of the ERA. This would require significant in-service training.
6   This letter was written on behalf of the governors and teachers of a middle school some of whose pupils had spent a week at a large outdoor education centre, under threat of closure.
7   On 25 September 1991, the Association of Heads of Outdoor Education Centres met with the parliamentary under-secretary of state responsible for schools who stated that the general schools budget would not be increased beyond 85 per cent. As a result there would always be 15 per cent central retention which would allow authorities to maintain centres as distinctive exceptions within that amount (unpublished notes of meeting). However, this 15 per cent must also cover other areas of provision such as music, libraries etc., and may not remove the threat of closure to many centres.
8   Although this HMI document is concerned with good practice in the primary area, nowhere are equal opportunity issues mentioned. It is pertinent to note, however, that the PE interim working group did draw attention to the importance of equal opportunities and special needs issues in PE in its report.
     The Autumn 1991 edition of the Journal of the Association of Head Teachers (*Head Teachers Review*) focuses specifically upon outdoor education.
9   There is evidence that competent and committed women teaching in outdoor education who challenge patriarchal values do so at their own considerable personal loss, as do committed women elsewhere in male-dominated work contexts (cf. Levi, 1991).
10   Evidence suggests that the number of women lecturers in teacher education in the area of outdoor education and women providers of outdoor adventure activities in Further and Higher Education may well be less than that in the early 1980s, which was already low (cf. Ball, 1986).
     The Basic Expedition Award (BETA) run by the Central Council for Physical Recreation is a basic leadership award in the outdoors and takes seriously both technical and interpersonal skills. There is a high percentage of women running this grass-roots course but significantly fewer involved in running more prestigious mountain leadership awards.
     The Get A Way girls' project, set up by women youth workers in Leeds in 1987, utilizes the BETA award. The aims of the project include:

● To encourage girls and young women to take up outdoor pursuits.
● To empower those groups of girls and young women who are

disempowered in society. This particularly includes Black and working-class young women with disabilities and young single mothers.
- To challenge the existing providers of outdoor activities to make what they offer girls and young women genuinely *accessible* in the widest sense.
- To further the use of outdoor pursuits in work with girls.

(Appleyard and Dare, 1989, p. 2)

Although the project has a vision for future work, its workers are largely financially insecure and spend valuable time fundraising.

11 Part of an interview with a PGCE student following an option in outdoor education in 1989 at Southampton University.

12 'It [OE] is not a subject but an approach to education encompassing all age groups and abilities . . . and crossing curricular boundaries' (HMI, 1977).

13 There is contradictory evidence regarding 'progressive', child-centred ideologies and their compatibility or otherwise with the values fostered through feminist informed pedagogy (Acker, 1988). Both are underpinned by philosophies which value and attempt to understand each individual's view and experiences and both are concerned to foster self-esteem in each pupil and collaboration and understanding between pupils (cf. Joyce, 1987; Rindell, 1988).

14 See Humberstone (1991b) in which the application of ecofeminism to the 'use' of natural assets by sporting cultures is explored.

15 This is not to suggest that technical competence is not important — it is of paramount importance in relation to hazardous activities. But the teacher needs to have knowledge and understanding of interpersonal skills and group dynamics in order to provide a creative safe environment (cf. Thomas, 1991).

16 This is borne out in relation to race and culture by the Reith Lecturer, Dr Jones, reader in genetics at University College, London, in his talk, 'Cousins under the Skin', in the series 'The Language of the Genes', BBC Radio 4, Wednesday 11 December 1991.

17 Despite there being a number of articles identifying how OE can 'fit' practically into the framework of the NC (cf. Stansfield, 1989) many outdoor educators have found difficulty in legitimating OE in the terms of the NC. This has been evident from meetings of executive members of an outdoor education association.

18 The HMI report 'Adventure Experiences for Young People from Urban Areas' (1991b) clearly details the diversity of settings in which adventure experiences have been made available, from mobile units travelling within deprived inner-city areas to the provision of expeditions to foreign locations for selected inner-city young people. Also, Humberstone (1986) describes adventurous experiences which are made available both in the natural environment and under cover.

19 I would suggest that many of these initiatives are largely driven by liberal ideologies; some like 'Adventure UK' which is now named 'The Foundation for Outdoor Adventure' came about from the recommendations of the Hunt report whose advocates are vigorously seeking funding to bring about the implementation of their mission of providing adventure experiences for all; others like 'Fairbridge Drake Society' are voluntary organizations again attempting to provide similar experiences to 'less privileged' young people.

20 A community worker, attending a Surrey LEA training day in OE, whose location includes a Travellers' community, not only works to include these people within the local white rural community, but also works, often under physical threat, with the men to challenge their sexism.

Barbara Humberstone

References

ACKER, S. (1988) 'Teachers, Gender and Resistance', *British Journal of Sociology of Education*, **9**, 3, pp. 307–22.

APPLEYARD, J. and DARE, S. (1989) *Get A Way Girls*, Appleyard and Dare.

BALL, D. (1986) 'The Outdoors and Gender', *Adventure Education*, **3**, 2, pp. 28–30.

BERNSTEIN, B. (1977) 'On the Classification and Framing of Educational Knowledge', in BERNSTEIN, B. (Ed.) *Class, Codes and Control*, London, Routledge and Kegan Paul.

BRADSHAW, C. and HUMBERSTONE, B. (1991) 'Dilemmas for Young Sports Women', in *Women and Sport*, Sports Council and Womens Sports Foundations, p. 8.

CONNELL, R.W. (1987) *Gender and Power*, Oxford, Polity Press.

DAVIES, A.M., HOLLAND, J. and MINHAS, R. (1990) *Equal Opportunities in the New Era*, Tufnell Press.

DEPARTMENT OF EDUCATION AND SCIENCE (1975) *Outdoor Education in the School Curriculum, Dartington Conference Study Report N496*, HMSO.

DEPARTMENT OF EDUCATION AND SCIENCE (1991a) *National Curriculum; Physical Education Working Group; Interim Report*, DES/Welsh Office.

DEPARTMENT OF EDUCATION AND SCIENCE (1991b) *Physical Education for Ages 5 to 16*, DES/Welsh Office.

DEWAR, A.M. (1991) 'Incorporation of Resistance?: Towards an Analysis of Women's Responses to Sexual Oppression in Sport', *International Review for Sociology of Sport*, **26**, 1, pp. 15–22.

DUNNING, E. (1986) 'Sport as a Male Preserve: Notes on the Social Sources of Masculine Identity and its Transformation', *Theory Culture and Society*, **3**, 1, pp. 79–90.

GIDDENS, A. (1982) *New Rules of Sociological Method*, London, Hutchinson.

GREEN, E., HEBRON, S. and WOODWARD, D. (1990) *Women's Leisure, What Leisure?* London, Macmillan.

HARGREAVES J. (1990) 'Gender on the Sports Agenda', *International Review for the Sociology of Sport*, **25**, 4, pp. 287–305.

HEAD TEACHERS REVIEW (1991) *The Great Outdoors . . . Outdoor Education*, National Association for Head Teachers, Autumn.

HER MAJESTY'S INSPECTORATE (1977) *The Curriculum 11–16*, London, HMSO.

HER MAJESTY'S INSPECTORATE (1991a) *Aspects of Primary Education: The Teaching and Learning of Physical Education*, London HMSO.

HER MAJESTY'S INSPECTORATE (1991b) *Adventure Experiences for Young People from Urban Areas*, London, HMSO.

HUMBERSTONE, B. (1986) 'Learning for a Change', in EVANS, J. (Ed.) *PE, Sport and Schooling: Studies in the Sociology of PE*, Lewes, Falmer Press, pp. 195–214.

HUMBERSTONE, B. (1990a) Warriors or Wimps? Creating Alternative Forms of PE', In MESSNOR, M. and SABO, S. (Eds) *Sport, Men and the Gender Order*, Champaign, IL, Human Kinetics. pp. 201–10.

HUMBERSTONE, B. (1990b) 'Gender, Change and Adventure Education', *Gender and Education*, **2**, 2, pp. 199–215.

HUMBERSTONE, B. (1991b) 'Rethinking Sport in the Natural Environment: Ecofeminism and the Creative Use of Natural Assets', in *Commission d'Etude du Sport Universitaire: The Changing Patterns of Recreation and Leisure*, Sheffield, pp. 142–8.

HUMBERSTONE, B. (1992) 'Outdoor Education in the National Curriculum: A Cross-Curricular Conundrum', in ARMSTRONG, N. (Ed.) *New Directions in Physical Education. Vol. 2: Towards a National Curriculum*, Champaign, IL, Human Kinetics (in press).

HUMBERSTONE, B. (forthcoming) 'Gender and Outdoor Education', in THOMAS, S. (Ed.) *'Perspectives' Outdoor Education*, Journal of School of Education, University of Exeter.

HUMBERSTONE, B. and LYNCH, P. (1992) 'Girls' Concepts of themselves and Their Experiences in Outdoor Education Programmes', in *Sport For All: Into the 90s. Proceedings of the 7th International Symposium for Comparative Physical Education and Sport*, Germany, Meyer und Meyer Verlag (in press).

HUNT, J. (1989) *In Search of Adventure: A Study of Opportunities for Adventure and Challenge for Young People*, Talbot Adair Press.

JAMES, B. and SAVILLE-SMITH, K. (1989) *Gender, Culture and Power*, Auckland, Oxford University Press.

JOYCE, M. (1987) 'Being a Feminist Teacher', in LAWN, M. and GRACE, G. (Eds) *Teachers: The Culture and Politics of Work*, London, Falmer Press, pp. 67–89.

KEIGHLEY, P. (1991) 'Education Out of Doors', *British Journal of Physical Education*, **22**, 2, pp. 32–6.

LEVI, J. (1991) 'Entering the Outdoor Education Profession — A High Risk Activity for Women?', *Adventure Education and Outdoor Leadership*, **8**, 1, pp. 7–8.

LOYNES, C. (1984) 'The Development of Outdoor Education at Stanway School', *Adventure Education*, **1**, 3, pp. 14–15.

MACDONALD, M. (1980) 'Schooling and the Reproduction of Class and Gender Relations', in BARTON, L., MEIGHAN, R. and WALKER, S. *Schooling, Ideology and the Curriculum*, Lewes, Falmer Press, pp. 29–48.

MCMORRIN, I. (1991a) 'Muffling the Call of the Wild', *Times Educational Supplement*, 19 April, p. 14.

MCMORRIN, I. (1991b) 'Facing Doubt: Some Thoughts on the Past, Present and Future of Outdoor Education', *Head Teachers Review: The Great Outdoors . . . Outdoor Education*, National Association for Head Teachers, Autumn, pp. 26–7.

MESSNOR, M. and SABO, D. (1990) *Sport, Men and the Gender Order: Critical Feminist Perspectives*, Champaign, IL, Human Kinetics.

MORTLOCK, C. (1984) *Adventure Education*, Cumbria, Cicerone Press.

NATIONAL CURRICULUM COUNCIL (1990) *Curriculum Guidance 3: The Whole Curriculum*, NCC.

REPORT OF THE ALTWOOD SCHOOL INQUIRY PANEL (1989) Royal County of Berkshire.

RINDELL, S. (1988) *Gender and Subject Choice in Two Rural Comprehensive Schools*, Unpublished PhD dissertation, University of Bristol.

ROBERTS, K., WHITE, G. and PARKER, H. (1974) *The Character Training Industry*, Devon, David and Charles.

SALMON, P. and CLAIRE, H. (1984) *Classroom Collaboration*, London, Routledge and Kegan Paul.

STANSFIELD, D. (1989) 'A Strategy for Implementing a Thematic Approach to Outdoor Education in the Modern Curriculum', *Adventure Education*, **6**, 4, pp. 19–22.

STANSFIELD, D. (1991) 'The Future of Cumbrian Outdoor Centres', *Adventure Education and Outdoor Leadership*, **8**, 2, pp. vi–vii.

SURREY COUNTY COUNCIL (1991) *Outdoor Education Policy*, June.

THOMAS, S. (1991) 'Safety Out of School', *British Journal of Physical Education*, **22**, 2, pp. 37–9.

THOMPSON, A. (1990) 'Outdoor Education at Belper School — Philosophy and Aims Behind a Programme which Runs Across the Curriculum', *Adventure Education*, **7**, 3, pp. 33–7.

Times Educational Supplement, (1991) 8 March, p. 1.

WALBY, S. (1990) *Theorizing Patriarchy*, Oxford, Blackwell.

WEINER, G. (1985) 'Equal Opportunities, Feminism and Girls' Education: Introduction', in WEINER, G. (Ed.) *Just a Bunch of Girls*, Milton Keynes, Open University Press, pp. 1–13.

WHITE, A. and BRACKENRIDGE, C. (1984) 'Who Rules Sport? Gender Divisions in the Power Structures of British Sports Organisations from 1960', Paper presented at the Olympic Scientific Conference, University of Oregon.

Barbara Humberstone

WHITE, J. (1988) 'Women in Leisure Service Management', in WIMBUSH, E. and TALBOT, M. (Eds) *Relative Freedoms*, Milton Keynes, Open University Press, pp. 147–60.

WHITSON, J. (1990) 'Sport in the Social Construction of Masculinity', in MESSNOR, M. and SABO, D. (Eds) *Sport, Men and the Gender Order*, Human Kinetics, pp. 19–30.

WIMBUSH, E. and TALBOT, M. (Eds) (1988) *Relative Freedoms: Women and Leisure*, Milton Keynes, Open University Press.

Post-Script: Physical Education Post ERA, in a Postmodern Society

John Evans and Brian Davies

We began this project with optimism and a sense of possibility and opportunity. We believed that the making of the NCPE constituted a moment of some significance in the history of physical education in England and Wales. We hoped that the principles of equity and equality might be established much more firmly in the official discourse of the subject, in time infusing the actions of teacher educators and physical education teachers in schools. Initially we were not disappointed. A commitment to 'equal opportunities' as 'a guiding and leading principle in the subject' was writ large in the text of the final report on the NCPE (DES/Welsh Office, 1991). Emancipatory principles appeared to have been on the verge of acceptance by the profession and established as key and defining elements in the curriculum of physical education.

However, very little of this material was included in the texts of the NCPE (DES, 1992; NCC, 1992) issued to teachers by the National Curriculum Council, the agency responsible for distributing National Curriculum documentation to schools. The consequences of this omission are that the expression of equity and equality principles in physical education will have to emerge, yet again, not from its official discourse but from the aspirations and activities of individual teachers and teacher educators. The pressing demands of the workplace always make this very difficult to achieve. Our hope must be that the final report on the NCPE will continue to be used as a resource and point of reference, alongside the 'official' NCPE documents, in any endeavour to implement the NCPE.

To the demolition of the place of emancipatory ideals in the physical education curriculum attributable to the conservative Right, we must now add the challenge of those of more liberal political persuasion to the egalitarian actions and initiatives in the curriculum given the dramatic changes which have taken place on the economic, social and cultural terrain of Britain and other post-industrial societies over the last forty years. Theorists of postmodernity (see, Best and Kellner, 1991) claim that trends in consumerism, mass culture and a decline of traditional institutions are bringing about major cultural re-orientations, the end of an era — a move from the modern to the postmodern society — which require new concepts and new theories.

We cannot here either document or interrogate the variety of voices that constitute 'the postmodern perspective' (see, Best and Kellner, 1991) or those which contest them. Whether postmodernism represents a mindless or a magical moment in the history of intellectual endeavour remains to be seen. Gilbert (1992, p. 53) is probably right to insist that at least for the moment we should avoid the temptation to dismiss it as 'mindless conformism', or to ignore its complexities, or to assume that superior judgmental authority which post-modernists question. As we see below, the defining characteristics of postmoder-nity may have important implications not only for theorists of the contemporary social world but also for teachers of physical education.

Analysts of the postmodern claim that the dramatic expansion in computer manufacturing, telecommunications, mass media, advertising, publishing, account-ing, along with the effect of computerization and developments in information processing have not only created new possibilities and problems in the social and cultural domains, but also changed the means of knowledge production, along with the forms of criteria of knowledge itself. Postmodernism is seen to have an 'epistemological effect of profound importance for the way knowledge is implicated in society' (Gilbert, 1992, p. 53). Whereas the theoretical discourses of modernism 'championed reason as the source of progress in knowledge and society, as well as the privileging locus of truth and the foundation of systematic knowledge' (Best and Kellner, 1991, p. 2), by contrast, postmodernism, it is claimed, subverts 'the notions of truth, meaning and subjectivity held to be the defining features of Western metaphysics' (Callinicos, 1990, quoted in Gilbert, 1992, p. 53). As Gilbert and others point out, 'modern thought' has 'legitimized itself in terms of "meta narratives" such as the dialectics of the Spirit, the hermeneutics of meaning, the emancipation of the rational or working subject, or the creation of wealth' and 'sought to ground knowledge in a fundamental unity, a privileged position of authority from which all knowledge could be categorized and assessed' (*ibid*, p. 54). However, postmodern theories of language and discourse have attacked the root assumptions of modern philosophy, its foundationalism and appeal to unifying principles of emancipation and truth. For example, Lyotard (1984, p. xxiv) has argued that all discourses are 'finite, locally determined language games, each with specific pragmatic criteria of appropriate-ness or valency'. Furthermore it is claimed that the dissolution of a unifying knowledge, and the fragmentation and instability of discourses in the cultural domain, is mirrored in personality and how the individual perceives his or her body and self. '[S]chizophrenia displaces alienation as the analytical metaphor' (Gilbert, 1992, p. 54). 'The immediacy of events, the sensationalism of the spec-tacle (political, scientific, military, as well as those of entertainment), becomes the stuff of which consciousness is forged' (Harvey, 1989, quoted in Gilbert, 1992, p. 55).

The relativism of this epistemological position is deeply worrying for anyone committed to emancipatory ideals. As Giddens (1991), points out, much post-structuralist and postmodernist analysis both denudes and offers little relevance to moral questions. Others claim that the moral response to the cultural changes of postmodernity is a damaging nihilism and narcissism (Luke and White, 1985); while, on a more positive note, Hall (1989, p. 55) claims that the pluralization of everyday life may 'expand the positionalities and identities available to ordinary people (at least in the industrialized world) in their everyday working, social, familial and sexual lives'.

Whatever the merits of these arguments we can not ignore them, nor the changes that have occurred on the social and cultural terrain and their significance for the expression of equality and equity in schools. Postmodernism seems to threaten the possibilities of a discourse of morality and concerted political action, both of which 'require some recognition of common interests and values derived from shared past experiences, as well as a desirable future sufficiently general as to have a broad appeal'. The fragmentation of culture and concomitantly of sensibilities may make this very difficult to attain (Gilbert, 1992, p. 53). It does challenge our conventional assumptions about knowledge, morality and subjectivity, and our assumptions about what the body and the self are, and therefore raises fundamental questions about essential elements of modern educational thought. As Gilbert (1992) and Giddens (1991) have argued, mass education in its recent forms has been a modernist project *par excellence*, with its stress on emancipation, rationality, individual autonomy and the unified self, and these authors go on to question the coherence, unity and usefulness of these concepts and ideals, upon which so much educational discussion has relied. Giddens (1991), for example, argues that an emancipatory politics, 'a generic outlook', is concerned above all with liberating individuals and groups; freeing them from constraints which adversely affect their life chances. Its project is to help individuals both shed 'shackles of the past, thereby permitting a transformative attitude towards the future' (*Ibid*, p. 211), and overcome 'the illegitimate domination of some individuals or groups by others'. Many of the authors in this book would endorse this concern. The pages of this text have expressed a concern with the social and cultural hierarchies of power that are transmitted in and through the curriculum of schooling and physical education within it. Our agenda has focused on divisions between 'others' — divisions of ethnicity gender, class, ability, and between ruling and subordinate groups; our objective has been to provide individuals with the information, knowledge and outlook that will help them reconstruct if not eliminate the relative differences between children which may negatively effect their life chances in physical education, sport and all other areas of life. The imperatives of justice, equality and participation lie at the heart of our actions and concerns. An emancipatory project such as this, in Giddens' (1991) formulation, is founded on a 'mobilising principle' long dear to the hearts of educators both traditional and progressive: the principle of autonomy. 'Emancipation means that collective life is organized in such a way that the individual is capable — in some sense or another — of free and independent action in the environments of her social life' (p. 213). Individuals are liberated from constraints placed on their behaviour 'as a result of exploitative, unequal or oppressive conditions'. As Giddens rightly goes on to stress, however, this does not render them free in any absolute sense. The basic conditions governing autonomy of action have to be worked out in terms of a thematic of justice (loc cit). For Giddens, however, the emancipatory project is incomplete. He argues that in the discourse of emancipatory politics how individuals and groups in a just order will actually behave is often left open. Since it is, above all else, concerned with 'overcoming exploitative, unequal or oppressive social relations, its main orientations tends to be "away from" rather than "towards". In other words, the actual nature of emancipation is given little flesh, save as the capacity of individuals to develop their potentialities within limiting framework of communal constraint' (loc cit).

We do not have to accept either the accuracy or the direction of Giddens' reading of the emancipatory ideal before acknowledging the challenges he presents to all teachers in search of equity and equality in programmes of physical education. If postmodernism does signify a decline of independent universal standards of morality and judgment, and if individuals can no longer centre their actions in a stable morality, then we are forced to ask 'what is the basis for our actions as physical educationalist?' and 'what forms of citizenship are to characterize the outcome of our endeavours as teachers in schools?' Is the struggle for equality and citizenship rights redundant in the absence of unified ideals? Have we to reconsider and reconstruct our emancipatory endeavours? It is certainly important to note, with Gilbert (1992), that the fragmentation of the postmodern may be less of a threat than first appears — arguably emancipatory projects have never been driven by unified ideals — and acknowledge with him that the problem may not be the diversity and fragmentation of culture but the nature of it. Furthermore, we have to ask, 'is the Semiotic society so narcotizing and fragmenting that people will cease to recognise established rights or the possibility of new ones?' (*ibid*, p. 61). We are also properly reminded that the focus on postmodernity is very much a first world and middle class phenomena which needs to be balanced with the recognition that large sections of the world's peoples remain dominated by modern industrial formations, and continue to draw inspiration from long standing cultural traditions. Even if postmodern developments themselves offer new possibilities for emancipatory action and citizenship conventional political action will continue to be essential elements of the social dynamic inside and outside schools (Giddens, 1991; Gilbert, 1992). Entitlements to civil and political rights and to social and welfare rights to certain material standards of living, increasingly conspicuous needs in the consumer society will, as Gilbert (1992) stresses, still have to be struggled for. In short, postmodernity neither diminishes nor makes redundant emancipatory politics and ideals.

Emancipatory politics are, however, a politics of *life chances*. (Giddens, 1991). In contrast, but not instead of, Giddens (1991) advocates a form of 'life politics', a politics of life style and self actualization, the concerns of which, he claims, would presage the development of forms of social order 'on the other side of modernity itself' (Giddens, 1991, p. 214). He offers little in the way of detail on what this other world may be. However, the claim is that in conditions of 'high modernity', what identity is, and how it should be expressed has become itself a matter of multiple options. In Giddens' terms, 'the more we "reflexively" "make ourselves" as persons, the more the very category of what a "person" or "human being" is comes to the fore' (*ibid*, p. 217). Thus neither the self nor the body can be taken as fixed because they have become deeply involved with modernity's reflexivity. If an emancipatory politic's objective is to 'free the body from the oppression to which it has fallen prey' (*ibid*, p. 218) it must recognize that in conditions of 'high modernity' the body becomes pro-active, 'less "docile" than ever before in relation to the self, since the two become intimately coordinated within the reflexive project of self identity' (*ibid*, p. 218). In the sphere of life politics the problem becomes how the individual is to make choices concerning strategies of bodily development in life planning. The body itself 'becomes more immediately relevant to the identity the individual promotes' (ibid, p. 218).

If 'the body' is increasingly privileged in the culture of postmodernity, then the process of education may have an increasingly important role to play particularly in the decisions children take concerning their own (and others') bodies. How are physical educationalists to act in this process? How are they to inform and intervene in this decision making process? 'Life politics' and its central concern with the body and the self, may be confused with and reduced to the crude and selfish individualism which is endemic and under accentuation at present in schooling and is liable to disintegrate into an education for self interest. For this reason Giddens is at pains to point out that we should avoid mistaking the new ethos of 'self discovery for the "old modern" aggrandizing individual'. We have to 'distinguish between new impulses towards personal growth, on the one hand, and capitalistic pressures towards personal advantage and material accumulation on the other' (*ibid*, p. 209). This is easier said than done.

Clearly neither the 'postmodern' nor a commitment to 'life politics' either dissolves or diminishes an emancipatory project or ideal. As Giddens (1991) points out, a commitment to life politics brings back to prominence precisely those moral and existential questions repressed by the core institutions of modernity; and commands a 'remoralizing of daily life'. Substantive questions on the agenda of life politics still centre upon human rights of personhood and individuality. He argues that 'all issues of life politics involve questions of right and obligations, demands for emancipatory rights do not therefore become less important, attempts to extend citizen rights, remain fundamental. 'Emancipatory politics will not come to an end as life politics moves to claim the overall political agenda; virtually all questions of life politics also raise problems of an emancipatory sort' (*Ibid*, p. 228). Whatever the merits of Giddens' conceptions of 'life politics' and the society this subsumes, neither theorists of the postmodern, nor teachers of physical education, can ignore the challenges he presents in his work. Given the continued dominance of a conservative discourse in the political and cultural domains, we must not relinquish emancipatory ideals, although we should in the years ahead consider seriously if and how they are to be reformulated and expressed in schools and elsewhere. Giddens gives some indication of the challenges that lie ahead.

> The capability of adopting freely chosen lifestyles, a fundamental benefit generated by a post-traditional order, stands in tension, not only with barriers to emancipation, but with a variety of moral dilemmas. No one should underestimate how difficult it will be to deal with these, or even how hard it is to formulate them in ways likely to command widespread consensus. How can we remoralize social life without falling prey to prejudice? The more we return to existential issues, the more we find moral disagreements; how can these be reconciled? If there are no transhistorical ethical principles, how can humanity cope with clashes of 'true believers' without violence? Responding to such problems will surely require a major reconstruction of emancipatory politics as well as the pursuit of life-political endeavours. (Opcit, p. 231)

There is agenda enough here for newly straitened and uncertain times in physical education in our schools.

John Evans and Brian Davies

References

BEST, S. and KELLNER, D. (1991) *Postmodern Theory, Critical Interrogations*, London, MacMillan.

CALLINICOS, A. (1990) 'Reactionary postmodernism?', in BOYNE, R. and RATTANSI, (Eds) *Postmodernism and Society*, London, MacMillan.

DEPARTMENT OF EDUCATION AND SCIENCE/WELSH OFFICE (1991) *Physical Education for Ages 5–16*, DES/Welsh Office, HMSO.

DEPARTMENT OF EDUCATION AND SCIENCE (1992) *Physical Education in the National Curriculum*, DES/Welsh Office, HMSO.

NATIONAL CURRICULUM COUNCIL (1992) *Physical Education Non Statutory Guidance*, York, National Curriculum Council.

GIDDENS, A. (1991) *Modernity and Self Identity*, Oxford, Basil Blackwell.

GILBERT, R. (1992) 'Citizenship, Education and Postmodernity', in *British Journal of Sociology of Education*, **13**, 1, pp. 52–69.

HALL, S. (1989) 'The meaning of new times,' in HALL, S. and JACQUES, M. (Eds) *New Times: The Changing Face of Politics in the 1990s*, London, Lawrence and Wishart.

HARVEY, D. (1989) *The Condition of Postmodernity: An Enquiry into the Origins of Cultural Change*, Oxford, Blackwell.

LUKE, T. and WHITE, S. (1985) *Critical Theory and Public Life*, Cambridge, Mass., MIT Press.

LYOTARD, J.F. (1984) *The Post Modern Condition: A Report on Knowledge*, Manchester, Manchester University Press.

Notes on Contributors

Len Barton is a Professor of Education at the University of Sheffield. He is the founder and editor of the International Journal, *Disability, Handicap and Society*. He has recently been a member of a series of seminars funded by the Rowntree Foundation exploring the issue of 'Researching Physical Disability'. His latest writings include a co-authored book — Cobett, J. and Barton, L. (1992) *Struggle for Choice: Young People with Special Needs in PE* (Routledge). His main research interest is in the Politics of Disability and Special Needs.

Bob Carroll is Director of the Centre for Physical Education and Leisure Studies at Manchester University. He has published widely in Physical Education and related areas and is co-author of a Research Report 'Sport and Recreation with Special Reference to Ethnic Minorities' (1991).

Brian Davies is a Professor of Education at University College, Cardiff. He was formerly a Professor of Education at King's College London, and a Lecturer in Sociology at the University of London Institute of Education and at Goldsmith's College, London after a period as a school teacher. He has written widely on the sociology of education and is author of *Education and Social Control* (1986) and the editor of an issue of *Educational Analysis* which dealt with *The State and Schooling* .

Patt Dodds is Associate Professor of Sport Pedagogy at the University of Massachusetts, Amherst. She taught in the (now defunct) undergraduate teacher preparation programme and currently teaches in the Physical Education Teacher Education (PETE) doctoral programme, doing research seminars on teaching, pre-service teacher education, in-service teacher development, and retrieval and review of teaching/teacher education research. Her research specializations are the socialization of physical education teachers, particularly during their pre-training and pre-service years, and the socialization of teacher educators, especially focusing on their formal and informal professional experiences prior to taking their first teacher education position.

John Evans is a Senior Lecturer in the Physical Education Department at the University of Southampton. He is author of *Teaching in Transition: The Challenge of Mixed Ability Grouping* (1986) and edited *Physical Education, Sport and*

Schooling (1986) and *Teachers, Teaching and Control in Physical Education* (1988) (Falmer Press). He has published widely in the sociology of education.

Peter Figueroa is a Senior Lecturer in the School of Education, University of Southampton, where he teachers Masters' courses in Multicultural and Anti-Racist Education, Curriculum Design and Development and Philosophy and Education. His interests also include policy issues, evaluation, comparative education, sociology and issues in social psychology. He has taught at the University of West Indies, the Australian National University, the University of Frankfurt and the University of Dar-es-Salaam. He is Jamaican settled in Britain with an English Wife and two young children, and author of *Education and the Social Construction of 'Race'* (Routledge, 1991).

Paula Halliday was formerly Adviser for Special Educational Needs in Salford LEA. Prior to that she was Headteacher and Head of Hostel at Lancasterian School, Manchester. She is author of *Teaching the Physically Disabled* as well as a variety of articles and distance learning materials on other aspects of Special Education. She is currently training for the priesthood in the Church of Ireland.

Phil Hodkinson taught in various secondary schools for twenty years. Since 1984 he has been directly involved with pre-vocational education, leading the introduction of CPVE in two different schools. From 1988 to 1991 he held the post of TVEI-related Lecturer in Education in the School of Education, Exeter University. He has written widely on educational issues related to the principles of pre-vocational education, and conducted several related research investigations. He is currently Senior Lecturer in Education at Crewe and Alsager College of Higher Education, and is co-directing, with Andy Sparkes, and ESRC-funded research project on Training Credits in Action.

Graeme Hollinshead was the Head of the Physical Education Department at a northern comprehensive school for seventeen years before becoming a Senior Master responsible for coordinating assessment in the school.

Barbara Humberstone is a temporary Senior Lecturer in Sociology at Portsmouth Polytechnic and an Equal Opportunities Consultant and independent researcher. She is Honorary Secretary of the National Association for Outdoor Education. She previously taught PE and Outdoor Education in secondary schools and in the University sector.

Sheila Scraton is a Reader in Feminist Studies in the Faculty of Cultural and Education Studies, Leeds Polytechnic. She began her teaching career as a PE teacher in a Liverpool comprehensive school before becoming Head of Physical and Leisure Activities at a sixth-form college. She has taught across a wide range of further and higher education and completed her doctorate in the area of Gender and PE. Currently she teaches Sociology and Leisure Studies and is course leader of a Masters programme in Leisure and Human Potential. Her research, academic and personal commitment is to feminism and to the development of anti-discriminatory theories, policies and practices in relation to gender, sexuality, 'race', class and disability.

Chris Shilling is a Lecturer in the Department of Sociology and Social Policy, University of Southampton. His main teaching interests are in the sociology of education, education policy and contemporary social theory. He is author of *Schooling for Work in Capitalist Britain*, (Falmer, 1989); joint author and editor of *The TVEI Story: Policy, Practice and Preparation for the Workforce* (Open University Press, 1990), and is author of *The Body and Social Theory* (Sage Press — Theory, Culture and Society Series).

Andrew Sparkes is a Lecturer in Education in the School of Education at the University of Exeter where he is also an Associate Director of the Physical Education Association Research Centre. His research interests include the study of educational innovation, the changing nature of teachers' work, the life histories of marginal groups, and the development of interpretive-critical methodologies. Andrew has published widely in these areas and is author of *Curriculum Change in Physical Education: Towards a Micropolitical Understanding* (Deakin University Press, 1990); editor of *Research in Physical Education and Sport: Exploring Alternative Visions* (Falmer Press, 1992); and co-editor of *Issues in Physical Education* (Cassell, 1991).

Margaret Talbot is Carnegie Professor and Assistant Dean in the Faculty of Cultural and Education Studies at Leeds Metropolitan University. Her current responsibilities include the management of the Carnegie National Sports Development Centre and the coordination of research across the Faculty. She was a member of the DES Physical Education Working Group on the National Curriculum, and chaired the sub-group on cross-curricular matters, including equal opportunities.

Sue Thomas is a Lecturer in Physical Education at the School of Education, Exeter University. She has taught Physical Education and Outdoor Education in comprehensive schools. Her main teaching and research interests are in the Sociology of the Physical Education curriculum.

Anne Williams is a Senior Lecturer in Physical Education and Senior Tutor for PGCE Courses at the University of Birmingham. Her publications include *Curriculum Gymnastics* and *Issues in Physical Education for the Primary Years* (Falmer Press). Her research interests centre on primary school physical education, and pupils' perceptions of physical education and gender issues.

Index

ability 13–14, 19–21, 24, 35, 49, 56, 58,
65, 67–70, 75, 81–3, 86, 88, 96–8,
108, 110, 112–14, 116, 118–19, 131,
139, 144, 147, 149, 173, 175, 177, 189,
206–7, 211, 218–19, 223, 227, 235
access 13–14, 19–20, 24, 29, 51, 55–7,
67–8, 74–5, 79, 81, 85, 97–8,
105–10, 112–14, 119–20, 127–30,
136, 140, 143, 149, 154, 156, 165, 171,
189, 206–12, 218–19, 227
accountability 15, 17, 44, 48, 106–7,
109–11, 125, 139
achievement 18, 20, 24, 29, 37, 67, 86, 97,
107, 110, 115–19, 136, 145–6, 173,
177, 196, 211
Acker, Sandra 133, 198, 199, 229
age 45, 52, 82, 118, 129
alienation 55, 108, 112, 151, 177, 179, 234
antiracism 90–100, 154, 155, 156, 164–5,
167–8, 189
Apple, M. 20, 48
Armstrong, N. 131
Arnot, Madeleine 4, 14, 25, 144, 154,
200
Askew, S. 130, 195
assessment 18, 32, 66–7, 83, 93, 95, 106,
108, 110–11, 116–18, 173–5, 197,
208–9, 211, 219
athleticism 57, 64–6, 107
athletics 79, 128, 145, 157, 160–1, 193
Atkinson, P. 22, 65
attainment 16–17, 18, 69, 100, 112,
116–18, 156, 171
attitude 30, 32–3, 35, 44, 48, 55, 59, 67,
69, 77–8, 86–7, 93–4, 97–8, 106,
125–6, 130, 132–6, 144–7, 164, 167,
186, 189–91, 199, 206, 208, 222
autonomy 176–8, 235

background 13, 20, 24, 56–7, 59–60, 66–8,
82, 85, 95, 97–8, 105, 114, 127, 129
Bagley, C. 95, 96
Bailey, C. 171, 174
Bain, L. 36, 50, 112
Ball, D. 218, 228
Ball, Stephen 19, 25, 56, 109–11, 116,
121, 142, 170, 175
Barton, Len 5, 43–52
Bayliss, T. 96, 155, 156
behaviour 30–3, 35, 67, 74, 76, 82, 84,
86–7, 93–4, 100, 114, 128, 131–4,
144, 146, 156, 163, 184–5, 189–90,
196
belief 30, 32, 76, 82, 85, 87, 91, 93, 97,
106, 114, 120, 158, 196, 199
Bernstein, B. 62, 225
Best, S. 233, 234
body
image 45, 47–8, 99, 145–6, 150–1, 196,
236–7
orientations and social class 55–70
Borsay, A. 45–6
Boulton, Pam 187, 188, 197–8
Bourdieu, Pierre 6, 58–62, 64, 156
Brah, A. 155, 166
Brannigan, C. 155, 165
Brisenden, S. 43, 44, 45
Brittan, Arthur 151, 195
Brittan, E.M. 95, 96
Brooker, N. 125, 132
Brown, C. 95, 96
Byrne, E. 12, 19–20, 23, 24

Campbell, A. 125, 132
Carrington, B. 8, 47, 50, 62, 95, 99,
154–6, 165
Carroll, Bob 7, 154–68, 170